ALTERNATIVES TO SUICIDE

ALTERNATIVES TO SUICIDE

Beyond Risk and Toward a Life Worth Living

Edited by

ANDREW C. PAGE

WERNER G.K. STRITZKE

ELSEVIER

ACADEMIC PRESS

An imprint of Elsevier

Academic Press is an imprint of Elsevier
125 London Wall, London EC2Y 5AS, United Kingdom
525 B Street, Suite 1650, San Diego, CA 92101, United States
50 Hampshire Street, 5th Floor, Cambridge, MA 02139, United States
The Boulevard, Langford Lane, Kidlington, Oxford OX5 1GB, United Kingdom

Notices

Knowledge and best practice in this field are constantly changing. As new research and experience broaden our understanding, changes in research methods, professional practices, or medical treatment may become necessary.

Practitioners and researchers must always rely on their own experience and knowledge in evaluating and using any information, methods, compounds, or experiments described herein. In using such information or methods they should be mindful of their own safety and the safety of others, including parties for whom they have a professional responsibility.

To the fullest extent of the law, neither the Publisher nor the authors, contributors, or editors, assume any liability for any injury and/or damage to persons or property as a matter of products liability, negligence or otherwise, or from any use or operation of any methods, products, instructions, or ideas contained in the material herein.

Library of Congress Cataloging-in-Publication Data
A catalog record for this book is available from the Library of Congress

British Library Cataloguing-in-Publication Data
A catalogue record for this book is available from the British Library

ISBN: 978-0-12-814297-4

For information on all Academic Press publications visit our website at https://www.elsevier.com/books-and-journals

Publisher: Nikki Levy
Editorial Project Manager: Megan Ashdown
Production Project Manager: Sujatha Thirugnana Sambandam
Cover Designer: Mark Rogers

Typeset by TNQ Technologies

Contents

Part 5 Epigenetics of suicidal behaviors

Contributors

Abigail Bray
Research Consultant School of Indigenous Studies, University of Western Australia, Crawley, Perth, WA, Australia

Julia D. Brown
School of Psychological Science, University of Western Australia, Perth, WA, Australia

Craig J. Bryan
National Center for Veterans Studies, The University of Utah, Salt Lake City, UT, United States

Heidi Bryan
Heidi Bryan Consulting, LLC, Neenah, WI, United States

Phoebe Carrington-Jones
Graduate School of Education, The University of Western Australia, Perth, WA, Australia

Sera Davidow
Western Massachusetts Recovery Learning Community, Holyoke, MA, United States

Pat Dudgeon
Professor, Poche Centre for Indigenous Health, School of Indigenous Studies, University of Western Australia, Crawley, Perth, WA, Australia

Thomas E. Ellis
Deptartment of Psychiatry and Behavioral Sciences, Baylor College of Medicine, Houston, TX, United States

T. Mark Ellison
School of Psychological Science, University of Western Australia, Perth, WA, Australia

Clemens Fartacek
Department of Crisis Intervention and Suicide Prevention, University Clinic of Psychiatry, Psychotherapy, and Psychosomatics; Paracelsus Medical University, Salzburg, Austria; Department of Clinical Psychology, University Clinic of Psychiatry, Psychotherapy, and Psychosomatics, Paracelsus Medical University, Salzburg, Austria

Nicolas Fay
School of Psychological Science, University of Western Australia, Perth, WA, Australia

Laura M. Fiori
McGill Group for Suicide Studies, Douglas Mental Health University Institute, McGill University, Montreal, QC, Canada

Sarah E. George
School of Psychological Science, University of Western Australia, Perth, WA, Australia

Patricia Gooding
School of Health Sciences, Division of Psychology and Mental Health, University of Manchester, Manchester, United Kingdom

Natasha A.R. Goods
School of Psychological Science, University of Western Australia, Perth, WA, Australia

Kamelia Harris
School of Health Sciences, Division of Psychology and Mental Health, University of Manchester, Manchester, United Kingdom

Dominique P. Harrison
School of Psychological Science, University of Western Australia, Perth, WA, Australia

Geoffrey R. Hooke
School of Psychological Science, University of Western Australia, Perth, WA, Australia

Abdul-Rahman Hudaib
Division of Psychiatry/UWA Medical School, The University of Western Australia, Perth, WA, Australia

Amy Joscelyne
School of Psychology, University of New South Wales (UNSW), Sydney, NSW, Australia

Shraddha Kashyap
School of Psychology, University of New South Wales (UNSW), Sydney, NSW, Australia

E. David Klonsky
University of British Columbia

Michael J. Kyron
School of Psychological Science, University of Western Australia, Perth, WA, Australia

David Lawrence
Graduate School of Education, The University of Western Australia, Perth, WA, Australia

Jason Y.S. Leong
School of Psychological Science, University of Western Australia, Perth, WA, Australia

Caroline Mazel-Carlton
Western Massachusetts Recovery Learning Community, Holyoke, MA, United States

Andrew C. Page
School of Psychological Science, University of Western Australia, Perth, WA, Australia

Martin Plöderl
Department of Crisis Intervention and Suicide Prevention, University Clinic of Psychiatry, Psychotherapy, and Psychosomatics; Paracelsus Medical University, Salzburg, Austria; Department of Clinical Psychology, University Clinic of Psychiatry, Psychotherapy, and Psychosomatics, Paracelsus Medical University, Salzburg, Austria

Günter Schiepek
Institute of Synergetics and Psychotherapy Research, Paracelsus Medical University, Salzburg, Austria

Werner G.K. Stritzke
School of Psychological Science, University of Western Australia, Perth, WA, Australia

Gustavo Turecki
McGill Group for Suicide Studies, Douglas Mental Health University Institute, McGill University, Montreal, QC, Canada

Roz Walker
Associate Professor, Poche Centre for Indigenous Health, School of Indigenous Studies, University of Western Australia, Crawley, Perth, WA, Australia

Tricia J. Wylde
Health Promotion Unit, University of Western Australia, Crawley, WA, Australia

Bita Zareian
University of British Columbia

Acknowledgment

In memory of Michael Chandler (1938–2019): A distinguished researcher and advocate

PART 1

Time for a paradigm shift

CHAPTER 1

Suicide is about life

Werner G.K. Stritzke, Andrew C. Page
School of Psychological Science, University of Western Australia, Perth, WA, Australia

San Francisco's Golden Gate Bridge is an iconic landmark. It is an engineering feat that speaks to the triumph of human ingenuity to overcome the obstacle to travel presented by the Bay. However, it has iconic status in a more tragic manner, as it has been a common location for attempted suicide. Each death is tragic, but there has been a study of the survivors of a suicide attempt on the Golden Gate Bridge and this study is revealing.

Seiden (1978) followed up the 515 individuals who, in the period up until 1978, had come to the bridge with the intention of killing themselves, but had been dissuaded by the highway patrol officers. Of this group, 35 individuals had proceeded to die by suicide. Despite the tragedy of each subsequent death, the overwhelming pattern was that 90% of people who had come to the bridge with the express purpose to die by suicide went on to live a life without future attempts. In fact, one of the few survivors of jumping, Kevin Hines, described that the very second he let go of the bridge, he knew that he had made a big mistake. These results are revealing, because the vast majority of those who had been at the brink of following through with a suicide attempt using a highly lethal method, nonetheless re-engaged with a life worth living without attempting to end their life again.

A more recent large study used the Swedish national registers to follow-up over 34,000 people admitted to hospital after deliberate self-harm (Runeson, Haglund, Lichtenstein, & Tidemalm, 2016). Although not all the self-harm events may have been a suicide attempt, less than 3.5% (i.e., 1182) went on to die by suicide during the follow-up period of up to 9 years (670 males and 512 females). Thus, death by suicide following an initial attempt is the rare exception rather than the rule. Yet, evidence also informs us that a history of prior attempts (especially multiple attempts) raises the risk level for a future attempt. But rather than seeking to understand what helps the vast majority of attempters (despite their increased risk level) to continue living and not die by suicide, which might hold the key to preventing future attempts, the conventional approach has been to focus instead on identifying risk status and those factors that may lead to a

Alternatives to Suicide
ISBN 978-0-12-814297-4
https://doi.org/10.1016/B978-0-12-814297-4.00001-7

future attempt. The problem with the latter approach is that there is now compelling evidence that it has not been effective (Franklin et al., 2017). First, the accuracy of a suicide 'expert' to predict a patient's future suicidal thoughts and behaviors based on a thorough assessment of risk factors is no better than the accuracy of a lay person flipping a coin. That is, after decades of trying, research has produced no meaningful advances in suicide prediction. Second, the World Health Organisation declared suicide prevention a "global imperative", because suicide rates in many countries have been increasing in recent years (WHO, 2014). For example in Australia, suicide is the leading cause of death for people aged 15 to 44 (AIHW, 2018). Third, our conventional approach to interventions with 'high risk' individuals by hospitalization (voluntary or not) has kept many a suicidal person alive, but does not appear to extend to making an individual's life worth living following discharge. In the first three months after discharge, the suicide rates of patients admitted with suicidal thoughts or behaviors are nearly 200 times the global suicide rate (Chung et al., 2017). If we are unable to predict suicide attempts at better than chance, if suicide rates are increasing rather than decreasing, and if the rates of death by suicide following discharge from conventional risk-centric inpatient interventions are so high that some have them described as a "nightmare and disgrace" (Nordentoft, Erlangsen, & Madsen, 2016), then is it not time for a paradigm shift?

Suicide is less about death and more about life

When we ask why people die by suicide, we tend to focus on death. We respond by beginning to try to predict the occurrence of death by suicide and once we have identified these risk factors we may then try to develop preventive strategies that address the relevant issues. For example, we may have noted that suffocation by inhalation of town gas was a common method of suicide and then we might seek ways to limit access to this means. In other words, we adopt a risk-management and mitigation approach.

Before considering the limitation of this approach, it is necessary to note that risk management has potentially live saving benefits. First, certain factors predict increased risk, and so it behooves us to monitor and manage them. Second, risk mitigation has demonstrated positive outcomes. For example, domestic gas is one of many examples (Sarchiapone, Mandelli, Iosue, Andrisano, & Roy, 2011) where restricting access to common means of suicide (e.g., firearms, pesticides) brings about temporary reductions in the rates of death by suicide. Thus, risk mitigation and management is necessary and valuable.

Nonetheless, asking the question "why do people die by suicide?" places the focus on death. When a particular means of suicide is controlled, it does not mean that suicide is no longer a problem. People will choose alternative methods. The changing strategies highlights that suicide is a motivational problem; some people are motivated to initiate their own deaths. By phrasing the question in the way we have done, we are then inclined to ask, why would a person want to be dead?

But this is where the perspectives of those with lived experience encourage a subtly different approach to the conventional risk-management and mitigation approach. It seems that people who wish to die by suicide tend to report less often that they want to be dead, but that *they no longer want to live*. There are aspects about their lives that they want terminated (e.g., psychological pain, relationship difficulties, trauma and adversity) and death seems to be the only way to achieve this outcome. But as so cogently put by Mazel-Carlton (2018), while there is usually something in the suicidal person's life that needs to stop, it is not one's heartbeat.

One way the question of "why do people die by suicide?" can be reformulated is, "why do some people perceive life as not worth living?" Or even more importantly, "why do most people who experience suicidal thoughts, or episodes of self-harm where they had the intention to die, go on living and re-engage with life despite adversity and pain?" This seemingly subtle change leads to a paradigm shift in the way that we would approach suicide. That is, no longer is the sole focus upon risk mitigation, but it shifts to strengthening resilience. No longer do we only focus on trying to manage depression and hopelessness, but we consider how to improve quality of life and a sense of flourishing. Not only do we ask a coroner to investigate a death by suicide to make recommendations on how to avoid it in the future, but we may ask services to report on how many people have they kept alive and to make recommendations on how we can broaden the impact. In research, we may not only investigate why people may wish to die, but we also consider why a person may wish to live. In public policy, we may not only ask questions such as, if the media were to publish this story could it increase the probability someone else might die, but broaden it to consider, how many more may live? In sum, while it is critically important to understand why people die by suicide, we must not neglect to examine why people do *not* die by suicide.

Ideation to action is only one pathway

If the primary lens through which we view suicide is one in which people who are considering suicide are planning death, then this risk-oriented approach will lead to an ideation-to-action framework. Such a model has made a significant contribution to the field, by encouraging a focus on the dynamic nature of predictors. That is, progression from suicidal ideation to potentially lethal action involves a series of steps or phases (e.g., Klonsky & May 2015; O'Connor & Kirtley, 2018). As such, each of these stages involves potentially distinct processes and the component processes have their own risk factors (Klonsky, Saffer, & Bryan, 2018). These stage-specific moderators can serve to facilitate movement between the stages of suicidal ideation to suicidal action (O'Connor, 2011). Various theories outline how the desire to die transitions from suicidal ideation to intent and to action (Joiner, 2005; Klonsky, May, & Saffer, 2016; O'Connor, 2011; Rudd, 2006). However, these transitions are likely to be non-linear (Chapter 6), and are influenced by dynamic and fluid changes in the relative balance between the wish to die and a wish to live (Brown, Steer, Henriques, & Beck, 2005; Kovacs & Beck, 1997). These themes will be explored in later chapters, but it is clear that dynamic shifts in the wish to live and wish to die are associated with changes in suicide risk, and each are related to different causal factors (Bryan, Rudd, Peterson, Young-McCaughan, & Wertenberger, 2016).

Notwithstanding the important contribution of the ideation-to-action framework, another potential limitation is that most ideators do not proceed to an attempt, and most suicide attempters proceed not to attempt suicide again (ten Have et al., 2009). The ideation-to-action framework is largely silent about the mediators and moderators of progression in this ideation to *non*-action pathway, or indeed, dynamic intersections between these two pathways. Hence, it is important to acknowledge that in addition to the factors that moderate and mediate ideation-to-action, there are also factors that moderate and mediate ideation-to-*non*-action toward death, and instead underpin ideation-to-*action toward life*.

Ideation to non-action is the most common pathway

If most people who attempt suicide have contemplated death, but then transition to strengthening and re-engaging with their desire for life, how did this occur? This transition from ideation to *non*-action is not clearly articulated within the current scope of the ideation-to-action framework. Likewise, as noted above, risk prediction is fraught with uncertainty and lacks specificity. Maybe prediction could be improved if we attempted to also understand the transition from ideation to non-action. What predictors would help us identify which people return to a life characterised by a strong wish to live and a weak wish to die? Or perhaps most importantly, we must identify and nourish those factors that help individuals who experience suicidal thoughts every day of their life, and who do have a plan and access to the means, but nonetheless (!) lead productive and meaningful lives without engaging in suicidal behavior. Those with lived experience teach us that balancing a wish to die with an equally strong (or perhaps fragile) wish to live may be as good as it gets (see Chapter 8 and Chapter 9). Since there are many more people along this ideation to non-action pathway than on the pathway leading from ideation to suicidal action, the analyses would not be plagued by the problems associated with low base rates that bedevil the quest for accurate 'prediction of suicide'.

A framework for understanding suicide and providing effective support to those contemplating it is bound to be inadequate unless it addresses the current mismatch between conventional risk-centric approaches to suicide and what suicidal people tell us they actually need. With respect to best practice and standards of care, this disconnect is apparent when considering the emphasis that is given to 'managing risk' - is it foremost on managing the patient's risk to die by suicide, or is it skewed toward managing the clinician's risk to be held liable in the event one of their patients dies by suicide? (Chapter 8). The way forward toward an alternative approach is challenging. But growing evidence suggests that the need for coercive interventions to save a person from themselves (e.g., holding on to a person about to climb over a protective barrier to jump from a bridge) is far less common, than the need to work collaboratively with a suicidal person so they can help themselves. This would be a daunting departure from the 'conventional wisdom' and status quo, because it requires accepting that suicidal thoughts may be chronic, plans to act on those thoughts once devised by the patient are here to stay, and respect for the patient's autonomy is paramount for freeing the resources and capabilities of patients to help themselves (e.g., Jobes, 2012).

The ethics of balancing risk-centric with life-oriented approaches to suicide

One example where we can see the implications of an overly risk-centric approach is in the ethics of research into suicide. Institutional review boards and ethics committees are charged with the important responsibility of ensuring that research, "maximizes possible benefits and minimizes possible harms for participants" (National Commission for the Protection of Human Subjects of Biomedical and Behavioral Research, 1979, p. 5; see also National Health and Medical Research Council, 2007). To this end, an ethics committee must weigh up both the potential harm as well as any potential benefits of research based "on the available evidence" (National Health and Medical Research Council, 2007, p. 15). However, ethics committees tend to appear to favor more of a risk-management approach. For instance, approximately two-thirds of members of ethics committees expressed concern that exposure to suicide-related material during a research project may increase suicidal thoughts and behaviors after participation (Lakeman & Fitzgerald, 2009a, 2009b). Those risk-averse beliefs and assumptions are well-intentioned, but if untested or contrary to available evidence, may do more harm than good (DuBois et al., 2012). There is now consistent evidence from recent meta-analyses that there are no iatrogenic risks of asking about suicidality in suicide related research even with high risk participants, but instead, there are significant benefits such as reductions in suicidal thoughts and behaviors following participation (Blades, Stritzke, Page, & Brown, 2018; DeCou & Schumann, 2018). Thus, the available evidence suggests that continuing with the status quo raises several ethical concerns. That is, an imbalance toward unsubstantiated concern prompting overly restrictive protection of the individual undermines the important ethical principles of justice and respect for the individual's autonomy. Injustice arises when potentially vulnerable participants are deprived of the opportunity to receive the substantiated benefits of participation. Autonomy is undermined because ethical guidelines explicitly allow for participants to assume a higher risk when providing informed consent if participation has been shown to offer direct benefits (The National Health and Medical Research Council, 2007).

With respect to understanding suicide and helping those contemplating it, what are the ethics of persevering with a predominantly risk and death focused approach, if suicidal individuals supposed to benefit from this approach are adamant that this does not meet their needs? (see Chapter 8 and Chapter 9). This speaks to the ethical principles of justice and patient autonomy. As reviewed above, the available evidence does not support confidence in continuing with a business-as-usual approach. Doing so fails to meet the ethical principle of justice by depriving suicidal people of alternative, evidence-based approaches that are more risk tolerant and collaborative, but are constrained by the 'expert wisdom' of standards of care heavily geared toward the clinician's need to limit exposure to legal liability. This paradox has been critiqued by Chapter 9 who quote from a press release by the American Psychological Association (2016), which first concludes that the state of the evidence produced by science in predicting suicide is no better than random guessing, but then recommends to not abandon current guidelines with the rationale "as most of these guidelines were produced by expert consensus, there is reason to believe that they may be useful and effective". Davidow and Mazel-Carlton describe the latter statement very kindly as "bold"; other synonyms of 'bold' include 'rash', 'reckless', and 'foolhardy'. For science to effectively inform understanding of suicide and its prevention, it must bridge this chasm between adhering to the status quo of standards of care grounded in fear of legal liability, and meeting the needs of suicidal sufferers who are wise to the clinician's dilemma and hence are reluctant to seek 'expert' help for fear of unwanted interventions and loss of autonomy, which ultimately would weaken their agency over re-engaging with a life worth living. Overcoming this impasse between the prevailing approach of focusing primarily on preventing a patient's death, where that often goes hand in hand with impinging on the patient's freedom and autonomy via unwanted or coercive interventions, and the patient's priority of finding ways and the strength to help themselves to move forward with *life*, is perhaps the foremost ethical challenge of advancing the field of suicidology.

However, some recent 'promising' research directions are — though again well intentioned - rather blunt in even further disenfranchising the patient from the process of collaborative risk assessment and management, in that they aim to circumvent the need for a trusting and open dialogue with the patient altogether. One response to the vexing problem of patients not admitting their suicidal thoughts or intent to health professionals has been the quest for implicit measures that might reveal the patient's suicidal risk without their conscious awareness (e.g., Harrison, Stritzke, Fay, Ellison, & Hudaib, 2014; Nock et al., 2010). As argued by Harrison and colleagues (Harrison, Stritzke, Fay, & Hudaib, 2018), this approach contrasts sharply with a collaborative approach where "the clinician and patient sit side-by-side and deconstruct the patient's suicidality" (Comtois et al., 2011, p. 965). In such a collaborative approach, the clinician is not seen as an adversary from whom information must be concealed, but as an ally who puts trust in the informed consent of the patient (Jobes, 2016). By contrast, using implicit measures is fraught with an adversarial dynamic if the patient's self-report is distrusted in favor of an indirect probe designed to bypass the patient's conscious control over what the patient may or may not want to disclose. Fortunately, the growing evidence shows that the widely used death/suicide implicit association test unequivocally reflects variability in a person's self-associations with life rather than death (Chapter 2). Thus, it might be reassuring for a patient to learn that their mind struggling with suicidal thoughts is in effect hard-wired to cling to life. On the other hand, it has been suggested that the future of accurate suicide risk prediction may benefit from relying on machine learning. Specifically, the aim is that "the machine determines the optimal algorithm for prediction" and replaces the need for "a human deciding which variables should be included and what the relationships among variables should be" (Franklin et al., 2017, p. 218). While this may be welcomed by the clinician who may hope to abrogate legal liability to the machine, the ethics of relying on such algorithms would be at least as murky as those debated for driverless cars (Smith, 2018). Even if we assume that algorithms should not bear responsibility for their actions (Rahwan et al., 2019), where does that leave the suicidal person who is seeking to find support (from other humans?) for staying on the path toward a life worth living? Is an unwanted or coercive intervention any more palatable if prompted by an app rather than the clinician?

Beyond risk and toward a life worth living

This volume brings together contributions from international experts in suicide research and practice, and importantly, also features prominently the viewpoints of those with lived experience, as well as the unique perspectives from within Indigenous cultures and refugee populations where suicide rates are disproportionately high. Although authors shine a light on a diverse range of circumstances and approaches to suicide risk, they provide a shared vision of how a safe path away from suicide must go beyond risk mitigation and include charting a course toward a life worth living that is characterized by respect for autonomy and firmly aligned with the needs of the suicidal person.

The next two chapters in this first section of the book review the conceptualization and assessment of *zest for life*, both at implicit and explicit levels of measurement. To effectively help suicidal people to embrace their life as worth living, it is important to monitor and track any signs of erosion of the zest for life, as well as understand its role as an antidote to risk during prevention and recovery.

The second section of the book presents theoretical advances and new evidence on the dynamic interplay between death-promoting and life-sustaining factors in determining suicide risk and resilience. This section begins with a review of the temporal dynamics of the wish to live and the wish to die using fluid vulnerability theory as a conceptual frame. This is followed by a chapter examining these dynamic processes using longitudinal data from an emergency care sample, as well as daily monitoring data of short term shifts in risk and resilience profiles from an inpatient sample, both of which are compared to the dynamic balance of the wish to live and the wish to die in a non-clinical sample. The next chapter in this section outlines a non-linear perspective on suicidal processes and reviews the principles of interventions and resilience to suicide guided by this framework. The last chapter in this section draws attention to different forms of connectedness, as the one protective factor that — despite the traditional predominant emphasis on risk factors — has featured in several prominent theories of suicide.

The third section of the book shifts the focus on the experience of the suicidal person. The authors of the first chapter pool their respective expertise stemming on the one hand from a long career as a researcher and clinician specializing in suicide, and on the other hand from a long journey to learn how to fully live despite a life-long struggle with suicidal ideation. Drawing on this synergy between patient and provider, they challenge the conventional risk-centric approach to working with suicidal persons as well-intentioned but misguided, and advocate for the need to embrace a strong collaborative alliance where empathic understanding of the suicidal wish, and respect for the patient's autonomy is essential. The subsequent chapter by members and facilitators of the *Alternatives to Suicide* approach developed by the Westerns Massachusetts Recovery Learning Community takes the central importance of autonomy a step further. As a reaction to not having their needs met by the conventional "suicide prevention industry", no clinicians are involved in their successful program by and for people with lived experience. After a decade of growth and now being emulated across the globe as far away as Australia, this provides the strongest argument yet that suicidal people continue living when given the space and community where they want to do that for themselves, free from the often traumatic restrictions on their autonomy that underpins the risk-centric care that professional helpers are legally bound to provide. The next chapter in this section reviews the limitations and merits of different approaches to conceptualizing psychological resilience to suicidal experience. The authors highlight the importance of involving *experts by experience* in investigating psychological resilience to suicide. In this context, one must also consider that mental health professionals who work with suicidal people may also have or have had suicidal experiences themselves. The last chapter in this section examining suicide risk and resilience through the lens of the suicidal person draws on the contextual analysis of suicide notes left prior to an attempt or completed suicide. The authors find that while there has been an extensive focus on identifying risk factors, a high proportion of notes also contain positive themes such as love and hope. The potential value of greater exploration of the balance between risk and protective factors in suicide notes is yet to be systematically examined.

The fourth section of the book examines the evidence base for what contributes to disproportionate rates of suicide among Indigenous and refugee populations. The first chapter in this section reviews the emerging international evidence base within Indigenous suicide research. The importance of self-determination and cultural continuity, along with the restoration of life-affirming Indigenous knowledge systems are vital to building resilience and providing holistic, strength-based, culturally safe approaches to suicide prevention. In the following chapter on refugees and suicide, the authors review how among forced migrants the experience of living in a state of sustained displacement leads to a corrosion of resilience. The high suicide rates among people with a refugee background are attributed less to a desire to die, nor necessarily to the great adversity and peril experienced as they had to flee their homes, but to their gradual and sustained thwarting of their quest for a better life. Finally, the book concludes with an update on the epigenetics of suicidal behaviors.

Conclusion

In conclusion, the present volume is a call for a new approach to suicide. Rather than a predominant focus on trying to understand why people die by suicide, we and our colleagues argue that we need also to understand why people who contemplate and even attempt suicide do not wish to live. This shift in thinking leads us away from a sole focus on risk mitigation and management, and toward working out what can be done to ensure that people have lives worth living.

References

American Psychological Association. (2016). *After decades of research, science is No better able to predict suicidal behaviors* [online] Retrieved from https://www.apa.org/news/press/releases/2016/11/suicidal-behaviors.aspx.

Australian Institute of Health and Welfare. (2018). *Deaths in Australia.* Retrieved on 10 June 2019 from https://www.aihw.gov.au/reports/life-expectancy-death/deaths-in-australia/contents/leading-causes-of-death.

Blades, C. A., Stritzke, W. G. K., Page, A. C., & Brown, J. D. (2018). The benefits and risks of asking research participants about suicide: A meta-analysis of the impact of exposure to suicide-related content. *Clinical Psychology Review, 64*, 1–12. https://doi.org/10.1016/j.cpr.2018.07.001. Epub 2018 Jul 5.

Brown, G. K., Steer, R. A., Henriques, G. R., & Beck, A. T. (2005). The internal struggle between the wish to die and the wish to live: A risk factor for suicide. *American Journal of Psychiatry, 162*, 1977–1979.

Bryan, C. J., Rudd, M. D., Peterson, A. L., Young-McCaughan, S., & Wertenberger, E. G. (2016). The ebb and flow of the wish to live and the wish to die among suicidal military personnel. *Journal of Affective Disorders, 202*, 58–66.

Chung, D. T., Ryan, C. J., Pavlovic, D. H., Singh, S. P., Stanton, C., & Large, M. M. (2017). Suicide rates after discharge from psychiatric facilities: A systematic review and meta-analysis. *JAMA Psychiatry, 74*, 694–702. https://doi.org/10.1001/jamapsychiatry.2017.1044.

Comtois, K. A., Jobes, D. A., O'Connor, S. S., Atkins, D. C., Janis, K., Chessen, C. E., et al. (2011). Collaborative assessment and management of suicidality (CAMS): Feasibility trial for next-day appointment services. *Depression and Anxiety, 28*(11), 963–972. https://doi.org/10.1002/da.20895.

DeCou, C. R., & Schumann, M. E. (2018). On the iatrogenic risk of assessing suicidality: A meta-analysis. *Suicide and Life-Threatening Behavior, 48*, 531–543. https://doi.org/10.1111/sltb.12368.

DuBois, J. M., Beskow, L., Campbell, J., Dugosh, K., Festinger, D., Hartz, S., et al. (2012). Restoring balance: A consensus statement on the protection of vulnerable research participants. *American Journal of Public Health, 102*, 2220–2225. https://doi.org/10.2105/AJPH.2012.300757.

Franklin, J. C., Ribeiro, J. D., Fox, K. R., Bentley, K. H., Kleiman, E. M., Huang, X., et al. (2017). Risk factors for suicidal thoughts and behaviors: A meta-analysis of 50 years of research. *Psychological Bulletin, 14*, 187–232. https://doi.org/10.1037/bul0000084.

Harrison, D. P., Stritzke, W. G. K., Fay, N., Ellison, T. M., & Hudaib, A. (2014). Probing the implicit suicidal mind: Does the death/suicide implicit association teat reveal a desire to die, or a diminished desire to live? *Psychological Assessment, 26*, 831–840. https://doi.org/10.1037/pas0000001.

Harrison, D. P., Stritzke, W. G. K., Fay, N., & Hudaib, A. (2018). Suicide risk assessment: Trust an implicit probe or listen to the patient? *Psychological Assessment, 30*, 1317–1329. https://doi.org/10.1037/pas0000577.

ten Have, M., de Graaf, R., van Dorsselaer, S., Verdurmen, J., van't Land, H., Vollebergh, W., et al. (2009). Incidence and course of suicidal ideation and suicide attempts in the general population. *Canadian Psychiatric Association Journal/La Revue de l'Association des psychiatres du Canada, 54*, 824–833.

Jobes, D. A. (2012). The Collaborative Assessment and Management of Suicidality (CAMS): An evolving evidence-based clinical approach to suicidal risk. *Suicide and Life-Threatening Behavior, 42*, 640–653. https://doi.org/10.1111/j.1943-278X.2012.00119.x.

Jobes, D. A. (2016). *Managing suicidal risk: A collaborative approach* (2nd ed.). The Guildford Press.

Joiner, T. (2005). *Why people die by suicide*. Cambridge, MA: Harvard University Press.

Klonsky, E. D., & May, A. M. (2015). The three-step theory (3ST): A new theory of suicide rooted in the "ideation-to-action" framework. *International Journal of Cognitive Therapy, 8*, 114–129. https://doi.org/10.1521/ijct.2015.8.2.114.

Klonsky, E. D., May, A. M., & Saffer, B. Y. (2016). Suicide, suicide attempts, and suicidal ideation. *Annual Review of Clinical Psychology, 12*, 307–330. https://doi.org/10.1146/annurev-clinpsy-021815-093204.

Klonsky, E. D., Saffer, B. Y., & Bryan, C. J. (2018). Ideation-to-action theories of suicide: A conceptual and empirical update. *Current Opinions in Psychology, 22*, 38–43. https://doi.org/10.1016/j.copsyc.2017.07.020.

Kovacs, M., & Beck, A. T. (1977). The wish to die and the wish to live in attempted suicides. *Journal of Clinical Psychology, 33*, 361–365.

Lakeman, R., & Fitzgerald, M. (2009a). Ethical suicide research: A survey of researchers. *International Journal of Mental Health Nursing, 18*, 10–17. https://doi.org/10.1111/j.1447-0349.2008.00569.x.

Lakeman, R., & Fitzgerald, M. (2009b). The ethics of suicide research: The views of ethics committee members. *Crisis, 30*, 13–19. https://doi.org/10.1027/0227-5910.30.1.13.

Mazel-Carlton, C. (2018). *Human rights: Expanding the conversation. Talk given at the 10th World hearing voices congress* (The Hague, Netherlands).

National Commission for the Protection of Human Subjects of Biomedical and Behavioral Research. (1979). *The belmont report: Ethical principles and guidelines for the protection of human Subjects of research-the national commission for the protection of human Subjects of biomedical and behavioral research*. US Government Printing Office (2017, June 14). Retrieved from https://www.hhs.gov/ohrp/regulations-and-policy/belmont-report/index.html.

National Health and Medical Research Council (Australia). (2007). *National statement on ethical conduct in human research 2007 (updated may 2015)*. Retrieved from https://www.nhmrc.gov.au/_files_nhmrc/publications/attachments/e72_national_statement_may_2015_150514_a.pdf.

Nock, M. K., Park, J. M., Finn, C. T., Deliberto, T. L., Dour, H. J., & Banaji, M. R. (2010). Measuring the suicidal mind: Implicit cognition predicts suicidal behavior. *Psychological Science, 21*, 511–517. https://doi.org/10.1177/0956797610364762.

Nordentoft, M., Erlangsen, A., & Madsen, T. (2016). Postdischarge suicides: Nightmare and disgrace. *JAMA Psychiatry, 73*, 1113–1114. https://doi.org/10.1001/jamapsychiatry.2016.2010.

O'Connor, R. C. (2011). The integrated motivational-volitional model of suicidal behavior. *Crisis, 32*, 295–298. https://doi.org/10.1027/0227-5910/a000120.

O'Connor, R. C., & Kirtley, O. J. (2018). The integrated motivational–volitional model of suicidal behaviour. *Philosophical Transactions Royal Society B, 373*, 20170268. https://doi.org/10.1098/rstb.2017.0268.

Rahwan, I., Cebrian, M., Obradovich, N., Bongard, J., Bonnefon, J.-F., Breazeal, C., et al. (2019). Machine behaviour. *Nature, 568*, 477–486. https://www.nature.com/articles/s41586-019-1138-y.

Rudd, M. D. (2006). Fluid vulnerability theory: A cognitive approach to understanding the process of acute and chronic suicide risk. In T. E. Ellis (Ed.), *Cognition and suicide: Theory, research, and therapy* (pp. 355–368). Washington, DC, US: American Psychological Association. https://doi.org/10.1037/11377-016.

Runeson, B., Haglund, A., Lichtenstein, P., & Tidemalm, D. (2016). Suicide risk after nonfatal self-harm: A national cohort study, 2000-2008. *Journal of Clinical Psychiatry, 77*, 240–246. https://doi.org/10.4088/JCP.14m09453.

Sarchiapone, M., Mandelli, L., Iosue, M., Andrisano, C., & Roy, A. (2011). Controlling access to suicide means. *International Journal of Environmental Research and Public Health, 8*, 4550–4562. https://doi.org/10.3390/ijerph8124550.

Seiden, R. H. (1978). Where are they now? A follow-up study of suicide attempters from the golden gate bridge. *Suicide and Life-Threatening Behavior, 8*, 1–13.

Smith, O. (2018). *A huge global study on driverless car ethics found the elderly are expendable.* Retrieved from https://www.forbes.com/sites/oliversmith/2018/03/21/the-results-of-the-biggest-global-study-on-driverless-car-ethics-are-in/#70ce0c674a9f.

World Health Organization. (2014). *Preventing suicide: A global imperative*. Retrieved on 10 June 2019 from https://www.who.int/mental_health/suicide-prevention/world_report_2014/en/.

CHAPTER 2

The implicit suicidal mind clings to life

Dominique P. Harrison[a], Werner G.K. Stritzke[a], Jason Y.S. Leong[a], T. Mark Ellison[a], Nicolas Fay[a], Abdul-Rahman Hudaib[b]
[a]School of Psychological Science, University of Western Australia, Perth, WA, Australia; [b]Division of Psychiatry/UWA Medical School, The University of Western Australia, Perth, WA, Australia

Fear of losing a patient to suicide weighs on the minds of health professionals dedicated to helping those who are not only in distress, but often despair of life itself. Beyond the traumatic impact losing a patient has on the clinician, the anxiety around suicide is kept on a slow burn by several inescapable factors surrounding patient safety. There is of course the worry about malpractice claims (Bongar & Sullivan, 2013; Jobes, Rudd, Overholser, & Joiner, 2008), not helped by the disconcerting conclusions from recent reviews that the ability to predict suicide attempts remains elusive and is little better than chance (Franklin et al., 2017). An overreliance on identification of risk factors and commonly used risk assessment scales that have poor predictive validity would provide false reassurance rather than effectively alley clinicians' worry about patient safety (Chan et al., 2016; Large et al., 2016). Arguably, the greatest fear of losing a patient to suicide stems from the clinician's need to rely on the patient honestly revealing their suicidal intent (Bryan & Rudd, 2006), while knowing that patients often make a suicide attempt after explicitly denying any suicidal thoughts or intent (Busch, Fawcett, & Jacobs, 2003; Fawcett et al., 1990).

When patients are unwilling to reveal their suicidal intentions for fear of unwanted clinical intervention, it would be advantageous for clinicians to have additional risk assessment tools that do not rely on patient self-report. Accessing the implicit suicidal mind with behavioral measures that elicit responses from individuals that are not easily controlled, lack intention, and are made with little awareness and greater automaticity, may provide insight into the strength of suicidal intent that is not apparent from patient self-report (Bargh, 1994; Nosek, Hawkins, & Frazier, 2011). One such measure to assess individuals' automatic, cognitive self-associations with death relative to life is the death/suicide Implicit

Alternatives to Suicide
ISBN 978-0-12-814297-4
https://doi.org/10.1016/B978-0-12-814297-4.00002-9

Association Test (d/s-IAT; Nock et al., 2010). The rationale underlying this computer-based reaction time task is that reaction time and accurate responses are facilitated when the combined concepts being measured are strongly associated in memory (e.g., self and death/suicide), and reaction time and accuracy are inhibited when the concepts are weakly associated in memory (e.g., self and life). Using a standard scoring algorithm (Greenwald, Nosek, & Banaji, 2003), a net difference d/s-IAT score between response latencies of self-associations with life and self-associations with death/suicide can be computed such that, for example, negative scores indicate individuals responded faster when self and death/suicide concepts are paired together and hence have a stronger self-association with death/suicide relative to life. Conversely, positive scores indicate individuals responded faster when self and life concepts are paired together and hence have a stronger self-association with life. Scores on the d/s-IAT have shown some promise in differentiating between high and low risk individuals, as well as prospectively predicting future suicide risk (e.g., Nock et al., 2010; Randall, Rowe, Dong, Nock, & Colman, 2013). However, these findings have not been consistently replicated (e.g., Barnes et al., 2017; Chiurliza et al., 2016; Harrison, Stritzke, Fay, & Hudaib, 2018).

In a study of emergency care patients, d/s-IAT scores distinguished suicide attempters from other psychiatrically distressed patients, and were associated with suicide-attempt status at presentation to the emergency department beyond explicit self-report predictors (Nock et al., 2010). However, in subsequent studies of emergency care patients, the d/s-IAT did not distinguish between patients who attempted suicide in the week prior to admission and patients who had not attempted suicide in the week prior to admission (Barnes et al., 2017), or between patients with suicidal ideation at intake who had no history of suicide attempts, and attempters who had made at least one suicide attempt in their lifetime prior to emergency care admission (Harrison et al., 2018). Likewise, in a sample of adolescents aged 13—19 years with a history of suicidal thoughts or behaviors admitted to short-term residential psychiatric treatment, there was no significant difference in death-IAT scores between ideators and attempters (Glenn et al., 2017). Finally, scores on a death-IAT and scores on a suicide-IAT were not associated with suicidal ideation in a large sample of US military service members (Chiurliza et al., 2016).

These findings cast doubt on the d/s-IAT's ability to reliably differentiate between individuals along different points on the ideation-to-action pathway to suicide (Klonsky & May 2015). The assumption that a history of suicide attempts would be more likely to strengthen implicit associations of self with death/suicide than merely thinking about it is not consistently supported by the available evidence. Although, when the d/s-IAT is administered immediately after an acute suicide attempt during emergency care, the d/s-IAT differentiated between individuals who were presenting with their first suicide attempt and those who had made multiple prior suicide attempts (Harrison et al., 2018). Compared to first time attempters, multiple attempters had significantly weaker self-associations with life relative to death/suicide. Harrison and colleagues speculated that multiple attempters may have relatively stronger existing memory traces formed after the repeated trauma associated with multiple past attempts. Hence, the acute and salient experience of a just survived brush with death may have activated those diminished implicit self-associations with life in multiple attempters to a greater extent than in first time attempters.

Similar to the equivocal results regarding the d/s-IAT's ability to reliably distinguish between relevant risk groups, evidence from longitudinal studies that the d/s-IAT may be useful in prospectively predicting suicidal thoughts and behavior above and beyond other risk indicators and self-reported intent is inconsistent. In two prospective studies with patient samples, the d/s-IAT predicted suicide attempts at six-month follow-up (Barnes et al., 2017; Nock et al., 2010). However, the prospective predictive utility of the d/s-IAT could not be replicated in a more recent study using a similar sample of emergency care patients that were followed up for the same six-month period (Harrison et al., 2018). Instead, explicit clinician and patient prediction outperformed the implicit measure and complemented each other in prospectively predicting different aspects of future suicide risk and resilience. Specifically, clinician estimates predicted death-promoting factors (i.e., suicidal ideation) and patient estimates predicted life-sustaining factors (i.e., desire to live and zest for life).

In sum, there is some initial evidence that the d/s-IAT is useful in prospectively predicting suicidal behavior, but results have been more equivocal regarding the d/s-IAT's ability to reliably distinguish between relevant risk groups. One limitation of most previous studies using the d/s-IAT was that the focus was primarily on investigating the practical clinical utility of this implicit tool, without much consideration given to what d/s- IAT scores reflect. Ultimately, for the d/s-IAT to have clinical utility, it is necessary to consider a conceptual model that could guide the interpretation of the presumed association between the implicit suicidal mind and suicidal thoughts, intentions, and behavior.

What underlies variations in d/s-IAT scores?

Harrison and colleagues outlined a conceptual model of the implicit suicidal mind grounded in contemporary theories of suicide (Harrison et al., 2018). A fundamental premise of the interpersonal theory of suicide is that humans are evolutionary wired to cling to life (Joiner, 2005). While it is rather common to think about suicide, few go on to make an attempt, and even fewer die by suicide. Joiner (2005) reasoned that because the instinctual inclination toward life and a strong drive for self-preservation is strongly ingrained, it is difficult for an individual to act on suicidal desire. Consequently, people do not naturally possess the capability to engage in serious self-harm, and therefore this is unlikely to occur unless they have first successfully "beaten down the instinct to live" (Joiner, 2005, p.24). Acquiring the capability to overcome the deep-rooted desire to live is aided by frequent instances of suicidal experience. Through repeated exposure to experiences that reduce an individual's fear of death and pain sensitivity, or the cognitive rehearsal of such experiences, can the hold on life be undermined and the capability for lethal self-harm strengthened (George, Page, Hooke, & Stritzke, 2016; Van Orden et al., 2010).

What then are the potential mechanisms that underlie variations in d/s-IAT scores? Given that humans have a strong ingrained desire to live, and the d/s-IAT is assumed to tap into automatic memory associations between self and attributes such as life and death, then one would expect that people would generally show stronger implicit self-associations with life than with death (Hypothesis 1). However, repeated self-associations with the prospect of one's own deliberate death, facilitated by acquiring greater pain tolerance and reduced fear of death, may diminish the automatic tendency to fear death and associated pain (Harrison et al., 2018). To the extent that new memory associations repeatedly associate the self with death in suicidal individuals, the implicit self-life association will be weakened and may lead to a stronger self-association with death than with life.

Thus, implicit suicide cognition, as measured by the d/s-IAT, may conceptually reflect a gradual movement away from the desire to live as an individual's self-association with life progressively weakens, but not necessarily to the extent that self-associations with life become weaker than self-associations with death/suicide. Although for some high-risk suicidal individuals who continue to gain suicidal experience, such as in a sample made up primarily of multiple attempters (e.g., Nock et al., 2010), their self-association with life may diminish to such an extent that it is no longer stronger than their self-association with death/suicide. This process of presumed malleability in implicit suicide cognition is consistent with the notion of cognitive sensitization (Beck, 1996), whereby frequent suicide-related experience leads to suicide related thoughts and behaviors becoming more accessible and active.

The more accessible and active the thoughts and behaviors become, the more easily and automatically they are triggered. That is, along the bipolar continuum of d/s-IAT difference scores, implicit death/suicide related cognitions may become favored over implicit life related cognitions. If the passive or deliberate exposure to experiences that facilitate the acquisition of the capability to engage in lethal self-harm is required to beat down the implicitly ingrained desire to cling to life, then the association between d/s-IAT scores and measures of suicide-related behavior will be partly mediated by the strength of an individual's acquired capability for suicide (Hypothesis 2).

If d/s-IAT scores reflect variability in the relative strength of self-associations with life and death, what then is the evidence for this presumed malleability of d/s-IAT scores? Perhaps the strongest evidence to date comes from an experimental priming study which tested the effects of success and failure priming conditions on subsequent performance on a d/s-IAT task (Tang, Wu, & Miao, 2013). In each condition, participants showed stronger self-associations with life than with death, but relative to a no priming control condition, success-related priming resulted in stronger self-life associations, and failure-related priming resulted in weaker self-life associations. This effect was more pronounced in participants high in internal locus of control compared to participants high in external locus of control. There is also longitudinal evidence that d/s-IAT scores can change over time. In a study of psychiatric inpatients with complex, treatment resistant disorders, a weak implicit self-association with life at admission became stronger over the course of treatment, and the stronger the association between self and life at admission, the lower was participants' suicidal ideation six weeks later at discharge (Ellis, Rufino, & Green, 2016). The same pattern of change in d/s-IAT scores from weaker self-associations with life at admission to stronger self-associations with life at discharge, and the same prospective association of stronger self-life associations at admission with lower suicidal ideation at discharge, was observed in adolescents with a history of suicidal thoughts and behaviors during short-term residential psychiatric treatment (Glenn et al., 2017).

Thus, there is clear evidence from experimental and longitudinal studies that implicit suicide-related cognitions as measured by the d/s-IAT are malleable over relatively short time periods. These changes were observed in adolescent and adult psychiatric inpatient samples (Ellis et al., 2016; Glenn et al., 2017). Importantly, these changes do not reflect a shift from an implicit self-association with death at intake to a self-association with life at discharge; they reflect a shift from weaker self-associations with life at the start of treatment to stronger self-associations with life at the end of treatment. In fact, at no time did high-risk suicidal patients show a stronger implicit self-association with death relative to life. This suggests that risk estimates based on the d/s-IAT reveal the extent of a diminished self-association with life rather than an implicit identification with death (Harrison, Stritzke, Fay, Ellison, & Hudaib, 2014).

Because the studies assessing patients at admission and discharge did not include a control condition of no treatment, it is not possible to attribute the changes in implicit suicidal cognitions to the treatment received. But given that it has been shown that implicit suicide-related cognitions are malleable, psychosocial treatments that improve individuals' coping skills and increase the salience of reasons for living may act to strengthen an individual's implicit identification with life. Glenn and colleagues (Glenn et al., 2017) concluded that shifts in the strength of implicit identification with death relative to life become apparent early in the development of suicidal thoughts and behaviors, rather than only after a long history of chronic suicidal thoughts and behaviors. It is plausible that, just as frequent or intense suicide-related experiences can undermine the ingrained implicit identification with life, a rekindling of a more positive outlook on and zestful engagement with life during treatment can enhance the belief there is a life worth living, and hence counter the shift toward a diminished implicit identification with life (Bryan, Rudd, Peterson, Young-McCaughan, & Wertenberger, 2016; Harrison et al., 2018, 2014; Jobes, 2016; Linehan, Goodstein, Nielsen, & Chiles, 1983). If the exposure to treatment or other supportive life affirming experiences facilitate the rekindling and enhancement of an individual's zest for life, then the association between d/s-IAT scores and measures of suicide-related ideation and behavior will be mediated by the strength of an individual's zest for life (Hypothesis 3).

In Hypothesis 2 we predicted that because the acquisition of capability to engage in lethal self-harm is required to beat down the implicitly ingrained desire to cling to life, the association between d/s-IAT scores and measures of suicide behavior should be partly mediated by the strength of an individual's acquired capability for suicide. In Hypothesis 3, we considered that this mediating effect of acquired capability in undermining the ingrained implicit identification with life, could be countered by an opposing mediating effect of zest for life which buffers the strength of implicit identification with life against the eroding effect of acquired capability, or enhances it with renewed vigor after implicit identification with life has been eroded. Whether the association between implicit self-associations with death/life and suicide risk is mediated by enhanced acquired capability for suicide or diminished zest for life, or both, can be tested using a multiple mediator model (Preacher & Hayes, 2008). Support for Hypothesis 2 requires that a stronger implicit self-association with life on the d/s-IAT will be associated with lower acquired capability for suicide, whereas higher acquired capability will be positively associated with suicide risk. Support for Hypothesis 3 requires that a stronger implicit self-association with life on the d/s-IAT will be associated with higher zest for life, whereas higher zest for life will be negatively associated with suicide risk. If both mediating pathways in the multiple mediator model are significant, this can be conceptualized as a 'tug of war' between competing forces mediating the association between implicit self-identification along a death-life continuum and suicide risk. Whereas higher acquired capability for suicide increases suicide risk, higher zest for life lowers suicide risk.

Does the death/suicide IAT reveal a desire to die, or a diminished desire to live?

Because the d/s-IAT is a relative measure of the strength of implicit identification with life and death, scores are computed as a net difference score (D-score) between response latencies of self-associations with life and self-associations with death/suicide (Greenwald et al., 2003). Therefore, it is arbitrary whether D-scores are computed in such a way that positive d/s-IAT scores reflect stronger self-associations with life, and negative d/s-IAT scores reflect stronger self-associations with death/suicide, or vice versa. Before reviewing d/s-IAT results across studies published to date with respect to Hypothesis 1 (that people generally would be expected to show stronger implicit self-associations with life than with death), it must be noted that in only three of the studies in Table 2.1 (Harrison et al., 2018, 2014; Violanti, Mnatsakanova, & Andrew, 2013) the IAT D-score was computed such that a positive IAT D-score represents a stronger self-association with life, and a

Table 2.1 Implicit scores, sample sizes, and sample type (including history of suicide attempts) across IAT studies.

Study	IAT	*D* Score	N	Sample
Barnes et al., 2017	Death/Suicide IAT			Veterans with a very high, self-reported, history of attempts (67.6%) and multiple attempts (42.8%)
	with recent attempt	-.44	44	
	without recent attempt	-.48	129	
	with follow-up attempt	-.29	27	
	without follow-up attempt	-.50	136	
Chiurliza et al., 2016	Death IAT	-.62	1548	Army recruits with an extremely low history of attempts (0.3%) and multiple attempts (0.1%), according to military records
	Suicide IAT	-.63	1548	
Ellis et al., 2016	Death IAT	-.49	118	In patients at a psychiatric hospital with a very high, self-reported, history of attempts (52.5%) and multiple attempts (31.5%)
	admission	-.48		
	discharge	-.59		
Glenn et al., 2017	Death IAT		275	Adolescents admitted to a short-term psychiatric treatment program with a high, self-reported, history of attempts (39.9%)
	with ideation and no attempt	-.28		
	with attempt (lifetime)	-.29		
	with attempt (past year)	-.24		
	with attempt (past month)	-.31		
	admission	-.28	275	
	discharge	-.35	250	
Harrison et al., 2014	Death/Suicide IAT[a]	-.47	408	Undergraduate students with a moderate, self-reported, history of attempts (14.3%) and multiple attempts (4.3%)
	with no attempt (lifetime)	-.48	357	
	with attempt (lifetime)	-.38	51	

Harrison et al., 2018	Death/Suicide IAT[a]	-.51	128	Patients presenting to the emergency department of a large hospital with a very high, self-reported, history of attempts (71.9%) and multiple attempts (60.9%)
	with no attempt	-.43	21	
	with single attempt	-.60	29	
	with multiple attempts	-.49	78	
	with recent single attempt	-.80	15	
	with recent multiple attempt	-.46	38	
Hussey et al., 2015	Death-identity IAT	-.34	42	Undergraduate students with no information provided on history of attempts
Nock et al., 2010	Death/Suicide IAT	_[b]	91	Patients presenting to the psychiatric emergency department of a large hospital, all of whom had a history of attempts
	D score $<$ 0 (life association)		69	
	D score $>$ 0 (death association)		22	
Price et al., 2009	Death IAT		26	Treatment-resistant depression patients with a moderate, self-reported, history of attempts (19%)
	Ketamine			
	baseline	-0.48		
	24hrs post-infusion	-0.28		
Price et al., 2014	Death IAT			Treatment-resistant unipolar major depression patients with a moderate, self-reported, history of attempts (28%)
	Ketamine		36	
	baseline	-0.39		Treatment-resistant unipolar major depression patients with a moderate-high, self-reported, history of attempts (38%)
	24 hrs post-infusion	-0.36		
	Midazolam		21	
	baseline	-0.54		
	24 hrs post-infusion	-0.39		

Continued

Table 2.1 Implicit scores, sample sizes, and sample type (including history of suicide attempts) across IAT studies.—cont'd

Study	IAT	*D* Score	N	Sample
Tang et al., 2013	Death/Suicide IAT		138	Undergraduate students with no information provided on history of attempts
	no priming	-0.41	24	
	priming (failure-related)	-0.24	20	
	priming (success-related)	-0.57	26	
Violanti et al., 2013	Suicide IAT[a]	–[b]	65	Police officers from several departments with no information provided on history of attempts
	D score < -0.15 (life association)		52	
	D score > -0.15 < 0.15 (neutral)		9	
	D score > 0.15 (death association)		4	

Note. [a]In three of the studies the IAT d-score was computed such that a positive IAT d-score represents a stronger self-association with life, and a negative IAT d-score represents a stronger self-association with death. Because the majority of Death/Suicide IAT studies computed the IAT d-score such that (somewhat counter intuitively) a negative IAT d-score represents a stronger self-association with life, and a positive IAT d-score represents a stronger self-association with death, the originally reported positive IAT d-scores in studies marked with the superscript 'a' were reversed for ease of interpretation across IAT d-scores in this table, so that a negative IAT d-score consistently denotes a stronger self-association with life across all studies included in the table.[b] In two of the studies no mean IAT d-score was reported. Authors only reported number of participants with a negative IAT d-score (stronger life association), or positive IAT d-score (stronger death association), or an IAT d-score at or near zero (interpreted as a 'neutral' association).

negative IAT D-score represents a stronger self-association with death. However, the majority of d/s-IAT studies computed the IAT D-score such that (somewhat counter intuitively) a negative IAT D-score represents a stronger self-association with life, and a positive IAT D-score represents a stronger self-association with death. Given this, the originally reported positive IAT D-scores in the three studies marked with the superscript 'a' were reverse scored for ease of interpretation across IAT D-scores in this table, so that a negative IAT D-score consistently denotes a stronger self-association with life across all studies in the table. In two studies, marked with the superscript 'b', no mean IAT D-score was reported. In these studies the authors only reported the number of participants with a negative IAT D-score (stronger life association), or positive IAT D-score (stronger death association), or an IAT D-score at or near zero (interpreted as a 'neutral' association).

Table 2.1 shows that, without exception, all studies report mean d/s-IAT scores reflecting a stronger implicit identification with life. This is consistent across clinical and non-clinical samples, including those at the highest end of the risk spectrum such as emergency care patients following an acute suicide attempt, or treatment resistant psychiatric patients with a history of suicidal ideation and attempts. For example, the frequency distribution of d/s-IAT scores in a non-clinical sample show that 91.2% had scores reflecting stronger implicit identification with life, and this proportion was very similar in those with a history of prior suicide attempts (88.2%; Harrison et al., 2014). Similarly, frequency graphs of IAT scores on both a death IAT and a suicide-IAT in a large sample of military recruits closely parallel the distribution reported by Harrison and colleagues (Chiurliza et al., 2016). Even among emergency care samples that include many patients with multiple prior suicide attempts, the vast majority have d/s-IAT scores reflecting stronger implicit identification with life than with death (e.g., 75.8% in Nock et al., 2010; and 83.6% in Harrison et al., 2018). Moreover, as noted earlier, when d/s-IAT scores were tracked in high-risk inpatients longitudinally from admission to discharge, they always reflected stronger implicit self-associations with life than with death, and this implicit identification with life gained strength over the course of inpatient care (Ellis et al., 2016; Glenn et al., 2017).

In sum, there is now compelling and consistent evidence in support of Hypothesis 1, that people generally show stronger implicit self-associations with life than with death. That is, the implicit suicidal mind, as measured by the d/s-IAT, clings to life. Thus, the "death/suicide' label of this IAT is somewhat of a misnomer (Harrison et al., 2018). Variability of d/s-IAT scores primarily reflects erosion or strengthening of a protective factor – attachment to life. This conclusion is consistent with results from a comparison of six versions of death related implicit association tests (Randall et al., 2013). IAT versions that only measured implicit identification with death, without considering the relative strength of implicit identification with life, did not predict future self-harm. Only a version of the IAT that measured self-associations with death *and life* predicted future self-harm, which led the authors to conclude that, when probing the implicit suicidal mind and conducting suicide risk assessments, it may be important to measure individuals' implicit - and perhaps explicit - associations with life. If behavioral responses on the d/s-IAT indeed tap into the strength of an individual's implicit attachment to life, we next address the question whether the association between implicit self-associations with death/life and suicide risk are mediated by the strength of self-reported zest for life, against the strength of self-reported acquired capability for suicide.

Is the association between the d/s-IAT and suicide risk mediated by zest for life or acquired capability for suicide, or both?

Using a multiple mediator model provides a means by which the strength of more than one mediating pathway between a predictor and outcome can be tested (Preacher & Hayes, 2008). Here we simultaneously test our Hypotheses 2 and 3 and hence the relative mediating influence of acquired capability and zest for life, respectively, on the association between d/s-IAT scores and various indicators of suicide risk.

Two further predictions from the perspective of the ideation-to-action framework (Klonsky, May, & Saffer, 2016) concern the relative influence of acquired capability and zest for life on suicide-specific indicators of risk and more general risk indicators. Suicide-specific, action oriented indicators, such as suicide intention and readiness, are more proximal to suicide attempts than suicide ideation or general risk factors such as depression. Furthermore, the interpersonal theory of suicide posits that acquired capability is a proximal causal antecedent of suicidal behavior facilitating the transition from suicidal desire to acting on that desire (Joiner, 2005; Van Orden et al., 2010). Hence, acquired capability for suicide is expected to be the stronger of the two opposing mediators for those indicators of risk signaling more advanced progression along the ideation-to-action pathway (i.e., intention, readiness, and attempts). By contrast, general risk indicators, such as psychological distress and depression, are more distal indicators of suicide risk. A person's zest for life may confer resilience to a greater extent to these more distal indicators of risk and the factors contributing to suicidal desire than to those contributing to suicidal action (Collins, Best, Stritzke, & Page; 2016; Collins, Stritzke, Page, Brown, & Wylde, 2018; Harrison et al., 2014; O'Connor & Nock, 2014). If this is the case, zest for life will be a stronger mediator of suicidal ideation and more general and distal indicators of risk compared to acquired capability.

Method

Participants

One hundred undergraduate students (68 female; $M_{age} = 19.96$ years, $SD = 6.62$) from the University of Western Australia participated for partial course credit. They were selected from a larger pool (N = 999) based on their answers to measures of acquired capability for suicide and zest for life. The screening sample was divided into ten acquired capability for suicide and ten zest for life decile groups, based on the mean scores for each measure. Five participants were recruited from each decile group to maximise variation across the range of acquired capability for suicide and zest for life scores. Of these, 71% were Caucasian, 20% Asian, 2% Aboriginal/Torres Strait Islander, and the remaining 7% were classified as other. Forty-one participants had experienced suicide ideation in the past year and 11 had a history of one or more suicide attempts in their lifetime. The University's ethics review board approved all procedures and informed consent was obtained from all participants.

Procedure and measures

Using individual desktop computers, participants completed the death/life IAT and questionnaires online in a counterbalanced order.

Death/life implicit association test (death/life IAT; Nock et al., 2010**).** The death/life IAT is a computer-based categorisation task that uses reaction time to measure an individual's automatic mental associations they hold about death/suicide and life. The task measures how long it takes an individual to categorize words associated with each of the following four categories: 'death/suicide' (deceased, die, dead, lifeless, and suicide); 'life' (alive, breathing, thrive, live, and survive); 'me' (myself, my, self, mine, and

I); and 'not me', (them, other, theirs, their, and they). The categorization task is completed under two conditions. In the first condition, words representing 'death/suicide' and 'me' are categorised using the same response key and words representing 'life' and 'not me' are categorised using an alternative response key. In the second condition, words representing 'death/suicide' and 'not me' are categorised using the same response key, and words representing 'life' and 'me' are categorised using an alternative response key. Responses are speeded when the combined categories are strongly associated in memory.

Reaction times to classify words in the 'death/suicide or me' and 'life or me' categories were recorded and analyzed using the standard IAT algorithm (Greenwald et al., 2003) to calculate a net difference 'death/life IAT' score. Positive death/life IAT scores indicate individuals responded faster when 'life' was paired with 'me' than when 'death/suicide' was paired with 'me', and hence have a stronger self-association with 'life' relative to 'death/suicide'.

Acquired capability for suicide. The 7-item Acquired Capability with Rehearsal for Suicide Scale (ACWRSS; George et al., 2016) assesses reductions in death-related fear, increases in pain tolerance, and mental rehearsal for suicide. Participants indicate their agreement to statements such as 'I have gone through in my mind what it would be like to die' and 'I can tolerate pain much more than I used to' using a 9-point scale ranging from *(0) = not at all* to *(8) = very strongly*. A high score represents a high capability for suicide. The ACWRSS has good internal consistency in non-clinical ($\alpha = 0.91$) and clinical ($\alpha = 0.88$) samples, and good 8-week test-retest reliability ($r = 00.85$) (George et al.; 2016). Internal consistency in the current sample was good ($\alpha = 0.81$).

Zest for life. This 12-item self-report measure (Chapter 3; George, Stritzke, Page, Brown, & Wylde) assesses a person's engagement with life and positive future outlook. Participants indicate their agreement to statements such as 'I feel less alive than I used to' and 'I have so much to look forward to' using a 9-point scale ranging from *(0) = not at all* to *(8) = very strongly*. Six items are reverse-scored, such that a high score represents high zest for life. The measure has excellent internal consistency across different samples ($\alpha = 0.95$ - 00.95; Collins, Best, Stritzke, & Page, 2016; 2018), and in the current sample ($\alpha = 0.95$).

Suicide risk measures. Suicide risk was assessed using four suicide-specific indicators of suicide risk (suicide ideation, suicide intention, suicide readiness, and suicide attempts) and two general indicators of suicide risk (depression and psychological distress). Measures of non-suicidal self-harm thoughts and attempts were included to ensure participants clearly distinguished self-harm thoughts and behaviors without the intent to die, from suicidal thoughts and behaviors with the intent to die (Nock, 2010).

Suicide-specific indicators of suicide risk. Four questions from the Self-Injurious Thoughts and Behaviors Interview (SITBI; Nock, Holmberg, Photos, & Michel, 2007) assessed suicide ideation (*'How many times in the past year have you thought about suicide?'*) and suicide attempts (*'How many times in your lifetime have you made an actual attempt to kill yourself, in which you had at least some intent to die?'*), as distinct from self-harm thoughts (*'How many times in the past year have you thought about purposely hurting yourself without wanting to die?'*) and self-harm attempts (*'How many times in your lifetime have you purposely attempted to hurt yourself without wanting to die?'*). Suicide ideation and self-harm thoughts were measured on a 6-point scale, with the following response options *(0) = Never, (1) = Once or twice a year, (2) = Once or twice a month, (3) = Once or twice a week, (4) = Three or four times a week, (5) = Almost every day*. Suicide attempts and self-harm attempts were measured on a 5-point scale, with the following response options *(0) = Never, (1) = Once, (2) = Twice, (3) = Three or four times, (4) = Five or more times*. The SITBI is suitable for use with non-clinical samples (Nock et al., 2007) and in self-report format (Latimer; Meade, & Tennant, 2013).

Two additional items assessed suicide readiness and suicide intention. Participants were asked to indicate their agreement with the statements, *'If I wanted to kill myself, I feel ready to do so'* and *'I have no intention of killing myself in the future'*, with responses ranging from *(0) = not at all to (8) = very strongly*. For the suicide readiness question, a high score represented high readiness for suicide. Responses for the suicide intention question were reverse-scored, so that a high score represented strong intention for suicide.

General indicators of suicide risk. Depression was assessed using the 7-item depression subscale of the Depression, Anxiety and Stress Scales-21 (DASS-21; Lovibond & Lovibond, 1995). Participants rate the frequency and severity of experiencing negative emotions over the previous week on a 4-point scale from *(0) = did not apply to me* to *(3) = applied to me very much, or most of the time*. The depression subscale of the DASS-21 demonstrates good construct validity with other measures of depression (Antony, Bieling, Cox, Enns, & Swinson; 1998) and has good internal consistency in non-clinical samples ($\alpha = 0.88$; Henry & Crawford, 2005; $\alpha = 0.83$: Norton, 2007) and in the current sample ($\alpha = 0.92$).

Psychological distress was assessed using the 10-item Kessler Psychological Distress Scale (K10; Kessler et al., 2002). Participants indicate the frequency of ten symptoms of psychological distress in the past four weeks on a 5-point scale ranging from *(0) = none of the time* to *(4) = all of the time*. The K10 can discriminate individuals with mood disorders from those without and has excellent internal consistency in non-clinical samples ($\alpha = 0.93$; Kessler et al., 2002) and in the current sample ($\alpha = 0.93$).

Overview of analyses

First, the distribution of death/life IAT scores was examined. Second, multiple mediation analyses were conducted using bootstrapping procedures (Preacher & Hayes, 2008) to test if the relationship between implicit self-associations with death/life and indicators of suicide risk is mediated by acquired capability for suicide and/or a diminished zest for life.

Bootstrapping resampling procedures produce two estimated analyses: the total indirect effect and the specific indirect effects. This involves repeatedly sampling from the dataset with replacement in order to estimate these effects. For each effect, bootstrapping produces a bias-corrected lower and upper confidence interval, based on stipulated confidence levels. To establish if an effect is significant, one examines the values corresponding to the lower and upper confidence intervals. If zero lies between the two values, this indicates no significant effect. If zero does not lie between the two values, a significant effect is indicated. The total indirect effect assesses if both mediators combined mediate the relationship between the death/life IAT and the indicators of suicide risk. A significant total indirect effect is not a prerequisite for investigating specific indirect effects (Preacher & Hayes, 2008). The specific indirect effects assess each mediator's unique ability to account for the effect of the death/life IAT on indicators of suicide risk, above and beyond the other mediator in the model. The specific indirect effects of each mediator are contrasted to determine if there is a significant difference in the mediators' ability to mediate the relationship between the death/life IAT and the indicators of suicide risk (Preacher & Hayes, 2008).

Results

Most participants exhibit an implicit self-association with life

Consistent with our review of the extant literature (see Table 2.1), the distribution of death/life IAT scores ($M = 0.42$, $SD = 0.30$) revealed that

93% of participants had a stronger self-association with life relative to death/suicide, supporting Hypothesis 1. The death/life IAT discriminated between participants with suicidal ideation in the past year ($M = 0.32$; $SD = 0.35$; $N = 41$) and those without ($M = 0.50$; $SD = 0.24$; $N = 59$), t (98), $3.00 = p < .05$; $d = 0.60$. Importantly, both groups exhibited a stronger self-association with life than with death, but this self-association with life is diminished in the group with recent suicidal ideation.

Is the association between the death/life IAT and suicide risk mediated by acquired capability for suicide and/or zest for life?

Multiple mediation analysis allows for the evaluation of competing hypotheses within a single model (Preacher & Hayes, 2008). Here we used bias corrected (BC) 95% CI bootstrapping based on 5000 samples to simultaneously evaluate two competing accounts of what mediates the relationship between implicit self-associations with death/life and indicators of suicide risk: acquired capability for suicide and zest for life. Mediation models for each of the six indicators of suicide risk, using standardised (β) regression coefficients, are shown in Figs. 2.1 and 2.2. In each of the models the death/life IAT is significantly negatively associated with acquired capability for suicide and significantly positively associated with zest for life. As predicted, a stronger implicit self-association with life was associated with lower acquired capability for suicide, which in turn predicted higher suicide risk. In addition, a stronger implicit self-association with life was also associated with higher zest for life, which in turn predicted lower suicide risk. Thus, the association between the death/life IAT and suicide risk is mediated by both acquired capability for suicide and zest for life, supporting Hypotheses 2 and 3.

Which is the stronger mediator of suicide risk: acquired capability or zest for life?

To determine the relative influence of acquired capability and zest for life on suicide-specific indicators of risk and more general risk indicators, two predictions are tested. First, acquired capability for suicide will be a stronger mediator of *suicide-specific* indicators of risk compared to zest for life. Second, zest for life will be a stronger mediator of *general* risk indicators compared to acquired capability.

Suicide-specific indicators of suicide risk. Examination of the direct effects in Fig. 2.1 shows the death/life IAT is significantly negatively associated with suicide ideation and suicide readiness, is marginally

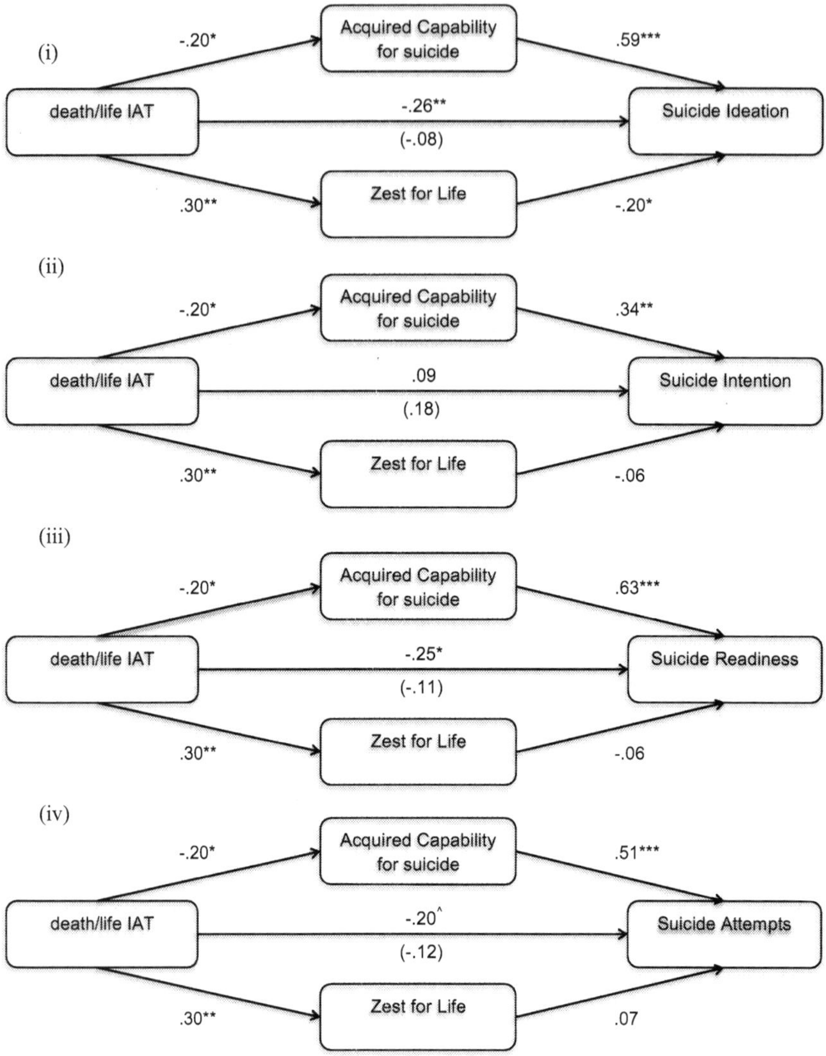

Fig. 2.1 Results of regression analyses for (i) Suicide Ideation (ii) Suicide Intention (iii) Suicide Readiness and (iv) Suicide Attempts, showing the direct and indirect pathways within the multiple mediation models. The numbers are standardized regression coefficients: $^{\wedge}p = .051$, $^{*}p < .05$, $^{**}p < .01$, $^{***}p < .001$.

negatively associated with suicide attempts ($p = .051$), and not significantly associated with suicide intention. Standardised regression coefficients of the associations between the mediators and the suicide-specific risk indicators reveal that acquired capability is three to eight times more strongly associated with each of these risk indicators than zest for life.

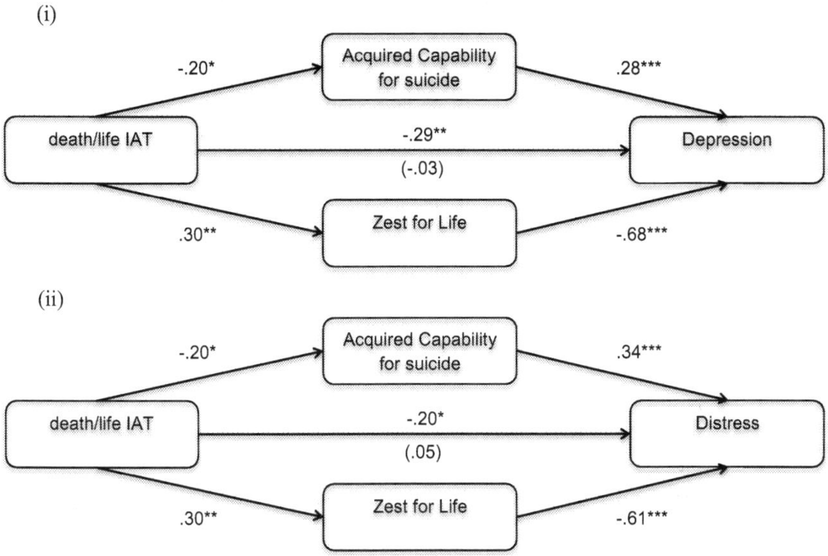

Fig. 2.2 Results of regression analyses for (i) Depression and (ii) Psychological Distress, showing the direct and indirect pathways within the multiple mediation models. The numbers are standardized regression coefficients: $*p < .05$, $**p < .01$, $***p < .001$.

Examination of the total and specific indirect effects shows that for suicide ideation acquired capability and zest for life (together and individually) are significant mediators of the relationship between the death/life IAT and suicide ideation (see Table 2.2). Contrasts of the indirect effects indicate no significant difference in influence between the two mediators on suicide ideation. For the more action-oriented suicide risk indicators (intentions, readiness, and attempts) only acquired capability is a significant mediator of the relationship between the death/life IAT and each risk indicator.

General indicators of suicide risk. Examination of the direct effects in Fig. 2.2 indicates the death/life IAT is significantly negatively associated with depression and psychological distress. Standardised regression coefficients of the associations between the mediators and the general risk indicators revealed zest was approximately two times more strongly associated with these risk indicators than acquired capability. As shown in Table 2.2, acquired capability and zest (together and individually) are significant mediators of the relationship between the death/life IAT and depression, and the death/life IAT and psychological distress. Contrasts of the indirect effects indicate that zest is a stronger mediator than acquired capability for both general risk indicators.

Table 2.2 Bootstrapping multiple mediation results of the suicide-specific indicators of suicide risk as outcome measures: Suicide ideation, suicide intention, suicide readiness, and suicide attempts.

	Suicide ideation				Suicide intention				Suicide readiness				Suicide attempts			
	L-CI	U-CI	PE	SE	L-CI	-CI	PE	SE	L-CI	U-CI	PE	SE	L-CI	U-CI	PE	SE
ACWRSS	-0.80	-0.01	**-.3[a]**	.20	.02	1.37	**.44[a]**	.32	-1.68	-0.03	**-.67[a]**	.41	-0.66	-0.01	**-.24[a]**	.16
Zest	-0.47	-0.05	**-.19[a]**	.10	-0.53	.77	.10	.32	-0.53	.27	-0.10	.20	-0.07	.20	.04	.06
Total indirect	-1.08	-0.13	**-.56[a]**	.24	-0.08	1.38	.54	.36	-1.56	-0.07	**-.77[a]**	.38	-0.55	.01	-0.19	14
Effect Contrast	-0.67	.19	-0.17	.21	-0.42	1.79	.35	.53	-1.92	.22	-0.58	.53	-0.81	.01	-0.28	.20

Note. L-CI, Lower CI; *U–CI*, Upper CI; *PE*, Point Estimate; *SE*, Standard Error; *ACWRSS*, Acquired Capability with Rehearsal for Suicide Scale; *Zest*, Zest for life.

[a] $p < .05$.

Table 2.3 Bootstrapping multiple mediation results of the general indicators of suicide risk as outcome measures: Depression and psychological distress.

	Depression				Distress			
	L-CI	U-CI	PE	SE	L-CI	U-CI	PE	SE
ACWRSS	-2.27	-0.04	**-.93***	.55	-4.21	-0.30	**-1.58***	.92
Zest	-6.01	-1.56	**-3.70***	1.12	-8.35	-2.11	**-4.90***	1.58
Total indirect effect	-7.53	-1.85	**-4.64***	1.43	-10.95	-2.75	**-6.48***	2.05
Contrast	-0.82	4.85	**2.77***	1.03	.28	6.27	**3.32***	1.57

Note. *L-CI*, Lower CI; *U-CI*, Upper CI; *PE*, Point Estimate; *SE*, Standard Error; *ACWRSS*, Acquired Capability with Rehearsal for Suicide Scale; *Zest*, Zest for life.
* $p < .05$.

Discussion

To die by suicide people must first defeat the strong desire for self-preservation. We hypothesised that this inbuilt desire to live will be reflected by implicit memory associations that favor life over death. Results from the current study support this prediction as the vast majority (93%) of our non-clinical sample had a stronger implicit self-association with life relative to death/suicide. Even participants who reported suicide ideation in the past year retained a positive self-association with life. However, their implicit self-association with life was diminished compared to those who had not experienced suicide ideation in the past year. This adds to the now compelling and consistent evidence that the bipolar d/s-IAT is best conceptualised as a measure tapping into the strength of a person's implicit attachment to life.

Participants with a lower implicit self-association with life had higher levels of suicide ideation in the past year, stronger feelings of readiness to die by suicide, and higher levels of current depression and psychological distress. They also had a higher number of prior suicide attempts in their lifetime ($p = .051$). Moreover, diminished implicit self-associations with life were associated with a higher capability to engage in suicidal behavior and a lower explicit desire to live.

If the implicit suicidal mind clings to life, as the evidence overwhelmingly indicates, we tested what competing influences might act to undermine or shore up this implicit hold on life. Specifically, grounded in the ideation-to-action framework, we predicted that acquired capability would be a stronger mediator of suicide-specific, action-oriented indicators of risk (intention, readiness, and attempts) than zest for life. Conversely, we expected that zest for life would be a stronger mediator of the ideation phase along the ideation-to-action pathway, and of the general indicators of risk such as depression and psychological distress, which are known to be robust predictors of ideation but less reliable predictors of attempts (May & Klonsky, 2016). Our results showed that for suicide ideation, acquired capability and zest for life combined and individually mediated the relationship between the death/life IAT and ideation. In contrast, for suicide intention, suicide readiness, and suicide attempts, only acquired capability was a significant individual mediator. The more proximal the indicators were to the behavioral enactment of suicide behavior (i.e., intention, readiness, attempts), the less of a mediating influence zest for life had.

However, the desire to live acts as a buffer against general indicators of suicide risk such as depression (Bagge, Lamis, Nadorff, & Osman, 2014) and psychological distress (Osman et al., 1993). We found that acquired capability and zest for life combined and individually mediated the relationship between the death/life IAT and depression and psychological distress, but as predicted, zest for life was the stronger mediator for both risk indicators. That is, the more distal a risk indicator is from suicide itself the more influential the role of zest for life. This is consistent with recent findings showing that reasons for living mediate the association of depressive symptoms and hopelessness with suicide ideation (Bagge et al., 2014). Zest for life also buffers the negative effects of experimentally-induced perceived burdensomeness and thwarted belongingness, that is, the interpersonal adversity that according to the interpersonal theory of suicide underlies suicidal desire (Collins et al., 2016). Moreover, there is longitudinal evidence that zest for life mediates the protective effects of mindfulness on suicidal ideation and intent eight weeks later, and these indirect effects were stronger at higher compared to lower levels of general (psychological distress) and suicide specific (perceived burdensomeness and thwarted belongingness) risk (Collins et al., 2018).

Results from our test of the multiple mediator model must be interpreted in the context of at least two limitations. First, the mediating role of acquired capability and zest for life must be replicated in clinical samples. Although capability to engage in suicidal behavior is presumed to be relatively stable once acquired (Joiner, 2005), implicit self-associations with life are malleable and can strengthen over the course of inpatient treatment (Ellis et al., 2016; Glenn et al., 2017). Therefore, bolstering zest for life offers a critical intervention target during clinical management of suicidal patients, and may be instrumental in reversing a weakening of the hard-wired implicit self-associations with life. Second, the cross-sectional design adopted here does not permit causal or temporal inferences regarding the mediating effect of acquired capability and zest for life on the relationship between the death/life IAT and suicide risk. Hence, the present findings will benefit from replication in clinical settings using longitudinal assessment outcomes.

Nevertheless, our findings have important theoretical and clinical implications. In a recent review, O'Connor and Nock (2014) noted a dearth of research into factors that offer protection against the risk of suicide. The extant literature on implicit assessment of the suicidal mind provides consistent evidence that an implicit probe such as the d/s-IAT offers insight into the protective influence of a person's implicit self-identification with life along the ideation-to-action pathway to suicide. As such, it may hold promise in monitoring the dynamic and fluctuating tension between the factors that encourage a suicidal act, and those that tip the balance in favor of life, without having to rely only on individuals' self-report.

Zest for life (assessed either at implicit or explicit levels of processing), along with positive community engagement, and optimism that experiences of burdensomeness, disconnectedness, defeat, and entrapment can be overcome, are life-oriented forces that remain largely unaccounted for in contemporary models of suicide. Our review and current results suggest that life-oriented implicit cognitions may apply a brake along the progression toward suicidal behavior, especially at the early pre-motivational stage and during ideation and intention formation. To the degree that the implicit suicidal mind clings to life, it may provide a critical safety barrier against death by suicide even when capability has been acquired and the volitional-motivational 'tug-of-war' is at an acute juncture (cf., O'Connor, 2011). Suicide risk assessments should routinely include measures of zest for life and protective factors, and interventions should go beyond risk-centric crisis management and aim to strengthen and sustain the desire to live (e.g., Kleiman & Beaver, 2013).

In conclusion, the implicit suicidal mind clings to life. Moreover, the association between implicit identification of self with life relative to death and suicide risk is mediated through two competing pathways: acquired capability for suicide and zest for life. The relative influence of each pathway varies depending on how specific and proximal, or general and distal, the risk indicators are to suicide itself. Whereas acquired capability is most influential for suicide-specific risk indicators further along the ideation-to-action pathway, zest for life is most influential at the earlier stages of the pathway and for general indicators of risk. We recommend that clinicians systematically assess the dynamic balance between acquired capability and the counterbalancing strength of life-oriented resilience factors. Suicide is as much about life as it is about death. It follows that theories of suicide must better account for the role of factors that contribute to the weakening or strengthening of the desire to persevere and (re)engage with life. In this chapter we have argued that the value of implicit tools of probing the suicidal mind lies perhaps less in having an alternative to clinical risk prediction, which otherwise is reliant on the accuracy of a person's self-report. Instead, implicit measures of the suicidal mind remind researchers and patients alike that humans are hard-wired to persevere, and despite adversity, can change the trajectory of the ideation-to-action pathway, where 'action' leads to the re-kindling and sustaining of a life worth living.

References

Antony, M. M., Bieling, P. J. J., Cox, B., Enns, M. W., & Swinson, R. P. (1998). Psychometric properties of the 42-item and 21-item versions of the Depression Anxiety Stress Scales in clinical groups and a community sample. *Psychological Assessment, 10*, 176–181. https://doi.org/10.1037/1040-3590.10.2.176.

Bagge, C. L., Lamis, D. A., Nadorff, M., & Osman, A. (2014). Relations between hopelessness, depressive symptoms and suicidality: Mediation by reasons for living. *Journal of Clinical Psychology, 70*, 18–31. https://doi.org/10.1002/jclp.22005.

Bargh, J. A. (1994). The four horsemen of automaticity: Awareness, intention, efficiency, and control in social cognition. In R. S. Wyer, Jr., & T. K. Scrull (Eds.), *Handbook of social cognition* (2nd ed., pp. 1–40). Hillsdale, NJ: Erlbaum.

Barnes, S. M., Bahraini, N. H., Forster, J. E., Stearns-Yoder, K. A., Hostetter, T. A., Smith, G.,., & Nock, M. K. (2017). Moving beyond self-report: Implicit associations about death/life prospectively predict suicidal behavior among veterans. *Suicide and Life-Threatening Behavior, 47*, 67–77. https://doi.org/10.1111/sltb.12265.

Beck, A. T. (1996). Beyond belief: A theory of modes, personality, and psychopathology. In P. M. Salkovskis (Ed.), *Frontiers of cognitive therapy* (pp. 1–25). New York, NY: Guilford Press.

Bongar, B., & Sullivan, G. (2013). *The suicidal patient: Clinical and legal standards of care* (3rd. ed.). Washington, DC: American Psychological Association.

Bryan, C. J., & Rudd, M. D. (2006). Advances in suicide assessment. *Journal of Clinical Psychology: In Session, 62*, 185–200, 0.1002/jclp.20222.

Bryan, C. J., Rudd, M. D., Peterson, A. L., Young-McCaughan, S., & Wertenberger, E. G. (2016). The ebb and flow of the wish to live and the wish to die among suicidal military personnel. *Journal of Affective Disorders, 202*, 58–66. https://doi.org/10.1016/j.jad.2016.05.049.

Busch, K. A., Fawcett, J., & Jacobs, D. G. (2003). Clinical correlates of inpatient suicide. *Journal of Clinical Psychiatry, 64*, 14–19. https://doi.org/10.4088/JCP.v64n0105.

Chan, M. K., Bhatti, H., Meader, N., Stockton, S., Evans, J., O'Connor, R. C., & Kendall, T. (2016). Predicting suicide following self-harm: Systematic review of risk factors and risk scales. *The British Journal of Psychiatry, 209*, 277–283. https://doi.org/10.1192/bjp.bp.115.170050.

Chiurliza, B., Hagan, C. R., Rogers, M. L., Podlogar, M. C., Hom, M. A., Stanley, I. H., et al. (2016). Implicit measures of suicide risk in a military sample. *Assessment*, 1–10. https://doi.org/10.1177/1073191116676363

Collins, K. R. L., Best, I., Stritzke, W. G. K., & Page, A. C. (2016). Mindfulness and zest for life buffer the negative effects of experimentally-induced perceived burdensomeness and thwarted belongingness: Implications for theories of suicide. *Journal of Abnormal Psychology, 125*, 704–714. https://doi.org/10.1037/abn0000167.

Collins, K. R., Stritzke, W. G., Page, A. C., Brown, J. D., & Wylde, T. J. (2018). Mind full of life: Does mindfulness confer resilience to suicide by increasing zest for life? *Journal of Affective Disorders, 226*, 100–107. https://doi.org/10.1016/j.jad.2017.09.043.

Ellis, T. E., Rufino, K. A., & Green, K. L. (2016). Implicit measure of life/death orientation predicts response of suicidal ideation to treatment in psychiatric inpatients. *Archives of Suicide Research, 20*, 59–68. https://doi.org/10.1080/13811118.2015.1004483.

Fawcett, J., Scheftner, W. A., Fogg, L., Clark, D. C., Young, M. A., Hedeker, D., & Gibbons, R. (1990). Time-related predictors of suicide in major affective disorder. *American Journal of Psychiatry, 147*, 1189–1194.

Franklin, J. C., Ribeiro, J. D., Fox, K. R., Bentley, K. H., Kleiman, E. M., Huang, X.,., & Nock, M. K. (2017). Risk factors for suicidal thoughts and behaviors: A meta-analysis of 50 years of research. *Psychological Bulletin, 143*, 187–232. https://doi.org/10.1037/bul0000084.

George, S. E., Page, A. C., Hooke, G. R., & Stritzke, W. G. K. (2016). Multifacet assessment of capability for suicide: Development and prospective validation of the acquired capability with rehearsal for suicide scale. *Psychological Assessment, 28*, 1452–1464. https://doi.org/10.1037/pas0000276.

Sarah E. George, Werner G. K. Stritzke, Andrew C. Page, Julia D. Brown, and Tricia J. Wylde. Zest for life: an antidote to suicide?.

Glenn, C. R., Kleiman, E. M., Coppersmith, D. D., Santee, A. C., Esposito, E. C., Cha, C. B., & Auerbach, R. P. (2017). Implicit identification with death predicts change in suicide ideation during psychiatric treatment in adolescents. *Journal of Child Psychology and Psychiatry, 58*, 1319–1329. https://doi.org/10.1111/jcpp.12769.

Greenwald, A. G., Nosek, B. A., & Banaji, M. R. (2003). Understanding and using the implicit association test: I. An improved scoring algorithm. *Journal of Personality and Social Psychology, 85*, 197–216. https://doi.org/10.1037/0022-3514.85.2.197.

Harrison, D. P., Stritzke, W. G. K., Fay, N., Ellison, T. M., & Hudaib, A. (2014). Probing the implicit suicidal mind: Does the death/suicide implicit association teat reveal a desire to die, or a diminished desire to live? *Psychological Assessment, 26*, 831–840. https://doi.org/10.1037/pas0000001.

Harrison, D. P., Stritzke, W. G. K., Fay, N., & Hudaib, A. (2018). Suicide risk assessment: Trust an implicit probe or listen to the patient? *Psychological Assessment*. https://doi.org/10.1037/pas0000577.

Henry, J. D., & Crawford, J. R. (2005). The short-form version of the depression anxiety stress scales (DASS-21): Construct validity and normative data in a large non-clinical sample. *British Journal of Clinical Psychology, 44*, 227–239. https://doi.org/10.1348/014466505 X29657.

Hussey, I., Daly, T., & Barnes-Holmes, D. (2015). Life is good, but death ain't bad either: Counter-intuitive implicit biases to death in a normative population. *The Psychological Record, 65*, 731–742. https://doi.org/10.1007/s40732-015-0142-3.

Jobes, D. A. (2016). *Managing suicidal risk: A collaborative approach* (2nd ed.). New York, NY: Guildford Press.

Jobes, D. A., Rudd, M. D., Overholser, J. C., & Joiner, T. E., Jr. (2008). Ethical and competent care of suicidal patients: Contemporary challenges, new developments, and considerations for clinical practice. *Professional Psychology: Research and Practice, 39*, 405–413. https://doi.org/10.1037/a0012896.

Joiner, T. (2005). *Why people die by suicide*. Cambridge, MA: Harvard University Press.

Kessler, R. C., Andrews, G., Colpe, L. J., Hiripi, E., Mroczek, D. K., Normand, S.-L. T., … Zaslavsky, A. (2002). Short screening scales to monitor population prevalences and trends in non-specific psychological distress. *Psychological Medicine, 32*, 959–976. doi: 10.1017'S0033291702006074.

Kleiman, E. M., & Beaver, J. K. (2013). A meaningful life is worth living: Meaning in life as a suicide resiliency factor. *Psychiatry Research, 210*, 934–939. https://doi.org/10.1016/j.psychres.2013.08.002.

Klonsky, E. D., & May, A. M. (2015). The three-step theory (3ST): A new theory of suicide rooted in the "ideation-to-action" framework. *International Journal of Cognitive Therapy, 8*, 114–129. https://doi.org/10.1521/ijct.2015.8.2.114.

Klonsky, E. D., May, A. M., & Saffer, B. Y. (2016). Suicide, suicide attempts, and suicidal ideation. Annual Review of Clinical Psychology, *12*, 307–330. https://doi.org/10.1146/annurev-clinpsy-021815-093204.

Large, M., Kaneson, M., Myles, N., Myles, H., Gunaratne, P., & Ryan, C. (2016). Meta-analysis of longitudinal cohort studies of suicide risk assessment among psychiatric patients: Heterogeneity in results and lack of improvement over time. *PLoS One, 11*(6), e0156322. https://doi.org/10.1371/journal.pone.0156322.

Latimer, S., Meade, T., & Tennant, A. (2013). Measuring engagement in deliberate self-harm behaviours: Psychometric evaluation of six scales. *BMC Psychiatry, 13*, 1–11. https://doi.org/10.1186/1471-244X-13-4.

Linehan, M. M., Goodstein, J. L., Nielsen, S. L., & Chiles, J. A. (1983). Reasons for staying alive when you are thinking of killing yourself: The Reasons for Living Inventory. *Journal of Consulting and Clinical Psychology, 51*, 276–286. https://doi.org/10.1037/0022-006X.51.2.276.

Lovibond, S. H., & Lovibond, P. F. (1995). *Manual for the depression anxiety and stress scales*. Sydney: Psychology Foundation.

May, A. M., & Klonsky, E. D.((2016). What distinguishes suicide attempters from suicide ideators? A meta-analysis of potential factors. *Clinical Psychology: Science and Practice, 23*, 5–20. https://doi.org/10.1111/cpsp.12136.

Nock, M. K. (2010). Self-injury. *Annual Review of Clinical Psychology, 6*, 339–363. https://doi.org/10.1146/annurev.clinpsy.121208.131258.

Nock, M. K., Holmberg, E. B., Photos, V. I., & Michel, B. D. (2007). Self-injurious thoughts and behaviors Interview: Development, reliability, and validity in an adolescent sample. *Psychological Assessment, 19*, 309–317. https://doi.org/10.1037/1040-3590.19.3.309.

Nock, M. K., Park, J. M., Finn, C. T., Deliberto, T. L., Dour, H. J., & Banaji, M. R. (2010). Measuring the suicidal mind: Implicit cognition predicts suicidal behavior. *Psychological Science, 21*, 511–517. https://doi.org/10.1177/0956797610364762.

Norton, P. J. (2007). Depression anxiety and stress scales (DASS-21): Psychometric analysis across four racial groups. *Anxiety, Stress & Coping, 20*, 253–265. https://doi.org/10.1080/10615800701309279.

Nosek, B. A., Hawkins, C. B., & Frazier, R. S. (2011). Implicit social cognition: From measures to mechanisms. *Trends in Cognitive Sciences, 15*, 152–159. https://doi.org/10.1016/j.tics.2011.01.005

Osman, A., Gifford, J., Jones, T., Lickiss, L., Osman, J., & Wenzel, R. (1993). Psychometric evaluation of the reasons for living inventory. *Psychological Assessment, 5*, 154–158. https://doi.org/10.1037/1040-3590.5.2.154.

O'Connor, R. C. (2011). Towards an integrated motivational-volitional model of suicidal behavior. In R. C. O'Connor, S. Platt, & J. Gordon (Eds.), *International handbook of suicide prevention: Research, policy and practice* (pp. 181–198). Chichester, United Kingdom: John Wiley & Sons.

O'Connor, R. C., & Nock, M. K. (2014). The psychology of suicidal behaviour. *The Lancet Psychiatry, 1*, 73–85. https://doi.org/10.1016/S2215-0366(14)70222-6.

Preacher, K. J., & Hayes, A. F. (2008). Asymptotic and resampling strategies for assessing and comparing indirect effects in multiple mediator models. *Behavior Research Methods, 40*, 879–891. https://doi.org/10.3758/BRM.40.3.879.

Price, R. B., Iosifescu, D. V., Murrough, J. W., Chang, L. C., Al Jurdi, R. K., Iqbal, S. Z.,., & Mathew, S. J. (2014). Effects of ketamine on explicit and implicit suicidal cognition: A randomized controlled trial in treatment-resistant depression. *Depression and Anxiety, 31*, 335–343. https://doi.org/10.1002/da.22253.

Price, R. B., Nock, M. K., Charney, D. S., & Mathew, S. J. (2009). Effects of intravenous ketamine on explicit and implicit measures of suicidality in treatment-resistant depression. *Biological Psychiatry, 66*, 522–526. https://doi.org/10.1016/j.biopsych.2009.04.029.

Randall, J. R., Rowe, B. H., Dong, K. A., Nock, M. K., & Colman, I. (2013). Assessment of self-harm risk using implicit thoughts. *Psychological Assessment, 25*, 714–721. https://doi.org/10.1037/a0032391.

Tang, J., Wu, S., & Miao, D. (2013). Experimental test of escape theory: Accessibility to implicit suicidal mind. *Suicide and Life-Threatening Behavior, 43*, 347–355. https://doi.org/10.1111/sltb.12021.

Van Orden, K. A., Witte, T. K., Cukrowicz, K. C., Braithwaite, S. R., Selby, E. A., & Joiner, T. (2010). The interpersonal theory of suicide. *Psychological Review, 117*, 575–600. https://doi.org/10.1037/a0018697.

Violanti, J. M., Mnatsakanova, A., & Andrew, M. E. (2013). Ideation in police officers: Exploring an additional measure. *Suicide Online, 4*, 33–41.

CHAPTER 3

Zest for life: an antidote to suicide?

Sarah E. George[a], Werner G.K. Stritzke[a], Andrew C. Page[a], Julia D. Brown[a], Tricia J. Wylde[b]
[a]School of Psychological Science, University of Western Australia, Perth, WA, Australia; [b]Health Promotion Unit, University of Western Australia, Crawley, WA, Australia

Life loves to be taken by the lapel and told, 'I'm with you, kid. Let's go.
Maya Angelou (author and poet).

It is estimated that worldwide one life is lost to suicide every 40 s (World Health Organization, 2014). While various risk factors play a role in death by suicide, suicide is ultimately about the erosion and exhaustion of the will to live (Shneidman, 1996). Not unlike Maya Angelou's often quoted approach to living life to the fullest, a life-oriented approach to prevention of suicide is about taking life by the lapel and finding ways to embrace it anew and be with it. This entails more than intervening to 'keep someone alive'. In this chapter we present evidence that a zestful life, characterized by active engagement with life accompanied by a positive outlook and free from recent depletions of enthusiasm and vigor for life, may be an important antidote to factors thought to proximally and causally antecede suicide.

While a zestful life is much more than just being alive, at the opposite end of the spectrum people may experience a state of 'devitalization' where one feels deprived of life, vigor, or effectiveness. For example, devitalization has been observed among children from traumatized asylum-seeking refugee families, where their life is in limbo for a prolonged period with an uncertain outcome. These children had become totally passive, immobile, lack tonus, and are withdrawn, mute, unable to eat and drink, incontinent and not reacting to physical stimuli or pain (Bodegård, 2005). In one sample of 23 treated children, about half had attempted suicide (Bodegård, 2005).

As Joiner (2005) noted, dying by suicide is not an easy thing to do, because humans have an evolutionarily ingrained, strong desire to live. Similarly, implicit measures of the suicidal mind suggest that humans are hard-wired to persevere (for a review, see Harrison et al. this volume).

Alternatives to Suicide
ISBN 978-0-12-814297-4
https://doi.org/10.1016/B978-0-12-814297-4.00003-0

This inbuilt desire to live is reflected in implicit memory associations that favor life over death. This is also the case even in high risk samples of multiple suicide attempters, such that implicit self-association with life are still stronger than implicit self-associations with death, but they are diminished compared to individuals without a history of suicidal ideation or attempts. While implicit life-death self-associations have been extensively studied, there are no explicit measures to assess zest for life, which capture all the key aspects of this constructs (i.e., engagement, positive outlook, and no diminished enthusiasm or vigor).

Assessment of one's level of engagement with and enthusiasm for life appears vital when evaluating risk. The interpersonal theory of suicide proposes that the will to live must be drained by thwarted interpersonal needs for suicidal desire to ensue (Joiner, 2005). Moreover, the theory also proposes that to act on this desire a person must have "beaten down the instinct to live" and acquired the capability to do so (Joiner, 2005, p. 24). Yet the theory does not make specific predictions about the role of such life-oriented factors.

In this chapter we test the role of zest for life against the deleterious impacts of the three causal factors proposed by the interpersonal theory (i.e., thwarted belongingness, perceived burdensomeness, acquired capability for suicide) using a prospective design. To achieve this aim it was first necessary to develop a new measure of zest for life, defined as engagement with life accompanied by a positive life outlook and free from recent depletions of enthusiasm and vigor for life.

Development of the Zest for Life Scale

Method

Participants and procedures. Six hundred and eleven undergraduate students (159 males and 452 females) who took part in a multi-sample series of studies on the acquired capability for suicide (George, Page, Hooke, & Stritzke, 2016) completed computer-based questionnaires in a supervised setting. Data were previously screened for invalid responding and six participants had been removed (George et al., 2016). Participant age ranged from 17 to 55 years ($M = 20.93$, $SD = 4.72$). Self-reported ethnicity was Caucasian Australian (67.1%), Asian (17.4%), European (6.8%), African (1.8%), Aboriginal Australian (0.4%) and Other (6.4%). This dataset was randomly divided into two samples of 200 and 411 participants. The first was used for an exploratory factor analysis, and the second was used for confirmatory factor analysis and the testing of convergent validity of interpretations. The research was approved by the institution's Human Research Ethics Committee.

Measures

Zest for Life. The Zest for Life Scale (ZLS) was developed from a pool of 26 items measuring connection to life. Twenty items were newly devised to capture a general sense of connection to and enthusiasm for life. Four items were adapted from the Survival and Coping Beliefs subscale of the Reasons for Living Inventory (Linehan, Goodstein, Nielsen, & Chiles, 1983) and two items were adapted from the 'Zest' subscale of the Values in Action Character Strengths Inventory (Peterson, Park, & Seligman, 2005). Items reflect engagement with life, a sense of living life to the fullest, and positive expectations for life (e.g., *"I am embracing life"; "I look forward to each new day"*). The scale also includes fourteen reverse-scored items designed to capture depletions in zest (e.g., *"Life feels more dull as time moves on"*). Respondents rate the degree to which each statement is true for them on a 9-point scale from *'Not at all'* (0) to *'Very strongly'* (8), with higher scores denoting heightened zest for life. The coefficient alpha for the 26-item version of the scale was 00.96 in the current sample.

Suicidal ideation and attempts. Two items adapted from the Self-Injurious Thoughts and Behaviors Interview (SITBI; Nock, Holmberg, Photos, & Michel, 2007) were used to assess frequency of suicidal ideation in the past year (*"How many times have you thought about suicide?"*) with six response options from *'never'* to *'almost every day,'* and history of suicide attempts (*"How many times in your lifetime have you made an actual attempt to kill yourself in which you had at least some intent to die?")* with five response options from *'never'* to *'five or more times.'* The SITBI is suitable for use in self-report format in non-clinical samples (Latimer, Meade, & Tennant, 2013).

Intent and readiness for suicide. Intent and readiness for lethal suicidal behavior were measured with two items (*"I have no intention of killing myself in the near future"* and *"If I wanted to kill myself, I feel ready to do so"*) on a 0–8 scale. The intention item is reverse-scored, such that high scores suggest higher intention for suicidal behavior. Both items demonstrate good test-retest reliability and are significantly associated with other indices of suicide risk including prior suicide attempts (George et al., 2016).

General psychological distress. The 10-item Kessler Psychological Distress Scale (K10; Kessler et al., 2003) measures emotional states experienced in the past four weeks on a 5-point scale from *'none of the time'* (1) to *'all of the time'* (5), with high scores denoting heightened general psychological distress. The K10 has construct validity with mental health diagnoses (Andrews & Slade, 2001). Normative cut-off scores for the Australian population are: low distress (10—15), moderate distress (16—21), high distress (22—29) and very high distress (30—50) (Cvetkovski, Reavley, & Jorm, 2012; Stallman, 2010). Total scores ranged from 10 to 46 and internal consistency for the current sample was excellent ($\alpha = 0.94$).

Meaning in Life Questionnaire (MLQ; Steger, Frazier, Oishi, & Kaler, 2006**).** The MLQ has two five-item subscales using a 7-point scale measuring search for and presence of meaning in life. The 'presence' subscale was used, where higher scores indicate heightened presence of meaning in life. The MLQ has good internal consistency and convergent and discriminant validity (Steger et al., 2006).

Data analytic strategy. Factor retention for the ZLS was first determined via parallel analysis using SPSS 21.0 and the syntax provided by O'Connor (O'Connor, 2000). Factors were retained when the Eigenvalues generated from the dataset were larger than the Eigenvalues from randomly generated correlation matrices (Hayton, Allen, & Scarpello, 2004; Horn, 1965). Principal axis factoring was selected over principal components analysis, as the latter assumes perfect measurement (Finch & West, 1997) and may lead to more spurious common variance (Comrey, 1988). Direct oblimin rotation was employed as it was anticipated that any factors that may emerge would be correlated (Tabachnick & Fidell, 2013). Items were retained if item factor loadings on the expected primary factor exceeded 0.45 (Meyers, Gamst, & Guarino, 2006), and if there was no evidence of cross-loading, specified *a priori* as a difference of at least 00.3 between the factor-loadings. As briefer scales are desirable for both research and clinical purposes, only the strongest loading items were then selected and the principal axis factoring was then run again with the reduced item set. To test the measurement model generated by the exploratory factor analysis, confirmatory factor analysis was next run with the second sample ($n = 411$) using AMOS.

Results

Sample characteristics. Mean levels of general psychological distress were at the low end of the high distress range ($M = 21.71$, $SD = 7.29$).

Nearly half of the sample (49.1%) reported suicide ideation in the past year, with 13.5% thinking about suicide on at least a monthly basis. At least one lifetime suicide attempt was reported by 13.4%, with 4.4% reporting multiple attempts.

Exploratory factor analysis of the ZLS. Item analysis did not reveal any skewness or problematic variances (Curran, West, & Finch, 1996). Parallel analysis of the 26 ZLS items yielded a two-factor solution. The first factor had an eigenvalue of 13.15, which was larger than the randomly generated eigenvalue (00.99). The second factor had an eigenvalue of 1.76, which was also larger than the corresponding random eigenvalue (00.85). All other eigenvalues were smaller than the corresponding randomly generated values, suggesting that only two factors should be retained.

Bartlett's test of sphericity was significant, indicating that inter-item correlations were sufficiently large for the analysis. Sampling adequacy was also excellent, as evidenced by the Keiser-Meyer-Olkin measure (KMO) of 00.95 (Field, 2009). Together, the factors accounted for 56.14% of the variance.

Given our aim to develop a brief measure, the principal axis factoring was then repeated using the top six items from each subscale.[1] Bartlett's test of sphericity was again significant and the KMO (00.93) indicated excellent sampling adequacy. Internal consistency for the 12-item scale was excellent ($\alpha = 0.93$).

As shown in Table 3.1, all items loaded cleanly on their respective factors, with loadings ranging from very good to excellent (Comrey & Lee, 1992). All reverse-coded items loaded strongly on the first factor, while all positively worded items loaded strongly on the second factor. Coefficient alphas for the two subscales were similarly strong for both the positively-worded ($M = 5.56$, $SD = 1.41$; $\alpha = 0.91$) and negatively-worded ($M = 5.81$, $SD = 1.82$, $\alpha = 0.92$) subscales.

Although the two factors reflected distinct aspects of zest for life, with one representing engagement with life and a positive outlook, and the other denoting depleted connection to life and diminished positive future thinking, the two subscales are also distinguished by positive versus negative wording. As reverse-coded items may introduce additional shared method covariance (Williams, Ford, & Nguyen, 2002, pp. 366–389), it is unclear whether the emergence of the two subscales reflects the presence of two distinct facets of zest, or is due to the presence of a reverse-coded method

[1] The reduced item set comprised ten newly devised items and two of the adapted items.

Table 3.1 Rotated two-factor principal axis factoring solution for the zest for life scale (n = 200).

Item	Factor 1	Factor 2
I Used to think of life as 'half full,' now it feels more like 'half empty.'	0.92	-0.10
I Feel less alive than I used to.	0.91	-0.05
Life seems to hold less for me than it used to.	0.80	0.07
Life feels more dull as time moves on.	0.76	0.07
I Never used to, but now I sometimes think 'why bother.'	0.74	-0.003
Life has become a drag.	0.69	0.19
I Am embracing life.	0.02	0.87
I Wake up in the morning and look forward to what life has in store for me.	-0.01	0.81
I Strive to participate fully in life, not just view it from the sidelines.	-0.05	0.76
I Look forward to each new day.	0.12	0.75
I Try to enjoy life no matter what.	-0.05	0.72
I Am looking forward to all that life has to offer.	0.18	0.68

Direct oblimin rotation was used. Bold values highlight the factor on which the item loads.

factor. Accounting for the influence of reverse-coded method covariance is recommended when testing the validity of multi-factor measurement models (DiStefano & Motl, 2006; Gignac, 2007), so we used confirmatory factor analysis in a separate sample to evaluate three measurement models: a parsimonious one-factor model, an oblique two-factor model, and a one-factor model with a latent reverse-coded method factor.

Confirmatory factor analysis. Using AMOS, the three models were identified by constraining the variances of all latent variables to 1.0 (Gignac, 2007). First, the 12 ZLS items were entered into the model as observed variables and were specified to load on one factor. Four fit indices were considered to determine model fit: the chi square, the root-mean-square error of approximation (RMSEA), the comparative fit index (CFI), and the Tucker-Lewis index (TLI). While a non-significant chi-square value indicates a good fit (Tabachnick & Fidell, 2013), this index is sensitive to sample size and may consequently underestimate fit (Brown, 2006). Given the large sample used, emphasis was placed on the other fit indices. RMSEA values under 0.08 are considered adequate, and values below 0.05 are considered good (Brown, 2006; Byrne, 2010; Hu & Bentler, 1999). CFI and TLI values between 0.90 and 0.95 are acceptable (Bentler, 1990), while values above 00.95 are good (Byrne, 2010).

Fit indices for the one-factor model were poor: χ^2 (54) = 412.42, $p < .001$; RMSEA = 0.127 (90% CI = 0.116, 0.139); CFI = 0.90, TLI = 0.87, suggesting that this model was an inadequate fit to the data. Therefore, the oblique two-factor model was next tested. The 12 items were each specified to load onto their respective positively- and negatively-worded factors and the factors were allowed to correlate, as they are expected to represent related facets of zest for life. The two-factor model was a good fit to the data, χ^2 (53) = 113.83, $p < .001$; RMSEA = 0.053 (90% CI = 0.039, 0.066); CFI = 0.98; TLI = 0.98, and was significantly better than the one-factor model, χ^2_{diff} (1) = 298.59, $p < .01$. However, the correlation between the two latent variables was very high (r = 00.83), indicating that 69% of the variance between the two factors was shared.

Lastly, a one-factor model with a reverse-coded method factor was tested. Here, all items were specified to load on a latent zest factor, and all reverse-scored items were also specified to load onto a latent method factor. This model, demonstrated good fit, χ^2 (48) = 104.97, $p < .001$; RMSEA = 0.054 (90% CI = 0.040, 0.068); CFI = 0.98; TLI = 0.98, that was also significantly better than the one-factor model, χ^2_{diff} (6) = 337.11, $p < .01$, but did not significantly differ from the oblique two-factor model, χ^2_{diff} (5) = 8.86, $p > .05$.

While the two-factor oblique model also displayed good fit, the two factors were highly correlated and distinguishable based on positive versus negative item wording, consistent with a reverse-coded method factor (Williams et al., 2002, pp. 366–389). Thus, the one-factor model with a latent reverse-coded method factor was deemed the best fit.

Cronbach's alpha was good for the full 12-item ZLS (α = 0.94), and for the positively- and negatively-worded item sets (α = 0.90 and α = 0.92, respectively). Inter-item correlations ranged from 00.40 to 00.73, suggesting that multicollinearity was not a concern (Field, 2009).

Associations between zest for life and suicide risk and resilience. Total zest for life scores were positively correlated with meaning in life (r = 0.63, $p < .01$), and negatively correlated ($ps < 0.01$) with suicide ideation (r = -0.56), suicidal intent (r = -0.33), readiness for lethal suicidal behavior (r = -0.47), and prior suicide attempts (r = -0.30).

In sum, the *Zest for Life Scale* (see appendix) has good construct and convergent validity as well as excellent internal consistency. We next used a prospective design to test the role of zest for life in relation to the three causal drivers of suicidal thoughts and behavior central to the interpersonal theory of suicide.

The mediating and moderating role of Zest for life in the prospective link from interpersonal risk factors and acquired capability to suicide risk

Method

Participants and procedures. Two-hundred and thirty-four university students (168 females, 66 males) who took part in a series of studies on the acquired capability for suicide (George et al., 2016) filled out an online survey on two occasions separated by an eight-week period. Data were previously screened for careless and inconsistent responding and three participants had been removed (George et al., 2016). The sample were undergraduate (65.8%) and postgraduate (34.2%) students ranging in age from 17 to 74 years (M = 25.78, SD = 10.35). Ethnicity included Caucasian Australian (60.3%), European (15%), Asian (14.9%), Oceanian (1.7%) and 'other' ethnic backgrounds (8.1%). The study had the institution's Human Research Ethics Committee approval.

Measures. Measures were administered at both time points and included measures of the interpersonal factors and acquired capability, and the measures already described above, except the SITBI item about suicide ideation was re-worded in the follow-up questionnaire to reflect events in the past four weeks. This captured the stressful period leading up to exams, and was consistent with the timeframe of the measure of general psychological distress (K10). Additionally, due to a clerical error, two ZLS items (*"I strive to participate fully in life, not just view it from the sidelines,"* and *"I try to enjoy life no matter what"*) were not included in this study. The measurement model of this 10-item measurement model was tested and demonstrated good fit both in this sample, χ^2 (29) = 69.18, $p < .001$; RMSEA = 0.077 (90% CI = 0.054, 0.101); CFI = 0.98, TLI = 0.97, and the previous independent sample ($n = 611$), χ^2 (29) = 66.39, $p < .001$; RMSEA = 0.046 (90% CI = 0.031, 0.061); CFI = 0.99, TLI = 0.99. The 10- and 12- item sets were also strongly correlated ($r = 0.99$, $p < .01$), suggesting that the versions are equivalent. Internal consistency at both baseline ($\alpha = 0.95$) and follow-up ($\alpha = 0.96$), and test-retest reliability was good ($r = 00.75$, $p < .01$).

Interpersonal Needs Questionnaire (INQ; Van Orden, Witte, Gordon, Bender, & Joiner, 2008**).** The INQ has six items about perceived burdensomeness (e.g., *"The people in my life would be better off if I were gone"*) and nine items about thwarted belongingness (e.g., *"I feel disconnected from other people"*) on a 7-point scale from 1 to 7. Higher scores suggest heightened levels of perceived burdensomeness and thwarted belongingness. Scores ranged from 15 to 90 at Time 1 and from 15 to 83 at Time 2. The INQ has good construct validity and internal consistency (Van Orden et al., 2008, 2012) and internal consistency in the current sample was excellent at both Time 1 (PB subscale $\alpha = 0.92$; TB subscale $\alpha = 0.91$) and Time 2 (PB subscale $\alpha = 0.94$; TB subscale $\alpha = 0.93$).

Acquired Capability with Rehearsal for Suicide Scale (ACWRSS; George et al., 2016**).** The 7-item ACWRSS measures three facets of acquired capability comprising two items measuring fearlessness of death (e.g., *"Even if I wanted to, killing myself is too scary to follow through with it"*), two items measuring pain tolerance (e.g., *"I can tolerate pain much more than I used to"*), and three items about preparation for suicide (e.g., *"I have considered whether some ways to kill myself would be easier than others"*). Items have a 9-point scale from 0 to 8, and higher scores denote heightened levels of acquired capability. The ACWRSS has good construct validity and internal consistency (George et al., 2016).

Data analytic strategy. First, to test the mediating role of zest for life in the relationships between the interpersonal factors and suicide ideation, and between the three acquired capability facets and indices of suicide risk along three steps of the motivational-volitional pathway to suicide (O'Connor & Nock, 2014), we ran several structural equation models using AMOS. To control for Type 1 error while obtaining an optimal estimate of indirect effects, 5000 bias-corrected bootstrapping samples were used (Jose, 2013). Second, moderation analyses were run using SPSS and PROCESS (version 2.16; Hayes, 2016) to test whether zest for life also buffers the adverse effects of perceived burdensomeness, thwarted belongingness, and acquired capability for suicide.

Results

Sample characteristics. Mean general psychological distress scores fell between the moderate and high bands at both baseline ($M = 21.43$, $SD = 8.07$) and eight-week follow-up ($M = 21.37$, $SD = 7.88$). At baseline, over half of the sample (50.9%) reported thinking about suicide in the past year, with over one-fifth (21.8%) reporting thinking about suicide at least once a month. At least one lifetime suicide attempt was endorsed by 14.1% of the sample, with 4.4% endorsing multiple prior attempts.

Does zest for life *mediate* the relationships between burdensomeness and thwarted belongingness and suicidal ideation?

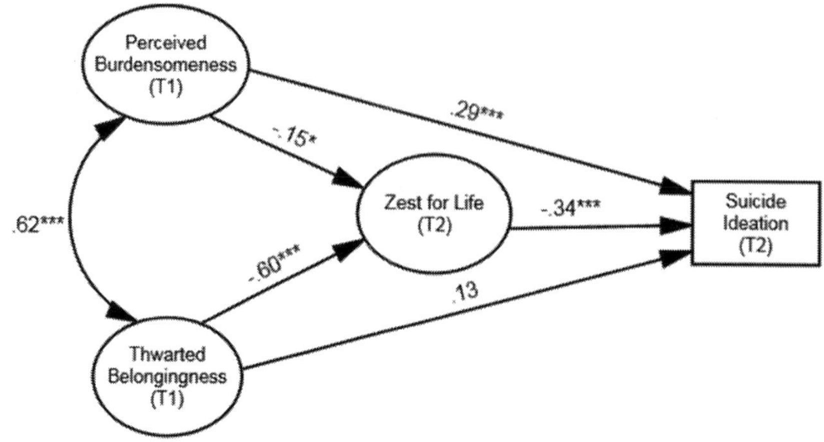

Fig. 3.1 Zest for life partly mediates the prospective relationships between the interpersonal factors and ideation ($n = 234$) *Note.* T1 = Time 1 (baseline); T2 = Time 2 (follow-up). $^{*}p < .05$, $^{***}p < .001$.

Baseline thwarted belongingness and perceived burdensomeness were each specified to predict suicidal ideation at follow-up both directly and indirectly via their relationships with zest for life at follow-up (see Fig. 3.1). This model had a good fit: χ^2 (288) = 611.70, $p < .001$; RMSEA = 0.069 (90% CI = 0.062, 0.077); CFI = 0.94, TLI = 0.93. Partly consistent with the interpersonal theory, perceived burdensomeness directly predicted suicide ideation (direct effect = 0.282, 95% CI: 0.065, 0.497, $p = .014$), though the direct effect of thwarted belongingness on ideation was not significant (direct effect = 0.085, 95% CI: 0.042, 0.209, $p = .17$). Baseline zest for life also partly mediated the relationship between perceived burdensomeness and suicidal ideation at follow-up (indirect effect = -0.051, 95% CI: 0.014, 0.116, $p = .009$), and fully mediated the relationship between thwarted belongingness and suicidal ideation at follow-up (indirect effect = 0.135, 95% CI: 0.067, 0.244, $p = .001$).

A hierarchical multiple regression confirmed that zest for life was not serving as a proxy for prior suicide ideation or general psychological distress. Zest for life at follow-up was significantly negatively associated with suicide ideation at follow-up after controlling for baseline suicide ideation, psychological distress, burdensomeness, and thwarted belongingness (β = -0.21, $p = .001$).

Does zest for life *moderate* the relationship between the interpersonal factors and suicidal ideation? Two moderation analyses were conducted using PROCESS (Hayes, 2016) to test the buffering influence of zest for life against the influence of (a) perceived burdensomeness and (b) thwarted belongingness on suicidal ideation. To maintain consistency with the mediation analyses, the interpersonal factors were measured at baseline and zest for life and suicidal ideation were measured at follow-up.

Zest for life significantly moderated the relationship between perceived burdensomeness and suicide ideation, F (3, 230) = 28.14, $p < .001$, $R^2 = 0.48$. Zest for life was significantly inversely related to suicide ideation, and the interaction between zest and burdensomeness also significantly negatively predicted ideation (Table 3.2). As shown in Table 3.2, the interaction was explored by examining the conditional effects of perceived burdensomeness on suicide ideation at three levels of zest for life (one standard deviation below the mean, at the mean, and above the mean). Perceived burdensomeness was significantly inversely related to suicide ideation at high levels of zest for life and was significantly positively associated with suicide ideation at low levels of zest, but was not significantly associated with ideation at mean levels of zest. The Johnson-Neyman technique revealed that the relationship between perceived

Table 3.2 Moderating effects of Zest for life in the prospective associations between interpersonal risk factors and suicidal ideation.

Predictor	**β**	***p***	**95% CI**
Perceived burdensomeness (PB)			
Zest for life	-0.20	< 0.001	-0.27, -0.13
PB	0.04	0.35	-0.05, 0.14
Zest x PB	-0.11	< 0.001	-0.15, 0.07
Conditional effects of PB for zest at:			
One *SD* below mean	0.23	< 0.001	0.14, 0.34
Mean	0.04	0.35	-0.05, 0.14
One *SD* above mean	-0.15	0.02	-0.28, -0.02
Thwarted belongingness (TB)			
Zest for life	-0.18	< 0.001	-0.24, -0.12
TB	0.09	.009	0.02, 0.15
Zest x TB	-0.11	< 0.001	-0.18, -0.05
Conditional effects of TB for zest at:			
One *SD* below mean	0.29	< 0.001	0.16, 0.41
Mean	0.09	0.009	0.02, 0.15
One *SD* above mean	-0.11	0.075	-0.24, 0.01

burdensomeness and suicide ideation was significant when zest for life was less than 0.41 standard deviations below the mean, and when zest for life was above 1.58 standard deviations above the mean.

Zest for life also significantly moderated the relationship between thwarted belongingness and suicide ideation, F (3, 230) = 28.14, $p < .001$, $R^2 = 0.48$. As indicated in Table 3.2, thwarted belongingness, zest for life, and their interaction significantly predicted ideation. The interaction was probed by examining the conditional effects of thwarted belongingness on suicide ideation again at three levels of zest for life. Thwarted belongingness was significantly positively related to suicide ideation at low and mean levels of zest for life, with the effect strongest at low levels of zest. At high levels of zest, the association between thwarted belongingness and suicide ideation was negative and fell outside the conventional criteria for significance ($p = .075$). The Johnson-Neyman technique revealed that the relationship between thwarted belongingness and suicide ideation was significant when zest for life was less than 0.19 standard deviations below the mean, and when zest for life was more than 1.96 standard deviations above the mean.

Does zest for life *mediate* the relationships between the three facets of acquired capability and three steps along the ideation-to-action pathway: (a) ideation, (b) intent, and (c) readiness for suicide? Three structural models were specified to test the mediating role of zest for life (Time 1) against the influence of the three acquired capability facets (Time 1) on three steps in the motivational-volitional pathway (O'Connor & Nock, 2014) from (a) suicide ideation to (b) intent to (c) readiness for lethal suicidal behavior (all Time 2) (Fig. 3.2). All models demonstrated good fit: Model (*a*) χ^2 (120) = 207.24, $p < .001$, RMSEA = 0.056 (90% CI = 0.043, 0.068), CFI = 0.97, TLI = 0.96; Model (*b*) χ^2 (120) = 213.94, $p < .001$, RMSEA = 0.058 (90% CI = 00.045, 0.070), CFI = 0.97, TLI = 0.96; Model (*c*) χ^2 (120) = 223.98, $p < .001$, RMSEA = 0.061 (90% CI = 0.048, 00.073), CFI = 0.97, TLI = 0.96.

Acquired capability: Preparation. Zest for life partly mediated the relationships between the preparation facet of acquired capability and both suicidal ideation (indirect effect = 0.205, 95% CI: 0.129, 0.305, $p < .001$; direct effect = 0.376, 95% CI: 0.236, 0.515, $p < .001$) and intent (indirect effect = 0.141, 95% CI: 0.053, 0.239, $p = .001$; direct effect = 0.241, 95% CI: 0.030, 0.412, $p = .027$). In contrast, the mediating effect of zest on the link between preparation and readiness fell outside the conventional criteria for significance (indirect effect = 0.086, 95% CI: 0.004, 0.195, $p = .062$),

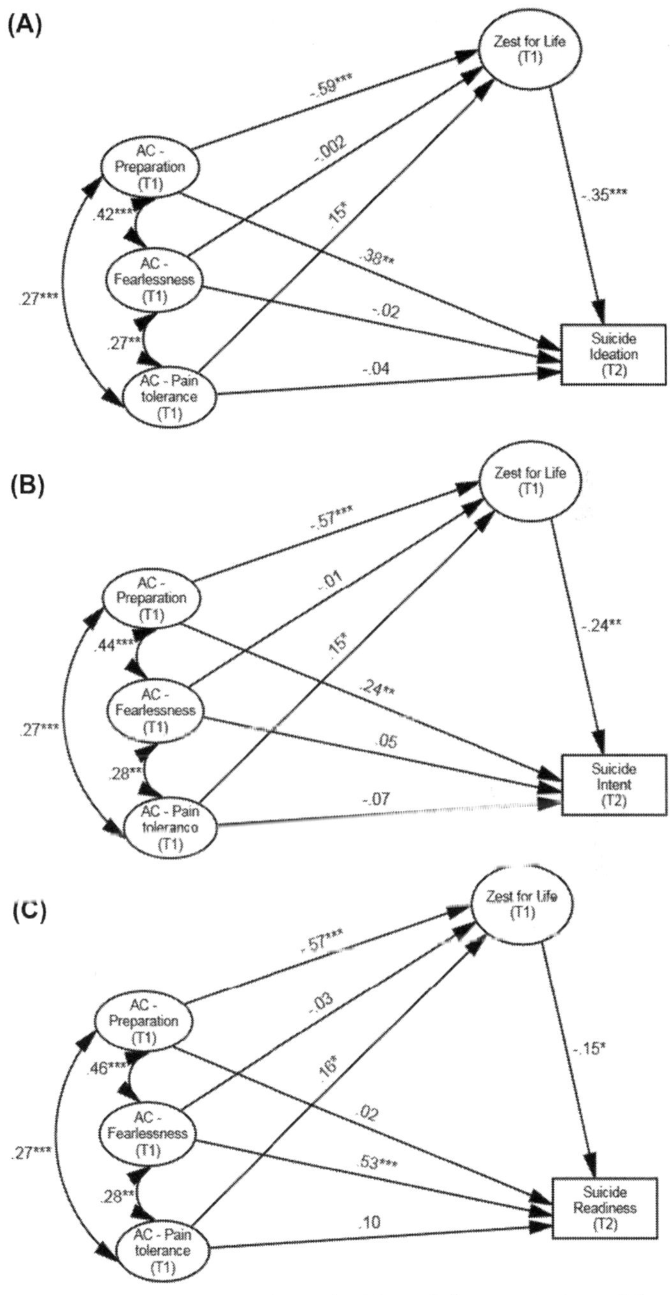

Fig. 3.2 Three mediation models of zest for life and the acquired capability facets in the pathway from (a) ideation to (b) intention to (c) readiness for suicide ($n = 234$). *Note.* AC = Acquired capability; T1 = Time 1 (baseline); T2 = Time 2 (follow-up) $^{*}p < .05$, $^{**}p < .01$, $^{***}p < .001$.

and the direct effect of the preparation facet on readiness was not significant (direct effect = 0.024, 95% CI: 0.188, 0.202, $p = .86$). Thus, the mediating influence of zest for life was strongest early in the ideation to action pathway, and diminished in strength in the subsequent stages from intention formation to readiness for suicide.

Acquired capability: Fearlessness of death. Zest did not mediate the associations between fearlessness of death and suicide ideation, intention, or readiness ($ps > 0.05$). Nor were the direct effects of fearlessness of death significant for the early stages in the ideation to action pathway (ideation and intention; $ps > 0.05$), but there was a strong direct effect of fearlessness on readiness for suicide (direct effect = 00.534, 95% CI: 0.315, 0.719, $p < .001$).

Acquired capability: Pain tolerance. Finally, zest for life fully mediated the relationships between the third facet of acquired capability (pain tolerance) and suicidal ideation (indirect effect = -0.052, 95% CI: 0.114, 0.001, $p = .054$), intention (indirect effect = -0.036, 95% CI: 0.095, -0.003, $p = .031$) and readiness (indirect effect = -0.023, 95% CI: 0.071, 0.001, $p = .063$), although the indirect effects for ideation and readiness fell just outside the criteria for significance. Notably, higher levels of pain tolerance were associated with higher levels of zest.

Pain tolerance is thought to increase readiness for engaging in suicidal behavior, although a recent review concluded that evidence is scant and does not include prospective studies (Kirtley, O'Carroll, & O'Connor, 2016). Inconsistent with the hypothesis that pain tolerance increases suicide-related behaviors, a recent study found that tolerance for psychological pain was higher among those who never attempted suicide compared to attempters (Meerwijk & Weiss, 2018). Moreover, there is evidence that physiological pain tolerance is *positively* associated with hope (Berg, Snyder, & Hamilton, 2008; Snyder et al., 2005), with the latter reflected in the positive outlook facet of zest for life. Those high in hope may seek out more challenging situations (Davidson, Wingate, Slish, & Rasmussen, 2010), thus encountering more pain and consequently heightening pain tolerance. Hence, it is possible that pain tolerance may indirectly *de*crease suicide ideation, intention, and readiness via its positive association with zest for life.

Does zest for life *moderate* the relationships between the mental preparation facet of acquired capability and suicidal ideation and intention?

Because of the strong negative association between mental preparation and zest for life (see Fig. 3.2), we further tested the role of zest as a protective factor in the relationship between mental preparation and suicide ideation and intent using moderation analyses. First, we tested if zest for life (Time 1) moderated the relationship between the mental preparation facet of acquired capability (Time 1) and suicide ideation (Time 2). This model was significant, F (3, 230) = 28.66, $p < .001$, $R^2 = 0.45$. As shown in Table 3.3, zest for life, mental preparation for suicide, and their interaction significantly prospectively predicted suicide ideation. Examining the conditional effects of mental preparation on suicide ideation at three levels of zest (one standard deviation below, at, and above the mean) showed that mental preparation was significantly positively related to suicide ideation at low and mean levels of zest for life, but not at high levels of zest. The Johnson-Neyman technique revealed that the relationship between mental preparation and suicide intention was significant when zest for life was less than 0.93 standard deviations above the mean.

Second, we tested if zest for life (Time 1) moderated the relationship between mental preparation (Time 1) and suicide intent (Time 2). This model was significant, F (3, 230) = 8.84, $p < .001$, $R^2 = 00.23$. As shown in Table 3.3, zest for life, mental preparation for suicide, and their

Table 3.3 Moderating effects of Zest for life in the prospective associations between the acquired capability facet of mental preparation and (a) Suicidal ideation and (b) Suicide intention.

Predictor	β	*p*	95% CI
(a) Suicidal ideation			
Zest for life	-0.15	< 0.001	-0.19, -0.09
Mental preparation	0.09	< 0.001	0.05, 0.13
Zest x mental preparation	-0.05	< 0.001	-0.07, -0.03
Conditional effects of mental preparation for zest at:			
One *SD* below mean	0.17	< 0.001	0.11, 0.23
Mean	0.09	< 0.001	0.05,0.13
One *SD* above mean	0.0009	0.97	-0.05, 0.05
(b) Suicidal intention			
Zest for life	-0.13	0.005	-0.21, -0.04
Mental preparation	0.11	0.005	0.03, 0.19
Zest x mental preparation	-0.08	< 0.001	-0.13, -0.04
Conditional effects of mental preparation for zest at:			
One *SD* below mean	0.25	< 0.001	0.15, 0.36
Mean	0.11	0.005	0.03, 0.19
One *SD* above mean	-0.03	0.57	-0.15, 0.08

interaction significantly prospectively predicted suicide intent. Examining the conditional effects of mental preparation on suicide intent at three levels of zest for life (one standard deviation below, at, and above the mean) showed that mental preparation was significantly positively related to suicide intention at low and mean levels of zest for life, but not at high levels of zest. The Johnson-Neyman technique revealed that the relationship between mental preparation and suicide intention was significant when zest for life was less than 0.34 standard deviations above the mean.

Discussion

Consistent with earlier proposals that the depletion of life-sustaining forces is central to suicide (Shneidman, 1996), we found that zest for life can act as a barrier against the deleterious effects of all three presumed causal factors of the interpersonal theory of suicide. While perceived burdensomeness directly predicted heightened suicide ideation at follow-up, thwarted belongingness did not. Importantly, and consistent with Joiner's proposal that the thwarting of the needs to contribute and belong is "life draining" (Joiner, 2005, p. 102), both interpersonal factors affected ideation indirectly via their inverse relationship with zest for life. Zest for life, in turn, negatively predicted suicide ideation, even after controlling for baseline ideation and general psychological distress capturing symptoms of both depression and anxiety (Andrews & Slade, 2001). This suggests that zest can counteract the influence of the thwarting of these interpersonal needs on future ideation.

Moderation analyses confirmed that zest for life 'buffers' (Johnson, Wood, Gooding, Taylor, & Tarrier, 2011) the adverse effects of both perceived burdensomeness and thwarted belongingness on suicidal desire. Both perceived burdensomeness and thwarted belongingness negatively predicted suicidal ideation at high levels of zest, but positively predicted ideation at low levels of zest, or in the case of thwarted belongingess also at mean levels of zest. Thus, heightened zest buffers against the adverse effects of burdensomeness and thwarted belongingness on the development of suicidal thinking.

Similarly, zest for life had a mediating influence on the impact of some of the key facets of acquired capability for suicide. However, consistent with the prediction from the interpersonal theory of suicide that acquired capability is necessary for the transition from suicidal thinking to *action* (Van Orden et al., 2010), the protective role of zest depended on which step in the motivational-volitional pathway toward suicide served as the criterion (cf., O'Connor & Kirtley, 2018). While zest for life negatively predicted subsequent suicidal ideation, intention, and readiness, these associations were of diminishing strength, respectively. Together with the buffering role of zest against the interpersonal antecedents of suicidal ideation, this suggests that zest primarily exerts its influence earlier in the ideation-to-action pathway during ideation and intention formation. Moreover, zest for life partly mediated the relationship between the *preparation* facet of acquired capability and the early steps of suicide ideation and intent, but did so only marginally for the later step of readiness, with the size of the indirect effect diminishing with each step closer to readiness.

Zest for life did not significantly mediate any of the associations between fearlessness of death and suicidal ideation, intent, or readiness. This is not unexpected given that fearlessness of death can also be fostered by zestful activities such as skydiving (Joiner, 2005). However, fearlessness of death had a significant direct effect on readiness, indicating that this facet of acquired capability acts directly, but not indirectly via zest, to amplify readiness for suicidal behavior. This is consistent with the interpersonal theory's proposal that fearlessness of death enhances readiness regardless of whether fearlessness is acquired passively through trauma exposure, pursuit of high risk leisure activities, deliberate non-suicidal self-injurious behavior, or active mental practice (Van Orden et al., 2010). Thus, zest for life appears not to counter fearlessness of death.

Zest for life mediated the relationships between pain tolerance and both suicide ideation and suicide intent, but consistent with previous evidence, pain tolerance was *positively* associated with zest. For example, other life-sustaining factors such as mastery (Christensen, Batterham, Mackinnon, Donker, & Soubelet, 2014) and hope (Davidson et al., 2010) are positively associated with acquired capability as measured by self-reported pain tolerance and fearlessness of death, and hope is also positively associated with physiological pain tolerance (Berg et al., 2008; Snyder et al., 2005). Davidson, Wingate, Rasmussen, and Slish (2009) suggest that those high in hope experience more pain since they may seek out more challenging situations. Those high in zest may similarly seek out challenging experiences with a greater probability of encountering more physical pain, consequently heightening pain tolerance. Conversely, heightened pain tolerance may facilitate greater engagement with and enjoyment of life by permitting one to experience challenging and novel situations. Additional research is needed to clarify the complex relationship between life-sustaining constructs such as zest for life, hope, and mastery and greater pain tolerance.

In sum, zest for life had a partial mediating role that was limited to the relationship between the *preparation* facet of acquired capability and the early steps of suicidal ideation and intent, but not further along the ideation-to-action pathway when readiness for behavioral action was the criterion. This 'buffering' effect of zest during the motivational phase of the pathway was again confirmed in that zest also moderated the adverse effects of mental preparation on subsequent heightened suicidal ideation and intent. Specifically, at high levels of zest, mental preparation did *not* significantly predict either suicide ideation or intent. Conversely, at low levels of zest, mental preparation was most strongly associated with both ideation and intent. Thus, erosion in zest for life amplifies the adverse effects of mental preparation on the solidification of suicidal desire and intention, but undiminished and strong zest confers protection.

Zest for life as an antidote to suicide

The present findings highlight the importance of accounting for the relationship between risk and resilience in theories of suicide (Klonsky & May 2015; Johnson et al., 2011). Zest for life may be eroded by unmet needs of belongingness and interpersonal effectiveness, or actively undermined by mental preparation for engaging in suicidal behavior. But to the extent that zest for life is strong, or is actively nourished during threat posed by the confluence of thwarted interpersonal needs and mental rehearsal to enact suicidal desire, it is potentially life-saving because it can stall or reverse progress toward suicide. As noted by O'Connor and Nock (2014), the refinement of psychological theories of suicide require programmatic testing of both risk and protective factors, and a better understanding of the factors that enable or impede behavioral enactment will inform the translation of this research into clinical practice.

In this chapter we have argued that suicide is best understood as an outcome of a process where life-sustaining strengths have been eroded and overcome by death-promoting proximal risk factors (Kovacs & Beck, 1977; Shneidman, 1996). While it is critically important to understand why people die by suicide, we must not neglect to examine why people do not die by suicide. That is, the ideation-to-action framework for research on the transition from suicidal thought to behavior is incomplete, unless complemented by better understanding of the ideation-to-*non*action path, which is the path taken by most ideators (ten Have et al., 2009). Here we have highlighted the critical importance of fostering engagement with life among those who are experiencing the thwarting of interpersonal needs and are engaging in mental preparation for suicidal action.

This paradigm shift from an almost exclusive risk-centric, 'death preventing' approach to one that is complemented by a life-focused and 'life sustaining' approach is also well-grounded in the perspectives voiced with ever increasing urgency by those with lived experience (see Ellis & Bryan, this volume; Davidow & Mazel-Carlton, this volume). As so cogently put by Heidi Bryan, even when the struggle with suicidal ideation is a life-long companion, "It's been a long journey to learn how to live fully and even while experiencing suicidal thoughts, but a journey worth taking" (Ellis & Bryan, this volume). There is much to be gained by putting life front and center when collaborating with those at risk. For example, in a recent study of 128 suicidal emergency care patients, who were monitored for a six-month period following discharge from the hospital, both the clinician and the patient provided a prediction at intake what the likelihood was that the patient will make a suicide attempt in the next six months (Harrison, Stritzke, Fay, & Hudaib, 2018). Clinician and patient predictions complemented each other in prospectively predicting *different* aspects of future suicide risk and resilience! Whereas clinician estimates of the likelihood of an attempt predicted future death-promoting factors (e.g., suicide ideation), patient estimates instead predicted future life-sustaining factors (e.g., zest for life). Thus, from the patients' point of view, the only significant predictor of a future suicide attempt was how strongly they had managed to re-connect with a life worth living.

There is increasing recognition that the "unique balance" between individuals' motivations for suicide and life-sustaining reasons may be a critical determinant of risk outcome (American Psychiatric Association, 2016; Fowler, 2012). For example, an index that computes the balance between the wish to die and the wish to live was found to uniquely predict suicide in a 10-year follow-up study of psychiatric outpatients (Brown, Steer, Henriques, & Beck, 2005). As the influence of zest for life appears to be most pronounced at the early ideation and intention formation phase of the pathway toward suicide, it suggests that dimished zest is an important target for suicide prevention. Indeed, enhanced engagement in life is a core strategy of community mental health initiatives, such as the Act-Belong-Commit program, which encourages individuals to stay mentally, physically, and socially active, while fostering purpose in life by setting goals and becoming involved in causes within the community (Anwar-McHenry, Donovan, Jalleh, & Laws, 2012; Donovan, James, Jalleh, & Sidebottom, 2006). Finally, as the assessment of zest for life enquires about engagement with life rather than suicide risk directly, it may be also useful in contexts where individuals may be reluctant to disclose suicidal intent (e.g., Kupers, 2005), but would welcome a caring conversation about what aspects of their life they need help with in taking it by the lapel and be told, *I'm with you, kid. Let's go.*

Appendix: the Zest for Life Scale (ZLS)

The following questions refer to *your thoughts and feelings* about ***life***. Please indicate how much you agree with the statements below by circling the number corresponding most closely how you feel about life at this time in your life. Your answers may range from AGREE NOT AT ALL (0) with the statement to AGREE VERY STRONGLY (8) with the statement.

		I agree with this statement …								
		Not at all								**Very strongly**
1.	I Look forward to each new day	0	1	2	3	4	5	6	7	8
2.	Life feels more dull as time moves on	0	1	2	3	4	5	6	7	8
3.	Life seems to hold less for me than it used to	0	1	2	3	4	5	6	7	8
4.	I Used to think about life as 'half full', now it feels more like 'half empty'	0	1	2	3	4	5	6	7	8
5.	I Feel less alive than I used to	0	1	2	3	4	5	6	7	8
6.	I Strive to participate fully in life, not just view it from the sidelines	0	1	2	3	4	5	6	7	8
7.	Life has become a drag	0	1	2	3	4	5	6	7	8
8.	I Wake up in the morning and look forward to what life has in store for me	0	1	2	3	4	5	6	7	8
9.	I Am embracing life	0	1	2	3	4	5	6	7	8
10.	I Am looking forward to all that life has to offer	0	1	2	3	4	5	6	7	8

(*Continued*)

11.	I Try to enjoy life no matter what	0	1	2	3	4	5	6	7	8
12.	I Never used to, but now I sometimes think 'why bother'	0	1	2	3	4	5	6	7	8

Reverse-scored items: 2, 3, 4, 5, 7, 12.

References

American Psychiatric Association. (2016). *Practice guidelines for the psychiatric evaluation of adults* (3rd ed.). Arlington: Author.

Andrews, G., & Slade, T. (2001). Interpreting scores on the kessler psychological distress Scale (K10). *Australian & New Zealand Journal of Public Health, 25*, 494–497. https://doi.org/10.1111/j.1467-842X.2001.tb00310.x.

Anwar-McHenry, J., Donovan, R. J., Jalleh, G., & Laws, A. (2012). Impact evaluation of the Act-Belong-Commit mental health promotion campaign. *Journal of Public Mental Health, 11*, 186–194. https://doi.org/10.1108/17465721211289365.

Bentler, P. (1990). Comparative fit indexes in structural models. *Psychological Bulletin, 107*, 238–246. https://doi.org/10.1037/0033-2909.107.2.238.

Berg, C. J., Snyder, C. R., & Hamilton, N. (2008). The effectiveness of a hope intervention in coping with cold pressor pain. *Journal of Health Psychology, 13*, 804–809. https://doi.org/10.1177/1359105308093864.

Bodegård, G. (2005). Pervasive loss of function in asylum-seeking children in Sweden. *Acta Pædiatrica, 94*, 1706–1707. https://doi.org/10.1080/08035250510036778.

Brown, T. A. (2006). *Confirmatory factor analysis for applied research*. New York, NY: Guilford Press.

Brown, G. K., Steer, R. A., Henriques, G. R., & Beck, A. T. (2005). The internal struggle between the wish to die and the wish to live: A risk factor for suicide. *American Journal of Psychiatry, 162*, 1977–1979. https://doi.org/10.1176/appi.ajp.162.10.1977.

Byrne, B. M. (2010). *Structural equation modeling with AMOS: Basic concepts, applications, and programming* (2nd ed.). New York: Routledge.

Christensen, H., Batterham, P. J., Mackinnon, A. J., Donker, T., & Soubelet, A. (2014). Predictors of the risk factors for suicide identified by the interpersonal-psychological theory of suicidal behaviour. *Psychiatry Research, 219*, 290–297. https://doi.org/10.1016/j.psychres.2014.05.029.

Comrey, A. L. (1988). Factor-analytic methods of scale development in personality and clinical psychology. *Journal of Consulting and Clinical Psychology, 56*, 754–761. https://doi.org/10.1037/0022-006x.56.5.754.

Comrey, A. L., & Lee, H. B. (1992). *A first course in factor analysis* (2nd ed.). Hillsdale, N.J.: L. Erlbaum Associates.

Curran, P. J., West, S. G., & Finch, J. F. (1996). The robustness of test statistics to non-normality and specification error in confirmatory factor analysis. *Psychological Methods, 1*, 16–29. https://doi.org/10.1037/1082-989X.1.1.16.

Cvetkovski, S., Reavley, N. J., & Jorm, A. F. (2012). The prevalence and correlates of psychological distress in Australian tertiary students compared to their community peers. *Australian and New Zealand Journal of Psychiatry, 46*, 457–467. https://doi.org/10.1177/0004867411435290.

Davidson, C. L., Wingate, L. R., Rasmussen, K. A., & Slish, M. L. (2009). Hope as a predictor of interpersonal suicide risk. *Suicide and Life-Threatening Behavior, 39*, 499–507. https://doi.org/10.1521/suli.2009.39.5.499.

Davidson, C. L., Wingate, L. R., Slish, M. L., & Rasmussen, K. A. (2010). The great black hope: Hope and its relation to suicide risk among African Americans. *Suicide and Life-Threatening Behavior, 40*, 170–180. https://doi.org/10.1521/suli.2010.40.2.170.

DiStefano, C., & Motl, R. W. (2006). Further investigating method effects associated with negatively worded items on self-report surveys. *Structural Equation Modeling, 13*, 440–464. https://doi.org/10.1207/s15328007sem1303_6.

Donovan, R. J., James, R., Jalleh, G., & Sidebottom, C. (2006). Implementing mental health promotion: The act-belong-commit mentally healthy WA campaign in Western Australia. *International Journal of Mental Health Promotion, 8*, 33–42. https://doi.org/10.1080/14623730.2006.9721899.

Field, A. (2009). *Discovering statistics using SPSS* (3rd ed.). Thousand Oaks, CA: Sage Publications Inc.

Finch, J. F., & West, S. G. (1997). The investigation of personality structure: Statistical models. *Journal of Research in Personality, 31*, 439–485. https://doi.org/10.1006/jrpe.1997.2194.

Fowler, J. C. (2012). Suicide risk assessment in clinical practice: Pragmatic guidelines for imperfect assessments. *Psychotherapy, 49*, 81–90. https://doi.org/10.1037/a0026148.

George, S. E., Page, A. C., Hooke, G. R., & Stritzke, W. G. K. (2016). Multifacet assessment of capability for suicide: Development and prospective validation of the acquired capability with rehearsal for suicide scale. *Psychological Assessment, 28*, 1452–1464. https://doi.org/10.1037/pas0000276.

Gignac, G. E. (2007). Multi-factor modeling in individual differences research: Some recommendations and suggestions. *Personality and Individual Differences, 42*, 37–48. https://doi.org/10.1016/j.paid.2006.06.019.

Harrison, D. P., Stritzke, W. G. K., Fay, N., & Hudaib, A.-R. (2018). Suicide risk assessment: Trust an implicit probe or listen to the patient? *Psychological Assessment, 30*, 1317–1329. https://doi.org/10.1037/pas0000577.

ten Have, M., de Graaf, R., van Dorsselaer, S., Verdurmen, J., van't Land, H., Vollebergh, W., et al. (2009). Incidence and course of suicidal ideation and suicide attempts in the general population. *Canadian Psychiatric Association Journal/La Revue de l'Association des psychiatres du Canada, 54*, 824–833.

Hayes, A. F. (2016). *My macros and code for SPSS and SAS*. Retrieved from http://afhayes.com/spss-sas-and-mplus-macros-and-code.html.

Hayton, J. C., Allen, D. G., & Scarpello, V. (2004). Factor retention decisions in exploratory factor analysis: A tutorial on parallel analysis. *Organizational Research Methods, 7*, 191–205. https://doi.org/10.1177/1094428104263675.

Horn, J. L. (1965). A rationale and test for the number of factors in factor analysis. *Psychometrika, 30*, 179–185. https://doi.org/10.1007/BF02289447.

Hu, L., & Bentler, P. M. (1999). Cutoff criteria for fit indexes in covariance structure analysis: Conventional criteria versus new alternatives. *Structural Equation Modeling, 6*, 1–55. https://doi.org/10.1080/10705519909540118.

Johnson, J., Wood, A. M., Gooding, P., Taylor, P. J., & Tarrier, N. (2011). Resilience to suicidality: The buffering hypothesis. *Clinical Psychology Review, 31*, 563–591. https://doi.org/10.1016/j.cpr.2010.12.007.

Joiner, T. E. (2005). *Why people die by suicide*. Cambridge, MA: Harvard University Press.

Jose, P. E. (2013). *Doing statistical mediation and moderation*. New York, NY: Guilford Press; US.

Kessler, R. C., Barker, P. R., Colpe, L. J., Epstein, J. F., Gfroerer, J. C., Hiripi, E., et al. (2003). Screening for serious mental illness in the general population. *Archives of General Psychiatry, 60*, 184–189. https://doi.org/10.1002/mpr.310.

Kirtley, O. J., O'Carroll, R. E., & O'Connor, R. C. (2016). Pain and self-harm: A systematic review. *Journal of Affective Disorders, 203*, 347–363. https://doi.org/10.1016/j.jad.2016.05.068.

Klonsky, E., & May, A. M. (2015). The three-step theory (3ST): A new theory of suicide rooted in the "ideation-to-action" framework. *International Journal of Cognitive Therapy, 8*, 114–129. https://doi.org/10.1521/ijct.2015.8.2.114.

Kovacs, M., & Beck, A. T. (1977). The wish to die and the wish to live in attempted suicides. *Journal of Clinical Psychology, 33*, 361–365. https://doi.org/10.1002/1097-4679.

Kupers, T. A. (2005). Toxic masculinity as a barrier to mental health treatment in prison. *Journal of Clinical Psychology, 61*, 713–724. https://doi.org/10.1002/jclp.20105.

Latimer, S., Meade, T., & Tennant, A. (2013). Measuring engagement in deliberate self-harm behaviours: Psychometric evaluation of six scales. *BMC Psychiatry, 13*. https://doi.org/10.1186/1471-244x-13-4.

Linehan, M. M., Goodstein, J. L., Nielsen, S. L., & Chiles, J. A. (1983). Reasons for staying alive when you are thinking of killing yourself: The Reasons for Living Inventory. *Journal of Consulting and Clinical Psychology, 51*, 276–286. https://doi.org/10.1037/0022-006X.51.2.276.

Meerwijk, E. L., & Weiss, S. J. (2018). Tolerance for psychological pain and capability for suicide: Contributions to suicidal ideation and behavior. *Psychiatry Research, 262*, 203–208. https://doi.org/10.1016/j.psychres.2018.02.005.

Meyers, L. S., Gamst, G., & Guarino, A. J. (2006). *Applied multivariate research: Design and interpretation*. London: SAGE Publications.

Nock, M. K., Holmberg, E. B., Photos, V. I., & Michel, B. D. (2007). Self-injurious thoughts and behaviors interview: Development, reliability, and validity in an adolescent sample. *Psychological Assessment, 19*, 309–317. https://doi.org/10.1037/1040-3590.19.3.309.

O'Connor, B. P. (2000). SPSS and SAS programs for determining the number of components using parallel analysis and Velicer's MAP test. *Behavior Research Methods Instruments & Computers, 32*, 396–402. https://doi.org/10.3758/bf03200807.

O'Connor, R. C., & Kirtley, O. J. (2018). The integrated motivational–volitional model of suicidal behaviour. *Philosophical Transactions Royal Society B, 373*(1754), 20170268. https://doi.org/10.1098/rstb.2017.0268.

O'Connor, R. C., & Nock, M. K. (2014). The psychology of suicidal behaviour. *Lancet Psychiatry, 1*, 27–39. https://doi.org/10.1016/S2215-0366(14)70222-6.

Peterson, C., Park, N., & Seligman, M. E. P. (2005). Assessment of character strengths. In G. P. Koocher, J. C. Norcross, & S. S. Hill (Eds.), *Psychologists' desk reference* (2nd ed., pp. 93–98). New York: Oxford University Press.

Shneidman, E. S. (1996). *The suicidal mind*. Oxford: Oxford University Press.

Snyder, C., Berg, C., Woodward, J. T., Gum, A., Rand, K. L., Wrobleski, K. K., et al. (2005). Hope against the cold: Individual differences in trait hope and acute pain tolerance on the cold pressor task. *Journal of Personality, 73*, 287–312. https://doi.org/10.1111/j.1467-6494.2005.00318.x.

Stallman, H. M. (2010). Psychological distress in university students: A comparison with general population data. *Australian Psychologist, 45*(4), 249–257. https://doi.org/10.1080/00050067.2010.482109.

Steger, M. F., Frazier, P., Oishi, S., & Kaler, M. (2006). The meaning in life questionnaire: Assessing the presence of and search for meaning in life. *Journal of Counseling Psychology, 53*, 80–93. https://doi.org/10.1037/0022-0167.53.1.80.

Tabachnick, B. G., & Fidell, L. S. (2013). *Using multivariate statistics* (6th ed.). Boston, MA: Pearson.

Van Orden, K. A., Cukrowicz, K. C., Witte, T. K., & Joiner, T. E., Jr. (2012). Thwarted belongingness and perceived burdensomeness: Construct validity and psychometric properties of the Interpersonal Needs Questionnaire. *Psychological Assessment, 24*, 197–215. https://doi.org/10.1037/a0025358.

Van Orden, K. A., Witte, T. K., Cukrowicz, K. C., Braithwaite, S. R., Selby, E. A., & Joiner, T. E., Jr. (2010). The interpersonal theory of suicide. *Psychological Review, 117*, 575–600. https://doi.org/10.1037/a0018697.

Van Orden, K. A., Witte, T. K., Gordon, K. H., Bender, T. W., & Joiner, T. E., Jr. (2008). Suicidal desire and the capability for suicide: Tests of the interpersonal-psychological theory of suicidal behavior among adults. *Journal of Consulting and Clinical Psychology, 76*, 72–83. https://doi.org/10.1037/0022-006x.76.1.72.

Williams, L. J., Ford, L. R., & Nguyen, N. (2002). *Basic and advanced measurement models for confirmatory factor analysis Handbook of research methods in industrial and organizational psychology*. Malden: Blackwell Publishing.

World Health Organization. (2014). *Preventing suicide: A global imperative* (Luxembourg: Author).

PART 2

To be or not to be

CHAPTER 4

The temporal dynamics of the wish to live and the wish to die among suicidal individuals

Craig J. Bryan
National Center for Veterans Studies, The University of Utah, Salt Lake City, UT, United States

The notion that suicidal individuals experience an internal struggle between the wish to live and the wish to die has been noted by clinicians and researchers for several decades (Brown, Steer, Henriques, & Beck, 2005; Evans & Farberow, 1988; Jobes & Mann, 1999; Kovacs & Beck, 1977; Neuringer & Lettieri, 1971; Shneidman, 1964; Stengel, 1964). This internal struggle between life and death has been described using several terms including the internal debate (Brown, Ten Have, et al., 2005; Kovacs & Beck, 1977), ambivalence (Jobes, 2016; Jobes & Mann, 1999), and suicidal mulling (Millner, Lee, & Nock, 2017). For the purposes of the present discussion, the term *suicidal ambivalence* will be used to refer to the psychological state of mixed—sometimes contradictory—feelings about life and death. This term and operationalization are used in order to align the concept of suicide-specific ambivalence with conceptualizations of general ambivalence used in other areas of psychology (e.g., Miller & Rollnick, 2012).

Suicidal ambivalence has traditionally been conceptualized on a unidimensional spectrum bookended by two opposing forces: life and death (Fig. 4.1). Consistent with this conceptualization, a common approach used by researchers is to assess the strength or salience of an individual's wish to live and their wish to die using separate scales, and then subtracting the former from the latter to create an ambivalence index, such that negative values indicate a stronger wish to live, positive values indicate a stronger wish to die, and zero values indicate ambivalence. For example, the first two items of the Scale for Suicide Ideation (SSI; Beck, Brown, & Steer, 1997) have been frequently used by researchers to quantify suicidal ambivalence. The SSI assesses the wish to live and the wish to die using a

Alternatives to Suicide
ISBN 978-0-12-814297-4
https://doi.org/10.1016/B978-0-12-814297-4.00004-2

Fig. 4.1 A unipolar structure of suicidal ambivalence.

three-point ordinal scale corresponding to the following response options: *none, weak,* and *strong*. Researchers subtract the (reversed) wish to live item score from the wish to die item score, resulting in an index score ranging from −2 (strong wish to live and no wish to die) to +2 (no wish to live and strong wish to die). The Suicide Status Form (SSF; Jobes, 2016) is another commonly-used tool for quantifying suicidal ambivalence using the same approach, although the SSF uses nine-point ordinal scales instead of three-point scales to assess each construct. Across both scales, researchers have found that negative values (i.e., stronger wish to live than wish to die) are correlated with less severe suicidal intent, hopelessness, self-hatred, emotional distress, and faster resolution of depression and suicidal ideation (Corona et al., 2013; Kovacs & Beck, 1977; Lento, Ellis, Hinnant, & Jobes, 2013; O'Connor, Jobes, Comtois, et al., 2012; O'Connor, Jobes, Yeargin, et al., 2012). Conversely, positive scores (i.e., stronger wish to die than wish to live) are correlated with more severe suicidal intent and emotional distress, slower resolution of suicidal ideation, and eventual death by suicide (Brown, Steer, et al., 2005; Corona et al., 2013; Kovacs & Beck, 1977; Lento et al., 2013; O'Connor, Jobes, Comtois, et al., 2012; O'Connor, Jobes, Yeargin, et al., 2012). Ambivalent states (i.e., equivalent or comparable levels of wish to live and wish to die) typically fall in between these two extremes.

Ambivalence implicates an inherently dynamic process characterized by vacillations between two opposing positions, in this case life and death. As a result of this competition between life and death, suicidal individuals are assumed to move back and forth on the ambivalence continuum, with suicidal behavior being highest at the extreme end of the spectrum characterized by the wish to die and the absence of the wish to live. An alternative perspective is to conceptualize suicidal ambivalence as a bidimensional construct, whereby the wish to live and the wish to die are separate, albeit correlated, dimensions (see Fig. 4.2). This perspective aligns with research supporting bidimensional structures for other constructs that are often presumed to be unidimensional, such as hope and hopelessness, optimism and pessimism, and negative and positive affect (Chang, Maydeu-Olivares, & D'Zurilla, 1997; Diener & Emmons, 1984;

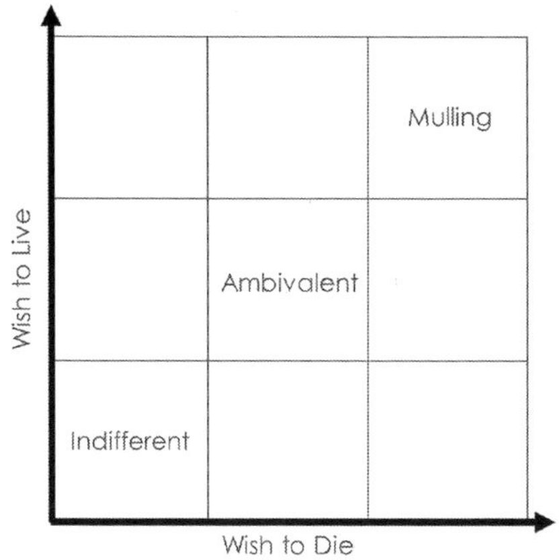

Fig. 4.2 A bidimensional structure of suicidal ambivalence.

Herzberg, Glaesner, & Hoyer, 2006; Osman et al., 2010). Because a bidimensional structure of suicidal ambivalence allows for the co-existence of a broader range of psychological states, it provides much greater nuance than a unidimensional structure. In Fig. 4.2, for example, three different configurations of suicidal ambivalence are possible: strong wish to live and strong wish to die, weak wish to live and weak wish to die, no wish to live and no wish to die.

Conceptually, these three combinations implicate very different psychological states. On one end of the spectrum, those experiencing neither a wish to live nor a wish to die may be best described as "indifferent," a psychological state that has not received much empirical attention but may reasonably be expected to be associated with "passive" suicide ideation including thoughts about death or remaining in a potentially life-threatening situation. On the other end of the spectrum is the combination of a strong wish to live and a strong wish to die, a psychological state characterized by intensely conflicting or opposing desires, consistent with Millner et al.'s (2017) descriptions of suicidal "mulling," which entails strong consideration of suicide attempts and "going back and forth in one's mind about whether to do it or not" (p. 5–6). In between these two extremes is the combination of a weak wish to live and a weak wish to die, which may reflect a psychological state that aligns with traditional conceptualizations of the internal debate. In the unidimensional approach, by comparison, these three combinations of the wish to live and the wish to die are considered equivalent because they all yield a total index score of zero. Experiencing the co-existence of a strong wish to live and a strong wish to die is therefore considered equivalent to experiencing the co-existence of no wish to live and no wish to die.

Consideration of the wish to live and the wish to die as separate constructs provides context for understanding the mechanisms that underlie the emergence of suicidal behaviors. For example, the death/suicide implicit association test is a computerized task that assesses an individual's automatic self-associations with death relative to life and has been shown to correlate with various indicators of suicide risk, to include future suicidal behavior (Nock & Banaji, 2007; Nock et al., 2010). Recent research indicates the association of performance on the task with these indicators of suicide risk is largely explained by a diminished wish to live rather than the presence of a wish to die (Harrison, Stritzke, Fay, Ellison, & Hudaib, 2014). In clinical settings, studies have similarly suggested that suicidal behaviors are driven to a larger degree by a diminished wish to live rather than a wish to die (Bryan, Rudd, Peterson, Young-McCaughan, & Wertenberger, 2016). A bidimensional structure may also provide context for the results of one study finding a different pattern than other studies using a unidimensional structure for suicidal ambivalence (Corona et al., 2013). In that study, psychiatric outpatients reporting a stronger wish to live at baseline showed better outcomes than patients reporting a stronger desire to die, as would be expected, but those reporting suicidal ambivalence showed the *worst* outcomes rather than falling in between the other two groups. One possible explanation for this finding is that ambivalent patients were experiencing a more pernicious type of suicidal ambivalence (e.g., suicidal mulling) than patients in other studies.

Another possible explanation is that the researchers did not fully account for the temporal dynamics of the wish to live and the wish to die. Specifically, patients in that study were classified based on the strength of their wish to live and wish to die at the outset of treatment only. It is possible that the relative balance between the wish to live and the wish to die changed over the course of treatment, such that some (or many) of the patients in this group experienced a strengthening of the wish to live and/or a weakening of the wish to die over time. The wish to live and the wish to die are not static; they change over time, especially in response to clinical intervention (Bryan, Mintz, Clemans, Leeson, et al., 2017; Bryan et al., 2016). Static classification of patients based on their scores at a single time point fails to capture these inherent temporal dynamics. Unfortunately, the majority of studies focused on suicidal ambivalence have used this static classification approach, even when using prospective designs (Brown, Ten Have, et al., 2005; Corona et al., 2013; Kovacs & Beck, 1977; Lento et al., 2013; O'Connor, Jobes, Comtois, et al., 2012; O'Connor, Jobes, Yeargin, et al., 2012). Conceptual models that account for the temporal dynamics of the wish to live and the wish to die are therefore needed.

The fluid vulnerability theory of suicide

The fluid vulnerability theory of suicide was first articulated by Rudd (2006) as a conceptual model for understanding the temporal processes by which suicide risk changes over time and, more importantly, for understanding the emergence of suicidal behaviors. In contrast to other contemporary theories of suicide, which have largely focused on identifying and studying the *content* of suicide risk states (i.e., *what* underlies the transition of suicidal thoughts to behaviors), the fluid vulnerability theory emphasizes the time course of suicide risk states (i.e., *how* and *when* does the transition from suicidal thoughts to behaviors occur). For example, the interpersonal-psychological theory (Joiner, 2007) posits that the combination of perceived burdensomeness and thwarted belongingness lead to active suicidal ideation. When these two variables co-occur with elevated capability for suicide, suicidal behavior can emerge. Various combinations of similar variables have been hypothesized by other suicide theories like the integrated motivational-volitional model (O'Connor & Kirtley, 2018) and the three step theory (Klonsky & May, 2015). Although research has provided some support for these hypothesized combinations of variables, recent meta analyses and reviews indicate the overall effects have been mixed and/or only modest in degree (Chu et al., 2017; O'Connor & Kirtley, 2018), suggesting only limited incremental utility beyond earlier theories of suicide. One potential reason for this finding is the limited attention paid to the temporal dynamics of suicide risk (Bryan & Rudd, 2016).

The wish to live as a component of the suicidal mode

A central tenet of the fluid vulnerability theory of suicide is that suicide risk is inherently dynamic, changing over time as a result of complex interactions among variables *within* individuals as well as *between* individuals and their environments. These interactions can be structurally organized using the suicidal mode (see Fig. 4.3). The suicidal mode is a

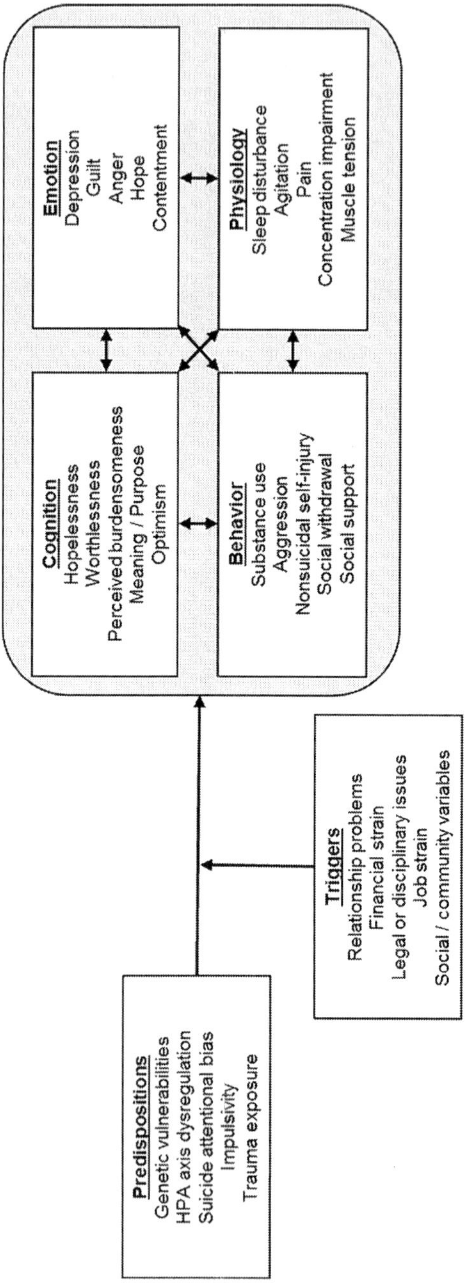

Fig. 4.3 The suicidal mode.

conceptual model that has guided the development of several empirically-supported treatments and interventions that reduce suicidal behaviors: cognitive behavioral therapy for suicide prevention (Brown, Ten Have, et al., 2005; Rudd et al., 2015), crisis response planning and safety planning (Bryan, Mintz, Clemans, Leeson, et al., 2017; Miller et al., 2017; Stanley et al., 2018); and the attempted suicide short intervention program (Gysin-Maillart, Schwab, Soravia, Megert, & Michel, 2016). The suicidal mode is also very similar to the biosocial theory that has been used to guide the development and refinement of dialectical behavior therapy, another effective treatment approach for suicide prevention (e.g., Linehan, Armstrong, Suarez, Allmon, & Heard, 1991; Linehan et al., 2006, 2015).

The suicidal mode organizes risk and protective factors into several domains: cognition, emotion, behavior, and physiology. These four domains are mutually influential, such that they are constantly pushing and pulling on one another. Activation and maintenance of these domains depends in part upon the nature of the individual's predisposing vulnerabilities within the context of his or her environment. Critically, an individual's predispositions are likely to be activated only in certain situations or environments, although individual differences in predisposing vulnerabilities dictate the breadth of situations and environments than may activate the suicidal mode. For example, some individuals may be vulnerable to suicidal thoughts and behaviors only within the context of intimate interpersonal relationships whereas other individuals may be vulnerable to suicidal thoughts and behaviors across many different contexts (e.g., financial strain, work-related conflict, trauma-related memories). Individuals who are easily activated across multiple contexts and situations are more likely to engage in repeat suicidal behaviors.

Within the suicidal mode, the wish to live can be conceptualized as a cognitive-affective state that entails life-sustaining beliefs and thought processes such as optimism (*Good things will happen to me*), hope (*Things will get better*), and purpose (*My life has meaning*), as well as positive emotional states like joy, happiness, and contentment. According to the suicidal mode, these cognitions and emotions should influence each other as well as an individual's behavior and physiological state. Indeed, research suggests that the experience of positive cognitive-affective states like perspective taking, planning ahead, and the ability to identify and flexibly employ coping strategies in response to adversity and stressful life experiences, are associated with a range of effects that should offset elevations in suicide risk (Fredrickson & Joiner, 2002; Fredrickson, Tugade, Waugh, & Larkin, 2003; Moskowitz, Folkman, & Acree, 2003; Reich, Blackwell, Simmons, & Beck, 2015; Stein, Folkman, Trabasso, & Richards, 1997; Tugade, Fredrickson, & Barrett, 2004). Kashdan, Uswatte, and Julian (2006) have further suggested that positive cognitive-emotional states may increase social engagement, another well-established protective factor for suicide. Physiologically, positive cognitive-affective states have also been associated with increased parasympathetic activation (Redwine et al., 2016), suggesting they may counteract the stress response. The wish to live is therefore one of many network components that comprise the suicidal mode and interact with multiple other risk and protective factors.

Fluctuations in the wish to live and the wish to die

Because suicide risk is inherently dynamic, an implication of the fluid vulnerability theory is that acute periods of risk elevation are followed by periods of resolution. These periods of risk elevation correspond to suicidal "crises" or suicidal "episodes," and can be understood as an activation of multiple domains of the suicidal mode, including the wish to die. Elevations in the wish to die would be expected to accompany elevations in other variables that cut across the various domains of the suicidal mode, such as hopelessness and/or perceived burdensomeness (cognition), depression and/or guilt (emotion), insomnia and agitation (physiological), and maladaptive coping strategies (behavior). Elevations in the wish to die may not always coincide with reductions in the wish to live, however, owing to the bidimensional nature of suicidal ambivalence.

According to Rudd (2006), periods of acute risk escalation are time-limited, typically lasting only a few minutes to hours in duration. Accumulating evidence using ecological momentary assessment (EMA) methods supports this assumption: fluctuations in suicidal ideation often occur rapidly, within the span of just three to 4 h (see Kleiman & Nock, 2018, for review). This up-and-down pattern reflects a process of homeostatic regulation. Homeostatic regulation implies the existence of a point of equilibrium, or a "set point," toward which the system is attracted. When a particular component of the system is higher than this set point at a given moment in time, that component will tend to decline during subsequent moments in time. Conversely, when a component of the system is lower than this set point at a given moment in time, that component will tend to increase during subsequent moments in time. As applied to suicidal ambivalence, individuals have a natural "set point" for the wish to live and the wish to die. In response to life stressors and change in the various components of the suicidal mode, the wish to live and the wish to die fluctuate around these set points, returning each time to its set point as a result of homeostatic regulation. Homeostatic regulation in both the wish to live and the wish to die have been empirically demonstrated (Bryan et al., 2016) and coincide with another central tenet of the fluid vulnerability theory: suicide risk returns to each individual's set point.

Homeostatic regulation of the wish to live and the wish to die

Consistent with the bidimensional structure of suicidal ambivalence described previously, fluctuations in the wish to live and the wish to die can occur independent of each other, such that an increase in one does not necessarily correspond with a decrease in the other (and vice versa). This does not rule out the possibility that, in some cases, fluctuations in the wish to live and the wish to die *do* correspond with each. The results of Bryan et al. (2016) support this possibility: the wish to live and the wish to die sometimes fluctuate in an uncoordinated manner but other times their fluctuations occur in a coordinated manner. Bryan and colleagues further found that the former situation (uncoordinated change) was associated with the occurrence of suicide attempts during or after treatment whereas the latter situation (coordinated change) was associated with the absence of suicide attempts. More specifically, the wish to die stabilized or regulated the wish to live, meaning that an elevated wish to die facilitated or supported the homeostatic balance of the wish to live. Among those patients who received brief cognitive behavioral therapy for suicide prevention (BCBT), a treatment shown to reduce suicide attempts by 60% among high-risk patients (Rudd et al., 2015), the wish to live also destabilized or dysregulated the wish to die, meaning that the wish to live disrupted the homeostatic balance of the wish to die. This latter finding is notable because it suggests that the wish to live enabled a process by which a new equilibrium could be established. Coordinated change processes in the wish to live and the wish to die therefore differentiated patients who attempted suicide as well as treatment group. To understand the practical implications of these findings, it is helpful to first discuss two aspects of homeostatic regulation: self-regulation and co-regulation.

The observed fluctuations in the wish to live and the wish to die implicate the existence of underlying self-regulatory processes. Self-regulation refers to the tendency of a system or a variable to return to its point of equilibrium. For most individuals, the set point for the wish to live is high and the set point for the wish to die is low, resulting in a set point that coincide with the upper left box of Fig. 4.2. For at-risk individuals, however, the set point for the wish to live is lower and the set point for the wish to die is higher, resulting in a set point that is below and to the right of the set point associated with nonsuicidal states. Nonsuicidal individuals therefore may experience a decline in the wish to live and/or an increase in the wish to die, but their self-regulatory processes would be expected to return them to top left box. Note that because the set point for these individuals is located in the top left region of the figure, deviations away from this set point are restricted to certain directions: down and to the right. By contrast, at-risk individuals whose set point lies in the center box could experience deviations from their set point in *all* directions, and would be expected to return to this box as a function of their self-regulatory processes. The differences in set points for nonsuicidal and at-risk individuals contributes to differences in the experience of these fluctuations; specifically, the restricted variability in the wish to live and the wish to die among nonsuicidal individuals is unlikely to be described as ambivalence, but the heightened variability among at-risk individuals is much more likely to be described as ambivalence or, in some cases, as an internal debate.

The magnitude of variability in the wish to live and the wish to die serves as an indicator of self-regulatory capacity. A considerable body of psychological research indicates, for example, that more extreme variability in a construct over time reflects compromised self-regulation whereas attenuated variability reflects greater self-regulation (Bänziger, Patel, & Scherer, 2014; Bryan & Rudd, 2017; Butner, Gagnon, Geuss, Lessard, & Story, 2015; Chow, Ram, Boker, Fujita, & Clore, 2005). These patterns are depicted in Fig. 4.4. As applied to suicidal ambivalence, larger (i.e., more extreme) fluctuations in the wish to live and the wish to die would therefore suggest less self-regulation whereas smaller (i.e., less extreme) fluctuations would suggest greater self-regulation. Several studies lend some support to this perspective. In both clinical and nonclinical settings, variability in suicidal ideation is more extreme among individuals

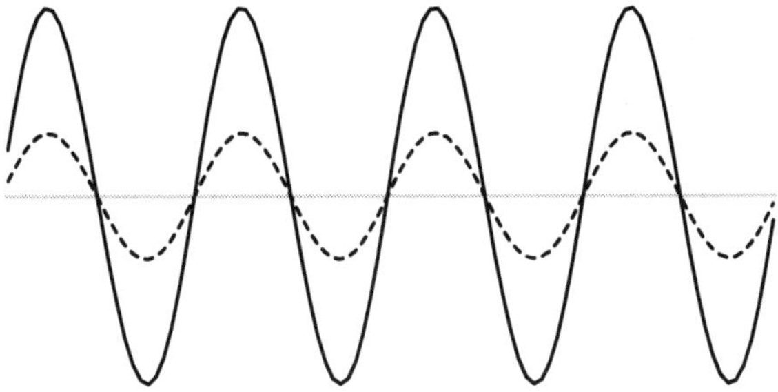

Fig. 4.4 The association of variability in a psychological construct and homeostatic regulation. Over time, more highly regulated systems show small smaller deviations from the mean whereas less regulated systems show larger deviations from the mean. As applied to suicide risk, lower risk individuals would be expected to experience smaller fluctuations in the wish to live and the wish to die because they have increased self-regulatory capacity, whereas higher risk individuals would be expected to experience larger fluctuations due to diminished self-regulatory capacity.

who have made multiple suicide attempts as compared to individuals who have never attempted suicide or made only one suicide attempt (Bryan & Rudd, 2017; Witte, Fitzpatrick, Joiner, & Schmidt, 2005). Considerable research indicates that individuals with a history of multiple suicide attempts experience deficits in self-regulation. Among patients who have made a first suicide attempt, impaired self-regulation also serves to predict the later occurrence of a second suicide attempt (Bryan, Johnson, Rudd, & Joiner, 2008).

According to the fluid vulnerability theory, these deficits in self regulation serve as a key vulnerability to repeat suicidal behavior (Rudd, 2006). By extension, the promotion of self-regulatory processes can prevent the emergence (and recurrence) of suicidal behaviors. Consistent with this hypothesis, empirically-supported treatments for the reduction of suicidal behaviors emphasize interventions that build and/or facilitate self-regulatory processes. For example, dialectical behavior therapy (Linehan, 1993) and BCBT (Bryan & Rudd, 2018) include skills training in self-monitoring, relaxation, mindfulness, and cognitive restructuring. These strategies are designed to help patients quickly detect when they are experiencing a deviation from their set point and how to effectively respond so they can more quickly return to this set point. Recent data further indicate that recall of these strategies by suicidal patients is associated with reductions in the magnitude of fluctuations in suicidal ideation post-intervention (Bryan et al., 2018), implicating enhanced self-regulation.

As noted previously, patients who do not attempt suicide show coordinated change patterns between the wish to live and the wish to die, such that the latter serves to co-regulate the former. Co-regulation refers to the tendency of one variable or component of a system to support or aid the regulation of another variable or component of the system. In other words, when the wish to die is elevated, the wish to live returns to its homeostatic set point much faster than when the wish to die is at or below its set point. To understand this pattern conceptually, consider an individual whose set point is in the center box of Fig. 4.2 (moderate wish to live and moderate wish to die). If this individual experiences an increase in his or her wish to die (i.e., moving to the right), they are also likely to experience a decline in the wish to live (i.e., moving down). This is because the wish to live and the wish to die, though separate constructs, can be nonetheless inversely related to each other, such that high levels of one tend to be correlated with low levels of the other. Because of homeostatic regulatory processes, we would expect that this individual would naturally return to the center box. The co-regulatory effect of the wish to die on the wish to live suggests, however, that the wish to live will return to its set point (i.e., moving upward) much faster than usual. This, in turn, would be accompanied by a faster than expected drop in the wish to live attributable to the inverse correlation of the wish to live and the wish to die. In other words, the faster than expected "correction" in the wish to live contributes to a faster than expected "correction" in the wish to die.

A different process would occur in reverse direction: an initial decline in the wish to die would be correlated with an increase in the wish to live. Because of co-regulatory effects, the wish to live's return to equilibrium would be *slower* than expected, meaning that the wish to die's return to equilibrium would also be slowed. Coordinated change processes between the wish to live and the wish to die therefore mean that suicidal individuals spend relatively briefer periods of time in higher risk states characterized by elevated wish to die and/or diminished wish to live, but spend relatively longer periods of time in lower risk states characterized by diminished wish to die and/or elevated wish to live. In addition to this specific change pattern, Bryan and colleagues found that patients who received BCBT also showed a second coordinated change process involving a co-*dys*regulating effect of the wish to live on the wish to die, whereby elevated wish to live counteracted or opposed the ability of the wish to die to return to its homeostatic set point. Returning to the hypothetical individual described in the previous paragraphs, all of the change processes outlined above would be the same, but with one additional dynamic: an elevated wish to live effectively neutralizes the homeostatic properties of the wish to die. A diminished wish to die therefore tends to remain diminished, which helps to maintain an elevated wish to live. In essence, patients in BCBT were pulled toward the upper left corner of Fig. 4.2.

Implications for suicide prevention

The findings of Bryan and colleagues highlight several important points about the temporal nature of the wish to live and the wish to die. First, the wish to live and the wish to die are inversely correlated with each other, but they are nonetheless separate constructs. Second, change patterns in the wish to live and the wish to die can sometimes occur in a highly coordinated manner and can sometimes occur in an uncoordinated manner. Third, change patterns significantly differ between individuals who engage in suicidal behaviors and those who do not, such that the latter demonstrate a greater degree of coordination. In particular, this coordinated change process is characterized by a co-regulatory effect of the wish to live on the wish to die. Fourth, change patterns significantly differ across patients receiving different types of treatment, such that those receive BCBT, a treatment that significantly reduces suicidal behavior, demonstrate a greater degree of coordination. In particular, this coordinated change process is characterized by a co-dysregulatory effect of the wish to live on the wish to die. Fifth, BCBT is associated with an overall strengthening of the wish to live combined with decreasing wish to die, although the former change process is much more pronounced.

Taken together, these conclusions suggest that treatments designed to reduce suicidal behaviors, and possibly suicide prevention strategies more broadly, may be more effective if they are able to foster coordinated change between the wish to live and the wish to die. One possible way to accomplish this is to teach patients how to recall and use strategies that foster or strengthen cognitive, affective, behavioral, and/or physiological states associated with the wish to live. The results of a recent clinical trial testing the efficacy of the crisis response plan (CRP), a brief (i.e., 30–60 min) suicide risk management strategy, for acutely suicidal patients (Bryan et al., 2018) supports this possibility. In that trial, two different versions of the CRP were compared to treatment as usual: a standard version of the CRP and an enhanced version. Both versions were identical to each other with respect to identifying personal indicators of an emerging crisis, self-regulatory strategies, sources of social support, and professional and crisis support services, but in the enhanced CRP, patients were also asked to identify their reasons for living. The addition of this component focused on reasons for living contributed to significantly larger improvements in hope and calmness (Bryan, Mintz, Clemans, Leeson, et al., 2017), two cognitive-affective states associated with the wish to live. Although the enhanced and standard CRP did not differ from each other with respect to overall effects on suicide attempts and suicidal ideation during follow-up (Bryan, Mintz, Clemans, Burch, et al., 2017), more frequent use of the enhanced CRP (but not the standard CRP) was correlated with less severe fluctuations in suicidal ideation (Bryan et al., 2018). The use of a procedure that explicitly focused on activating a patient's wish to live within the context of an elevated wish to die therefore strengthened psychological states associated with the wish to live and was correlated with greater regulation of suicidal thoughts.

BCBT uses a range of procedures similarly designed to elicit a patient's wish to live in the midst of suicidal episodes characterized by an extreme wish to die, although these hypothesized effects on the wish to live have not yet been explicitly tested. For example, a procedure contained within BCBT is the *survival kit*, which entails the creation of a container (usually a shoe box or envelope) that can be filled with physical reminders of positive experiences in life. Patients often fill the container with pictures of loved ones, trinkets or souvenirs from vacations or trips, inspirational quotes or passages, and other mementos. Patients are then instructed to review these items and recall the stories or meaning associated with them, especially during periods of acute crisis. BCBT also teaches patients to effectively use *cognitive reappraisal* skills in order to respond to stressful situations with more balanced and/or positive interpretations, thereby offsetting negative cognitive-affective states and reducing the tendency to employ maladaptive coping strategies. In many cases, the reappraisal process entails the recall of positive memories or other forms of evidence that contradict the hopelessness, entrapment, and despair that is associated with the wish to die. BCBT also employs *mindfulness* skills training, a procedure shown to boost positive emotions (Jain et al., 2007) and reduce cognitive reactivity (Lynch, Chapman, Rosenthal, Kuo, & Linehan, 2006). Finally, BCBT uses *activity planning* to increase the patient's engagement in meaningful activities, often within a social context, that elicit positive cognitive-affective states, thereby reinforcing the wish to live a meaningful life.

Summary and future directions

Further research is needed to more clearly understand how these specific procedures—and potentially other procedures—strengthen the wish to live and other related cognitive-affective states. In the meantime, accumulating data suggest that relatively simple and straightforward treatments and intervention strategies can change the ebb and flow of the wish to live and the wish to die among at-risk patients, and in some cases, lead to reductions in suicidal behavior. In particular, treatments that include an explicit focus on recalling reasons for living and experiencing positive cognitive-affective states, even in the midst of psychological distress and despair, appear to be especially beneficial for shifting a patient's homeostatic equilibrium toward life and away from death. In summary, continued examination of the ebb and flow of the wish to live and the wish to live holds considerable promise for advancing and refining suicide prevention.

References

Bänziger, T., Patel, S., & Scherer, K. R. (2014). The role of perceived voice and speech characteristics in vocal emotion communication. *Journal of Nonverbal Behavior, 38*, 31–52.

Beck, A. T., Brown, G. K., & Steer, R. A. (1997). Psychometric characteristics of the scale for suicide ideation with psychiatric outpatients. *Behaviour Research and Therapy, 35*, 1039–1046.

Brown, G. K., Steer, R. A., Henriques, G. R., & Beck, A. T. (2005). The internal struggle between the wish to die and the wish to live: A risk factor for suicide. *American Journal of Psychiatry, 162*, 1977–1999.

Brown, G. K., Ten Have, T., Henriques, G. R., Xie, S. X., Hollander, J. E., & Beck, A. T. (2005). Cognitive therapy for the prevention of suicide attempts: A randomized controlled trial. *Journal of the American Medical Association, 294*, 563–570.

Bryan, C. J., Johnson, L. G., Rudd, M. D., & Joiner, T. E. (2008). Hypomanic symptoms among first-time suicide attempters predict future multiple attempt status. *Journal of Clinical Psychology, 64*, 519–530.

Bryan, C. J., May, A. M., Rozek, D. C., Williams, S. R., Clemans, T. A., Mintz, J., et al. (2018). Use of crisis management interventions among suicidal patients: Results of a randomized controlled trial. *Depression and Anxiety*. Available ahead of print online.

Bryan, C. J., Mintz, J., Clemans, T. A., Burch, T. S., Leeson, B., Williams, S., et al. (2017). Effect of crisis response planning on patient mood and clinician decision making: A clinical trial with suicidal US soldiers. *Psychiatric Services, 69*, 108–111.

Bryan, C. J., Mintz, J., Clemans, T. A., Leeson, B., Burch, T. S., Williams, S. R., et al. (2017). Effect of crisis response planning vs. contracts for safety on suicide risk in US Army soldiers: A randomized clinical trial. *Journal of Affective Disorders, 212*, 64–72.

Bryan, C. J., & Rudd, M. D. (2016). The importance of temporal dynamics in the transition from suicidal thought to behavior. *Clinical Psychology: Science and Practice, 23*, 21–25.

Bryan, C. J., & Rudd, M. D. (2017). Nonlinear change processes during psychotherapy characterize patients who have made multiple suicide attempts. *Suicide and Life-Threatening Behavior*. Available online at https://onlinelibrary.wiley.com/doi/abs/10.1111/sltb.12361.

Bryan, C. J., & Rudd, M. D. (2018). *Brief cognitive-behavioral therapy for suicide prevention*. New York, NY: Guilford Press.

Bryan, C. J., Rudd, M. D., Peterson, A. L., Young-McCaughan, S., & Wertenberger, E. G. (2016). The ebb and flow of the wish to live and the wish to die among suicidal military personnel. *Journal of Affective Disorders, 202*, 58–66.

Butner, J. E., Gagnon, K. T., Geuss, M. N., Lessard, D. A., & Story, T. N. (2015). Utilizing topology to generate and test theories of change. *Psychological Methods, 20*, 1–25.

Chang, E. C., Maydeu-Olivares, A., & D'Zurilla, T. J. (1997). Optimism and pessimism as partially independent constructs: Relationship to positive and negative affectivity and psychological well-being. *Personality and Individual Differences, 23*, 433–440.

Chow, S. M., Ram, N., Boker, S. M., Fujita, F., & Clore, G. (2005). Emotion as a thermostat: Representing emotion regulation using a damped oscillator model. *Emotion, 5*, 208–225.

Chu, C., Buchman-Schmitt, J. M., Stanley, I. H., Hom, M. A., Tucker, R. P., Hagan, C. R., et al. (2017). The interpersonal theory of suicide: A systematic review and meta-analysis of a decade of cross-national research. *Psychological Bulletin, 143*, 1313–1345.

Corona, C. D., Jobes, D. A., Nielsen, A. C., Pedersen, C. M., Jennings, K. W., Lento, R. M., et al. (2013). Assessing and treating different suicidal states in a Danish outpatient sample. *Archives of Suicide Research, 17*, 302–312.

Diener, E., & Emmons, R. A. (1984). The independence of positive and negative affect. *Journal of Personality and Social Psychology, 47*, 1105–1117.

Evans, G., & Farberow, N. L. (1988). *The encyclopedia of suicide*. New York, NY: Facts on File.

Fredrickson, B. L., & Joiner, T. E. (2002). Positive emotions trigger upward spirals toward emotional well-being. *Psychological Science, 13*, 172–175.

Fredrickson, B. L., Tugade, M. M., Waugh, C. E., & Larkin, G. R. (2003). What good are positive emotions in crises? A prospective study of resilience and emotions following the terrorist attacks on the United State on September 11th, 2001. *Journal of Personality and Social Psychology, 84*, 365–376.

Gysin-Maillart, A., Schwab, S., Soravia, L., Megert, M., & Michel, K. (2016). A novel brief therapy for patients who attempt suicide: A 24-months follow-up randomized controlled study of the attempted suicide short intervention program (ASSIP). *PLoS Medicine, 13*, e1001968.

Harrison, D. P., Stritzke, W. G., Fay, N., Ellison, T. M., & Hudaib, A. R. (2014). Probing the implicit suicidal mind: Does the death/suicide implicit association test reveal a desire to die, or a diminished desire to live? *Psychological Assessment, 26*, 831–840.

Herzberg, P. Y., Glaesmer, H., & Hoyer, J. (2006). Separating optimism and pessimism: A robust psychometric analysis of the revised life orientation test (LOT-R). *Psychological Assessment, 18*, 433–438.

Jain, S., Shapiro, S. L., Swanick, S., Roesch, S. C., Mills, P. J., Bell, I., et al. (2007). A randomized controlled trial of mindfulness meditation versus relaxation training: Effects on distress, positive states of mind, rumination, and distraction. *Annals of Behavioral Medicine, 33*, 11–21.

Jobes, D. A. (2016). *Managing suicidal risk: A collaborative approach*. New York, NY: Guilford Publications.

Jobes, D. A., & Mann, R. E. (1999). Reasons for living versus reasons for dying: Examining the internal debate of suicide. *Suicide and Life-Threatening Behavior, 29*, 97–104.

Joiner, T. E. (2007). *Why people die by suicide.* Cambridge, MA: Harvard University Press.

Kashdan, T. B., Uswatte, G., & Julian, T. (2006). Gratitude and hedonic and eudaimonic well- being in Vietnam war veterans. *Behaviour Research and Therapy, 44*, 177–199.

Kleiman, E. M., & Nock, M. K. (2018). Real-time assessment of suicidal thoughts and behaviors. *Current Opinion in Psychology, 22*, 33–37.

Klonsky, E. D., & May, A. M. (2015). The three-step theory (3ST): A new theory of suicide rooted in the "ideation-to-action" framework. *International Journal of Cognitive Therapy, 8*, 114–129.

Kovacs, M., & Beck, A. T. (1977). The wish to die and the wish to live in attempted suicides. *Journal of Clinical Psychology, 33*, 361–365.

Lento, R. M., Ellis, T. E., Hinnant, B. J., & Jobes, D. A. (2013). Using the suicide index score to predict treatment outcomes among psychiatric inpatients. *Suicide and Life-Threatening Behavior, 43*, 547–561.

Linehan, M. (1993). *Cognitive-behavioral treatment of borderline personality disorder.* New York, NY: Guilford Press.

Linehan, M. M., Armstrong, H. E., Suarez, A., Allmon, D., & Heard, H. L. (1991). Cognitive-behavioral treatment of chronically parasuicidal borderline patients. *Archives of General Psychiatry, 48*, 1060–1064.

Linehan, M. M., Comtois, K. A., Murray, A. M., Brown, M. Z., Gallop, R. J., Heard, H. L., et al. (2006). Two-year randomized controlled trial and follow-up of dialectical behavior therapy vs therapy by experts for suicidal behaviors and borderline personality disorder. *Archives of General Psychiatry, 63*, 757–766.

Linehan, M. M., Korslund, K. E., Harned, M. S., Gallop, R. J., Lungu, A., Neacsiu, A. D., et al. (2015). Dialectical behavior therapy for high suicide risk in individuals with borderline personality disorder: A randomized clinical trial and component analysis. *JAMA Psychiatry, 72*, 475–482.

Lynch, T. R., Chapman, A. L., Rosenthal, M. Z., Kuo, J. R., & Linehan, M. M. (2006). Mechanisms of change in dialectical behavior therapy: Theoretical and empirical observations. *Journal of Clinical Psychology, 62*, 459–480.

Miller, W. R., & Rollnick, S. (2012). In *Motivational interviewing: Helping people change* (3rd ed.). New York: Guilford Press.

Millner, A. J., Lee, M. D., & Nock, M. K. (2017). Describing and measuring the pathway to suicide attempts: A preliminary study. *Suicide and Life-Threatening Behavior, 47*, 353–369.

Moskowitz, J. T., Folkman, S., & Acree, M. (2003). Do positive psychological states shed light on recovery from bereavement? Findings from a 3-year longitudinal study. *Death Studies, 27*, 471–500.

Neuringer, C., & Lettieri, D. J. (1971). Cognition, attitude, and affect in suicidal individuals. *Suicide and Life-Threatening Behavior, 1*, 106–124.

Nock, M. K., & Banaji, M. R. (2007). Prediction of suicide ideation and attempts among adolescents using a brief performance-based test. *Journal of Consulting and Clinical Psychology, 75*, 707–715.

Nock, M. K., Park, J. M., Finn, C. T., Deliberto, T. L., Dour, H. J., & Banaji, M. R. (2010). Measuring the suicidal mind: Implicit cognition predicts suicidal behavior. *Psychological Science, 21*, 511–517.

O'Connor, R. C., & Kirtley, O. J. (2018). The integrated motivational–volitional model of suicidal behaviour. *Philosophical Transactions of the Royal Society B, 373*, 20170268.

O'Connor, S. S., Jobes, D. A., Comtois, K. A., Atkins, D. C., Janis, K., Chessen, E., et al. (2012). Identifying outpatients with entrenched suicidal ideation following hospitalization. *Suicide and Life-Threatening Behavior, 42*, 173–184.

O'Connor, S. S., Jobes, D. A., Yeargin, M. K., FitzGerald, M. E., Rodríguez, V. M., Conrad, A. K., et al. (2012). A cross-sectional investigation of the suicidal spectrum: Typologies of suicidality based on ambivalence about living and dying. *Comprehensive Psychiatry, 53*, 461–467.

Osman, A., Gutierrez, P. M., Barrios, F., Wong, J. L., Freedenthal, S., & Lozano, G. (2010). Development and initial psychometric properties of the University of Texas at san Antonio future disposition inventory. *Journal of Clinical Psychology, 66*, 410–429.

Redwine, L., Henry, B. L., Pung, M. A., Wilson, K., Chinh, K., Knight, B., et al. (2016). A pilot randomized study of a gratitude journaling intervention on HRV and inflammatory biomarkers in Stage B heart failure patients. *Psychosomatic Medicine, 78*, 667–676.

Reich, C. M., Blackwell, N., Simmons, C. A., & Beck, J. G. (2015). Social problem solving strategies and posttraumatic stress disorder in the aftermath of intimate partner violence. *Journal of Anxiety Disorders, 32*, 31–37.

Rudd, M. D. (2006). Fluid vulnerability theory: A cognitive approach to understanding the process of acute and chronic risk. In T. E. Ellis (Ed.), *Cognition and suicide: Theory, research, and therapy* (pp. 355–368). Washington, DC: American Psychological Association.

Rudd, M. D., Bryan, C. J., Wertenberger, E., Peterson, A. L., Young-McCaughon, S., Mintz, J., et al. (2015). Brief cognitive behavioral therapy effects on post-treatment suicide attempts in a military sample: Results of a 2-year randomized clinical trial. *American Journal of Psychiatry, 172*, 441–449.

Sneidman, E. S. (1964). Suicide, sleep, and death: Some possible interrelations among cessation, interruption, and continuous phenomena. *Journal of Consulting Psychology, 28*, 95–106.

Stein, N., Folkman, S., Trabasso, T., & Richards, T. A. (1997). Appraisal and goal processes as predictors of psychological well-being in bereaved caregivers. *Journal of Personality and Social Psychology, 72*, 872–884.

Stanley, B., Brown, G. K., Brenner, L. A., Galfalvy, H. C., Currier, G. W., Knox, K. L., et al. (2018). Comparison of the safety planning intervention with follow-up vs usual care of suicidal patients treated in the emergency department. *JAMA Psychiatry, 75*, 894–900.

Stengel, E. (1964). *Suicide and attempted suicide.* Oxford, UK: Penguin Books.

Tugade, M. M., Fredrickson, B. L., & Barrett, L. F. (2004). Psychological resilience and positive emotional granularity: Examining the benefits of positive emotions on coping and health. *Journal of Personality, 72*, 1161–1190.

Witte, T. K., Fitzpatrick, K. K., Joiner, T. E., & Schmidt, N. B. (2005). Variability in suicidal ideation: A better predictor of suicide attempts than intensity or duration of ideation? *Journal of Affective Disorders, 88*, 131–136.

CHAPTER 5

Daily monitoring of the wish to live and the wish to die with suicidal inpatients

Natasha A.R. Goods, Andrew C. Page, Werner G.K. Stritzke, Michael J. Kyron, Geoffrey R. Hooke
School of Psychological Science, University of Western Australia, Perth, WA, Australia

A striking aspect of suicide is that the rates of successful attempts are dramatically smaller than those of suicidal thoughts (Klonsky, May, & Saffer, 2016). Contemplating, mulling over, and considering plans to end one's life mostly do not result in a fatal outcome. That people can have repetitive and intrusive thoughts about killing themselves, even with an intense wish to die, but without acting on it, points to the existence of potentially restraining factors. As outlined by Bryan (this volume), one such factor is the wish to live. As he and others have noted, a wish to live is not the bipolar opposite of a wish to die (Bryan, Rudd, Peterson, Young-McCaughan, & Wertenberger, 2016; Kovacs & Beck, 1977). The wish to live and wish to die are partially independent constructs, such that circumstances can arise so a moderate or even intense wish to live can co-occur with an elevated wish to die. The co-occurrence of these two wishes pits competing motivations against one another, leading to a state of ambivalence.

An ambivalent motivational space is uncomfortable and impels a resolution with one competing desire winning out. For example, an approach-avoidance conflict is an ambivalent state which is ultimately resolved by an action in one direction or the other (Corr, 2013). Thus, the ambivalent motivational state when both the wish to live and wish to die are elevated is not a permanent mode of being. Rather, it is inherently unstable and dynamic. As such, the concept of ambivalence is eminently compatible with fluid vulnerability theory (Rudd, 2006). This theory draws attention to the dynamic nature of suicidal risk; observing that the probability of transition from suicidal ideation to action is not solely a function of a trait-like property of the individual or the environment, but varies as a function of variable factors. Fluid vulnerability theory is not necessarily incompatible with the existence of enduring diatheses, but it highlights the importance of

Alternatives to Suicide
ISBN 978-0-12-814297-4
https://doi.org/10.1016/B978-0-12-814297-4.00005-4

understanding risk and resilience factors that raise and lower the probability of suicidal action.

Understanding the dynamic balance between the wish to live and wish to die has promise as a unique predictor of suicide risk status (Brown, Steer, Henriques, & Beck, 2005). The present chapter will summarize an investigation of this interplay in samples at different levels of suicide risk tested across time. The time period in these samples will first be months, but then, the temporal focus will shift to the level of days. The first aim is to examine response profiles reflecting differences in the dynamic balance of the wish to live and the wish to die, and to determine whether the identified profiles differ on their level of suicidal risk and resilience. The second aim is to examine how the dynamic balance of the wish to live and the wish to die may shift over time. The first sample used cross-sectional data from a large non-clinical sample of university students (Goods et al., 2019). This provides a baseline against which shifts in the dynamic balance of the wish to live and the wish to die in high-risk clinical samples can be compared. The second sample included patients recruited from an emergency care department with elevated suicide risk at the time of admission (Goods et al., 2019; Harrison, Stritzke, Fay, & Hudaib, 2018). These patients had been admitted because of a suicide attempt, or had reported suicidal ideation at intake. The relative strength of the wish to live and wish to die were assessed at intake and then re-assessed three and six months following discharge. We then present analyses of response profiles in a sample of psychiatric inpatients. Specifically, the patients' wish to live and wish to die was monitored over a period of three days following the first day on which a patient had reported suicidal ideation.

The dynamic balance of the wish to live and the wish to die in a non-clinical sample

Using latent profile analyses, Goods et al. (2019) found that the most common latent profile (80%) of the relative strength of university students' wish to live and wish to die reflected a strong orientation toward life and a weak orientation toward death. This was unsurprising as one would expect that a relatively healthy sample of young people would be characterized by a wish to live. However, in the remaining one-fifth of the sample, a moderately strong wish to live was matched by a comparable wish to die. These "ambivalent" participants reported both more suicidal risk and less psychological wellbeing than their predominant "wish to live" counterparts. That is, ambivalent participants had elevated levels of perceived burdensomeness (i.e., feeling they are a burden on others), thwarted belongingness (i.e., feeling they do not belong), and acquired capability for suicide (George, Page, Hooke, & Stritzke, 2016). The Interpersonal Theory of Suicide posits that the simultaneous endorsement of these three constructs signals an elevated risk of suicide (Joiner, 2005). Compared to the wish to live participants, ambivalent participants also exhibited reduced psychological wellbeing as indicated by lower scores on a scale of flourishing (cf., Huppert & So, 2013).

In sum, when the wish to live is assessed alongside the wish to die in a non-clinical sample, the dynamic balance between the two is characterized by a predominant wish to live in four of five participants. But equally important, and equally non-surprising given increasing evidence that university students are at particularly high risk for suicidal thoughts and behaviors (e.g., Lageborn, Ljung, Vaez, & Dahlin, 2017), one in five of the participants had a balanced latent profile indicating moderately strong suicidal ambivalence. There was no latent profile reflecting a predominant wish to die, or a disengaged profile, where participant report very low or zero levels in both the wish to live and the wish to die. The absence of this latter profile is interesting, because it suggests that generally people in a non-clinical population are not neutral or disengaged about life or death. Rather, to the extent that the balance between the two is dynamic, this variability occurs with at least some level of intensity one way or the other or as tension between the two motivational forces.

The dynamic balance of the wish to live and the wish to die in emergency care patients

In contrast to the non-clinical population, the most common (80%) latent response profile among emergency care patients who were at high acute risk of suicide at hospital admission reflected a strong orientation toward death and weak orientation toward life (Goods et al., 2019). The remainder had either a moderate ambivalent profile (13%) or a weak wish to live profile (7%). It is noteworthy that, like in the non-clinical sample, no disengaged profile emerged where both the wish to live and the wish to die were very low. The same patients were re-assessed three and six months after discharge. After three months, their wish to live and wish to die response profiles showed both a growing wish to live and a weakening wish to die. Importantly, at the six-month follow-up, the percentage of patients

(80%) endorsing a strong wish to live and a weak wish to die was comparable to the percentage of individuals with the same predominant wish to live profile in the non-clinical sample. Thus, after a six-month recovery period, most people in the previously suicidal group had a similar level and relative balance of the wish to live and the wish to die as a non-suicidal group. However, a minority of people continued to report a strong desire to die, or a moderate desire to die with a co-occurring moderate desire to live. It is important to consider the level of potential suicidal resilience among these different groups.

By six months, patients with a strong wish to live and weak wish to die reported the highest levels of zest for life (cf., Harrison, et al., 2018; Linehan Goodstein, Nielsen, & Chiles, 1983). In contrast, those who still had a strong predominant wish to die reported the lowest levels of zest for life, with the ambivalent patients reporting intermediate levels of zest for life. Thus, a gradual shift in the dynamic balance of the wish to live and the wish to die in favor of a strengthening and consolidation of a predominant wish to live is reflected in a broader strengthening of zest for and hence re-engagement with life.

So far, we summarized recent findings of differences in the dynamic balance of the wish to live and the wish to die across a non-clinical and an acute emergency care sample, as well as changes in this relative balance over a six-month period in the clinical sample. Next, we examine the relative strength of the wish to live and the wish to die among a psychiatric inpatient sample, but do so over a three day period. An inpatient sample provides the opportunity to have daily contact with a patient and thus allows the dynamic nature of the wish to live and the wish to die to be examined with a different degree of temporal resolution capturing short-term fluidity and stability.

Daily monitoring of the wish to live and the wish to die in an inpatient setting

A psychiatric inpatient sample is arguably different from both an emergency care and non-clinical sample because inpatients are deliberately removed from daily life stressors, where the inpatient stay, in Australia, can be a few weeks in duration (Australian Institute of Health and Welfare, 2018). In contrast, patients considered at-risk of suicide in an emergency department are only provided a temporary reprieve while the decision is made regarding the best course of action. In Australia, 72% of patients spent 4 h or less in the emergency department (Australian Institute of Health and Welfare, 2017), with the average stay of mental health or suicidal patients between five and 6 h (Fry & Brunero, 2004). Thus, while patients presenting to an emergency department are often discharged within the same day, psychiatric inpatients can be provided ongoing intervention in an environment temporarily removed from external life stressors. This 'time out' does not only provide a reprieve from the daily grind of ongoing hassles and distress, but also from the pressure of making immediate decisions or the need to urgently resolve the current crisis. As such, response profiles of the dynamic balance of the wish to live and the wish to die in an inpatient sample may also include some that reflect this disengaged state of mind. Accordingly, unlike in non-clinical samples and those in acute, ambulatory clinical care, one would expect some proportion of inpatients to endorse both a weak desire to live and weak desire to die (i.e., temporarily disengaged from thinking about life or death).

One benefit of using an inpatient sample is the opportunity of having daily contact with patients. As mentioned earlier, fluid vulnerability theory (FVT) posits that suicide risk is inherently dynamic and waxes and wanes over time (Rudd, 2006). Therefore, suicide risk and protective factors should be monitored regularly (Bryan & Rudd, 2016). As such, we sought to monitor the wish to live and the wish to die across a daily interval for three days to examine the potential stability and variability of the inpatients' relative balance in both desires. This three-day monitoring period was triggered on the first day a patient reported suicidal ideation during their inpatient stay.

While it is not yet clear what the optimal temporal resolution for monitoring may be, daily monitoring of inpatients' suicide ideations for a week yielded five overarching ideation profiles representing either stability or different trajectories of change in ideation scores, and the greatest fluctuations occurred immediately after elevated suicidal ideation (Restifo, Kashyap, Hooke, & Page, 2015). Further, endorsing strong ideations for two-consecutive days resulted in an increased risk of self-harming behavior (Restifo et al., 2015), relative to a profile in which the suicidal ideation dropped over this two day period. Thus, while the sensitivity of change of inpatients' wish to live and wish to die is currently unknown, it appears reasonable that daily monitoring for a brief period of time may be sufficient in identifying both the stability and the variability of inpatients' self-reported wish to live and wish to die.

We first allocated patients to one of four possible response profiles reflecting a two-dimensional matrix based on the relative strength of their wish to live and wish to die (cf., Kovacs & Beck; 1977). By assuming a multidimensional relationship between the wish to live and wish to die we could examine the potentially independent changes of both desires over time.

The first aim was to investigate the patients demonstrating *stability,* by examining those who remained in the same response profile for three consecutive days. Patients with stable profiles were compared on their level of psychological distress, suicidal ideation, and psychological wellbeing. Since inpatients' levels of distress and wellbeing are reliable indicators of functioning (Newnham, Hooke, & Page, 2010; Page, Cunningham, & Hooke, 2016) and predictors of self-harming behavior (Restifo et al., 2015), we examined the clinical relevance of particular profiles in this motivational space. First, we examined the relationship between the variables of interest and the two imbalanced profiles (i.e., strong wish to live and weak wish to die group, or strong wish to die and weak wish to live group) to see how the two profiles compared on indicators of risk and wellbeing. It would be expected that those with a strong, predominant wish to live would exhibit less risk and greater wellbeing than those with a strong, predominant wish to die. Next, we examined the relationship between the variables of interest and the two balanced profiles (i.e., Ambivalent and Disengaged) to identify how patients with an equal magnitude of both desires (but of varying intensity) compare, and also to examine how the imbalanced and balanced profiles compared. Little is known about the distinctions between ambivalent and disengaged patients. It may be that disengaged patients represent less risk due to having a 'time out' which permits them a moment's pause from the inner turmoil that ambivalent patients experience, or, it may be that disengaged patients represent heightened risk by virtue of 'dropping out of life', while ambivalent patients may be more strongly attached to life.

The second aim was to investigate the patients demonstrating *variability* in the wish to live and wish to die, that is, patients who shifted between response profiles over the three days. Evidence suggests that the wish to live and the wish to die are sensitive to change over long periods of time (Bryan et al., 2016; Goods et al., 2019), however it remains uncertain as to whether patients' wish to live and wish to die fluctuate in a meaningful way over briefer periods. If patients do shift between profiles, we aimed to assess whether trajectories of change indicate improvement by patients shifting directly toward a predominant wish to live (in a similar manner to the emergency department patients we had studied over a six month period), or whether patients transition through one of the two balanced profiles (i.e., ambivalent and disengaged) as an intermediate step before they transition toward a greater desire for life. Alternatively, intermediate balanced profiles may indicate a continued fluid recovery status with an equal or greater probability of dropping back to a predominant wish to die profile.

Method

Participants

Patients were recruited from a private psychiatric hospital. The present sample was selected from the total number of inpatients admitted between 15 January 2017 and 15 July 2017 ($N = 1043$). To be selected, patients were required to have three day minimum admissions and they had to answer questions pertaining to their current wish to live and wish to die. The final sample consisted of 602 patients with an average age of 36.81 ($SD = 15.66$), and most identifying as female (69.9%). The mean length of stay was 18.38 days ($SD = 13.13$). Over half of the sample were single (56.8%), followed by married/de facto (30.9%), divorced/separated (11.0%), and widowed (1.3%). The most common principal diagnosis was an affective disorder (47.3%), followed by an anxiety or stress disorder (18.6%), personality disorder (8.3%), a substance use disorder (6.8%), and the remainder had other disorders.

Procedure and measures

Ethics approval was obtained from the Human Research Ethics Board. All patients admitted to the psychiatric inpatient hospital were invited to answer a question assessing their suicidal ideation over the past 24 h; *"I have thoughts about killing myself"*, assessed on a 6-point scale from 0 *(At no time)* to 5 *(All of the time)*. If a patient endorsed any score equal to or greater than one (i.e., experiencing at least some suicidal ideation) they were prompted to indicate their current wish to live and wish to die (e.g., *"my wish to live has been"* and *"my wish to die has been"*). Both items were assessed on a 4-point scale from 0 *(None)* to 3 *(Strong)*. Patients were requested to complete these two items for the duration in which they endorsed suicidal ideations, and for the two days following their discontinued endorsement. Patients answered these questions as part of a daily assessment monitoring patient progress via electronic tablet devices available in their room.

DI-5 Daily Index (Dyer, Hooke, & Page, 2014**).** This five-item scale measures affective psychological distress in the preceding 24 h. The items include feelings of depression, anxiety, worthlessness, not coping, and thoughts about killing one's self. The DI-5 has excellent internal consistency (Day 1 - $\alpha = 0.86$; Day 7 $- \alpha = 0.89$), test-retest reliability, validity, and demonstrated sensitivity to change within an inpatient sample (Dyer et al., 2014). We removed the ideation item from the general distress scale to avoid confounding of the two constructs. This yielded a four-item general distress index and a single suicide-specific ideation rating. All items were rated on a 6-point scale from 0 *(At no time)* to 5 *(All of the time),* with higher scores indicating higher frequencies. The four-item distress index had good internal consistency at Time 1, Time 2, and Time 3 ($\alpha = 0.77$, $\alpha = 0.83$, $\alpha = 0.85$), which was comparable to the internal consistency achieved by the full DI-5 index ($\alpha = 0.79$, $\alpha = 0.85$, $\alpha = 0.87$) and the published reliability (Dyer et al., 2014).

WHO-5 Wellbeing Index (Bech, Gudex, & Johansen, 1996; Newnham et al., 2010**).** This five-item scale measures positive wellbeing over the past 24 h, including feelings of cheerfulness, calmness, freshness, feeling active, and belief that life is filled with interesting things. Rated on a 6-point scale from 0 *(At no time)* to 5 *(All of the time),* higher scores indicate greater wellbeing, with a score of 11 or higher indicating positive wellbeing in an inpatient sample (Newnham et al., 2010). This scale has good internal consistency ($\alpha = 0.89$), validity, and demonstrated sensitivity to change within an inpatient setting (Newnham et al., 2010).

Results

Little's Missing Completely at Random analysis (Little, 1988) showed that cases were missing completely at random for the Wish to Die items [χ^2 (8) $= 8.13$; $p = 0.42$], the Wish to Live items [χ^2 (8) $= 3.15$; $p = 0.92$], and the suicidal ideation item [χ^2 (5) $= 7.32$, $p = .20$]. It also showed items were missing completely at random for the DI-4 scale [χ^2 (5) $= 5.23$, $p = 0.38$] and the WHO-5 scale [χ^2 (7) $= 6.75$; $p = 0.45$]. Expectation maximization was used to impute missing data.

We distributed patients into four profiles based on the relative strength of their wish to live and wish to die (cf., Kovacs & Beck, 1977). Scores of two and three were defined as 'strong', and scores of zero and one were defined as 'weak'. Since wish to live and wish to die are the dimensions, we will use the term *Strong Wish to Live* to refer to people with the high scores on the wish to live item and low scores on the wish to die item. Likewise, *Strong Wish to Die* will describe people with high scores on the wish to die item and low scores on the wish to live item. The two remaining profiles are *Ambivalent* (with high ratings on both the wish to live and wish to die items) and *Disengaged* (with low ratings on both items).

On the first day that inpatients endorsed suicidal ideation (i.e., Time 1) 313 patients were classified in the Strong Wish to Die profile, 138 patients in the Strong Wish to Live profile, 85 patients in the Disengaged profile, and 66 patients in the Ambivalent profile.

Comparing patients who remain stable in one of the four response profiles on variables of distress, suicidal ideation, and wellbeing

Nearly 62% of the sample ($N = 391$) remained stable in their profile for three consecutive days. The largest group had a Strong Wish to Die profile ($N = 197$), followed by patients with a Strong Wish to Live profile ($N = 111$), and two smaller groups of patients with a Disengaged profile ($N = 39$) or an Ambivalent profile ($N = 24$). These groups were compared on indicators of suicidal risk and wellbeing.

Psychological Distress. Mean distress scores for each of the four stable profile groups are shown in Fig. 5.1. A 4 (profile groups) × 3 (time) mixed model ANOVA showed there was a significant main effect of group, F (3, 367) = 104.94, $p < .001$, $\eta^2_{\text{partial}} = 0.46$. The Stable Wish to Die group reported the most distress, while the Stable Wish to Live group reported the least distress, with the Stable Ambivalent group and the Stable Disengaged group reporting intermediate distress levels. The two extreme groups were significantly different in distress from the two intermediate groups and from each other, whereas the two intermediate groups did not significantly differ in distress on any of the three days ($p = .805$, $p = .678$, $p = .269$, respectively). There was also a significant main effect for time, F (1 0.91, 699.91) = 25.25, $p < .001$, $\eta^2_{\text{partial}} = 0.06$, with a general trend of groups showing some decrease in distress. There was no significant group by time interaction, F (5.72, 699.91) = 0.56, $p = .750$, $\eta^2_{\text{partial}} = 0.01$.

Suicidal Ideation. Mean suicidal ideation scores for each of the four stable profile groups are shown in Fig. 5.2. A 4 (profile groups) × 3 (time) mixed model ANOVA showed there was a significant main effect of group, F (3, 367) = 223.76, $p < .001$, $\eta^2_{\text{partial}} = 0.65$, such that the Stable Wish to Die group reported the highest level of suicidal ideation and the Stable

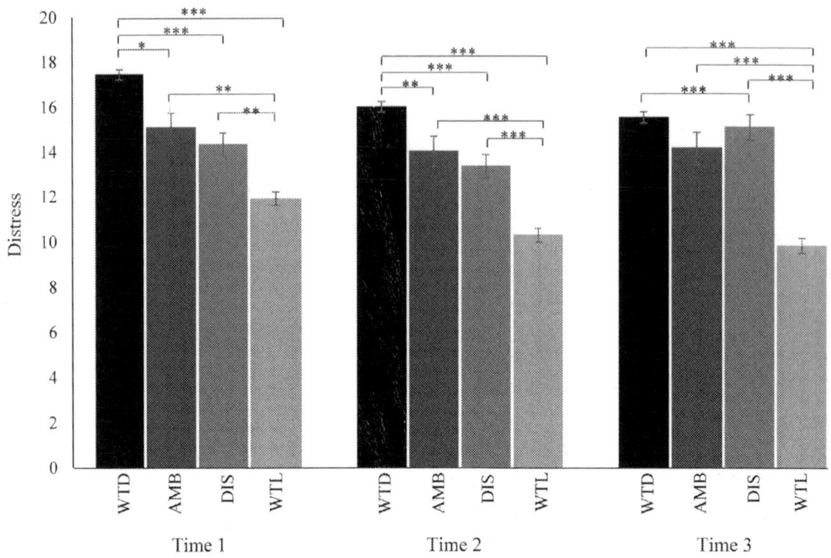

Fig. 5.1 Mean difference scores representing distress levels for each stable group across three days. *Note. AMB*, Stable Ambivalent Group; *DIS*, Stable Disengaged Group; *WTD*, Stable Wish to Die Group; *WTL*, Stable Wish to Live Group. $^{*}p < 0.05$. $^{**}p < 0.01$. $^{***}p < 0.001$.

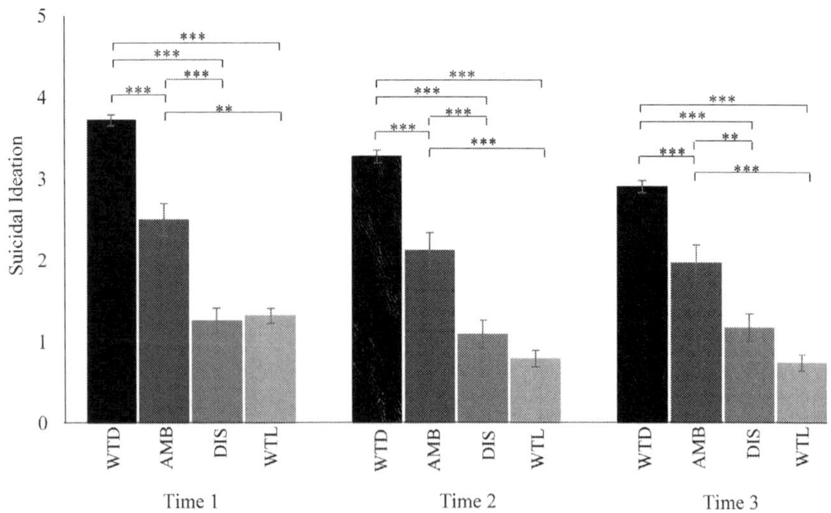

Fig. 5.2 Mean difference scores representing suicidal ideation levels for each stable group across three days. *Note. AMB*, Stable Ambivalent Group; *DIS*, Stable Disengaged Group; *WTD*, Stable Wish to Die Group; *WTL*, Stable Wish to Live Group$^{*}p < 0.05$. $^{**}p < .01$. $^{***}p < .001$.

Wish to Live group reported the lowest level. However, unlike for distress scores where the Stable Ambivalent and Stable Disengaged groups had similar intermediate scores, the Stable Ambivalent group had significantly higher suicidal ideation scores than the Stable Disengaged group at each of the three time points (see Fig. 5.2). In fact, the suicidal ideation scores of the Stable Disengaged group were not significantly different from the Stable Wish to Live group on any of the three days ($p = .927$, $p = .246$, $p = .082$, respectively), whereas the suicidal ideation scores for the Stable Ambivalent group were closer to the Stable Wish to Die group than to the Stable wish to Live group (see Fig. 5.2). Thus, based on the suicidal ideation scores, the Stable Ambivalent group was associated with a significantly higher risk than the Stable Disengaged group which was similarly low to the Stable Wish to Live group.

There was also a significant group by time interaction, F (5.89, 720.62) $= 2.98$, $p = .007$, $\eta^2_{\text{partial}} = 0.02$. To investigate this interaction further, the effect of time was examined separately for each group. Both the Stable Wish to Die group [F (2, 392) $= 42.79$, $p < .001$, $\eta^2_{\text{partial}} = 0.18$] and the Stable Wish to Live group [F (2, 220) $= 28.10$, $p < .001$, $\eta^2_{\text{partial}} = 0.20$] significantly decreased in suicidal ideation over the three days. In contrast, both the Stable Ambivalent group [F (1.58, 36.40) $= 2.47$, $p = .109$, $\eta^2_{\text{partial}} = 0.10$] and the Stable Disengaged group [F (2, 76) $= 0.61$, $p = .548$, $\eta^2_{\text{partial}} = 0.02$] showed no change in their ideation levels.

While this would suggest a good risk prognosis for patients in the Stable Disengaged group given that their ideation scores are low and not different from the Stable Wish to Live group, the risk profile for patients in the Stable Ambivalent group is more uncertain. Although their ideation scores are lower than those from the Stable Wish to Die group on each of the three days, they remain at that heightened level, whereas the ideation scores for the Stable Wish to Die group show a steady decrease over time.

Psychological Wellbeing. Mean psychological wellbeing scores for each of the four stable profile groups are shown in Fig. 5.3. A 4 (profile group) x 3 (time) mixed model ANOVA showered there was a significant main effect of group, F (3, 367) $= 41.18$, $p < 0.001$, $\eta^2_{\text{partial}} = 0.25$, such that the Stable Wish to Live group reported the most psychological wellbeing and the Stable Wish to Die group reported the least psychological wellbeing. Although the Stable Ambivalent group had higher wellbeing scores than the Stable Disengaged group on each of the three days, this was not significant ($p = 0.058$, $p = 0.503$, $p = 0.681$). However, it is

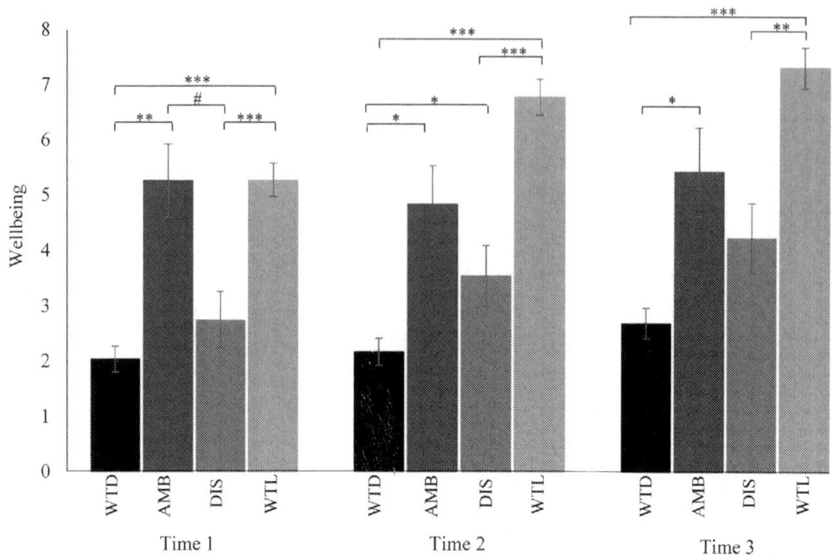

Fig. 5.3 Mean difference scores representing wellbeing levels for each stable group across three days. *Note. WTD*, Stable Wish to Die Group; *AMB*, Stable Ambivalent Group; *DIS*, Stable Disengaged Group; *WTL*, Stable Wish to Live Group. $^{*}p < .05$. $^{**}p < .01$.$^{***}p < .001$. # = 00.058.

noteworthy that the higher wellbeing scores of the Stable Ambivalent group were similar to the high scores of the Stable Wish to Live group ($p = 1.00$, $p = 0.167$, $p = 0.265$), and the lower wellbeing scores of the Stable Disengaged group were generally more similar to the low wellbeing scores of the Stable Wish to Die group ($p = 0.340$, $p = 0.034$, and $p = 0.110$, respectively) (see Fig. 5.3). Thus, based on the psychological wellbeing scores, the ambivalent patients appear to be faring better than the disengaged patients whose wellbeing is similarly low as in those with a predominant wish to die.

There was also a significant group by time interaction, F (5.24, 640.65) = 5.25, $p < 0.001$, $\eta^2_{\text{partial}} = 0.04$. To investigate this interaction further, the effect of time was once more examined separately for each group. The Stable Wish to Die group [F (1.75, 343.25) = 15.54, $p < 0.001$, $\eta^2_{\text{partial}} = 0.07$], the Stable Wish to Live group [F (1.80, 198.37) = 18.45, $p < 0.001$, $\eta^2_{\text{partial}} = 0.14$] and the Stable Disengaged group [F (1.40, 53.29) = 4.76, $p = 0.22$, $\eta^2_{\text{partial}} = 0.11$] all increased their wellbeing levels over the three days. Only the Stable Ambivalent group did not show any significant change, F (1.23, 28.20) = 0.90, $p = .37$,

$\eta^2_{\text{partial}} = 0.04$. Thus, while the Stable Ambivalent group had comparable wellbeing levels to the Stable Wish to Live group, it was the Stable Disengaged group which demonstrated a consistent increase in wellbeing.

In sum, ambivalent and disengaged patients reported similar levels of intermediate distress, but ambivalent patients were higher in suicidal ideation, yet also showed a trend for higher wellbeing which did not change over time. In contrast, there was some steady increase in wellbeing over the three days within the disengaged patients. This pattern is consistent with the hypothesis that ambivalent patients' heightened wish to live, which balances out a simultaneously heightened wish to die, is experienced as a positive step and hence moderate level of wellbeing. On the other hand, this degree of wellbeing, like the level of suicidal ideation scores, remained precariously poised and unchanging over the three days in the ambivalent group, whereas wellbeing steadily improved in the disengaged group. This suggests that an ambivalent profile is perhaps a more uncertain state, whereas for the disengaged profile change may be steadier and less volatile.

How do patients shift between the four profiles over the three-day period?

While many (61.6%) patients remained stable in their profile across the three days, a substantial number (38.4%) shifted between profiles during this time. First, we will examine the transition patterns of patients who were in one of the two imbalanced profiles at Time 1 (i.e., the Strong Wish to Die profile and the Strong Wish to Live profile).

Fig. 5.4 shows that of the 313 patients in the Strong Wish to Die profile at Time 1, only 34 (10.9%) transitioned to the Strong Wish to Live profile by Time 3, indicating there is a low probability of patients with a predominant wish to die shifting to a profile reflecting a predominant wish to live in only three days. Of the 77 patients who showed an *early* shift away from the Strong Wish to Die profile (i.e., at Time 2), 24 (31.2%) transitioned to the Strong Wish to Live profile at Time 3. Alternatively, of the 39 patients who showed a *late* shift away from the Wish to Die profile (i.e., at Time 3), 10 (25.6%) transitioned to the Strong Wish to Live profile. Thus, while the overall likelihood of shifting from a Strong Wish to Die profile at Time 1 to a Strong Wish to Live profile at Time 3 was low, the earlier the shift the greater the odds. However, a late shift away

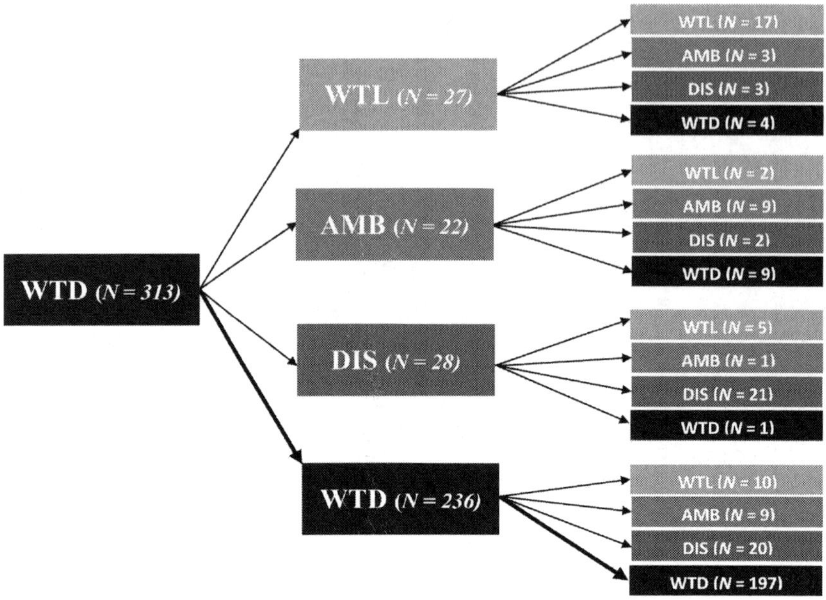

Fig. 5.4 Flow chart showing the trajectory of change of patients who endorsed a weak wish to live and strong wish to die at time one. *Note. AMB* = Ambivalent; *DIS* = Disengaged; *WTD* = Wish to Die; *WTL* = Wish to Live.

from the Strong Wish to Die profile was still beneficial to about one in four patients.

Fig. 5.5 shows that of the 138 patients in the Strong Wish to Live profile at Time 1, only two (1.4%) ended up in the Strong Wish to Die profile at Time 3. Thus, substantially fewer patients transitioned from the Strong Wish to Live profile to the Strong Wish to Die profile than vice versa. Of the 18 patients who showed an *early* shift away from the Strong Wish to Live profile (i.e., at Time 2), more than twice shifted back to the Strong Wish to Live profile at Time 3 ($N = 8$; 44.4%) compared to maintaining or shifting to the Strong Wish to Die profile ($N = 4$; 22.2%) Alternatively, of the nine who showed a *late* shift away from the Strong Wish to Live profile (i.e., at Time 3), only two (22.2%) ended up in the Strong Wish to Die profile. Thus, while any shift away reduced the likelihood of a patient ending up in the Strong Wish to Live profile, there remained a greater probability of them returning to the Strong Wish to Live profile compared to shifting to the Strong Wish to Die profile.

Next, we will examine what happens when patients with a greater orientation toward life or death shift toward one of the two intermediate

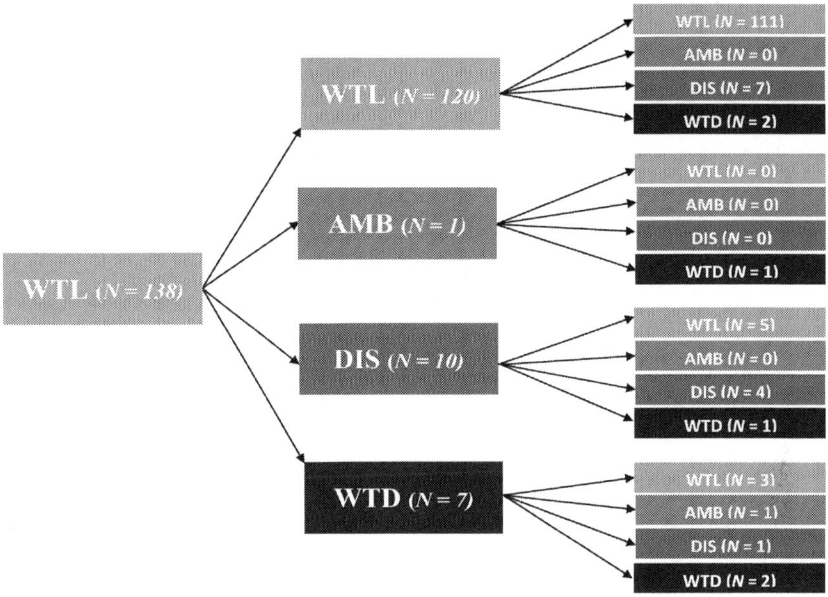

Fig. 5.5 Flow chart showing the trajectory of change of patients who endorsed a strong wish to live and weak wish to die at time one. *Note. AMB* = Ambivalent; *DIS* = Disengaged; *WTD* = Wish to Die; *WTL* = Wish to Live.

profiles (i.e., Ambivalent or Disengaged). Fig. 5.4 shows that of the 28 patients (8.9%) who shifted from the Strong Wish to Die profile to the Disengaged profile at Time 2, five times more shifted to the Strong Wish to Live profile at Time 3 than back to the Strong Wish to Die profile ($N = 5$; 17.9%, $N = 1$; 3.6%, respectively). Conversely, of the 22 patients who shifted from the Strong Wish to Die profile to the Ambivalent profile at Time 2, only two shifted to the Strong Wish to Live profile at Time 3 whereas nine returned to the Strong Wish to Die profile. Thus, a shift to the Disengaged profile has a better prognosis than a shift to the Ambivalent profile.

An analogous pattern of results was found when examining patients in the Strong Wish to Live profile, as half of the 10 patients who shifted to the Disengaged profile at Time 2 returned to the Strong Wish to Live profile at Time 3, but only one shifted to the Strong Wish to Die profile (see Fig. 5.5). Only one patient from the Strong Wish to Live profile shifted to the Ambivalent profile at T2, and this patient transitioned to the Strong Wish to Die profile at Time 3. Thus, these pattern of results suggest that a disengaged profile is a more stable intermediate profile on the transition toward life than an ambivalent profile, which is more precariously fluid and volatile in its progress.

Lastly, we will examine the transition patterns of patients who belong to either the Ambivalent profile (see Fig. 5.6) or Disengaged profile (see Fig. 5.7). Although patients in the Ambivalent or the Disengaged profile at Time 1 had an almost equal probability of shifting to the Wish to Live profile by Time 3 (33.3% and 35.3%, respectively), twice as many ambivalent patients shifted to the Strong Wish to Die profile at Time 3 compared to disengaged patients (19.7% and 9.4%, respectively). Thus, this is consistent with the notion that disengaged patients have a better prognosis in terms of recovery pattern than ambivalent patients, regardless of whether the disengagement was a starting or intermediate profile.

Discussion

Inpatients were distributed into one of four profiles based on the relative strength of their wish to live and wish to die: Strong Wish to Live, Strong Wish to Die, Ambivalent, and Disengaged. Most (61.6%) patients remained stable in their profile over three days, with the majority belonging to the

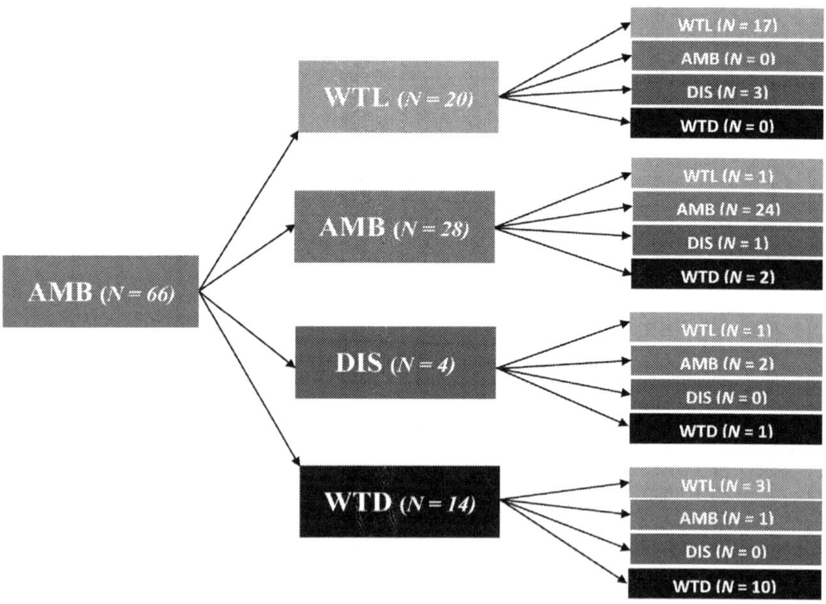

Fig. 5.6 Flow chart showing the trajectory of change of patients who endorsed a strong wish to live and strong wish to die at time one. *Note. AMB* = Ambivalent; *DIS* = Disengaged; *WTD* = Wish to Die; *WTL* = Wish to Live.

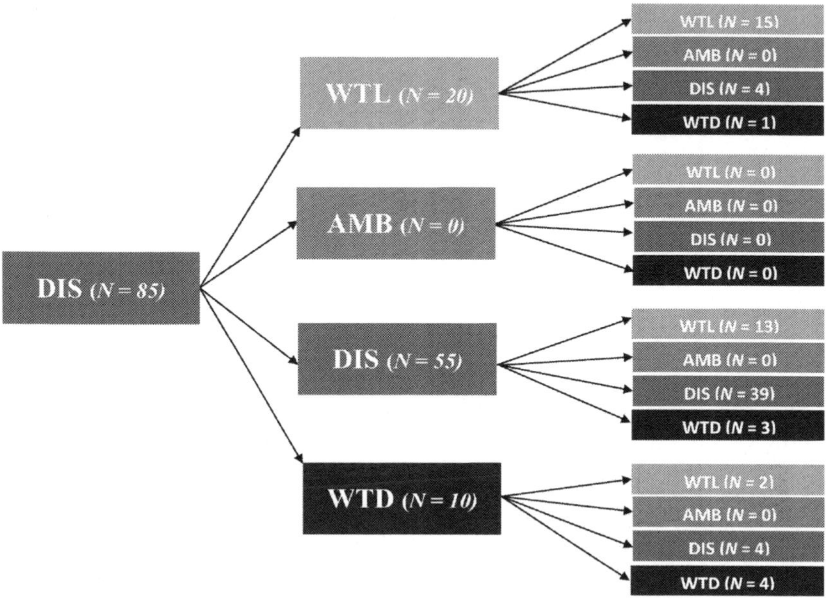

Fig. 5.7 Flow chart showing the trajectory of change of patients who endorsed a weak wish to live and weak wish to die at time one. *Note. AMB* = Ambivalent; *DIS* = Disengaged; *WTD* = Wish to Die; *WTL* = Wish to Live.

Stable Strong Wish to Die profile. This is not unexpected for an inpatient sample, given that potential harm to self is often a particularly salient consideration when opting for a psychiatric inpatient admission. Despite profile stability being the most common pattern, over one-third of patients shifted between the profiles over three days.

Toward a multidimensional and fluid conceptualization of suicidal desire

It is important to note that the patients' wish to live and wish to die scores were distributed across the entire bi-dimensional motivational space, and hence yielded four distinct profiles. These profiles reflected different degrees of either reciprocal activation of desires where one was dominant over the other, or co-activation of desires where both desires were present at equal magnitude. Furthermore, along this co-activation axis, patients differed on whether the two desires where balanced at a high degree of intensity (ambivalence) or at a low degree of intensity (disengagement) (cf., Cacioppo & Berntson, 1994). This supports the theoretical premise that the wish to live and the wish to die should be considered in conjunction and conceptualized as separate dimensions (cf., Bryan et al., 2016). Indeed, together with the evidence for an ambivalent profile in non-clinical and emergency care samples reviewed earlier in the chapter, the present findings of psychiatric inpatients with both ambivalent and disengaged profiles, confirm that a solely risk-centric approach, which only monitors a person's wish to die and disregards the strength of a person's concurrent wish to live, is not only theoretically untenable, but potentially detrimental to best practice in patient care and risk prevention. These advances in our understanding of the importance of a life-oriented approach to managing risk in suicidal individuals are also much more aligned with the lived experience perspective (see chapters by Ellis and Bryan, and by Mazel-Carlton and Davidow, this volume). That is, a long overdue paradigm shift is needed from the narrow focus on death and dying to a more balanced approach which meets the need of at-risk individuals to find the support and means to nourish their wish to *live* and re-engage with their life as worth living, while respecting their experience of a simultaneous wish to die.

In addition to being multidimensional, suicidal desire is dynamic and fluid. It is dynamic because the relative strength of the wish to live and the wish to die can vary over time, and it is fluid because shifts in the relative balance can occur over periods of months or days, and likely even hours. This is particular pertinent when the wish to live and the wish to die are balanced at equal levels of intensity. Inspection of the ambivalent and disengaged patients shows that distinguishing these two presentations is clinically meaningful. In terms of risk, the disengaged patients not only had less suicidal ideation than their ambivalent counterparts, but their ideation levels were similarly low to those with a strong wish to live. Using cut-off scores for the suicidal ideation items established by Restifo et al. (2015) to predict self-injury from daily monitoring of temporal trajectories of suicidal ideation, the suicidal ideation scores of both the disengaged and ambivalent patients are associated with a lower risk of subsequent self-injury (4%) compared to patients with a Strong Wish to Die profile (18%). This is despite ambivalent patients having similarly high wish to die scores as Strong Wish to Die patients! Moreover, the ideation scores for the disengaged and ambivalent patients were below the threshold of three on the scale, which classified them as "remitting" patients, in contrast to the Strong Wish to Die group who were above this threshold, which classified them as 'non-remitting" patients (for cut-off scores, see Restifo et al., 2015).

Although the ambivalent patients reported higher levels of suicidal ideation than the disengaged patients, they also reported higher levels of wellbeing. This is consistent with the notion that ambivalence is experienced with some level of volatile intensity between competing states. This combination of higher suicidal ideation and higher wellbeing, with the latter remaining stable over the three days, contrasted with the disengaged patients who had lower suicidal ideation along with lower wellbeing, but their wellbeing was increasing to a moderate level over the three days. Thus, the motivational balance for ambivalent patients occurs at a higher level of intensity which might make the balance more precarious as a weakening in one dimension could quickly intensify the impact of the already strong and then predominant weight of the other. In contrast, the low intensity motivational balance for disengaged patients is consistent with a timeout from the struggle. As such, the more gradual increase in wellbeing from low levels is perhaps a promising sign of the inpatient stay facilitating a slow but gradual recovery from an overwhelming crisis state.

Examination of the recovery trajectories over time also showed that of the two balanced profiles suicidal ambivalence is a more fluid and transient state. Only 36% of ambivalent patients remained in this profile for the full three days, whereas more of the disengaged patients (46%) maintained their respective profile during the three days.

Encouragingly, when ambivalent patients did shift away from their conflicted state they were more likely to transition toward life (i.e., Strong Wish to Live profile; 33%) than toward death (i.e., Strong Wish to Die profile; 20%). Disengaged patients showed a similar pattern of movement toward life (35%), but compared to the proportion of ambivalent patients who had transitioned to a Strong Wish to Die profile, less than half did so from a disengaged profile (20% vs. 9%, respectively). Hence, both profiles had a similar likelihood of transitioning toward life, but those with an ambivalent profile were at greater risk of shifting toward a predominant wish to die profile. This suggests again that ambivalent patients are more precariously fluid in their recovery than disengaged patients.

The same pattern of ambivalence being associated with a more precarious fluid risk trajectory, and disengagement with a more gradual and steady shift toward a Wish to Live Profile, was apparent when examining the trajectories of those patients who had a Strong Wish to Die profile at Time 1, but had shifted to one of the two balanced profiles at Time 2. If the shift was to the Ambivalent profile, patients were four times more likely to revert back to the Strong Will to *Die* profile than to move to the Strong Wish to Live profile. In contrast, if the shift was to the Disengaged profile, patients were five times more likely to shift the Strong Wish to *Live* profile than to revert back to the Strong Wish to Die profile.

While the disengaged patients appeared to be on a more promising short-term trajectory than the ambivalent patients, the patients who had a Strong Wish to Live profile, as expected, reported the lowest level of suicidal ideation and highest level of psychological wellbeing. Moreover, 80% of the Strong Wish to Live patients remained stable in their profile for the three days. For the few that did shift away, patients who started in the Strong Wish to Live profile had a higher probability than any other patients to re-align with their initial profile.

In stark contrast, patients who maintained a Strong Wish to Die profile (63%) had the highest level of suicidal ideation and the lowest level of psychological wellbeing compared to the other stable groups. Based on published cut-off scores for daily inpatient monitoring of suicidal ideation (Restifo et al., 2015), patients with a stable Strong Wish to Die profile over a period of at least two consecutive days have the highest risk of self-harm.

Conclusions

There is now growing and compelling evidence that the longstanding practice of conceptualizing and monitoring suicidal desire only as the strength of the wish to die, without regard to also enquiring about a potentially competing wish to live, is neither theoretically sound nor clinically aligned with the experience of at-risk individuals or suicidal patients. The relative strength of the wish to live and the wish to die is variable, and changes in this relative balance are associated with different trajectories of risk and resilience. It is therefore essential to pay greater attention to the patients' struggle to (re)engage with a life worth living and the need to shore up their wish to live, despite a wish to die that for some remains ever present (notwithstanding health professionals' anxiety to eliminate it in their clients). Importantly, this multidimensional approach to understanding the dynamic interplay of risk and resilience aligns well with meeting the needs of those with lived experience who advocate for a more collaborative, patient-centered approach, where the suicidal person can have the space and support to find ways of keeping alive, and wanting to do that for themselves.

References

Australian Institute of Health and Welfare. (2017). *Emergency department care 2016–17: Australian hospital statistics.* Canberra: AIHW. Health services series no. 80. Cat. no. HSE 194.

Australian Institute of Health and Welfare. (2018). *Admitted patient care 2016-17: Australian hospital statistics.* Canberra: AIHW. Health services series no. 84. Cat. no. HSE 201.

Bech, P., Gudex, C., & Johansen, K. (1996). The WHO (ten) well-being index: Validation in diabetes. *Psychotherapy and Psychosomatics, 65*, 183–190. https://doi.org/10.1159/000289073.

Brown, G. K., Steer, R. A., Henriques, G. R., & Beck, A. T. (2005). The internal struggle between the wish to die and the wish to live: A risk factor for suicide. *American Journal of Psychiatry, 162*, 1977–1979. https://doi.org/10.1176/appi.ajp.162.10.1977.

Bryan, C. J., & Rudd, M. D. (2016). The importance of temporal dynamics in the transition from suicidal thought to behavior. *Clinical Psychology: Science and Practice, 23*, 21–25. https://doi.org/10.1111/cpsp.12135.

Bryan, C. J., Rudd, M. D., Peterson, A. L., Young-McCaughan, S., & Wertenberger, E. G. (2016). The ebb and flow of the wish to live and the wish to die among suicidal military personnel. *Journal of Affective Disorders, 202*, 58–66. https://doi.org/10.1016/j.jad.2016.05.049.

Cacioppo, J. T., & Berntson, G. (1994). Relationship between attitudes and evaluative space: A critical review, with emphasis on the separability of positive and negative substrates. *Psychological Bulletin, 115*, 401–423. https://doi.org/10.1037//0033-2909.115.3.401.

Corr, P. J. (2013). Approach and avoidance behaviour: Multiple systems and their interactions. *Emotion Review, 5*, 285–290. https://doi.org/10.1177/1754073913477507.

Dyer, K., Hooke, G., & Page, A. C. (2014). Development and psychometrics of the five item daily index in a psychiatric sample. *Journal of Affective Disorders, 152*, 409–415. https://doi.org/10.1016/j.jad.2013.10.003.

Fry, M., & Brunero, S. (2004). The characteristics and outcomes of mental health patients presenting to an emergency department over a twelve month period. *Australian Emergency Nursing Journal, 7*, 21–25. https://doi.org/10.1016/S1328- 2743(05)80027-6.

George, S. E., Page, A. C., Hooke, G. R., & Stritzke, W. G. (2016). Multifacet assessment of capability for suicide: Development and prospective validation of the acquired capability with rehearsal for suicide scale. *Psychological Assessment, 28*, 1452–1464. https://doi.org/10.1037/pas0000276.

Goods, N. A. R., Page, A. C., Stritzke, W. G. K., Harrison, D. P., Hudaib, A., & Fay, N. (2019). *Latent profile and transition analysis of the wish to live and wish to die in emergency care patients at risk of suicide compared to a non-clinical sample* (Manuscript in preparation).

Harrison, D. P., Stritzke, W. G., Fay, N., & Hudaib, A. R. (2018). Suicide risk assessment: Trust an implicit probe or listen to the patient? *Psychological Assessment, 30*, 1317–1329. https://doi.org/10.1037/pas0000577.

Huppert, F. A., & So, T. T. C. (2013). Flourishing across Europe: Application of a new conceptual framework for defining well-being. *Social Indicators Research, 110*, 837–861. https://doi.org/10.1007/s11205-011-9966-7.

Joiner, T. E. (2005). *Why people die by suicide.* Cambridge, MA: Harvard University Press.

Klonsky, E. D., May, A. M., & Saffer, B. Y. (2016). Suicide, suicide attempts, and suicidal ideation. *Annual Review of Clinical Psychology, 12*, 307–330. https://doi.org/10.1146/annurev-clinpsy-021815-093204.

Kovacs, M., & Beck, A. T. (1977). The wish to die and the wish to live in attempted suicides. *Journal of Clinical Psychology, 33*, 361–365. https://doi.org/10.1002/1097-4679(197704)33:2<361::AID-JCLP2270330207>3.0.CO;2-H.

Lageborn, C. T., Ljung, R., Vaez, M., & Dahlin, M. (2017). Ongoing university studies and the risk of suicide: A register-based nationwide cohort study of 5 million young and middle-aged individuals in Sweden, 1993–2011. *BMJ Open, 7*, 1–8. https://doi.org/10.1136/bmjopen-2016-014264.

Linehan, M. M., Goodstein, J. L., Nielsen, S. L., & Chiles, J. A. (1983). Reasons for staying alive when you are thinking of killing yourself: The reasons for living inventory. *Journal of Consulting and Clinical Psychology, 51*, 276–286. https://doi.org/10.1037/0022-006X.51.2.276.

Little, R. J. (1988). A test of missing completely at random for multivariate data with missing values. *Journal of the American Statistical Association, 83*, 1198–1202. https://doi.org/10.1080/01621459.1988.10478722.

Newnham, E. A., Hooke, G. R., & Page, A. C. (2010). Monitoring treatment response and outcome using the World Health Organization's wellbeing index in psychiatric care. *Journal of Affective Disorders, 122*, 139–146. https://doi.org/10.1016/j.jad.2009.06.005.

Page, A. C., Cunningham, N. K., & Hooke, G. R. (2016). Using daily monitoring of psychiatric symptoms to evaluate hospital length of stay. *BJPsych Open, 2*, 341–345. https://doi.org/10.1192/bjpo.bp.116.003814.

Restifo, E., Kashyap, S., Hooke, G. R., & Page, A. C. (2015). Daily monitoring of temporal trajectories of suicidal ideation predicts self-injury: A novel application of patient progress monitoring. *Psychotherapy Research, 25*, 705–713. https://doi.org/10.1080/10503307.2015.1006707.

Rudd, M. D. (2006). Fluid vulnerability theory: A cognitive approach to understanding the process of acute and chronic suicide risk. In T. E. Ellis (Ed.), *Cognition and suicide: Theory, research, and therapy* (pp. 355–368). Washington, DC, US: American Psychological Association. https://doi.org/10.1037/11377-016.

CHAPTER 6

Alternatives to suicide: a nonlinear dynamic perspective

Clemens Fartacek[a,b] Martin Plöderl[a,b], Günter Schiepek[c]
[a]Department of Crisis Intervention and Suicide Prevention, University Clinic of Psychiatry, Psychotherapy, and Psychosomatics; Paracelsus Medical University, Salzburg, Austria; [b]Department of Clinical Psychology, University Clinic of Psychiatry, Psychotherapy, and Psychosomatics, Paracelsus Medical University, Salzburg, Austria; [c]Institute of Synergetics and Psychotherapy Research, Paracelsus Medical University, Salzburg, Austria

Introduction

Suicidal behavior is a public health problem, with approximately 788 000 annual deaths worldwide (WHO, 2015). Suicidal behavior results from a specific process, the "suicidal process", which implies progression of suicidality over time (e.g., Van Heeringen, 2001). A better understanding of the suicidal process may lead to the development of more effective prevention and intervention strategies. Therefore, several suicidologists have suggested modeling suicidal processes within the theoretical framework of nonlinear dynamic systems (NDS), because NDS may provide new perspectives on clinically relevant questions about the prediction of suicide phenomena and the mechanisms of change in suicidality (e.g., Rogers, 2003; Schiepek et al., 2011).

The aim of the chapter at hand is to outline an NDS perspective on suicidal processes and to discuss principles of interventions as well as resilience to suicide within this framework. Before addressing this, we would like to introduce some basic concepts of NDS (for a detailed description see Haken & Schiepek, 2006; Salvatore & Tschacher, 2012; Stam, 2005; Strunk & Schiepek, 2006) and specify this perspective for suicidal processes. Finally, a number of implications for suicide research are outlined.

Nonlinear dynamic systems

Theories of NDS, also termed self-organization theories or chaos and complexity theories, are a family of interdisciplinary theories describing, measuring, and explaining processes of NDS in different fields of science

Alternatives to Suicide
ISBN 978-0-12-814297-4
https://doi.org/10.1016/B978-0-12-814297-4.00006-6

(e.g., mathematics, physics, chemistry, psychology). Regardless of the subject of the research field, NDS share four structural properties (Strunk & Schiepek, 2014): First, these systems are dissipative, i.e., they consume and exchange energy with the environment, and they are driven by so-called control parameters; second, they combine positive activating and negative inhibiting feedback loops (mixed feedback); third, they consist of at least one variable in the case of discrete processes or of at least three variables in continuous processes; and finally, there is at least one nonlinear relationship between the variables.

Some of these theories deal with pattern formations in systems containing large amounts of interrelated elements (e.g., the human brain). Under specific conditions – described by so-called control parameter values (e.g., the supply of energy in physical systems) – the dynamics of previously independent (sometimes stochastically) acting system elements are synchronized to coherent collective patterns. According to Synergetics, a well-established theory of NDS (Haken, 2004), such phenomena result from the interactions of these system elements (e.g., cognitions, emotions, behaviors) on a relatively microscopic level, which then lead to the emergence of order structures — so-called order parameters — at a relatively macroscopic level (e.g., syndromes). The other way round, order parameters enslave the system elements, leading to a circular-causal process between macroscopic and microscopic levels. Therefore, order parameters describe the behavior of many components or subsystems of a system (information compression).

The dynamics of order parameters are also referred to as attractors since they "attract" trajectories (sequences of system states) and restrict the system dynamics to their pattern. Deviating input or system states from this pattern are damped away, as can be demonstrated by simple mathematical systems such as the Verhulst system (see Fig. 6.1). In other words, attractors regulate and organize the system's dynamics and make them resistant against internal fluctuations and external disturbances. There are four main types of attractors in NDS (Stam, 2005): Fixed-point attractors (i.e., regulation toward a steady state), limit cycles (i.e., regulation toward closed loops); torus attractors (i.e., regulation toward a three-dimensional periodic or quasi-periodic limit cycle with a donut-like shape), and chaotic or strange attractors (see below). Such patterns neither result from input nor external sources, but are produced by processes within the system itself, so that they are referred to as self-organizing (Haken & Schiepek, 2006; Strunk & Schiepek, 2006).

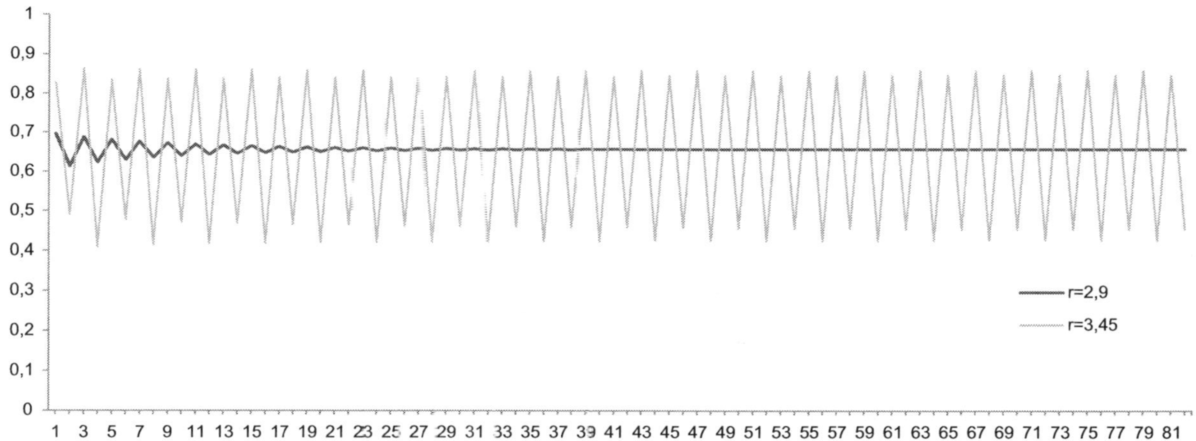

Fig. 6.1 Illustration of a fixed-point and a periodic oscillation (period 4) of the Verhulst dynamics. The Verhulst system is a discrete nonlinear dynamic system ($x_{n+1} = rx_n - rx_n^2$), originally designed to describe population dynamics. r represents the control parameter, x the population size (y-axis), and n the number of iterations (x-axis). The iteration process starts at an initial value of $x = 0.6$. Depending on the control parameter setting, different attractors emerge. At a control parameter setting of $r = 2.9$ (bold line) and after transient behaviors at the beginning, the system regulates toward a constant value (fixed-point attractor). At a parameter setting of $r = 3.45$ (thin gray line), an oscillation between the four values emerges.

Some behaviors of NDS are referred to as complex, i.e., behaviors which cannot be predicted in the long run, even if the generating system operates completely deterministically and is known in detail (Strunk & Schiepek, 2014). The most prominent type of complex behavior is deterministic chaos, which became known as the butterfly effect in the 1960s through meteorologist Lorenz (1963). Chaotic attractors are complex behaviors between regularity and noise that cannot be predicted in the long run because even smallest differences in initial conditions would lead to an exponential divergence of the trajectories over time (see Fig. 6.2). Furthermore, during chaotic phases, the system does not visit a state twice, although it shows a stable but 'strange' pattern in the phase space (see Fig. 6.3).

So-called phase transitions (outside of physics also known as order or pattern transitions) are another characteristic of non-linear dynamic systems with reference to transitions from one order parameter to another. As predicted by Synergetics, such order transitions are primed and accompanied by critical fluctuations (Haken & Schiepek, 2006) and occur when control parameters (e.g., energy-flow in physical systems) drive attractors out of existing equilibrium states (non-equilibrium phase transitions) (see Fig. 6.4). During phase transitions, systems are in an unstable state where even minimal input from the outside or even internal fluctuations can be crucial for the system's next emerging attractor. Therefore, NDS in a phase transition are not predictable.

NDS may also produce a landscape of coexisting order parameters, i.e., a phenomenon that is referred to as bi- or multi-stability (see Fig. 6.4). In other words, the system is able to create two or more order parameters with the same set of parameter values. Depending on the impact of specific input or internal fluctuations as well as the attraction (basin) of the competing patterns, the system will manifest one of the potentially available order parameters.

Furthermore, Synergetics postulates the principle of embodied system history for human systems like brains or minds (Haken & Schiepek, 2006). According to this principle, the more frequently specific order parameters emerge, the more accessible they become and the stronger their attraction gets. In terms of the potential landscape metaphor, the landscape itself changes as a function of the use of the landscape (experience): The ball that is moving around in this landscape (current system behavior) modifies the shape of the landscape. With each emergence of an order parameter, its accessibility (metaphorically expressed by flattening the repellor and

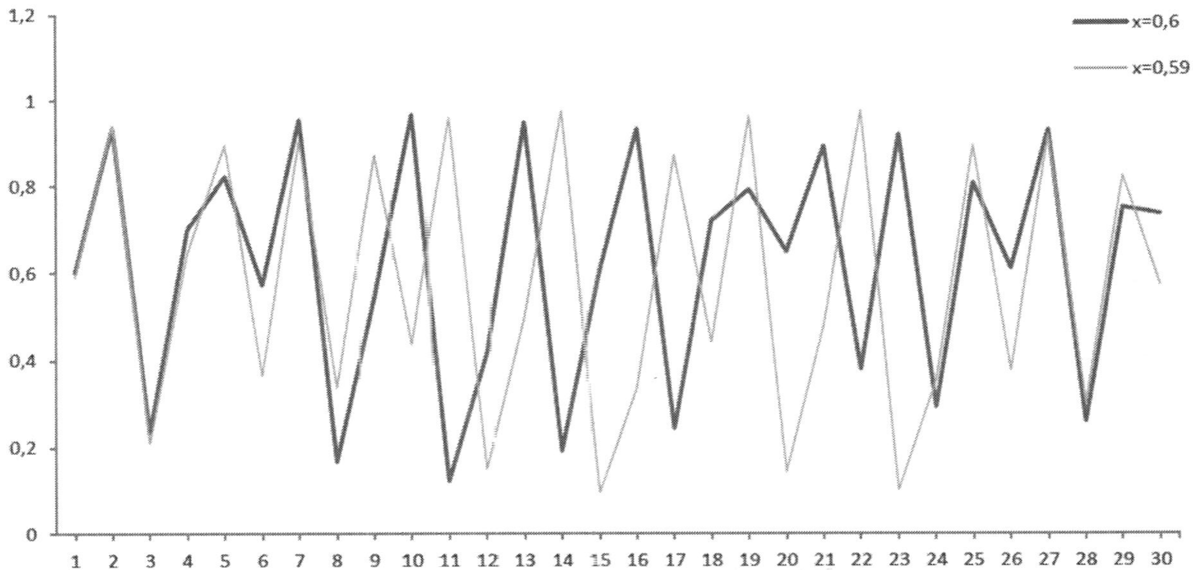

Fig. 6.2 Illustration of sensitive dependency of the dynamics ("butterfly effect") of the Verhulst system (see Fig. 6.1 for more details). At a control parameter value of $r = 3.894$, one dynamic starts at an initial value of $x = 0.6$ (bold line) and the other at an initial value of $x = 0.59$ (thin line). Although the initial values differ only slightly, they diverge exponentially after the 10th iteration.

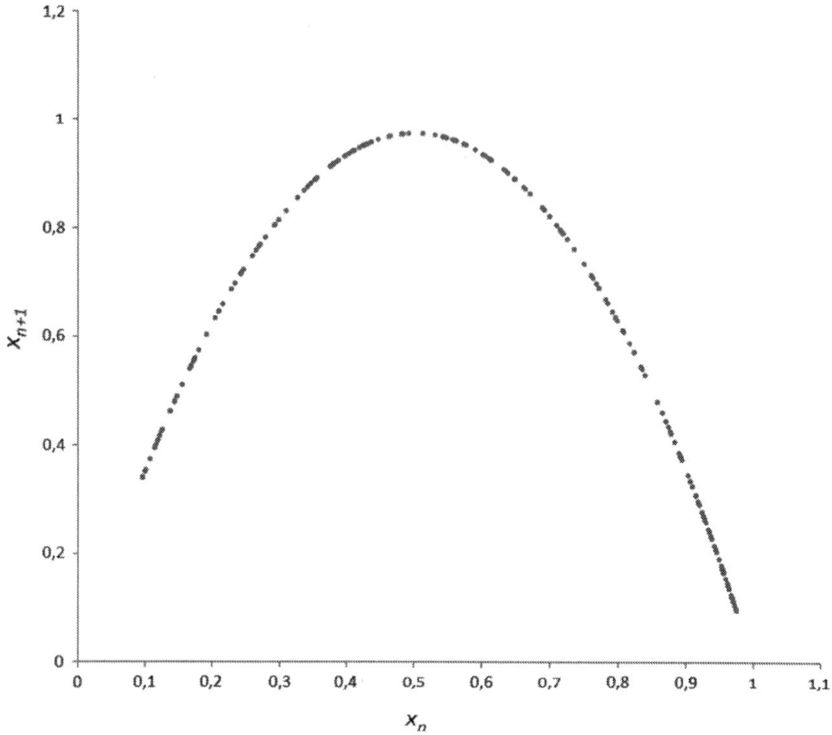

Fig. 6.3 The parabolic attractor of the Verhulst dynamics in a two-dimensional phase space (x_n vs. x_{n+1}) at a parameter value of $r = 3.9$.

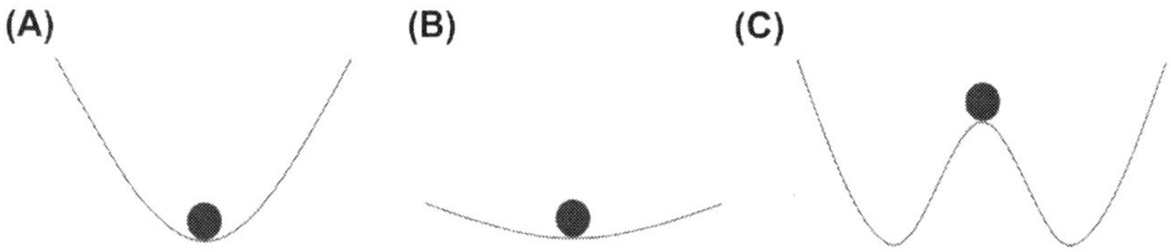

Fig. 6.4 A model of phase transitions and the (in)stability of system states as illustrated by the metaphor of potential landscape. In (A), the ball in the valley symbolizes a stable state (i.e., order parameter): External disturbances and internal fluctuations bring the ball into motion, but it rolls back into the valley. The deeper the valley and the wider its basin, the higher the stability and attractive force of an order parameter. In (B), the control parameter is set in a way that the valley is flattened. The attraction of the order parameter diminishes. In (C), the control parameter is set in a way that two distinct valleys appear. At the top of a mountain (i.e., the repellor) the system becomes extremely unstable: Smallest fluctuations and minimal input determine into which valley (i.e., which order parameter) the ball will roll next. Altogether, the sequence of potential landscapes from (A) to (C) illustrates a transition from mono-to bi-stability as a result of changes in control parameters.

expanding the basin of the order parameter) and its intensity and duration (metaphorically expressed by an increasing depth of the potential valley) would increase (Schiepek, Eckert, Aas, Wallot, & Wallot, 2015).

Nonlinear dynamics of suicidal processes

Modeling psychopathological processes with NDS has been suggested by numerous scholars (e.g., Yang & Tsai, 2013). From an NDS-viewpoint, dysfunctional mental states and disorders were considered order parameters that reduce the degrees of freedom in the dynamics of cognitions, emotion, and behaviors (e.g., depression), which are referred to as cognition-emotion-behavior (CEB) patterns in Synergetics. These order parameters make the system resistant against internal fluctuations and disturbances from the outside (e.g., interventions or scheme non-conforming information) (Haken & Schiepek, 2006). Whereas healthy minds remain poised to switch order parameters depending upon stimulation and demands (Schiepek et al., 2015), during psychopathological episodes, individuals are caught in the basin of one or very few dysfunctional order parameters (see Fig. 6.5). Successful therapeutic processes are associated with order transitions from fixed pathological order states to healthy ones (Schiepek et al., 2015).

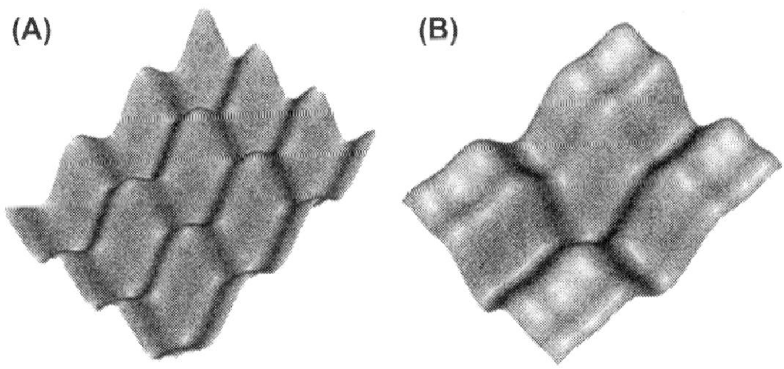

Fig. 6.5 Potential landscapes representing the transition from a healthy to a pathological state. The landscapes illustrate the transition from a multi-stability (A) — associated with flexibility and adaptability (cf. Kashdan & Rottenberg, 2010) switching between several order parameters depending upon stimulation and demands — into a nearby mono-attractor state (B), representing the emergence of a pathological state that reduces the degrees of freedom of cognitions, emotion, and behavior (e.g., depression). *(Reproduced with permission from Haken, H., & Schiepek, G. (2010). Synergetik in der Psychologie: Selbstorganisation verstehen und gestalten [Synergetics of psychology: Understanding and facilitating self-organisation] (second ed.), p. 45. © Hogrefe.)*

Indeed, this was found in several empirical studies (e.g., Heinzel, Tominschek, & Schiepek, 2014; Schiepek et al., 2013; Schiepek, Tominschek, & Heinzel, 2014).

Several suicidologists have suggested modeling suicidal processes within the framework of NDS (e.g., Bryan & Rudd, 2017; Fartacek, Schiepek, Kunrath, Fartacek, & Plöderl, 2016; Rogers, 2003; Schiepek et al., 2011). This suggestion can be underpinned by analogies between the known characteristics of suicidal processes and the dynamic properties of NDS. For example, according to the organizing function of order parameters, specific states are expected to emerge during suicidal processes in which the degrees of freedom of mental and behavioral dynamics are reduced and which exhibit resistance to disturbances. The analogy to the phenomenology of acute suicidal states is obvious. Pavulans, Bolmsjö, Edberg, and Öjehagen (2012) describe acute suicidal states as specific states of mind immediately prior to suicidal behavior in which the wish to live is no longer accessible, and in which arguments against suicide may switch to pro-suicide arguments, where no help can be sought or accepted, and where suicide is seen as the only way out. The phenomenon of acute suicidal states has also been described by other suicidologists. Hendin, Al Jurdi, Houck, Hughes, and Turner (2010) describe a distinct, time-limited psychological state, termed as "suicide crisis", that typically precedes suicidal behaviors and leaves clients feeling out of control and which signifies acute danger of suicide. According to Yaseen, Gilmer, Modi, Cohen, and Galynker (2012), this state is characterized by frantic hopelessness, ruminative flooding, and near-psychotic somatization, and enables the transition from suicidal ideations to suicidal behavior. Wenzel and Beck (2008) describe a state of attentional fixation immediately before suicidal behavior occurs. In this state, clients are preoccupied with the idea that suicide is the only way out of their problems. They act like they are in trance or in an "out-of-the-ordinary" state of mind, dissociative, like an automaton (Maltsberger, 2004; Michel & Gysin-Maillart, 2015; Orbach, 1994). This state is also termed "suicidal mode" (Michel, 2011; Pavulans et al., 2012), which was conceptualized as a specific cognitive-affective behavioral-physiological network of schemata (Rudd, 2000). In Synergetics, the suicidal mode would be considered a specific order parameter or CEB pattern that reduces the degrees of freedom in the dynamics of cognitions, emotion, and behaviors (Schiepek et al., 2015).

In the suicidal process, acute suicidal states are likely to be preceded by other suicide-related states. Considering these states to be specific order parameters as well, the suicidal process could be understood as a cascade of order transitions within a nonlinear dynamic framework. For example, Pöldinger (1968) describes a stage of "consideration". In this stage, suicide is considered as one potential solution among others. Here, unlike in acute suicidal states, control over suicidal thoughts is completely preserved. Furthermore, various authors describe a state of ambivalence in the suicidal process, in which an inner struggle takes place between the desire to live and the desire to die (e.g., Pöldinger, 1968; Shneidman, 1993). Arguments against suicide (e.g., staying alive for one's children) are weighed against arguments in favor of suicide (e.g., to end one's suffering) as the wish to live and the wish to die are balanced against one another (Bryan, this volume). The disappearance of the wishes to live could dissolve this ambivalence and could be indicative of the transition into an acute suicidal state and suicidal behavior (Bryan, Rudd, Peterson, Young-McCaughan, & Wertenberger, 2016).

In NDS, one would expect strong fluctuations in system dynamics, which could indicate critical instabilities before phase transitions. In line with this, ecological monitoring studies found considerable fluctuations in suicidality (e.g., Kleiman et al., 2017). A hint for phase transitions in the suicidal process is also provided by studies that found a positive correlation between the degree of affective variability with the frequency and severity of suicidality (Palmier-Claus et al., 2013; Palmier-Claus, Taylor, Gooding, Dunn, & Lewis, 2012). Affective variability could be indicative of critical fluctuations in phases of order transitions (Strunk & Schiepek, 2014). For suicidal processes, the ambivalent state, where the wish to live and the wish to die are both elevated may be also indicate critical instability (Goods et al. this volume).

Another analogy between NDS and suicidal phenomena can be drawn from studies that found a sensitization to future suicidal episodes by past ones. According to the principle of embodied system history (Haken & Schiepek, 2006), with each emergence of an attractor its accessibility, intensity, and duration will increase in future crises (see above). This is supported by empirical studies which found that past suicidal behavior increases the risk of future suicidal behavior (Beghi, Rosenbaum, Cerri, & Cornaggia, 2013). Furthermore, suicidal crises are more easily triggered, more intensively experienced, and last longer in multiple attempters compared to single and non-attempters (Joiner & Rudd, 2000; Witte, Fitzpatrick, Joiner, & Schmidt, 2005). Therefore, in addition to control parameter configurations or the timing and intensity of disturbances (depending on the stability of states), the principle of embodied system history might also explain individual differences in the duration of suicidal processes (e.g., Deisenhammer, Strauss, Kemmler, Hinterhuber, & Weiss, 2009).

Nonlinear dynamic relationships between input and output are typical for NDS. Indeed, nonlinear relations between stressors and the emergence of suicidality were described by several authors (Mishara, 2006; Ramsay, 1997; Schiepek et al., 2011). For example, massive stress at one moment could have no effect on suicidality, while at other times even the smallest stressors could lead to severe suicidality. Such dynamics would not be surprising in NDS. The impact of external inputs depends, above all, on the degree of stability or instability of the system. Even small disturbances can trigger a phase transition at instability points, while massive disturbances at stable states have no effect if the basin of the dominating attractor cannot be overcome (see Fig. 6.4).

The inability to predict suicidal behavior may also be a characteristic feature of nonlinear dynamics. Suicide research has concentrated almost exclusively on the long-term prediction of suicide behavior, but only with modest success (Glenn & Nock, 2014). Despite decades of research, predicting suicide is still not possible with satisfying specificity and sensitivity (e.g., Large, Galletly, Myles, Ryan, & Myles, 2017). This failure is, from an NDS perspective, not only a consequence of lacking epistemic knowledge (e.g., unspecific or unknown risk factors) or aleatory processes (random noise), but also a consequence of the inherent complexity of the underlying system (Plöderl & Fartacek, 2018). Whereas some types of attractors (e.g., fixed-point attractors) enable long-term predictions if their control parameters are known and remain stable or controllable (which cannot be taken for granted in living systems), complex dynamics such as chaos or order transitions cannot be predicted in the long term, even if the generating system would operate in a completely deterministic fashion and is known in detail.

Implications of NDS on suicide risk assessment

According to the analogies between the dynamic properties of suicidal processes and NDS as described above, acute suicidal states can be understood as order parameters, and the process up to that point can be described as a cascade of order transitions between different suicide-related states. This perspective has considerable implications for suicide risk assessment.

According to the complexity of suicidal processes, the long-term prediction of suicidal behavior over years is a utopian aim. Instead, suicidology should focus on short-term prediction of suicidal behavior. This complies with the need for warning signs as promoted by Rudd et al. (2006) that are conceived as the earliest recognizable signs pointing to suicidal behavior in the near future. According to an NDS model, three types of warning signs would be appropriate for monitoring: (1) specific markers of suicide-related states; (2) the control parameters of suicide-related states; and (3) critical fluctuations and other related precursors during transitions into these states.

First, assuming a cascade of order transitions in the suicidal process, suicide-related states (e.g., state of ambivalence, acute suicidal states) could serve as precursors of suicidal behavior and be therefore used for risk assessment. The warning signs postulated by Rudd et al. (2006) (e.g., hopelessness, no reason for living) may turn out to be specific markers of suicide-related states. Second, the emergence of suicide-related order parameters and the shape of the corresponding landscapes strongly depend on the set of control parameters. Knowing the values of the relevant control parameters and their critical thresholds (e.g., through high-frequency monitoring) could support risk assessment. Depending on the control parameter settings, one would know about the available repertoire of order parameters. A control parameter setting that indicates the presence of acute suicidal states in a multi-stable potential landscape would indicate a risk for its emergence under the influence of external disturbances (e.g., stressors) and the attraction of the available attractors (see below for hypotheses concerning possible control parameters of suicidal processes).

Finally, critical fluctuations in the suicidal process could serve as warning signs. This approach was inspired by common practices in geophysics used for short-term predictions of rare but extreme events, such as earthquakes or tsunamis, which are based on continuous monitoring of appropriate signals and the identification of nonlinear precursors of such extreme events (Albeverio, Jentsch, & Kantz, 2006). If we assume that acute suicidal states correspond to the activation of a specific order parameter, critical fluctuations can be expected before a transition into an acute suicidal state occurs and may thus be deemed observable precursors. In terms of limitations, it cannot be supposed that critical fluctuations are highly specific features of acute suicidal states. Critical fluctuations occur at phases where a system is unstable and where slightest external disturbances or internal fluctuations can trigger the emergence of the next attractor of the system. This could be an acute suicidal state, but also a qualitatively different state. In addition to critical fluctuations, a synchronization between the relevant system elements would be expected in the course of the emergence of order parameters (Haken, 2004). Therefore, such synchronization patterns might also serve as precursors for suicide-related states (for detailed information on various algorithms see Schiepek et al., 2015; Dako et al., 2012).

Ways out of and resilience to suicidal states

According to the title of the book *Alternatives to Suicide: Beyond Risk and Toward a Life Worth Living,* the question arises how ways out of suicidal states or alternative routes on the way to suicide can be facilitated within a nonlinear dynamic framework. Based on the theory of Synergetics, the exit from the suicidal process requires the realization of conditions for self-organized order transitions of dysfunctional, pathological order parameters into functional, healthy ones. Schiepek, Eckert, Honermann, and Weihrauch (2001) formulated generic principles describing the process of realizing these conditions for the benefit of psychotherapeutic processes (for a detailed description see Schiepek et al., 2015). These principles are not a phase model, but instead are criteria that are permanently relevant in psychotherapy, though they are of different relevance to different process stages (Schiepek et al., 2015).

Specifying the generic principles for suicidal processes, suicidal states must be destabilized before new states can emerge. This requires stable boundary conditions (generic principle *stability conditions*). For example, an adequate treatment setting contributes to this (e.g., inpatient treatment), in which the clients feel safe (e.g., distance from stressors) and relieved (e.g., professional support). Referring to Bowlby's attachment theory (Bowlby, 1973), it is necessary to establish a *secure base* for the clients. This requires a good therapeutic relationship between client and therapist that is based, for example, on a shared understanding of the clients' mental pain and meaning of the suicidal crisis (referred to as a collaborative approach; Jobes, 2006).

For treatment planning, dysfunctional order parameters must first be identified (generic principle *identification of relevant system patterns*). These typically emerge as CEB (cognition-emotion-behavior) patterns (Schiepek et al., 2015). A heuristic that we have been testing during the last years is called idiographic system modeling, which allows for identifying the most important suicide-related components and their interrelations within a personal system (e.g., cognitions, emotions, resources, risk factors, coping strategies) (see Box 6.1). From our experience, and in line with suicide research, intolerable psychological pain, hopelessness, entrapment, sleep disorders, or neglect of personal resources are often interrelated by positive and negative feedback loops.

Idiographic system models often reveal plausible targets in CEB patterns for therapeutic interventions (e.g., system elements with many interrelations) that can contribute to the destabilization and amplification of fluctuations of dysfunctional order parameters (generic principle

Box 6.1 The method of idiographic system modeling

In a cooperative interview, a list of important psychological and social variables of the system under consideration is composed. Starting off at a general picture of the client's life in the last couple of months, the therapist takes notes throughout the interview on important factors such as psychological problems, problem-solving methods, coping strategies, and impact on social life. These notes will form the basic components of the idiographic system model that is to be developed (Schiepek et al., 2015). Any topic that is subjectively important to the client can be used to create this model. It is advisable to use the client's language in order for client and therapist to create mutual understanding and producing the client's very own individual model. After the interview, all components are checked for their terminology and content in order to make sure that clients can find themselves in these components. It is important that the components are expressed as variables with values that can change throughout time. In a perfect case, therapist and client manage to capture all important bio-psycho-social aspects of the client's life presenting a risk for suicide, Incorporating cognitions, emotions, motives, behavior, physiological states and more, yet by using the client's own language and terminology.

Subsequently, the inter-connections of these variables are mapped, creating a personal landscape of relevant aspects of the client's mental functioning — the idiographic system model (ISM). Using a flipchart, variable A is written down and the list is then checked for other variables that are connected to it. Writing down a second connected variable B, both are linked with an arrow and a + or − sign, indicating whether there is a positive relation (same directedness: increase in A leads to increase in B and decrease in A leads to decrease in B) or a negative relation (opposite directedness: increase in A leads to decrease in B and decrease in A leads to increase in B) (as example see Schiepek, Stöger-Schmidinger, Aichhorn, Schöller, & Aas, 2016).

destabilization and amplification of fluctuations). It is assumed that several methods or techniques are equally functional in this regard, so that therapists can freely choose according to their experience, personal preferences, and style (Schiepek et al., 2015). Those interventions are most effective that focus on the control parameters (generic principle *identification of control parameters*). If treatment could focus on the control parameters, the potential landscape would change, which would lead to phase transitions into other order states. Despite their importance, control parameters of suicidal processes are not yet known. With regard to their identification, the distinction between order parameters and control parameters plays an important role. The criterion for this differentiation is the reference to different time scales. Control parameters change on a slower time scale than the variables or states of a system. Therefore, Schiepek et al. (2017) suggest that in psychological systems control parameters can be interpreted as traits or dispositions that change on a slower time scale than the order parameters or states of a system. Potential hypotheses for control parameters of therapeutic change are provided by the integrative nonlinear dynamic model of psychotherapeutic change processes described by Schiepek et al. (2017). For example, such control parameters could be emotion regulation abilities, capacities for mentalization, problem-solving competence, or self-efficacy. Some of these potential control parameters were also key targets in established therapeutic approaches to reduce suicidal behavior (e.g., dialectic behavioral therapy, mentalization-based treatment, cognitive behavioral treatment of suicidality). Moreover, suicidological literature provides a number of suicide risk factors that might change on a slower time scale than acute suicidal states (e.g., psychache, meaningfulness, entrapment, reasons for living, burdensomeness). Therefore, studies are needed to distinguish between control parameters and order parameters within suicide risk factors. Until then, we recommend evaluating interventions for each client in real time by using continuous electronic feedback systems (e.g., Kashyap, Hooke, & Page, 2015; Kyron, Hooke, & Page, 2018; Restifo, Kashyap, Hooke, & Page, 2015).

From an NDS perspective, it is also necessary to personalize interventions in a dynamic sense, because interventions need good timing (generic principles: *kairos, resonance, and synchronization*). This is especially necessary during phases of critical instability. In these moments, the system is in an unstable state and sensitive to change, because the attractive force of attractors is reduced. For the identification of such phases, electronic diaries such as the Synergetic Navigation System (i.e., a web-based and app-based monitoring system that provides feedback on system stability in real time through analysis algorithms; for a detailed description see Schiepek et al., 2015) are helpful. Such feedback systems can be optimized by the use of individualized questionnaires (Haynes, Mumma, & Pinson, 2009). To realize the latter, we combine idiographic system modeling and the Synergetic Navigation System (Fartacek, Plöderl, & Schiepek, 2015). Here, important suicide-related components (e.g., cognitions, emotions, resources, risk factors, coping strategies) are derived from the variables of idiographic system modeling, and by using the questionnaire editor of the Synergetic Navigation System, a personalized process questionnaire can be designed.

In a system that is far from equilibrium and close to an instability point, two or more order parameters are potentially realized in an equally likely degree (Schiepek et al., 2015). However, there are situations in which certain patterns should be avoided and not left to chance (e.g., the suicidal mode). To steer an order transition in a desired direction (generic principle *purposeful symmetry breaking*), certain forms of assistance can be provided, e.g., some structural elements of a new order state can be realized in, for instance, role-play, imagination exercises, or through the activation of personal resources. This can cause a partial realization of structural elements of the order parameter and may, according to the enslaving principle, result in the emergence of the full order parameter (Schiepek et al., 2015).

Relapse prevention is a key issue in suicide prevention, because once a suicidal crisis has emerged, individuals have an increased lifetime risk for further suicidal crises, especially in suicide attempters (Beghi et al., 2013). An explanation is provided by Michel (2011), who describes the suicidal mode as a learned and stored state of mind used for dealing with psychosocial crises. In line with this, Shneidman (1993) has described suicidality as a (lifelong) pattern for coping with unbearable and hopeless life circumstances. This raises the question of how relapse risks can be reduced and resilience to future suicidal crises can be developed (generic principle: *stabilization of new patterns*).

Usual definitions of resilience resemble the stability of system dynamics during or after disturbances. Resilience is seen as a response to different adversities, ranging from ongoing daily hassles to major life events (Fletcher & Sarkar, 2013). Ryff, Love, Essex, and Singer (1998) defined resilience as the capacity to maintain or recover high well-being in the face of life's adversities. Resilience may come in form of a positive adaptation which must be conceptually appropriate to the experienced adversity and must be examined in terms of the domains assessed and the stringency of criteria used. Related concepts are coping, hardiness, or even autopoiesis, which means the reproduction of the structure of a living system. All these concepts refer to stability and homeostasis, which implies that the system under consideration (e.g., individuals, families, groups, even societies) should be able to return to the former existing attractor after any short-term or enduring disturbances. In the context of Synergetics, this stability can be basically explained in two ways: (1) Resilience implicates that existing (non-suicidal) order parameters (valleys) should be deepened and their basins should be broadened so that even violent disruptions and disturbances will not, metaphorically, "kick the ball out of the valley". (2) Stable control parameter values. In therapy, for example, this can be facilitated by creating idiographic system models of individual recovery processes and the determinants of healthy states (Strunk & Schiepek, 2014), which might deepen the understanding of these processes and may enhance the capability for mentalization and self-awareness.

From a developmental perspective, destabilization is not only a reaction to stressors but a basic characteristic of development transients, which are sometimes even triggered by the developing system itself (e.g., human personality) (Lichtwarck-Aschoff, van Geert, Bosma, & Kunnen, 2008). This perspective respects the inevitable fluctuating situational demands of life and manifests itself as a cascade of order transitions enabling periods of stability and instability. Accordingly, crises could be part of life and a prerequisite for the development of new modes and personal growth. Therefore, "good therapy" not only aims to ensure that clients survive such crises, but also tries to develop new coping strategies with clients that allow to manage future crises and to substitute their suicidal mode. In this sense, safety plan interventions (Stanley & Brown, 2012) target the early detection of and coping with emerging suicidal processes. The more often such strategies succeed, the larger the basin of functional modes gets, while the basin of the suicidal mode loses its attraction. This can be facilitated by the relapse prevention task, where the skills learned in therapy are played through imagination of past and future suicidal crises.

Outlook

As outlined in this chapter, from an NDS perspective, acute suicidal states can be understood as order parameters of an underlying nonlinear dynamic system and the process up to that point as a cascade of order transitions between different suicide-related states. This perspective has considerable implications for suicide risk assessment and treatment of suicidal clients. Long-term predictions are a utopian goal due to complex behaviors (e.g., chaos, phase transitions) of NDS. Instead, short-term prediction should receive more attention and should be expanded by new approaches (e.g., monitoring of nonlinear precursors). Successful treatment requires the realization of conditions for self-organized order transitions of the suicidal mode into functional, healthy regimes. This change process can be guided by generic principles already applied in psychotherapeutic research. In such a model, resilience can be understood, on the one hand, through the stability of the order parameter regimes associated with health and their corresponding control parameters settings. On the other hand, resilience to suicidality is associated with the development of alternative modes for coping with future crises.

Because of the substantial implications of the NDS model in understanding suicidal processes, its empirical investigation is, in our opinion, of high relevance. Appropriate research designs are based on the identification of dynamic features of NDS in relevant processes. Therefore, continuous and high-frequent assessments of suicidal processes with equidistant sampling rates (time-sampling) are required. Time-sampling procedures can be realized using electronic diaries (e.g., ecological momentary assessment, Synergetic Navigation System). These methods have already been applied in suicidology. For ethical reasons, it is important to note that the few available studies reveal no indication for iatrogenic effects of high-frequency monitoring on suicidality (Blades, Stritzke, Page, & Brown, 2018; Law et al., 2015).

The identification of prototypical dynamics of NDS like chaos in process data is based on nonlinear time series analysis. Unfortunately, classical algorithms that enable the identification of chaos, such as the estimation of fractal dimensionality, require very long, highly resolved, and stationary time series data (Grassberger & Procaccia, 1983). However, stationarity, i.e., invariant statistical characteristics across time (Molenaar & Campbell, 2009), cannot be assumed in human systems, and therefore also not in suicidal processes. Furthermore, the compliance needed for assessing thousands of measures is unrealistic even in highly motivated clients.

Another, probably more feasible hypothesis of NDS, would predict critical fluctuations during order transitions into another order parameter (Haken, 2004; Haken & Schiepek, 2006). As described above, from an

NDS perspective, suicidal states may be viewed as specific order parameters, and before the emergence of suicidal states, increased critical fluctuations in the suicidal process would be expected. To test this hypothesis, complexity algorithms are required that are capable of measuring critical fluctuations and can be applied to short, coarse-grained and non-stationary time series. Proposed algorithms are the dynamic complexity (Schiepek & Strunk, 2010), permutation entropy (Bandt & Pompe, 2002), or recurrence plots (Webber & Zbilut, 1994). As a prerequisite for the investigation of this hypothesis, studies are necessary to determine the optimal sampling rate for tracking the suicidal processes. If the sampling rate is set too low, the process would be too coarse-grained, and relevant information about the process could be lost. If the sampling rate is set too high, the participants would be unnecessarily overloaded. Furthermore, empirically valid definitions and assessments of suicidal states are necessary. Although there are some indications of different suicide-related states in the suicidal process, a detailed empirical (qualitative and quantitative) investigation and a conceptual operationalization of what constitutes these states is not yet available (for first suggestions concerning acute suicidal states see Rogers, Galynker, Yaseen, DeFazio, & Joiner, 2017).

In a next step, the actual positive impact of real-time process feedback about critical fluctuations on suicide risk assessment and treatment of suicidal clients must be clarified in further studies. As mentioned above, from a nonlinear dynamic perspective, feedback on critical instabilities in suicidal dynamics could be helpful for suicide risk assessment and the treatment of suicidal clients, because they hint at moments sensitive to therapeutic change as well as the emergence of suicidal states. Furthermore, the investigation of control parameters of suicidal states would be crucial for suicidal risk assessment and therapy of suicidal clients. Despite their importance, control parameters of suicidal processes are not yet known. Since experimental designs under laboratory conditions are difficult in the context of suicidology (but see Collins, Best, Stritzke, & Page, 2016; George, Collins, Cao, Stritzke, & Page, 2017), micro-longitudinal data collected via electronic diaries could provide a methodological alternative. Such data allows the investigation of temporal relationships between potential control parameters and qualitative changes in system dynamics. According to Haken and Schiepek (2006), an important hint for the identification of control parameters in time series could be that control parameters would be expected to change more slowly than order parameters and order parameters would change more slowly than enslaved elements.

Regarding the need for further research on an NDS model of suicidal processes, the importance of electronic diaries has already been mentioned. Independent of an NDS perspective, there are a number of other suicidological research topics whose investigation could be driven forward with such micro-longitudinal data (see Kleiman & Nock, 2018). Moreover, electronic diaries can be useful for the treatment of suicidal clients in several ways. For example, continuous monitoring of suicidality could improve suicide risk assessment, because suicide risk is not always assessed the same by clients and clinicians (Bewick, McBride, & Barkham, 2006). If electronically assessed suicidality is reported to the clinician on a regular basis, errors in judgment could be corrected. Furthermore, process feedback allows for an early identification of non-responders, thereby enabling the modification of treatment in real time. Also, it is likely that the feedback to clients themselves as well as joint reflections on the process also contribute to improvement (Harmon, Hawkins, Lambert, Slade, & Whipple, 2005). Data from monitoring could be useful in helping accurately reconstruct the process between treatment sessions in detail with reduced recall bias (e.g., enhanced recall of information that is congruent with one's mood, and vice versa). This might reveal forgotten positive experiences that convey a sense of hope (Wenze & Miller, 2010). Moreover, the data may give insights into activities that may benefit clients' emotional well-being and thus support an experience of self-efficacy and encourage self-management skills (Wichers et al., 2011) that might lead to a reduction in hopelessness (Wenzel & Beck, 2008). Additionally, process feedback may draw attention to environmental contingencies and triggers (Wenze & Miller, 2010). This might improve the quality of case formulation, behavior modification, and the client's episodic memory for triggers or warning signs (Lynch, Chapman, Rosenthal, Kuo, & Linehan, 2006). Repeated self-assessments may also increase emotional awareness and competencies in meta-cognition, as well as the awareness of suicide-specific warning signs. This is concordant with studies that found a positive association between continuous monitoring and aspects of emotion regulation (Kauer et al., 2012; Reid et al., 2013). Furthermore, continuous self-monitoring allows for combining with tele-health applications, which might improve outcomes (Kasckow et al., 2015).

To sum up, the NDS approach to the suicidal process may open up novel and powerful new theoretical ways to understand the risk and resiliency for suicidality and may establish the basis for more effective suicide prediction and interventions.

References

Albeverio, S., Jentsch, V., & Kantz, H. (2006). *Extreme events in nature and society*. Heidelberg: Springer.

Bandt, C., & Pompe, B. (2002). Permutation entropy: A natural complexity measure for time series. *Physical Review Letters, 88*(17), 174102. https://doi.org/10.1103/PhysRevLett.88.174102.

Beghi, M., Rosenbaum, J. F., Cerri, C., & Cornaggia, C. M. (2013). Risk factors for fatal and nonfatal repetition of suicide attempts: A literature review. *Neuropsychiatric Disease and Treatment, 9*, 1725–1736.

Bewick, B. M., McBride, J., & Barkham, M. (2006). When clients and practitioners have differing views of risk: Benchmarks for improving assessment and practice. *Counselling and Psychotherapy Research, 6*(1), 50–59.

Blades, C. A., Stritzke, W. G. K., Page, A. C., & Brown, J. D. (2018). The benefits and risks of asking research participants about suicide: A meta-analysis of the impact of exposure to suicide-related content. *Clinical Psychology Review, 64*, 1–12.

Bowlby, J. (1973). Attachment and loss. In *Separation, anxiety, and anger* (Vol. 2). New York: Hogarth Press.

Bryan, C. J., & Rudd, M. D. (2017). Nonlinear change processes during psychotherapy characterize patients who have made multiple suicide attempts. *Suicide and Life-Threatening Behavior, 48*(4), 386–400.

Bryan, C. J., Rudd, M. D., Peterson, A. L., Young-McCaughan, S., & Wertenberger, E. G. (2016). The ebb and flow of the wish to live and the wish to die among suicidal military personnel. *Journal of Affective Disorders, 202*, 58–66.

Collins, K. R. L., Best, I., Stritzke, W. G. K., & Page, A. C. (2016). Mindfulness and zest for life buffer the negative effects of experimentally-induced perceived burdensomeness and thwarted belongingness: Implications for theories of suicide. *Journal of Abnormal Psychology, 125*(5), 704–714.

Dakos, V., Carpenter, S. R., Brock, W. A., Ellison, A. M., Guttal, V., Ives, A. R., et al. (2012). Methods for detecting early warnings of critical transitions in time series illustrated using simulated ecological data. *PLoS One, 7*(7), e41010.

Deisenhammer, E. A., Strauss, R., Kemmler, G., Hinterhuber, H., & Weiss, E. M. (2009). The duration of the suicidal process: How much time is left for intervention between consideration and accomplishment of a suicide attempt? *Journal of Clinical Psychiatry, 70*(1), 19–24.

Fartacek, C., Plöderl, M., & Schiepek, G. (2015). Idiographisches systemmonitoring in der Suizidprävention. In I. Sammet, G. Dammann, & G. Schiepek (Eds.), *Der therapeutische Prozess: Forschung für die Praxis* (pp. 82–94). Stuttgart: Kohlhammer.

Fartacek, C., Schiepek, G., Kunrath, S., Fartacek, R., & Plöderl, M. (2016). Real-time monitoring of nonlinear suicidal dynamics: Methodology and a demonstrative case report. *Frontiers in Psychology, 7*(130). https://doi.org/10.3389/fpsyg.2016.00130.

Fletcher, D., & Sarkar, M. (2013). Psychological resilience: A review and critique of definitions, concepts, and theory. *European Psychologist, 18*, 12–23.

George, S. E., Collins, K. R. L., Cao, T., Stritzke, W. G. K., & Page, A. C. (2017). An experimental test of the 'interpersonal' in the interpersonal theory of suicide. *Journal of Experimental Psychopathology, 8*(4), 332–346. https://doi.org/10.5127/jep.060316.

Glenn, C. R., & Nock, M. K. (2014). Improving the short-term prediction of suicidal behavior. *American Journal of Preventive Medicine, 47*(3), 176–180. https://doi.org/10.1016/j.amepre.2014.06.004.

Grassberger, P., & Procaccia, I. (1983). Characterization of strange attractors. *Physical Review Letters, 50*(5), 346–349. https://doi.org/10.1103/PhysRevLett.50.346.

Haken, H. (2004). *Synergetics: Introduction and advanced topics.* Berlin: Springer.

Haken, H., & Schiepek, G. (2006). *Synergetik in der Psychologie: Selbstorganisation verstehen und gestalten: Hogrefe göttingen.*

Harmon, C., Hawkins, E. J., Lambert, M. J., Slade, K., & Whipple, J. S. (2005). Improving outcomes for poorly responding clients: The use of clinical support tools and feedback to clients. *Journal of Clinical Psychology, 61*(2), 175–185. https://doi.org/10.1002/jclp.20109.

Haynes, S. N., Mumma, G. H., & Pinson, C. (2009). Idiographic assessment: Conceptual and psychometric foundations of individualized behavioral assessment. *Clinical Psychology Review, 29*(2), 179–191. https://doi.org/10.1016/j.cpr.2008.12.003.

Heinzel, S., Tominschek, I., & Schiepek, G. (2014). Dynamic patterns in psychotherapy-discontinuous changes and critical instabilities during the treatment of obsessive compulsive disorder. *Nonlinear Dynamics, Psychology, and Life Sciences, 18*, 155–176.

Hendin, H., Al Jurdi, R. K., Houck, P. R., Hughes, S., & Turner, J. (2010). Role of intense affects in predicting short-term risk for suicidal behavior: A prospective study. *The Journal of Nervous and Mental Disease, 198*(3), 220–225. https://doi.org/10.1097/NMD.0b013e3181d13d14.

Jobes, D. A. (2006). *Managing suicidal risk: A collaborative approach.* New York: Guilford Press.

Joiner, T. E., & Rudd, M. D. (2000). Intensity and duration of suicidal crisis vary as a function of previous suicide attempts and negative life events. *Journal of Consulting and Clinical Psychology, 68*(5), 909.

Kasckow, J., Gao, S., Hanusa, B., Rotondi, A., Chinman, M., Zickmund, S., et al. (2015). Telehealth monitoring of patients with schizophrenia and suicidal ideation. *Suicide and Life-Threatening Behavior.* https://doi.org/10.1111/sltb.12154.

Kashdan, T. B., & Rottenberg, J. (2010). Psychological flexibility as a fundamental aspect of health. *Clinical Psychology Review, 30*, 865–878. https://doi.org/10.1016/j.cpr.2010.03.001.

Kashyap, S., Hooke, G. R., & Page, A. C. (2015). Identifying risk of deliberate self-harm through longitudinal monitoring of psychological distress in an inpatient psychiatric population. *BMC Psychiatry, 15*, 81. https://doi.org/10.1186/s12888-015-0464-3.

Kauer, S. D., Reid, S. C., Crooke, A. H. D., Khor, A., Hearps, S. J. C., Jorm, A. F., et al. (2012). Self-monitoring using mobile phones in the early stages of adolescent depression: Randomized controlled trial. *Journal of Medical Internet Research, 14*(3), e67. https://doi.org/10.2196/jmir.1858.

Kleiman, E. M., & Nock, M. K. (2018). Real-time assessment of suicidal thoughts and behaviors. *Current Opinion in Psychology, 22*, 33–37.

Kleiman, E. M., Turner, B. J., Fedor, S., Beale, E. E., Huffman, J. C., & Nock, M. K. (2017). Examination of real-time fluctuations in suicidal ideation and its risk factors: Results from two ecological momentary assessment studies. *Journal of Abnormal Psychology, 126*(6), 726.

Kyron, M. J., Hooke, G. R., & Page, A. C. (2018). Daily assessment of interpersonal factors to predict suicidal ideation and non-suicidal self-injury in psychiatric inpatients. *Journal of Consulting and Clinical Psychology, 86*(6), 556–567. https://doi.org/10.1037/ccp0000305.

Large, M., Galletly, C., Myles, N., Ryan, C. J., & Myles, H. (2017). Known unknowns and unknown unknowns in suicide risk assessment: Evidence from meta-analyses of aleatory and epistemic uncertainty. *BJPsych Bulletin, 41*, 160–163.

Law, M. K., Furr, R. M., Arnold, E. M., Mneimne, M., Jaquett, C., & Fleeson, W. (2015). Does assessing suicidality frequently and repeatedly cause harm? A randomized control study. *Psychological Assessment, 27*(4), 1171.

Lichtwarck-Aschoff, A., van Geert, P., Bosma, H., & Kunnen, S. (2008). Time and identity: A framework for research and theory formation. *Developmental Review, 28*, 370–400.

Lorenz, E. N. (1963). Deterministic nonperiodic flow. *Journal of the Atmospheric Sciences, 20*(2), 130–141. https://doi.org/10.1175/1520-0469(1963)020<0130:DNF>2.0.CO;2.

Lynch, T. R., Chapman, A. L., Rosenthal, M. Z., Kuo, J. R., & Linehan, M. M. (2006). Mechanisms of change in dialectical behavior therapy: Theoretical and empirical observations. *Journal of Clinical Psychology, 62*(4), 459–480. https://doi.org/10.1002/jclp.20243.

Maltsberger, J. T. (2004). The descent into suicide. *The International Journal of Psychoanalysis, 85*(3), 653–668.

Michel, K. (2011). Neurobiology and patient-oriented models of suicide—a contradiction? In K. E. Michael, & D. Jobes (Eds.), *Building a therapeutic alliance with the suicidal patient* (pp. 183–203). Washington, DC: American Psychological Association.

Michel, K., & Gysin-Maillart, A. (2015). *Assip—attempted suicide short intervention program: A manual for clinicians*. Hogrefe Publishing.

Mishara, B. L. (2006). A dynamic developmental model of suicide. *Human Development, 39*(4), 181–194. https://doi.org/10.1159/000278445.

Molenaar, P. C., & Campbell, C. G. (2009). The new person-specific paradigm in psychology. *Current Directions in Psychological Science, 18*(2), 112–117. https://doi.org/10.1111/j.1467-8721.2009.01619.

Orbach, I. (1994). Dissociation, physical pain, and suicide: A hypothesis. *Suicide and Life-Threatening Behavior, 24*(1), 68–79.

Palmier-Claus, J. E., Ainsworth, J., Machin, M., Dunn, G., Barkus, E., Barrowclough, C., et al. (2013). Affective instability prior to and afterthoughts about self-injury in individuals with and at-risk of psychosis: A mobile phone based study. *Archives of Suicide Research, 17*(3), 275–287. https://doi.org/10.1080/13811118.2013.805647.

Palmier-Claus, J. E., Taylor, P., Gooding, P., Dunn, G., & Lewis, S. (2012). Affective variability predicts suicidal ideation in individuals at ultra-high risk of developing psychosis: An experience sampling study. *British Journal of Clinical Psychology, 51*(1), 72–83. https://doi.org/10.1111/j.2044-8260.2011.02013.x.

Pavulans, K. S., Bolmsjö, I., Edberg, A.-K., & Öjehagen, A. (2012). Being in want of control: Experiences of being on the road to, and making, a suicide attempt. *International Journal of Qualitative Studies on Health and Well-Being, 7*.

Plöderl, M., & Fartacek, C. (2018). Known but unpredictable—an argument for complexity. *BJPsych Bulletin, 42*(2), 89-89.

Pöldinger, W. (1968). *Die Abschätzung der Suizidalität: Eine medizinisch-psychologische und medizinisch-soziologische Studie*. In Huber Hans (Ed.). Switzerland: Bern.

Ramsay, R. (1997). Chaos theory and crisis intervention: Toward a new meaning of equilibrium in understanding and helping people in crisis. *Child and Family, 1*(3), 23–35.

Reid, S. C., Kauer, S. D., Hearps, S. J., Crooke, A. H., Khor, A. S., Sanci, L. A., et al. (2013). A mobile phone application for the assessment and management of youth mental health problems in primary care: Health service outcomes from a randomised controlled trial of mobile type. *BMC Family Practice, 14*(1), 84. https://doi.org/10.1186/1471-2296-12-131.

Restifo, E., Kashyap, S., Hooke, G. R., & Page, A. C. (2015). Daily monitoring of temporal trajectories of suicidal ideation predict self-injury: A novel application of patient progress monitoring. *Psychotherapy Research, 25*(6), 705–713. https://doi.org/10.1080/10503307.2015.1006707.

Rogers, J. R. (2003). The anatomy of suicidology: A psychological science perspective on the status of suicide research. *Suicide and Life-Threatening Behavior, 33*(1), 9–20. https://doi.org/10.1521/suli.33.1.9.22783.

Rogers, M. L., Galynker, I., Yaseen, Z., DeFazio, K., & Joiner, T. E. (2017). An overview and comparison of two proposed suicide-specific diagnoses: Acute suicidal affective disturbance and suicide crisis syndrome. *Psychiatric Annals, 47*(8), 416–420.

Rudd, M. D. (2000). The suicidal mode: A cognitive-behavioral model of suicidality. *Suicide and Life-Threatening Behavior, 30*(1), 18–33. https://doi.org/10.1111/j.1943-278X.2000.tb01062.x.

Rudd, M. D., Berman, A. L., Joiner, T. E., Nock, M. K., Silverman, M. M., Mandrusiak, M., et al. (2006). Warning signs for suicide: Theory, research, and clinical applications. *Suicide and Life-Threatening Behavior, 36*, 255–262.

Ryff, C. D., Singer, B., Dienberg Love, G., & Essex, M. J. (1998). Resilience in adulthood and later life. In J. Lomranz (Ed.), *Handbook of aging and mental health* (pp. 69–96). New York: Plenum.

Salvatore, S., & Tschacher, W. (2012). Time dependency of psychotherapeutic exchanges: The contribution of the theory of dynamic systems in analyzing process. *Frontiers in Psychology, 25*(3), 253. https://doi.org/10.3389/fpsyg.2012.0025.

Schiepek, G., Eckert, H., Aas, B., Wallot, S., & Wallot, A. (2015). *Integrative psychotherapy: A feedback-driven dynamic systems approach.* Boston, MA: Hogrefe International Publishers.

Schiepek, G., Eckert, H., Honermann, H., & Weihrauch, S. (2001). Ordnungswandel in komplexen dynamischen Systemen: Das systemische Paradigma jenseits der Therapieschulen. *Hypnose und Kognition, 18*(1/2), 89–117.

Schiepek, G., Fartacek, C., Sturm, J., Kralovec, K., Fartacek, R., & Plöderl, M. (2011). Nonlinear dynamics: Theoretical perspectives and application to suicidology. *Suicide and Life-Threatening Behavior, 41*(6), 661–675. https://doi.org/10.1111/j.1943-278X.2011.00062.x.

Schiepek, G. K., Stöger-Schmidinger, B., Aichhorn, W., Schöller, H., & Aas, B. (2016). Systemic case formulation, individualized process monitoring, and state dynamics in a case of dissociative identity disorder. *Frontiers in Psychology, 7*, 1545.

Schiepek, G., & Strunk, G. (2010). The identification of critical fluctuations and phase transitions in short term and coarse-grained time series—a method for the real-time monitoring of human change processes. *Biological Cybernetics, 102*(3), 197–207. https://doi.org/10.1007/s00422-009-0362-1.

Schiepek, G., Tominschek, I., & Heinzel, S. (2014). Self-organization in psychotherapy: Testing the synergetic model of change processes. *Frontiers in Psychology, 5*, 1–11. https://doi.org/10.3389/fpsyg.2014.01089.

Schiepek, G., Tominschek, I., Heinzel, S., Aigner, M., Dold, M., Unger, A., et al. (2013). Discontinuous patterns of brain activation in the psychotherapy process of obsessive-compulsive disorder: Converging results from repeated fmri and daily self-reports. *PLoS One, 8*(8), e71863. https://doi.org/10.1371/journal.pone.0071863.

Schiepek, G. K., Viol, K., Aichhorn, W., Hütt, M.-T., Sungler, K., Pincus, D., et al. (2017). Psychotherapy is chaotic—(Not only) in a computational world. *Frontiers in Psychology, 8*, 379.

Shneidman, E. S. (1993). *Suicide as psychache: A clinical approach to self-destructive behavior.* New York: Jason Aronson.

Stam, C. J. (2005). Nonlinear dynamical analysis of EEG and MEG: Review of an emerging field. *Clinical Neurophysiology, 116*(10), 2266–2301.

Stanley, B., & Brown, G. K. (2012). Safety planning intervention: A brief intervention to mitigate suicide risk. *Cognitive and Behavioral Practice, 19*(2), 256–264. https://doi.org/10.1016/j.cbpra.2011.01.001.

Strunk, G., & Schiepek, G. (2006). *Systemische Psychologie: Eine Einführung in die komplexen Grundlagen menschlichen Verhaltens*. München: Elsevier.

Strunk, G., & Schiepek, G. (2014). *Therapeutisches Chaos: Eine Einführung in die Welt der Chaostheorie und der Komplexitätsforschung* (Göttingen: Hogrefe).

Van Heeringen, K. (2001). *Understanding suicidal behaviour: The suicidal process approach to research, treatment, and prevention* (Vol. 68). John Wiley & Sons Inc.

Webber, C. L., & Zbilut, J. P. (1994). Dynamical assessment of physiological systems and states using recurrence plot strategies. *Journal of Applied Physiology, 76*(2), 965–973.

Wenzel, A., & Beck, A. T. (2008). A cognitive model of suicidal behavior: Theory and treatment. *Applied and Preventive Psychology, 12*(4), 189–201. https://doi.org/10.1016/j.appsy.2008.05.001.

Wenze, S. J., & Miller, I. W. (2010). Use of ecological momentary assessment in mood disorders research. *Clinical Psychology Review, 30*(6), 794–804. https://doi.org/10.1016/j.cpr.2010.06.007.

WHO. (2015). *Suicide data*. Retrieved 10.04.2018 http://www.who.int/gho/mental_health/suicide_rates/en/.

Wichers, M., Simons, C., Kramer, I., Hartmann, J., Lothmann, C., Myin-Germeys, I., et al. (2011). Momentary assessment technology as a tool to help patients with depression help themselves. *Acta Psychiatrica Scandinavica, 124*(4), 262–272. https://doi.org/10.1111/j.1600-0447.2011.01749.x.

Witte, T. K., Fitzpatrick, K. K., Joiner, T. E., & Schmidt, N. B. (2005). Variability in suicidal ideation: A better predictor of suicide attempts than intensity or duration of ideation? *Journal of Affective Disorders, 88*(2), 131–136.

Yang, A. C., & Tsai, S.-J. (2013). Is mental illness complex? From behavior to brain. *Progress in Neuro-Psychopharmacology and Biological Psychiatry, 45*, 253–257. https://doi.org/10.1016/j.pnpbp.2012.09.015.

Yaseen, Z. S., Gilmer, E., Modi, J., Cohen, L. J., & Galynker, I. I. (2012). Emergency room validation of the revised suicide trigger scale (STS-3): A measure of a hypothesized suicide trigger state. *PLoS One, 7*(9), e45157.

CHAPTER 7

Connectedness and suicide

Bita Zareian, E. David Klonsky
University of British Columbia

Most theories of suicide focus on factors that cause suicide ideation and attempts, such as pain, hopelessness, and social isolation, as opposed to factors that make life worth living (Klonsky, Saffer, & Bryan, 2018). Similarly, research has focused far more on risk factors for suicide than protective factors (O'Connor & Nock, 2014). However, most people who develop suicide ideation do not make suicide attempts, and most people who make suicide attempts do not go on to die by suicide (Klonsky, May, & Saffer, 2016). In short, most people struggling with suicidality end up living long, productive lives.

Even and especially for those struggling with painful adversities and emotions, it is important to understand what makes life worth living and what keeps people alive. In this chapter we focus on one such construct: connectedness. First, we briefly describe the role of connectedness in major suicide theories; second, we review at length the empirical research on four forms of connectedness that are protective against suicide; third, we conclude by considering contemporary perspectives on connectedness and its measurement.

Connectedness in major theories of suicide

While seminal theories of suicide have focused on risk factors and causes of suicide, they also have implications for factors that might protect individuals from suicide ideation and attempts. For instance, Durkheim (1951) suggests that low social integration causes reduced sense of meaning and purpose in life, which in turn elevates suicide risk. His theory suggests that having connections with other individuals, such as a spouse, as well as with one's larger community and society, acts as a protective factor against suicide by giving the individual a reason to live. More recent theories of suicide have also focused on the importance of having a sense of connection to other

Alternatives to Suicide
ISBN 978-0-12-814297-4
https://doi.org/10.1016/B978-0-12-814297-4.00007-8

people as a protective factor against suicide. Joiner (2005) explains in his interpersonal theory of suicide that suicide ideation develops when an individual has a sense of thwarted belongingness and burdensomeness, suggesting once again that feelings of belonging to one's loved ones, and perhaps in a broader sense, to society, might protect the individual from suicide ideation.

However, connection to other *people* might not be the only form of connection that protects individuals from suicide. Durkheim (1951), for instance, suggests that being connected to a religion can protect an individual against suicide by giving a sense of meaning to the individual's life. Klonsky and May (2015) also consider connections beyond those to people in their Three-Step Theory (3ST) of suicide. The first part of the theory states that individuals who experience both pain and hopelessness are at risk of developing suicide ideation. However, the second part of the theory suggests that, in those experiencing pain and hopelessness, connectedness is protective against escalating suicide ideation. Their definition of connectedness is intentionally broad, and includes connections to a job, role, values, community, or any sense of purpose or meaning that may make life worth living even in the presence of pain (Klonsky & May, 2015). Thus, there are many forms of connectedness that hold promise as protective factors against suicide and provide reasons to live.

Empirical research on four forms of connectedness that are protective against suicide

While theories have been enormously helpful in conceptualizing the protective role of connectedness against suicidal thoughts and acts, it is of course necessary to conduct research and assess the validity of these theoretical perspectives. In this chapter we focus on four types of connectedness that appear to be protective against suicide: (a) a sense of purpose and meaning in life, (b) relationships, (c) religiosity, and (d) employment. While these variables can overlap, they each appear to have unique roles in protecting against suicide, and thus are discussed separately.

Sense of meaning and purpose in life

Many theorists have emphasised the importance of meaning of life for individuals' mental health (Frankl, 1985; Seligman, 2011; Wong, 2012). Almost all of these theories point to the fact that life can have different meanings for different people: what people perceive as meaningful in life varies significantly from person to person. Indeed, empirical research supports the notion of individualized meanings of life (Glaw, Kable, Hazelton, & Inder, 2017). Glaw et al. (2017) found that while there were many factors that participants endorsed as variables that give meaning to their lives, relationship were the most important and the most frequently endorsed. Relatedly, Debats (1999) found that the most important reasons for living for all participants were relationships, lifework, personal well-being, and self-actualization, and among those, the most frequently endorsed one among both patients and non-patients was relationships. Similarly, another group of researchers found that relationships were the most endorsed area of meaning in life, specifically among patients (Volkert, Schulz, Brütt, & Andreas, 2014). Taken together, two conclusions can be drawn from this work: first, relationships contribute to meaning of life for most people; and second, a variety of other factors also can contribute to meaning of life and can vary from person to person.

Additional research appears to support a third take-home message: reduced meaning in life is robust predictor of mental health problems, depression, and suicide risk. One study found that individuals with mental health problems find less meaning in life, and those with depression find even fewer reasons to live compared to individuals with non depressive forms of mental health problems (Volkert et al., 2014). Lower senses of purpose and meaning have also been linked to eating disorders (Marco, Cañabate, Pérez, & Llorca, 2017) and histories of childhood abuse (Lamis, Kapoor, & Evans, 2018). In addition, research has found that having a sense of meaning and purpose in life is negatively correlated with suicide ideation (Harlow, Newcomb, & Bentler, 1986). Similar results have been found among children, adolescents, and older adults (Heisel & Flett, 2016; Tan, Chen, Xia, & Hu, 2018; Wilchek-Aviad, 2015). Likewise, individuals with histories of suicide attempts report fewer life goals and purposes than those without a history of suicide attempt (Rodríguez, Salvador, & García-Alandete, 2017). All in all, research suggest that stronger perceptions of meaning in life and sense of purpose are protective factors against mental health problems generally and suicide ideation and attempts specifically.

Relationships

A great deal of research has focused on loneliness and isolation as risk factors for suicide ideation and attempt. For instance, research has found that individuals who live on their own are at heightened risk of suicide attempt, in comparison to individuals who live with family members (Denney, 2010). Conversely, having to care for a young child seem to act as a protective factor against suicide attempt (Denney, 2010). However, the extent to which living with others acts as a protective factor against suicide depends on many specifics, such as the nature of the relationships to others and the family structure and dynamics (Frey & Cerel, 2015).

Marriage. One form of relationship that has been studied frequently in relation to suicide risk is marriage. Research has most often found that individuals who are married are less likely to attempt suicide (Cheng, Chen, Chen, & Jenkins, 2000; Denney, Rogers, Krueger, & Wadsworth, 2009; Duberstein, Conwell, Conner, Eberly, & Caine, 2004) than those who are divorced, separated, or never married (Boardman, Grimbaldeston, Handley, Jones, & Willmott, 1999; Denney et al., 2009). Divorced individuals seem to be at the highest risk of suicide in comparison to other non-married groups of individuals (i.e., widowed and never married) and married individuals (Kyung-Sook, SangSoo, Sangjin, & Young-Jeon, 2018), suggesting that rejection of connectedness may be particularly harmful. In contrast, results for widowed individuals is mixed (Denney et al., 2009; Kposowa, 2000; Park, Lee, & Kim, 2018; Smith, Mercy, & Conn, 1988), with some studies suggesting that these individuals are not at a greater risk of suicide than married individuals (Kposowa, 2000).

Interestingly, the relationship between suicide and marital status may vary by key demographic factors. A few studies find that marriage is a stronger protective factor for males than females (Cantor & Slater, 1995; Denney et al., 2009; Kposowa, 2000). A recent meta-analysis found that divorce and widow-status increased suicide risk for men more than women (Kyung-Sook et al., 2018). Furthermore, this study found that age was also acting as a moderator variable, with non-married individuals (i.e., single, divorced, widowed) younger than 65 years old, especially females, at greater risk of suicide compared to non-married older than 65 years old. In other words, marriage seems most protective for younger individuals.

Of course, the quality of the relationship between romantic partners is also a variable that should be considered in assessing the relationship between marital status and suicide. As mentioned before, divorced individuals have the highest risk of suicide in comparison to individuals with other marital status, such as never-married individuals (Kyung-Sook et al., 2018), suggesting that perhaps conflict that results from divorce might contribute to the risk of suicide. Similarly, recent separation, recent bereavement, and having conflict and difficulties in relationships with the romantic partner all significantly increased the risk of suicide (Bastia & Kar, 2009; Boardman et al., 1999; Duberstein, 2004; Gururaj, Isaac, Subbakrishna, & Ranjani, 2004). These findings suggest that, while being married protects the individuals from suicide, having conflict in that relationship can have the reverse effect.

Parenthood. In addition to marriage, having children has been found to act as a protective factor against suicide (Denney, 2010). This relationship appears to be especially true for parents with younger children (Qin & Mortensen, 2003). Similar to the protective effect of marriage on risk of suicide, there seems to be a gender difference in the relationship between parenthood and suicide: mothers benefit from the protective effect of having children more than fathers (Krüger, Priebe, Fritsch, & Mundt, 2017; Qin & Mortensen, 2003). In their research, Qin and Mortensen (2003) found that for men, having children acted as protective factor only during the first year after the child's birth; in contrast, mothers were protected against suicide even when the children had reached the age of 18. Similarly, Krüger et al. (2017) found that while incarcerated mothers were at lower risk of suicide attempt in comparison to incarcerated females without children, incarcerated fathers did not differ from their childless male counterparts in risk of attempting suicide. Furthermore, research suggests that not only is having any children protective, but having more children is correlated with a reduced risk of suicide, a relationship that also seems to be stronger in females (Qin & Mortensen, 2003).

Another important factor in the association between parenthood and suicide is the quality of the parent-child relationship. Unfortunately, the research on the effect of parent-child relationship quality on parent's suicide risk is thin. One study found that, for parents without a history of mental illness, having a child diagnosed with a mental illness increases the risk of suicide (Qin & Mortensen, 2003), suggesting that the stress and relationship difficulties associated with raising a child with mental health problems, nullifies the protective effect of having a child. Furthermore, parents' suicide attempts are reported to frequently have been preceded by a conflict with a child or a conflict with the spouse about children (Cerel, 2006). More research is needed to further clarify the protective role of parenting against suicide.

Family Factors. Though living with (as opposed to without) family members appears to be protective against suicide (e.g., Boardman et al., 1999; Duberstein, 2004), there are many family composition variables that appear to influence suicide risk. In general, having larger families is protective against suicide, presumably because they afford more and richer opportunities for connection (Denney, Rogers, Krueger, & Wadsworth, 2009). However, being an oldest sibling increases risk for suicide, as does having more siblings (Çetin, 2001). More research is needed to clarify the sibling characteristics that increase and decrease suicide risk. Similarly, the relationship between suicide and number of parents at home is not clear. Some studies have found that children in one parent families are at increased risk of suicide attempt (Hollis, 1996). However, other studies have found that the number of parents that a child lives with is unrelated to suicide risk once other variables, such as age and gender, are controlled for (Lin, Lin, Hsieh, & Chang, 2014).

Extensive research suggests that the quality of family relationships is important for suicide risk. Research has consistently found a negative correlation between quality of parent-child relationship and suicide ideation in children (Chiu, Tseng, & Lin, 2017; Feng, Waldner, Cushon, Davy, & Neudorf, 2016; Lardier Jr, Barrios, Garcia-Reid, & Reid, 2016). For instance, Feng et al. (2016) found that school children who reported an excellent relationship with their parents were less likely to have suicide ideation in comparison to children who had moderate or poor relationship with their parents, suggesting that good parent-child relationship can protect against suicide ideation. Relatedly, Barzilay et al. (2015) found that while the effect of belongingness to parents was significantly related to suicide ideation, sense of belonging to peers was not. This finding emphasizes the importance of parent-child relationship in risk of suicide. Moreover, research has found that quarrelsome and disharmonious family environments significantly contribute to risk of suicide ideation (Chiu et al., 2017), even after controlling for variables such as depression (Hollis, 1996; Lin et al., 2014); thus, the relationship between parents not only affects the relationship of the parents with their child, but the child's suicide risk.

Social support. Apart from the family, one's extended social network also seems to play a role in protecting against suicide (King & Merchant, 2008). Johnson et al. (2002) found that, after controlling for demographic variables, not having close friends, having difficulty making new friends, and frequent argument and anger toward friends are associated with attempting suicide in late adolescence and early adulthood. Relatedly, among adolescent psychiatric inpatients, low level of close friendship and higher levels of peer rejection were associated with suicide ideation (Prinstein, Boergers, Spirito, Little, & Grapentine, 2000). There also seems to be some gender differences in the association between social network and suicidality among adolescent (Bearman & Moody, 2004; Kerr, Preuss, & King, 2006). A study found that adolescent girls, and not adolescent boys, were more likely to have suicide ideation if they were isolated from their peers or had intransitive friendships (Bearman & Moody, 2004). Furthermore, while attending a school with dense social networks protected adolescent girls from suicide ideation, it protected adolescent boys from suicide attempt (Bearman & Moody, 2004).

Apart from the effect of peer support in protecting adolescents from suicide, feeling of connectedness with school defined as "the belief by students that adults in the school community care about students' learning and about them as individuals" (Waters & Cross, 2010) seems to also protect adolescents from suicide ideation and attempt (Kidger, Araya, Donovan, & Gunnell, 2012; Marraccini & Brier, 2017). One study found that perceived teacher support decreased the risk of suicide among Latino adolescents by 23% (De Luca, Wyman, & Warren, 2012). Similarly, a study on South African adolescents showed that higher perceived teacher support was associated with lower risk of suicide (Peltzer, 2008). Therefore, it seems like, perceiving the support of adults other than the parents in adolescent's life can act as another barrier against suicide.

Social support seems to also act as a protective factor for adults (Endo et al., 2014; Hollingsworth et al. 2018; Xie et al., 2018). A study found that social connectedness, as measured by the number of past and present affiliations with social groups, and social support, measured by items such as "My friends really try to help me" (Zimet, Dahlem, Zimet, & Farley, 1988), were both inversely associated with suicide ideation, and both relationships were mediated by perceived burdensomeness among adults (Hollingsworth et al., 2018). However, this study has not differentiated between the effectiveness of different sources of support, and therefore, it is not clear whether the effectiveness of social support in this study is only because of perceived support from family members, or that other sources of support are also contributing to its protective effect. A study that has differentiated between sources of support found that in a sample of adults in Japan, lifetime and current suicide ideation were both associated with lower perceived social support and lower satisfaction with the quality of received support (Endo et al., 2014), and that other than family support, perceiving support from the neighbors, was the only factor negatively associated with suicide ideation (Endo et al., 2014). A study, assessing the role involvement in organized community groups as a proxy of social support, and the role of having a sense of community in protecting against suicide ideation, found that both social support and having a sense of community were correlated with lower level of suicide ideation at baseline; further, after controlling for host of other variables, higher availability of social support was associated with lower likelihood of developing suicide ideation in the follow up (Handley et al., 2012).

Similar relationships between social support and suicide has been found in older adults (Chang, Chan, & Yip, 2017). A longitudinal study in older age adults found that smaller social network size was associated with an increased likelihood of developing suicide ideation in the follow up (Lapierre et al., 2012). Relatedly, another study found that older adults who have higher number of friends and relatives or have more frequent visits from friends or relatives were less likely to have thoughts of death or suicide ideation (Bartels et al., 2002). Moreover, in a sample of older adults, participation in community activities was associated with reduced likelihood of having suicide ideation (Saïas, Beck, Bodard, Guignard, & Roscoät, 2012).

Therapeutic alliance. There is evidence for the effectiveness of different types of therapies in reducing suicide ideation and attempt (Lieb, Zanarini, Schmahl, Linehan, & Bohus, 2004; Liberman & Eckman, 1981). However, because very different approaches from very different theoretical backgrounds have been found to be effective in reducing suicide ideation, some have suggested that a factor common to these different therapies may account for at least some of their effectiveness: therapeutic alliance (Dunster-Page, Haddock, Wainwright, & Berry, 2017; Michel et al., 2011). One study showed that, across both behavioral and non-behavioral forms of therapy, therapist-rated therapeutic alliance was associated with reduced risk of suicide attempt among clients (Bedics, Atkins, Harned, & Linehan, 2015). Similarly, a study assessing the effect of the Attempted Suicide Short Intervention Program on patients with a recent suicide attempt found that better therapeutic alliance predicted lower suicide ideation at 12-month and 24-month follow-ups (Gysin-Maillart, Schwab, Soravia, Megert, & Michel, 2016). Furthermore, perceiving the therapeutic relationship as collaborative has been found to be associated with decreased suicide ideation (Ilgen et al., 2009). A meta-analytic review of the relationship between therapeutic alliance and suicidal thoughts and behaviors found that the risk of both suicide ideation and attempt is reduced by a stronger therapeutic alliance (Dunster-Page et al., 2017). Results suggest that a strong and positive relationship between therapist and client is a protective factor against suicide.

Religion

Decades of research suggests that religiosity is associated with reduced risk of suicide ideation and suicide attempt (Dervice et al., 2004; Martin, 1984; Kleiman & Liu, 2014). There have been several proposed direct and indirect mechanisms examined through which religiosity may act as a protective factor against suicide (Gearing & Lizardi, 2009).

Increased social connectedness. Being affiliated with a religious group and clergy can expands one's social network and can increase the perceived quality of relationships within the social network (Ellison & George, 1994). Furthermore, it has been suggested that being connected to "religious professionals" provides an additional layer of social support (Ellison, Vaaler, Flannelly, & Weaver, 2006). As explored extensively in previous sections, research has shown that an increase in social connectedness can act a protective factor against suicide. Based on these findings, it seems reasonable to think that religiosity can act as a buffer against suicide ideation and attempt via increasing opportunities for social support. Consistent with this hypothesis, a study found that public religiousness, and not private religiousness, was associated with reduced suicide ideation, and this relationship was mediated by the extent of social support (Robins & Fiske, 2009).

Relatedly, another study found that those who felt closer to their church members and interacted with their church members more frequently had a reduced likelihood of suicide ideation. However, frequency of interaction with church members was rendered insignificant when closeness to church members was controlled for (Chatters, Taylor, Lincoln, Nguyen, & Joe, 2011). Interestingly, this study found that those with a history of suicide attempt were more likely to report more frequent interactions with their church members, suggesting that, perhaps, individuals with a history of suicide attempt, seek an increase connectedness to life through interacting with their church members (Chatters et al., 2011).

Fear of punishment and moral objection to suicide. Most religions consider suicide a sin and prescribe punishments for an individual who attempts suicide. As a result, strong religious beliefs might act as a protective factor against suicidality (Gearing & Lizardi, 2009). Consistent with this hypothesis, research has found that religions that consider suicide unforgivable and a greater sin, like Islam, are associated with lower suicide rates than religions that are more forgiving of suicide, like Hinduism (Ineichen, 1998). Furthermore, moral objection to suicide is one of the variables that have been found to be negatively associated with both suicide ideation and suicide attempt, and the associations remained significant after controlling for demographic variables and other religion-related variables (Dervice et al., 2004; Dervice at al., 2011; Jongkind, van den Brink, Schaap-Jonker, van der Velde, & Braam, 2018). Furthermore, moral objections to suicide has also been found to be associated with lower levels of suicide risk factors such as depression, hopelessness, impulsivity, and anxiety, lower likelihood of suicide attempts, and more reasons for living (Lizardi et al., 2008).

Sense of meaning and purpose in life. Durkheim (1951) proposed that one of the factors contributing to the protective effect of religion against suicide is meaning and purpose. In other words, religion may provide individuals with an enhanced sense of purpose and meaning in life. Stack (1983) suggests that religion can provide meaning and purpose for one's suffrage. Religion depicts life's ups and downs as tests from God. Therefore, individuals with strong religious beliefs are likely to see their problems and pains not merely as reasons for unhappiness but as an integral part of a larger, meaningful context (Stack, 1983). In a qualitative study of individuals with psychotic disorders, half of these participants reported that religion is a protective factor for them against suicide because it gives them hope and a sense of meaning in life. Similarly, quantitative research suggests that giving meaning to life is one of the most important factors that contributes to protective effect of religion against suicide (Heisel & Flett, 2008).

Reduced risk factors for suicide. Gearing and Lizardi (2009) proposed that being religious can indirectly reduce risk of suicide attempt by reducing maladaptive behaviors and substance abuse that increase risk. Research has also supported this idea showing that those who are more religious are less likely to be aggressive (Mann, Bortinger; Oquendo, Currier, Li, & Brent, 2005), smoke (Martin, Kirkcaldy, & Siefen, 2003), and drink alcohol (Marsiglia, Ayers, & Hoffman, 2012), all of which has been linked to suicidal thoughts and behaviors.

Type of religion. Not all religions protect against suicide ideation and attempt to the same extent (Gearing & Lizardi, 2009). Suicide seem to be less prevalent among countries with majority Muslims or Jewish population (Levav & Aisenberg, 1989; Stack & Kposowa, 2011), and some research has shown that risk is lower among Muslims in comparison to Jewish populations (Levav & Aisenberg, 1989). Reasons for differences among religions are not completely clear. However, there might be several explanations. One possible explanation is that religions differ in how strictly they prohibit suicide. While suicide is considered a sin in Chritianity, Islam, and Judaism, the Christian prohibitions against suicide seem less strict as compared to Islam and Judaism (Gearing & Lizardi, 2009). For instance, while historically suicide has been considered a sin in Christianity (Gearing & Lizardi, 2009), the current view of Catholic Church (1994) is that for an act to be considered a sin, the executer of the act should be mentally competent. As a result, Gearing and Lizardi (2009) suggest that since suicide most often is considered a result of a mental illness, some Christians might not interpret it as a sin. However, this is not always the case in Islam and Judaism. In Judaism, some orthodox sources consider suicide a sin greater than homicide (Herring, 1984). Similarly, Quran considers suicide a great sin, and some Islamic countries still consider suicide as a crime (Al-Jahdali et al., 2004). This might result in both reduced suicide rates out of fear of punishment and stigma, as well as potential under-reporting of suicide in these countries (Al-Harrasi, Al Maqbali, & Al-Sinawi, 2016). On the other hand, some religions such as Hinduism have a less clear stance on suicide. Gearing and Lizardi (2009) explain that while suicide is discouraged in Hinduism, Hinduism's philosophy of reincarnation might suggest a more tolerant stance on suicide. The fact that suicide rates are higher in religions such as Hinduism, which has a more ambivalent stance on suicide (Kamal & Loewenthal, 2002), compared to religions that do consider suicide a sin (Ineichen, 1998; Kamal & Loewenthal, 2002) support the idea that religious conviction and fear of punishment in afterlife may protect against suicide.

God representation. Jongkind et al. (2018) define God representation as a "mental representation of personal relationship with God, and cognitions and emotions toward God". Previous research has shown that being fearful of God, feeling wronged by God, and believing in a punishing God are associated with negative mental health outcomes, such as depression, general anxiety disorder, social anxiety disorder, paranoia, and obsessive-compulsive disorder (Braam et al., 2008; Braam et al., 2014; Schaap-Jonker, van der Velde, Eurelings-Bontekoe, & Corveleyn, 2017; Silton, Flannelly, Galek, & Ellison, 2014). Conversely, having a positive perspective of God has been shown to be associated with more positive mental health outcomes and less sever mental health problems (Braam et al., 2008, 2014; Schaap-Jonker et al., 2017; Silton et al., 2014). Although the relationship between suicidality and God representation has not been thoroughly investigated, one study found that God representation was significantly related to suicide ideation; specifically, a positive and supportive God representation was associated with less suicide ideation, whereas a passive, angry, and anxiety-provoking God representation was associated with more suicide ideation (Jongkind et al., 2018). After controlling for demographic and other religion variables, the relationship between God representation and suicide ideation remained significant.

Religious salience. People who identify as belonging to a religion may still have important differences in religious salience, defined as the extent to which religion is significant in individual's day to day life (Jongkind et al., 2018). Religious salience has been found to be negatively correlated with suicide ideation (Jongkind et al., 2018; Kralovec, Kunrath, Fartacek, Pichler, & Ploderl, 2018). However, the protective effect of religious salience against suicide does not appear to remain once other demographic and religion-related variables are controlled for (Jongkind et al., 2018), suggesting that the relationship between religious salience and suicide ideation is mediated by third variables, such as social support or frequency of religious attendance (Edgell, Tranby, & Mather, 2013; Rushing, Corsentino; Hames, Sachs-Ericsson, & Steffens, 2013).

Frequency of religious attendance. While some studies have not found an association between frequency of religious attendance and suicidal thoughts and behavior (Jongkind et al., 2018), other studies find that frequency of religious attendance it related to reduced likelihood of suicide attempt, even after controlling for the role of perceived social support (Rasic et al., 2009; VanderWeele, Li, Tsai, & Kawachi, 2016). Consistent with this latter finding, a longitudinal study found that individuals who had higher frequency of religious attendance were prospectively less likely to attempt suicide, even after controlling for physical and mental health problems, social support, and socioeconomic status (Rasic, Robinson, Bolton, Bienvenu, & Sareen, 2011). Furthermore, a retrospective study found that those who died by suicide were less likely to have had religious participation compared to those who had died by natural causes — a difference that remained reliable even when controlling for social support (Nisbet, Duberstein, Conwell, & Seidlitz, 2000).

Frequency of prayer. Findings regarding the protective nature of praying on suicide risk is mixed. Whereas some studies have found that frequency of prayers is negatively correlated with suicide ideation (Kralovec et al., 2018), other studies have not found an association between private religious practices such as prayer and suicide related variables (Rushing, Corsentino, Hames, Sachs-Ericsson, & Steffens, 2013). Jongkind et al. (2018) found that frequency of prayers was inversely correlated with suicide ideation, suggesting a protective effect, however this relationship was rendered nonsignificant once demographic variables and other aspects of religiosity were controlled for. Results suggest that frequency of prayers may not have a direct relationship to or effect on suicide ideation.

Demographic moderators. Some demographic variables such as age and gender seem to affect the relationship between religiosity and suicide. For example, the protective effect of religion may be most pronounced among older adults (Wu, Wang, & Jia, 2015). A possible explanation is that older adults have suffered many losses of connection (e.g., children moving out, losing job due to retirement, deaths of friends) that increase their suicide risk; as a result, religion plays a stronger protective factor against suicide in this population (Wu et al., 2015). However, studies in elderly population has shown that the protective effect of religiosity on suicide ideation is only partially explained by increased social support (Rushing et al., 2013), suggesting that other aspects of religiosity such as perceived meaning in life help religion protect against suicide in this population.

Gender also appears to moderate the relationship between suicide and religion. For instance, Ozdel et al. (2009) found that among suicide attempters, females but not males were more likely to have lower religious beliefs. Similarly, another study found that religion was a stronger protective factor against suicide ideation in females, in comparison with males (Kralovec et al., 2018). For instance, frequency of religious attendance and prayers, as well as believing in the existence of god, was inversely associated with suicide ideation in females, but not in males. Furthermore, almost all aspects of religiosity were associated with increased belongingness in females, and with reduced capability for suicide in males (Kralovec et al., 2018), suggesting that religiosity might be acting as protective factor against suicidality through different pathways in different genders.

Employment

Literature on the relationship between employment and suicide has mostly focused on assessing employment as a risk factor for suicide. In fact, unemployment has consistently been found to be associated with elevated risk of suicide (Kraut & Walld, 2003; Milner, Page, & LaMontagne, 2014). These studies suggest that employment on its own can act as a protective factor against suicide ideation. Some have suggested that particular factors related to employment, such as type of employment or security of employment, are also important for suicide risk; the available research on these factors is reviewed below.

Type of occupation and skill. A recent meta-analytic review of suicide rates among different vocations found that clerical support workers and highly skilled managers had lower rates of suicide, suggesting that these types of jobs can potentially act as protective factors against suicide (Milner, Spittal, Pirkis, & LaMontagne, 2013). Furthermore, they found that, jobs requiring low skill levels were associated with elevated risk of suicide. Interestingly, however, jobs requiring higher skill levels were not associated with reduced risk of suicide in comparison to the average rate of suicide across different occupations.

Job security. Studies assessing the relationship between job security and suicide consistently find that individuals with low job security are at greater risk of suicide (Han, Chang, Won, Lee, & Ham, 2017; Kraut & Walld, 2003; Min, Park, Hwang, & Min, 2015). For instance, in a study across Europe, higher expectation of job loss in next 12 months was associated with elevated risk of suicide (Yur'yev, Värnik, Värnik, Sisask, & Leppik, 2012). This suggests that having a sense of stability and job security might act as a protective factor against suicide. Furthermore, some of these studies found that the relationship between job security and suicide was much stronger among male participants (Han et al., 2017; Yur'yev et al., 2012), hinting at a gender difference in the association between suicide and job security.

Connection to job. Connection to a job or a sense of responsibility to others can have an important protective role against suicide (Jobes & Mann, 1999). Some jobs more than others induce a sense of camaraderie and purpose, and come with strong organizational and social support at work. Examples may include soldiers in military, firefighters, and police (Stanley, Hom, & Joiner, 2016). These jobs can protect against suicide in multiple ways. Not only do they offer a strong sense of belonging and purpose, which can act as a protective factor against suicide, but because they can give individuals a sense of purpose and may reduce the sense of perceived burdensomeness that sometimes motivates suicide (Stanley et al., 2016).

Research on the relationship between military personnel and suicide has provided some evidence for this argument. For instance, several aspects of military life seem to protect soldiers from suicide, including: leadership, positive military attitudes, and unit cohesion (Hourani et al., 2018). Relatedly, among US Air Force personnel, dissatisfaction with lifestyle associated with being an Air Force employee was a predictor of suicide ideation among males, and this relationship was strongest among married men (Langhinrichsen-Rohling, Snarr, Slep, Heyman, & Foran, 2011).

Furthermore, among female employees of the Air Force, satisfaction with the workplace relationship was a predictor of suicide ideation. Notably, the associations between these workplace variables and suicide risk indicators remain even after controlling for family support and social support (Langhinrichsen-Rohling et al., 2011).

Contemporary perspectives on connectedness and its measurement

Recently, Klonsky et al. (2016) advocated for a particular framework to inform all of suicide research, theory, intervention, and prevention: The Ideation-to-Action Framework. This framework emphasizes that a) the development of suicide ideation and b) the progression from suicide ideation to potentially lethal suicide attempts are separate processes with separate explanations and predictors. Therefore, to better understand suicide and prevent suicide attempts, we need to gain a better understanding of the distinct factors that contribute to these distinct processes, and any intervention should be clear about which of its mechanisms are meant to reduce ideation and which are meant to impede the transition from ideation to attempts (Klonsky et al., 2016).

More recent theories of suicide, such as the interpersonal theory (Joiner, 2005), integrated motivational-volitional (O'Conner, 2011), and Three-Step Theory of suicide (Klonsky & May 2015), are positioned within this framework. These perspectives are sometimes collectively referred to as ideation-to-action theories of suicide (Klonsky et al., 2016). Of note, connectedness plays a prominent role in each of these theories.

Joiner's interpersonal theory of suicide posits that for an individual to develop suicide ideation, they need to perceive reduced sense of belonging to others (i.e., thwarted belongingness) and to perceive themselves as a burden to others (i.e., perceived burdensomeness; Joiner, 2005). This theory further explains that for an individual to progress from suicide ideation to suicide attempt, they need to develop acquired capability for suicide. Joiner (2005) explains that attempting suicide involves overcoming fears of pain, injury, and death that are barriers to attempting suicide. One way individuals overcome this fear, is through habituation to pain and anxiety associated with harming oneself through experiences such as non-suicidal self injury. This habituation to fear and anxiety associated with suicide attempt, in known as acquired capability for suicide.

In Joiner's theory, both factors required for the development of suicidal desire, thwarted belongingness and perceived burdensomeness, involve connectedness to others. Joiner suggests that the presence of either can cause passive suicidal ideation, but that the combination of thwarted belongingness and perceived burdensomeness is particularly pernicious and likely to lead to active suicidal desire.

The second ideation-to-action theory of suicide is the integrated motivational-volitional model (O'Connor, 2011). O'Connor (2011) proposes that the motivational phase (i.e., suicide ideation) is a product of feeling entrapped, where killing oneself is seen as the only avenue through which the individual can escape. These feelings of being trapped are often the result of defeat and humiliation experienced in one's life. The transition from defeat and humiliation to entrapment and from entrapment to suicide ideation are facilitated by specific moderators (O'Connor; 2011). Faced with defeat and humiliation, factors such as lower problem-solving abilities, less effective coping skills, or having negative cognitive biases, can act as moderators through which the individuals might develop feelings of entrapment. In turn, motivation moderators, factors such as thwarted belongingness, burdensomeness, and low social support, result in the development suicide ideation as a solution to feeling entrapped (O'Connor, 2011). Finally, progression from motivation phase to volitional phase, or in other words progression from suicide ideation to attempt, is facilitated by volitional moderators, which according to O'Connor (2011) are factors such as impulsivity, access to means, and fearlessness about death.

Once again, we can see the prominent role of connectedness in developing suicide ideation. The role of connectedness is specially pronounced in motivational moderators that helps individuals progress from feeling entrapped to developing suicide ideation. According to O'Connor (2011), having connection to other individuals can offer avenues other than suicide through which the individual can escape entrapment, and as a result can prevent or alleviate suicide ideation.

The Three-Step Theory of suicide (Klonsky & May 2015), is the most recent ideation-to-action theory of suicide. In this theory, Klonsky and May (2015) suggest that pain and hopelessness are both required for development of suicide ideation. However, to progress from moderate suicide ideation to strong suicide ideation, one's pain needs to outweigh one's connectedness. The Three-Step Theory defines pain and connectedness more broadly than previous theories of suicide. In the context of Three-Step Theory, pain can result from myriad sources, including social isolation, perceived burdensomeness, thwarted belongingness, feelings of entrapment, or even physical pain. Connectedness is also defined more broadly and includes factors such as connection to other people, a job, a role, or anything that gives a sense of purpose and meaning to life (Klonsky & May 2015). Finally, to progress from suicide ideation to attempt, one needs to have capability to attempt suicide. Capability can be acquired capability as defined by Joiner (2005) in interpersonal theory, or can be practical capability (e.g., access to firearms) or dispositional capability (e.g., low pain sensitivity).

Once again, we can observe the importance of connectedness in developing suicide ideation. According to Three-Step Theory, reduced connectedness can result in psychological pain, and as a result, can contribute to development of suicide ideation. Reduced connectedness can also reduce hope for a better future. At the same time, strong connectedness can act as a protective factor against developing strong suicide ideation in those otherwise experiencing pain and hopelessness. Even for someone who experiences pain in day to day life, and who is hopeless about the pain stopping, a sense of strong connectedness can make life worth living.

Given the prominent role of connectedness in theories of suicide, careful thought has gone into delineating and measuring this construct. There have been some recent efforts to develop measures of connectedness that are well-matched to the forms of connectedness highlighted in recent theories of suicide. For instance, Van Orden, Cukrowicz, Witte, and Joiner (2011) developed Interpersonal Needs Questionnaire (INQ) to assess perceived burdensomeness and thwarted belongingness, variables that in interpersonal theory of suicide (Joiner, 2005) contribute to development of suicide ideation. While INQ has been used extensively to measure connectedness in the context of suicide research, it only focuses on connectedness to other individuals and does not address connection to other aspects in individuals' life that can give them a sense of purpose and meaning, and as a result, might prevent them from developing suicide ideation. As Klonsky and May's (2015) Three-Step Theory of suicide proposes, individuals can feel connected to life through a sense of connection to others as well as factors such as roles, projects or interests. However, this definition of connectedness is broader than other definitions, and a challenge will be to develop a measure that covers the entire construct and not just a part. So far research has used the INQ belongingness subscale to measure connectedness for the purpose of testing the Three-Step Theory (Klonsky & May 2015).

Even beyond the Three-Step Theory, there is a need to develop sufficiently broad measures of connectedness. Over and over again connectedness features prominently in theories of suicide, though in different forms. Moreover, as illustrated in our research review, connectedness can be conceptualized in different ways — connection to people, to religion, to employment, to a sense of meaning — and each of these versions of connection have been found to be protective against suicide risk. Therefore, a useful next step in the field might be to develop a measure of connection that is sufficiently broad and multi-dimensional, and that can therefore cover the different forms of connectedness that have been emphasized in theories and examined in various studies on suicide risk. Through better measurement we can better understand how individuals perceive and value connection in their lives, and the role that these connections play not just in suicide risk but in contributing to a life that feels meaningful and worth living.

References

Al-Harrasi, A., Al Maqbali, M., & Al-Sinawi, H. (2016). Surviving a suicide attempt. *Oman Medical Journal, 31*(5), 378–380. https://doi.org/10.5001/omj.2016.74.

Al-Jahdali, H., Al-Johani, A., Al-Hakawi, A., Arabi, Y., Ahmed, Q. A., Altowirky, J., et al. (2004). Pattern and risk factors for intentional drug overdose in Saudi Arabia. *Canadian Journal of Psychiatry, 49*(5), 331–334. https://doi.org/10.1177/070674370404900509.

Bartels, S. J., Coakley, E., Oxman, T. E., Constantino, G., Oslin, D., Chen, H., et al. (2002). Suicidal and death ideation in older primary care patients with depression, anxiety, and at-risk alcohol use. *American Journal of Geriatric Psychiatry, 10*(4), 417–427. https://doi.org/10.1097/00019442-200207000-00008.

Barzilay, S., Feldman, D., Snir, A., Apter, A., Carli, V., Hoven, C. W., & Wasserman, D. (2015). The interpersonal theory of suicide and adolescent suicidal behavior. *Journal of Affective Disorders, 183*, 68–74.

Bastia, B. K., & Kar, N. (2009). A psychological autopsy study of suicidal hanging from Cuttack, India: Focus on stressful life situations. *Archives of Suicide Research, 13*(1), 100–104.

Bearman, P. S., & Moody, J. (2004). Suicide and friendships among American adolescents. *American Journal of Public Health, 94*(1), 89–95.

Bedics, J. D., Atkins, D. C., Harned, M. S., & Linehan, M. M. (2015). The therapeutic alliance as a predictor of outcome in dialectical behavior therapy versus nonbehavioral psychotherapy by experts for borderline personality disorder. *Psychotherapy, 52*(1), 67–77. https://doi.org/10.1037/a0038457.

Boardman, A. P., Grimbaldeston, A. H., Handley, C., Jones, P. W., & Willmott, S. (1999). The north staffordshire suicide study: A case–control study of suicide in one health district. *Psychological Medicine, 29*(1), 27–33.

Braam, A. W., Schaap-Jonker, H., Mooi, B., Ritter, D.d., Beekman, A. T. F., & Deeg, D. J. H. (2008). God image and mood in old age: Results from a community-based pilot study in The Netherlands. *Mental Health, Religion & Culture, 11*(2), 221–237. https://doi.org/10.1080/13674670701245274.

Braam, A. W., Schaap-Jonker, H., van der Horst, Marleen, H. L., Steunenberg, B., Beekman, A. T. F., et al. (2014). Twelve-year history of late-life depression and subsequent feelings to god. *American Journal of Geriatric Psychiatry, 22*(11), 1272–1281. https://doi.org/10.1016/j.jagp.2013.04.016.

Cantor, C. H., & Slater, P. J. (1995). Marital breakdown, parenthood, and Suicide. *Journal of Family Studies, 1*(2), 91–102.

Catholic Church. (1994). *United States of America: United States Catholic conference*. Inc Libreria Editrice Vaticana.

Cerel, J. (April 2006). Suicide attempts in parents of minor children. In *Paper presented at the annual conference of the American Association of Suicidology, Seattle, WA*.

Çetin, F.Ç. (2001). Suicide attempts and self-image among Turkish adolescents. *Journal of Youth and Adolescence, 30*(5), 641–651.

Chang, Q., Chan, C. H., & Yip, P. S. (2017). A meta-analytic review on social relationships and suicidal ideation among older adults. *Social Science & Medicine, 191*, 65–76.

Chatters, L. M., Taylor, R. J., Lincoln, K. D., Nguyen, A., & Joe, S. (2011). Church-based social support and suicidality among african americans and black caribbeans. *Archives of Suicide Research, 15*(4), 337–353. https://doi.org/10.1080/13811118.2011.615703.

Cheng, A. T. A., Chen, T. H. H., Chen, C., & Jenkins, R. (2000). Psychosocial and psychiatric risk factors for suicide: Case–control psychological autopsy study. *The British Journal of Psychiatry, 177*(4), 360–365. https://doi.org/10.1192/bjp.177.4.360.

Chiu, Y. C., Tseng, C. Y., & Lin, F. G. (2017). Gender differences and stage-specific influence of parent–adolescent conflicts on adolescent suicidal ideation. *Psychiatry Research, 255*, 424–431.

De Luca, S. M., Wyman, P., & Warren, K. (2012). Latina adolescent suicide ideations and attempts: Associations with connectedness to parents, peers, and teachers. *Suicide and Life-Threatening Behavior, 42*(6), 672–683. https://doi.org/10.1111/j.1943-278X.2012.00121.x.

Debats, D. L. (1999). Sources of meaning: An investigation of significant commitments in life. *Journal of Humanistic Psychology, 39*(4), 30–57.

Denney, J. T. (2010). Family and household formations and suicide in the United States. *Journal of Marriage and Family, 72*(1), 202–213.

Denney, J. T., Rogers, R. G., Krueger, P. M., & Wadsworth, T. (2009). Adult suicide mortality in the United States: Marital status, family size, socioeconomic status, and differences by sex. *Social Science Quarterly, 90*(5), 1167–1185. https://doi.org/10.1111/j.1540-6237.2009.00652.x.

Dervic, K., Carballo, J., Baca-Garcia, E., Galfalvy, H., Mann, J., Brent, D., et al. (2011). Moral or religious objections to suicide may protect against suicidal behavior in bipolar disorder. *Journal of Clinical Psychiatry, 72*(10), 1390–1396. https://doi.org/10.4088/JCP.09m05910gre.

Dervic, K., Oquendo, M. A., Grunebaum, M. F., Ellis, S., Burke, A. K., & Mann, J. J. (2004). Religious affiliation and suicide attempt. *American Journal of Psychiatry, 161*(12), 2303–2308. https://doi.org/10.1176/appi.ajp.161.12.2303.

Duberstein, P. R., Conwell, Y., Conner, K. R., Eberly, S., & Caine, E. D. (2004). Suicide at 50 years of age and older: Perceived physical illness, family discord and financial strain. *Psychological Medicine, 34*(1), 137–146. https://doi.org/10.1017/S0033291703008584.

Dunster-Page, C., Haddock, G., Wainwright, L., & Berry, K. (2017). The relationship between therapeutic alliance and patient's suicidal thoughts, self-harming behaviours and suicide attempts: A systematic review. *Journal of Affective Disorders, 223*, 165–174. https://doi.org/10.1016/j.jad.2017.07.040.

Durkheim, E. (1951). In G. Simpson, J. A. Spaulding, & G. Simpson (Eds.), *Suicide: A study in sociology*.

Edgell, P., Tranby, E. P., & Mather, D. M. (2013). Profiles of anticipated support: Religion's place in the composition of Americans' emotional support networks. *Journal for the Scientific Study of Religion, 52*(2), 293–308.

Ellison, C. G., & George, L. K. (1994). Religious involvement, social ties, and social support in a southeastern community. *Journal for the Scientific Study of Religion, 33*(1), 46–61. https://doi.org/10.2307/1386636.

Ellison, C. G., Vaaler, M. L., Flannelly, K. J., & Weaver, A. J. (2006). The clergy as a source of mental health assistance: What americans believe. *Review of Religious Research, 48*(2), 190–211.

Endo, G., Tachikawa, H., Fukuoka, Y., Aiba, M., Nemoto, K., Shiratori, Y., et al. (2014). How perceived social support relates to suicidal ideation: A Japanese social resident survey. *International Journal of Social Psychiatry, 60*(3), 290–298.

Feng, C. X., Waldner, C., Cushon, J., Davy, K., & Neudorf, C. (2016). Suicidal ideation in a community-based sample of elementary school children: A multilevel and spatial analysis. *Canadian Journal of Public Health, 107*(1), 100–105.

Frankl, V. E. (1985). *Man's search for meaning*. Simon and Schuster.

Frey, L. M., & Cerel, J. (2015). Risk for suicide and the role of family: A narrative review. *Journal of Family Issues, 36*(6), 716–736.

Gearing, R. E., & Lizardi, D. (2009). Religion and suicide. *Journal of Religion and Health, 48*(3), 332–341. https://doi.org/10.1007/s10943-008-9181-2.

Glaw, X., Kable, A., Hazelton, M., & Inder, K. (2017). Meaning in life and meaning of life in mental health care: An integrative literature review. *Issues in Mental Health Nursing, 38*(3), 243–252.

Gururaj, G., Isaac, M. K., Subbakrishna, D. K., & Ranjani, R. (2004). Risk factors for completed suicides: A case-control study from Bangalore, India. *Injury Control and Safety Promotion, 11*(3), 183–191.

Gysin-Maillart, A., Schwab, S., Soravia, L., Megert, M., & Michel, K. (2016). A novel brief therapy for patients who attempt suicide: A 24-months follow-up randomized controlled study of the attempted suicide short intervention program (ASSIP). *PLoS Medicine, 13*(3), e1001968. https://doi.org/10.1371/journal.pmed.1001968.

Han, K.-M., Chang, J., Won, E., Lee, M.-S., & Ham, B.-J. (2017). Precarious employment associated with depressive symptoms and suicidal ideation in adult wage workers. *Journal of Affective Disorders, 218*, 201–209.

Handley, T. E., Inder, K. J., Kelly, B. J., Attia, J. R., Lewin, T. J., Fitzgerald, M. N., et al. (2012). You've got to have friends: The predictive value of social integration and support in suicidal ideation among rural communities. *Social Psychiatry and Psychiatric Epidemiology, 47*(8), 1281–1290. https://doi.org/10.1007/s00127-011-0436-y.

Harlow, L. L., Newcomb, M. D., & Bentler, P. M. (1986). Depression, self-derogation, substance use, and suicide ideation: Lack of purpose in life as a mediational factor. *Journal of Clinical Psychology, 42*(1), 5–21.

Heisel, M. J., & Flett, G. L. (2008). Psychological resilience to suicide ideation among older adults. *Clinical Gerontologist, 31*(4), 51–70. https://doi.org/10.1080/07317110801947177.

Heisel, M. J., & Flett, G. L. (2016). Does recognition of meaning in life confer resiliency to suicide ideation among community-residing older adults? A longitudinal investigation. *American Journal of Geriatric Psychiatry, 24*(6), 455–466. https://doi.org/10.1016/j.jagp.2015.08.007.

Hollingsworth, D. W., Slish, M. L., Wingate, L. R., Davidson, C. L., Rasmussen, K. A., O'Keefe, V. M., et al. (2018). The indirect effect of perceived burdensomeness on the relationship between indices of social support and suicide ideation in college students. *Journal of American College Health, 66*(1), 9–16.

Herring, B. (1984). *Jewish ethics and Halakhah for our time: sources and commentary, 1*. KTAV Publishing House, Inc.

Hollis, C. (1996). Depression, family environment, and adolescent suicidal behavior. *Journal of the American Academy of Child & Adolescent Psychiatry, 35*(5), 622–630.

Hourani, L. L., Williams, J., Lattimore, P. K., Morgan, J. K., Hopkinson, S. G., Jenkins, L., et al. (2018). Workplace victimization risk and protective factors for suicidal behavior among active duty military personnel. *Journal of Affective Disorders, 236*, 45–51.

Ilgen, M. A., Czyz, E. K., Welsh, D. E., Zeber, J. E., Bauer, M. S., & Kilbourne, A. M. (2009). A collaborative therapeutic relationship and risk of suicidal ideation in patients with bipolar disorder. *Journal of Affective Disorders, 115*(1), 246–251. https://doi.org/10.1016/j.jad.2008.07.019.

Ineichen, B. (1998). The influence of religion on the suicide rate: Islam and hinduism compared. *Mental Health, Religion & Culture, 1*(1), 31–36. https://doi.org/10.1080/13674679808406495.

Jobes, D. A., & Mann, R. E. (1999). Reasons for living versus reasons for dying: Examining the internal debate of suicide. *Suicide and Life-Threatening Behavior, 29*(2), 97–104.

Johnson, J. G., Cohen, P., Gould, M. S., Kasen, S., Brown, J., & Brook, J. S. (2002). Childhood adversities, interpersonal difficulties, and risk for suicide attempts during late adolescence and early adulthood. *Archives of General Psychiatry, 59*(8), 741–749.

Joiner, T. (2005). *Why people die by suicide.* Cambridge, MA, US: Harvard University Press.

Jongkind, M., van den Brink, B., Schaap-Jonker, H., van der Velde, N., & Braam, A. W. (2018). Dimensions of religion associated with suicide attempt and suicide ideation in depressed, religiously affiliated patients. *Suicide and Life-Threatening Behavior.* https://doi.org/10.1111/sltb.12456.

Kamal, Z., & Loewenthal, K. M. (2002). Suicide beliefs and behaviour among young Muslims and Hindus in the UK. *Mental Health, Religion & Culture, 5*(2), 111–118.

Kerr, D. C., Preuss, L. J., & King, C. A. (2006). Suicidal adolescents' social support from family and peers: Gender-specific associations with psychopathology. *Journal of Abnormal Child Psychology, 34*(1), 99–110.

Kidger, J., Araya, R., Donovan, J., & Gunnell, D. (2012). The effect of the school environment on the emotional health of adolescents: A systematic review. *Pediatrics, 129*(5), 925–949.

King, C. A., & Merchant, C. R. (2008). Social and interpersonal factors relating to adolescent suicidality: A review of the literature. *Archives of Suicide Research, 12*(3), 181–196.

Kleiman, E., & Liu, R. (2014). Prospective prediction of suicide in a nationally representative sample: Religious service attendance as a protective factor. *British Journal of Psychiatry, 204*(4), 262–266. https://doi.org/10.1192/bjp.bp.113.128900.

Klonsky, E. D., & May, A. M. (2015). The three-step theory (3ST): A new theory of suicide rooted in the 'ideation-to-action' framework. *International Journal of Cognitive Therapy, 8*(2), 114–129. https://doi.org/10.1521/ijct.2015.8.2.114.

Klonsky, E. D., May, A. M., & Saffer, B. Y. (2016). Suicide, suicide attempts, and suicidal ideation. *Annual Review of Clinical Psychology, 12*, 307–330.

Klonsky, E. D., Saffer, B. Y., & Bryan, C. J. (2018). Ideation-to-action theories of suicide: A conceptual and empirical update. *Current Opinion in Psychology, 22*, 38–43.

Kposowa, A. J. (2000). Marital status and suicide in the national longitudinal mortality study. *Journal of Epidemiology & Community Health, 54*(4), 254–261. https://doi.org/10.1136/jech.54.4.254 (1979-).

Kralovec, K., Kunrath, S., Fartacek, C., Pichler, E., & Ploderl, M. (2018). The gender-specific associations between Religion/Spirituality and suicide risk in a sample of austrian psychiatric inpatients. *Suicide and Life-Threatening Behavior, 48*(3), 281–293. https://doi.org/10.1111/sltb.12349.

Kraut, A., & Walld, R. (2003). Influence of lack of full-time employment on attempted suicide in Manitoba, Canada. *Scandinavian Journal of Work, Environment & Health*, 15–21.

Krüger, S., Priebe, S., Fritsch, R., & Mundt, A. P. (2017). Burden of separation and suicide risk of prisoners with minor children. *International Journal of Law and Psychiatry, 52*, 55–61.

Kyung-Sook, W., SangSoo, S., Sangjin, S., & Young-Jeon, S. (2018). Marital status integration and suicide: A meta-analysis and meta-regression. *Social Science & Medicine, 197*, 116–126. https://doi.org/10.1016/j.socscimed.2017.11.053.

Lamis, D. A., Kapoor, S., & Evans, A. B. (2018). Childhood sexual abuse and suicidal ideation among bipolar patients: Existential but not religious well-being as a protective factor. *Suicide and Life-Threatening Behavior*. https://doi.org/10.1111/sltb.12438.

Langhinrichsen-Rohling, J., Snarr, J. D., Slep, A. M. S., Heyman, R. E., & Foran, H. M. (2011). Risk for suicidal ideation in the US Air Force: An ecological perspective. *Journal of Consulting and Clinical Psychology, 79*(5), 600.

Lapierre, S., Boyer, R., Desjardins, S., Dubé, M., Lorrain, D., Préville, M., et al. (2012). Daily hassles, physical illness, and sleep problems in older adults with wishes to die. *International Psychogeriatrics, 24*(2), 243–252. https://doi.org/10.1017/S1041610211001591.

Lardier, D. T., Jr., Barrios, V. R., Garcia-Reid, P., & Reid, R. J. (2016). Suicidal ideation among suburban adolescents: The influence of school bullying and other mediating risk factors. *Journal of Child and Adolescent Mental Health, 28*(3), 213–231.

Levav, I., & Aisenberg, E. (1989). Suicide in Israel: Crossnational comparisons. *Acta Psychiatrica Scandinavica, 79*(5), 468–473. https://doi.org/10.1111/j.1600-0447.1989.tb10289.x.

Liberman, R. P., & Eckman, T. (1981). Behavior therapy vs insight-oriented therapy for repeated suicide attempters. *Archives of General Psychiatry, 38*(10), 1126–1130. https://doi.org/10.1001/archpsyc.1981.01780350060007.

Lieb, K., Zanarini, M. C., Schmahl, C., Linehan, M. M., & Bohus, M. (2004). Borderline personality disorder. *The Lancet, 364*(9432), 453–461.

Lin, F. G., Lin, J. D., Hsieh, Y. H., & Chang, C. Y. (2014). Quarrelsome family environment as an enhanced factor on child suicidal ideation. *Research in Developmental Disabilities, 35*(12), 3245–3253.

Lizardi, D., Dervic, K., Grunebaum, M., Burke, A., Mann, J., & Oquendo, M. (2008). The role of moral objections to suicidal to suicide in the assessment patients. *Journal of Psychiatric Research, 42*(10), 815–821. https://doi.org/10.1016/j.jpsychires.2007.09.007.

Mann, J. J., Bortinger, J., Oquendo, M. A., Currier, D., Li, S., & Brent, D. A. (2005). Family history of suicidal behavior and mood disorders in probands with mood disorders. *American Journal of Psychiatry, 162*(9), 1672–1679. https://doi.org/10.1176/appi.ajp.162.9.1672.

Marco, J. H., Cañabate, M., Pérez, S., & Llorca, G. (2017). Associations among meaning in life, body image, psychopathology, and suicide ideation in Spanish participants with eating disorders. *Journal of Clinical Psychology, 73*(12), 1768–1781. https://doi.org/10.1002/jclp.22481.

Marraccini, M. E., & Brier, Z. M. (2017). School connectedness and suicidal thoughts and behaviors: A systematic meta-analysis. *School Psychology Quarterly, 32*(1), 5.

Marsiglia, F. F., Ayers, S. L., & Hoffman, S. (2012). Religiosity and adolescent substance use in central mexico: Exploring the influence of internal and external religiosity on cigarette and alcohol use. *American Journal of Community Psychology, 49*(1), 87–97. https://doi.org/10.1007/s10464-011-9439-9.

Martin, W. T. (1984). Religiosity and United States suicide rates, 1972-1978. *Journal of Clinical Psychology*, 40(5), 1166–1169. https://doi.org/10.1002/1097-4679(198409)40:5<1166::AID- JCLP2270400507>3.0.CO;2-T.

Martin, T., Kirkcaldy, B., & Siefen, G. (2003). Antecedents of adult wellbeing: Adolescent religiosity and health. *Journal of Managerial Psychology, 18*(5), 453–470. https://doi.org/10.1108/02683940310484044.

Michel, K. (2011). General aspects of therapeutic alliance. In K. Michel, D. A. Jobes, K. Michel, & D. A. Jobes (Eds.), *Building a therapeutic alliance with the suicidal patient* (pp. 13–28). Washington, DC, US: American Psychological Association. https://doi.org/10.1037/12303-001.

Milner, A., Page, A., & LaMontagne, A. D. (2014). Cause and effect in studies on unemployment, mental health and suicide: A meta-analytic and conceptual review. *Psychological Medicine, 44*(5), 909–917.

Milner, A., Spittal, M. J., Pirkis, J., & LaMontagne, A. D. (2013). Suicide by occupation: Systematic review and meta-analysis. *The British Journal of Psychiatry, 203*(6), 409–416.

Min, K. B., Park, S. G., Hwang, S. H., & Min, J. Y. (2015). Precarious employment and the risk of suicidal ideation and suicide attempts. *Preventive Medicine, 71*, 72–76.

Nisbet, P. A., Duberstein, P. R., Conwell, Y., & Seidlitz, L. (2000). The effect of participation in religious activities on suicide versus natural death in adults 50 and older. *The Journal of Nervous and Mental Disease, 188*(8), 543–546.

O'Connor, R. C. (2011). Towards an integrated motivational–volitional model of suicidal behaviour. *International handbook of suicide prevention: Research, policy and practice, 1*, 181–198.

O'Connor, R. C., & Nock, M. K. (2014). The psychology of suicidal behaviour. *Lancet Psychiatry, 1*, 73–85.

Ozdel, O., Varma, G., Atesci, F. C., Oguzhanoglu, N. K., Karadag, F., & Amuk, T. (2009). Characteristics of suicidal behavior in a turkish sample. *Crisis, 30*(2), 90–93. https://doi.org/10.1027/0227-5910.30.2.90.

Park, S. K., Lee, C. K., & Kim, H. (2018). Suicide mortality and marital status for specific ages, genders, and education levels in South Korea: Using a virtually individualized dataset from national aggregate data. *Journal of Affective Disorders, 237*, 87–93.

Peltzer, K. (2008). Social support and suicide risk among secondary school students in Cape Town, South Africa. *Psychological Reports, 103*(3), 653–660. https://doi.org/10.2466/PR0.103.7.653-660.

Prinstein, M. J., Boergers, J., Spirito, A., Little, T. D., & Grapentine, W. L. (2000). Peer functioning, family dysfunction, and psychological symptoms in a risk factor model for adolescent inpatients' suicidal ideation severity. *Journal of Clinical Child Psychology, 29*(3), 392–405.

Qin, P., & Mortensen, P. B. (2003). The impact of parental status on the risk of completed suicide. *Archives of General Psychiatry, 60*(8), 797–802.

Rasic, D. T., Belik, S. L., Elias, B., Katz, L. Y., Enns, M., Sareen, J., et al. (2009). Spirituality, religion and suicidal behavior in a nationally representative sample. *Journal of Affective Disorders, 114*(1–3), 32–40.

Rasic, D., Robinson, J. A., Bolton, J., Bienvenu, O. J., & Sareen, J. (2011). Longitudinal relationships of religious worship attendance and spirituality with major depression, anxiety disorders, and suicidal ideation and attempts: Findings from the baltimore epidemiologic catchment area study. *Journal of Psychiatric Research, 45*(6), 848–854. https://doi.org/10.1016/j.jpsychires.2010.11.014.

Robins, A., & Fiske, A. (2009). Explaining the relation between religiousness and reduced suicidal behavior: Social support rather than specific beliefs. *Suicide and Life-Threatening Behavior, 39*(4), 386–395. https://doi.org/10.1521/suli.2009.39.4.386.

Rodríguez, S. P., Salvador, J. M., & García-Alandete, J. (2017). The role of hopelessness and meaning in life in a clinical sample with non-suicidal self-injury and suicide attempts. *Psicothema, 29*(3), 323–328.

Rushing, N., Corsentino, E., Hames, J., Sachs-Ericsson, N., & Steffens, D. (2013). The relationship of religious involvement indicators and social support to current and past suicidality among depressed older adults. *Aging & Mental Health, 17*(3), 366–374. https://doi.org/10.1080/13607863.2012.738414.

Saïas, T., Beck, F., Bodard, J., Guignard, R., & Roscoät, E.d. (2012). Social participation, social environment and death ideations in later life. *PLoS One, 7*(10). https://doi.org/10.1371/journal.pone.0046723.

Schaap-Jonker, H., van der Velde, N., Eurelings-Bontekoe, E. H. M., & Corveleyn, J. M. T. (2017). Types of god representations and mental health: A person-oriented approach. *The International Journal for the Psychology of Religion, 27*(4), 199–214. https://doi.org/10.1080/10508619.2017.1382119.

Seligman, M. E. (2011). Flourish: A visionary new understanding of happiness and well-being. *Policy, 27*(3), 60–61.

Silton, N. R., Flannelly, K. J., Galek, K., & Ellison, C. G. (2014). Beliefs about god and mental health among american adults. *Journal of Religion and Health, 53*(5), 1285–1296. https://doi.org/10.1007/s10943-013-9712-3.

Smith, J. C., Mercy, J. A., & Conn, J. M. (1988). Marital status and the risk of suicide. *American Journal of Public Health, 78*(1), 78–80.

Stack, S. (1983). The effect of religious commitment on suicide: A cross-national analysis. *Journal of Health and Social Behavior, 24*(4), 362–374. https://doi.org/10.2307/2136402.

Stack, S., & Kposowa, A. J. (2011). Religion and suicide acceptability: A cross-national analysis. *Journal for the Scientific Study of Religion, 50*(2), 289–306. https://doi.org/10.1111/j.1468- 5906.2011.01568.x.

Stanley, I. H., Hom, M. A., & Joiner, T. E. (2016). A systematic review of suicidal thoughts and behaviors among police officers, firefighters, EMTs, and paramedics. *Clinical Psychology Review, 44*, 25–44.

Tan, L., Chen, J., Xia, T., & Hu, J. (2018). Predictors of suicidal ideation among children and adolescents: Roles of mental health status and meaning in life. *Child and Youth Care Forum, 47*(2), 219–231. https://doi.org/10.1007/s10566-017-9427-9.

Van Orden, K. A., Cukrowicz, K. C., Witte, T. K., & Joiner, T. E. (2011). Thwarted belongingness and perceived burdensomeness: Construct validity and psychometric properties of the interpersonal needs Questionnaire. *Psychological Assessment, 24*(1), 197–215.

VanderWeele, T. J., Li, S., Tsai, A. C., & Kawachi, I. (2016). Association between religious service attendance and lower suicide rates among US women. *JAMA Psychiatry, 73*(8), 845–851. https://doi.org/10.1001/jamapsychiatry.2016.1243.

Volkert, J., Schulz, H., Brütt, A. L., & Andreas, S. (2014). Meaning in life: Relationship to clinical diagnosis and psychotherapy outcome. *Journal of Clinical Psychology, 70*(6), 528–535.

Waters, S., & Cross, D. (2010). Measuring students' connectedness to school, teachers, and family: Validation of three scales. *School Psychology Quarterly, 25*(3), 164.

Wilchek-Aviad, Y. (2015). Meaning in life and suicidal tendency among immigrant (Ethiopian) youth and native-born Israeli youth. *Journal of Immigrant and Minority Health, 17*(4), 1041–1048. https://doi.org/10.1007/s10903-014-0028-5.

Wong, P. T. P. (2012). *The human quest for meaning: Theories, research, and applications* (2nd ed.). New York: Routledge. https://doi.org/10.4324/9780203146286.

Wu, A., Wang, J., & Jia, C. (2015). Religion and completed suicide: A meta-analysis. *PLoS One, 10*(6), e0131715. https://doi.org/10.1371/journal.pone.0131715.

Xie, P., Wu, K., Zheng, Y., Guo, Y., Yang, Y., He, J., … Peng, H. (2018). Prevalence of childhood trauma and correlations between childhood trauma, suicidal ideation, and social support in patients with depression, bipolar disorder, and schizophrenia in southern china. *Journal of Affective Disorders, 228*, 41–48. https://doi.org/10.1016/j.jad.2017.11.011.

Yur'yev, A., Värnik, A., Värnik, P., Sisask, M., & Leppik, L. (2012). Employment status influences suicide mortality in Europe. *International Journal of Social Psychiatry, 58*(1), 62–68.

Zimet, G. D., Dahlem, N. W., Zimet, S. G., & Farley, G. K. (1988). The multidimensional scale of perceived social support. *Journal of Personality Assessment, 52*(1), 30–41.

PART 3

Through the lens of the suicidal person

CHAPTER 8

Collaborative movement from "preventing suicide" to recovering desire to live

Thomas E. Ellis[a], **Heidi Bryan**[b]
[a]Deptartment of Psychiatry and Behavioral Sciences, Baylor College of Medicine, Houston, TX, United States; [b]Heidi Bryan Consulting, LLC, Neenah, WI, United States

> *… such hideous fantasies [of suicide], which cause well people to shudder, are to the deeply depressed mind what lascivious daydreams are to persons of robust sexuality*
>
> ***Styron (1990, p. 53).***

A number of autobiographical accounts have been published by individuals who have experienced suicidal crises, and much is to be gained from reading them. In *Night Falls Fast,* for example, psychologist Kay Jamison (Jamison, 1999) speaks of a "loss of fundamental innocence" that occurred when she first began to give serious consideration to suicide as "the only solution possible to an unendurable level of mental pain" due to her bipolar illness. Prior to this, she notes, "I knew death only in the most abstract of senses; I never imagined it would be something to arrange or seek" (p. 5).

Like Jamison, many mental health professionals (especially younger ones) will confess to bewilderment at the very idea of someone's taking active steps toward ending his or her own life. Needless to say, a helper's feeling bewildered by a patient's psychological experience does little to facilitate that individual's feeling understood and working in close alliance with that helper, especially around such a sensitive issue as suicide.

Indeed, it was this very bewilderment that led me (TE) to pursue a specialty focus in suicidology that extended through most of a 40-year career. This seemed a noble cause at the time, although I have since come to see it as an "arrogant ignorance;" for it is easy for a professional who has never experienced the awful reality of a suicidal crisis, with all good intentions, to provide "help" with statements like, "That sounds painful; tell me more," statements that are seemingly empathic, but in

Alternatives to Suicide
ISBN 978-0-12-814297-4
https://doi.org/10.1016/B978-0-12-814297-4.00008-X

reality conceal that helper's fundamental view that "It makes no sense for a person to attempt or die by suicide." It reminds me of a remark I once heard at a lecture by the Zen Buddhist philosopher Alan Watts: "Let me help you lest you drown, said the monkey, placing the fish safely up a tree."

Although reading gifted authors like Jamison and conducting multiple studies of the suicidal mind helped me to move in the direction of Orbach's instructive to "develop empathy for the suicidal wish," (Orbach, 2001), my patients at the Menninger Clinic in Houston stand alone as my best teachers. The typical patient at Menninger brings with him or her a lifelong history of struggles with multiple psychiatric disorders and failures of therapies, whether pharmacological, psychological, or both. Multiple diagnoses are the rule rather than the exception, including mood disorders, severe anxiety, substance-related disorders, and personality disorders that cause severe damage to relationships in personal and work arenas. Treatment histories generally include trials of multiple drugs from various drug classes, often in combination; neurostimulation treatments such as electroconvulsive therapy (ECT); multiple hospitalizations (sometimes involuntary); and years (sometimes decades) of psychotherapy. Younger patients, while experiencing fewer years of treatment hardships, often report a numbing sense of meaninglessness, purposelessness, and cynicism that challenge even the most seasoned therapists' fundamental assumption that life is worth living. It is clear to anyone paying attention that these patients have not "failed treatment" due to any lack of desire or effort; rather, the treatments, even when offered by competent, caring professionals, have failed them. In such a context, it is virtually impossible to maintain the position that considering suicide "makes no sense."

It is my view that the commonest mistake by well-meaning helpers seeking to prevent loss of life due to suicide is to assume that their agenda to save a life is shared by an individual simply because he or she is in their office. It is crucial for the clinician to realize that it is the choice to live itself that makes no sense to an individual who sees no viable alternatives for relief from suffering.

A lived experience perspective

I (HB) have struggled with suicidal ideation all my life; I am an attempt survivor who lost her brother to suicide. It's been a long journey to learn how to live fully and even while experiencing suicidal thoughts, but a journey worth taking. I was struggling with wanting to die even as I began my work in suicide prevention. Then, at a conference, I met Dr. Kenneth Tullis. He asked me whether I thought one could become addicted to suicidal thoughts and behaviors. I suddenly realized that this was what I had been doing — I'd been using suicide much like I previously used alcohol. Whenever I was stressed or upset, I knew I could turn my thoughts to suicide and it would calm and soothe me. I can always kill myself, I'd think. It provided an escape plan. Because I was in recovery for alcoholism, I was able to apply the principles of addiction recovery to my thoughts of suicide.

Although this helped, from time to time suicidal thoughts returned. I was seeing a therapist shortly after my brother died. At first it was bumpy, and we didn't talk much about my suicidality because I thought he didn't get it. However, somewhere along the line, we began talking about it. On my own, I learned about cognitive distortions, automatic thinking, and how to combat those thoughts (Ellis & Newman, 1996), and I learned that I could talk to my therapist openly about it and we'd figure it out — what worked and what didn't. It organically became a collaborative process. Now, when the thoughts pop up and don't leave, I'm able to discuss them either with my therapist or my husband and that's usually sufficient to manage them. I don't fight them as much; I also try not to judge them. They are part of my life, my being, so I accept them for what they are and do my best to maintain a healthy life so as not to invite them to stay and take root.

Theoretical context

Consistent with the general thrust of this volume (see Introduction), we seek here to describe a therapeutic perspective on suicide that moves away from a near exclusive focus on "what's wrong" and preventing suicidal behaviors, toward an emphasis on cultivating deeper empathic insight into the individual's experience of suicide, in service of a deeper, more effective relationship between the professional helper and the individual. This is not in any way to abandon a commitment to saving lives, nor to deny contributions of psychological impairments to suicidality (see, for example, Ellis & Rutherford, 2008), but to seek a more balanced perspective in hopes of enhancing therapeutic processes.

Building blocks for a less exclusively pathology-oriented perspective on suicide can be found in at least three bodies of work. In his groundbreaking work on Rational-Emotive Behavior Therapy (REBT), Albert Ellis (no relation) (1994) posited that, while disturbed emotion and behavior can be reduced by modifying "irrational" thinking, it is important not to lose sight of intrinsic human strengths. Ellis maintained that, although human beings do seem "hard-wired" for irrationality, they also are born with a drive to grow and develop their innate potentialities (Bernard, Froh, DiGiuseppe, Joyce, & Dryden, 2010). Beyond "rational" thinking, human happiness also is characterized by a variety of healthy behaviors, including those Ellis described as "vital absorption." Examples of activities to be cultivated and nurtured are loving (feeling absorbed in other people), creating (getting absorbed in things and activities), and philosophizing (getting absorbed in ideas) (Bernard et al., 2010). This perspective is reflected in current developments in behavioral activation therapy (Hopko, Ryba, McIndoo, & File, 2016), which enjoys considerable empirical support in the treatment of clinical depression.

Equally ground-breaking has been Marsha Linehan's work on reasons for living. Linehan is famous (infamous?) for offering validation for the experience of suicidal patients with borderline personality disorder with comments like, "If I had your life, I think I'd be suicidal, too!" In a seminal research paper, Linehan and colleagues noted, "Focusing on adaptive, life-maintaining characteristics of nonsuicidal people is similar to the approach proposed by Viktor Frankl (1959) and others, who have asked: How did the survivors of the Nazi concentration camps maintain their will to live? Investigators and survivor testimonials have pointed to beliefs about life and expectations for the future as instrumental in keeping many alive through extremes of painful life stress (Linehan, Goodstein, Nielsen, & Chiles, 1983) (p. 277).

A third, more recent body of work, Acceptance and Commitment Therapy (ACT), has focused less specifically on suicide but offers as much or more to understanding and addressing suicide therapeutically. A close cousin of cognitive behavior therapy (CBT), ACT has distinguished itself through its emphasis on recognizing human suffering as an inexorable aspect of the human condition (Hayes, 2005). Here, the primary focus shifts from getting rid of negative mood states to pursuing a fulfilling life consistent with one's most cherished values (McKay, Forsyth, & Eifert, 2010). This model places experiential avoidance (EA) at the center of emotional and behavioral disorders; avoidance strategies, which may range from repressed grief to addictions, while intended to relieve misery, are commonly seen only to worsen suffering in the long run. In a study designed to test the notion that suicidal ideation and behavior may be viewed as the ultimate form of experiential avoidance, Ellis and Rufino (2016) found that EA predicted suicidal ideation, even after controlling for other major correlates of suicidal ideation, such as depression, hopelessness, and prior suicide attempts. The ACT model is consistent with the perspective presented here that suicidality can be approached as a "normal" effort by an individual to relieve suffering, and that therapy preferably shifts its focus away from getting rid of certain emotions and eliminating suicidal thoughts and behavior to helping an individual to clarify what is really important to him or her and finding ways to pursue it.

Finally, it behooves one seeking to optimize the working relationship between clinicians and suicidal individuals to attend to a body of work that is largely overlooked by clinicians and suicide researchers alike: psychological *reactance*. This principle is epitomized by the cartoon showing a man saying to his wife, "I suddenly have an urge to juggle machetes," while standing next to a street sign reading, "Absolutely NO machete juggling." The caption reads, "The Essence of Human Nature."

Psychological reactance is an aversive affective reaction in response to efforts at behavioral control that impinge on freedom and autonomy (Brehm & Brehm, 1983). Reactance occurs when a person feels that someone or something is taking away his or her choices or limiting the range of alternatives. Reactance can cause the person to adopt or strengthen a view or attitude that is contrary to what was intended; it also increases resistance to persuasion. Psychotherapists and clients alike will recognize this as the "digging in the heels syndrome."

Indeed, this phenomenon seems to be human nature; examples abound, both in the laboratory (Brehm & Brehm, 1983) and in the natural world. Consider prohibition, Romeo and Juliet, teen smoking, gun control, and a variety of prohibited unhealthy behaviors. This is one reason why well-intentioned efforts to save a person's life, whether by therapists, family members, or friends, backfire. "You must not kill yourself," is experienced as a roadblock to the one course of action that the individual sees as a possible route to relief from suffering. Thus, a more collaborative approach is needed, as now recognized in a variety of quarters (Ellis, 2004; Jobes, 2016).

A lived experience critique

In reflecting on ways that conventional approaches fall short of what suicidal people actually need, I [HB] recalled a recent visit with my new psychiatrist. (I had recently relocated.) I liked him. He adjusted my medications, and I felt better; but when the topic of my suicidality came up, I turned my head away and inwardly thought, "Ah yes, this is why I didn't want to see a new doctor." It was almost as if I could see the muscles and sphincters clenching. "Suicide? Did you say suicide? Do you have a plan? Do you have a time frame? Do you have access to enact your plan or other ways?" "Do we need to do something about this?"

For me, as someone who struggles with chronic suicidality, this wasn't helpful. Yes, I have a plan, I've always had a plan; once it's in your head, you can't simply erase it. *But just because I talk about suicide doesn't mean it is imminent.* Although I recognize that clinicians must do a reasonable risk assessment, it sometimes seems as if the risk they are managing is more their own (liability) than the patient's. It's like a knee-jerk reaction — I say suicide and you say, "Yikes! Do we need to hospitalize her?" The end result is that I don't even want to bring it up.

It's ironic that almost the last person I feel like talking to about my suicidality is the one person who is supposed to be the most helpful for it. The perspective presented in this paper calls for clinicians to balance the assessment of lethality, imminence, and safety with exploring suicidal thinking openly, calmly, and frankly. Maybe if you asked why I felt that way, or what's going on that I would feel that way, how long have I been feeling that way instead of my plan, timeframe, etc., I'd be more willing to talk with you. You'd find out all that information anyway, without showing that you almost panic as soon as you hear the word suicide. I understand it's a tough word, and you probably feel responsible for keeping me alive. But you aren't — I am. In doing so, patients like me will be much more open to bringing the subject up the next time if need be.

I have talked with other attempt survivors who say the same thing. A friend of mine once told me her doctor would always pull out a safety contract as soon as she said suicide and my friend said she'd "sign the damn thing just to get her off her back." She knew the safety contract was to make the doctor feel better, not her. It can be exhausting to explain your chronic suicidality, and often you can tell the professionals aren't hearing you — they're focusing so much on keeping you alive that they sometimes lose sight of how to help you not want to kill yourself. Plus, one can be thinking about wanting to die but not want to actually go through with it. It's the same as thinking about having a chocolate sundae but not indulging in it because you're on a diet or have diabetes.

Finding a doctor with whom you can talk openly about your thoughts, discuss how they started, find out why they started, what's going on to prompt it all, can be a difficult process but one that's worth the time and energy. Again, like so many others with lived experience have said, working together, educating each other about suicide, is the best way to help suicidal people.

The foregoing overview is not presented as an exhaustive review of tributaries to the growing stream of alternative approaches to suicide, but to provide the reader with a sense of where this development originated and how it might be further enhanced. The following sections offer more specific thoughts on potential approaches for therapist and client that might be helpful as an individual moves from looking for a way out to cultivating a way forward.

Implications for practice

Other authors in this volume [cites] outline problems with what we might characterize as the "conventional" approach to suicidal patients, so that will not be repeated here. Suffice it to say that conventional approaches prioritize prevention, sometimes to the neglect of a full acknowledgment and understanding of the patient's experience. At risk of setting up a bit of a straw man, let us consider what might be considered a conventional (and, we might add "common-sense") approach to working therapeutically with a suicidal individual (Chapters 1 and 9).

1. Priority one: Keep the patient alive (with or without the individual's consent).
2. Make the environment safe.
3. Provide encouragement and attempt to inspire hope.
4. Utilize support systems.
5. Mitigate modifiable risk factors (e.g., reducing depressive symptoms via medication and/or psychotherapy).
6. Encourage adherence.

Such an approach has been shaped largely by a medical model, in which an alliance with the patient, while desirable, is considered secondary to the implementation of procedures to achieve the goal, in this case, preservation of life. While commendable and consistent with a generally agreed upon standard of care, professionals and (more so) patients are aware of limitations that often limit success and sometimes actually precipitate failure. This approach has been described as the "therapist responsibility" model (Ellis, 2004). While eschewing the opposite extreme, the "client responsibility" model, Ellis (2004) proposed a third, "collaborative," model that recognizes crucial, complimentary roles that clinicians and their clients play in approaching the problem of suicide effectively.

For illustration, imagine the six items above through the eyes of an individual whose wish to die is substantially greater than his or her wish to live. Every item, even the seemingly innocuous third one, become distasteful and alienating; for all are contrary to the individual's experience of hopelessness and the relief seemingly offered by death. Indeed, perhaps the most basic shortcoming of a "common sense" approach to the suicidal individual is that it is the *provider's* common sense that is being considered, not the individual's. Indeed, it is common sense *to the individual* that nothing will help (perhaps nothing has helped up to this point) and that the only solution, therefore, is death. Thus, attempts to "provide encouragement and inspire hope," however well-intentioned, become yet more evidence to the individual that the provider is, at best, clueless, or, at worst, minimizing or dismissing the depth of his or her suffering and sense of hopelessness. Conventional interventions such as safeguarding the environment and utilizing the support system may be experienced as coercive efforts to implement an unwanted agenda, rather than the compassionate acts that they are intended to be.

Where does this leave the helper – endorsing the individual's hopelessness or even his or her view of death as the only solution? This distasteful alternative is obviously unacceptable, and leads many to adhere to the conventional approach, drawbacks and all. However, consider the following stance as an alternative:

1. Priority one: Pursue a therapeutic alliance as the *sine qua non* of working effectively with a suicidal individual (Michel & Jobes, 2011).
2. Seek to gain and convey understanding of the reality and validity of the individual's suffering and desire for relief.
3. Endeavor to build a partnership toward the *shared* goal of helping the individual to obtain relief from suffering and begin movement toward a life that he or she feels is worth living.
4. To allow time for this work to be accomplished, collaboratively develop a plan for safety to ensure that the individual survives the current or anticipated crises. Safety planning might potentially include involvement of significant others and even agreements regarding nonconsensual actions such as hospitalization, should the individual become unable to care for himself or herself (such as during a psychotic episode).

5. Collaboratively implement evidence-based, suicide-specific therapeutic strategies.

Let us now explore each aspect of the above "stance" in greater detail.

Pursue a therapeutic alliance

The therapeutic alliance may at first seem to be a "no-brainer" that is so obvious that it scarcely needs to be discussed. Human attachment is widely recognized as a fundamental aspect of emotional well-being and effective coping (e.g., Allen, 2013). From this perspective, it is no surprise that the therapeutic alliance has consistently emerged as one of, if not the, strongest predictor of psychotherapy outcomes (Norcross & Lambert, 2011). Conveying empathy, a key aspect of developing such an alliance, is one of the first skills taught in counseling and psychotherapy training programs and comes naturally to many clinicians. But what of empathy for the suicidal wish itself (Orbach, 2001)? Many clinicians chafe at the prospect of expressing understanding – not to mention acceptance – of suicidal thoughts and urges, for fear of somehow implying that suicide is okay, acceptable, or even desirable, and thereby nudging the client in the opposite direction from the one the clinician desires.

It is important to be clear about what empathic "acceptance" and "understanding" do and do not mean in this context; for far from condoning or endorsing suicide, what the helper needs to convey here is that suicidality is present, is based on frustrated needs that may or may not be fully understood at this time, and that suicidal thinking will not be judged morally nor rejected in knee-jerk fashion. In other words, there is no presumption that the individual's suicidality is illogical, unreasonable, or irrational, nor that suicidality must be "taken off the table if we are to work together" (a pre-condition for a surprising number of clinicians). This distinction between acceptance and endorsement is not obvious to many professionals; yet it is crucial if a helper is to feel and express true empathy to the suicidal individual and avoid alienating him or her from the earliest stages of the relationship.

Seek to gain and convey understanding of the reality and validity of the individual's suffering and desire for relief

The above stance requires active steps by the clinician to develop empathic understanding of suicidality, notably by reading first-person accounts, such as those by Kay Jamison (1995), William Styron (1990), and Sylvia Plath (1971). Another means is to devote time, perhaps through imagery, to vividly imagining being "in the client's shoes," including childhood traumas, current stressors, symptoms of mood disorder, lack of social support, and other sources of suffering in the client's life. It is also well worth engaging actively where possible with individuals active in the growing "lived experience" movement, such as in the recently formed division of the American Association of Suicidology (www.suicidology.org).

Eschewing a knee-jerk rejection of suicide can be tricky for helpers, who of course tend to be strongly convinced that life is almost always preferable to death. One means of conveying acceptance and objectivity to a suicidal client is described in a section of *Choosing to Live* (Ellis & Newman, 1996), titled, "Advantages of Suicide – Are You Kidding?" The answer to the question should be, "No, I am not kidding. You are not stupid; we both need to be clear that you have valid reasons for wanting to kill yourself, and we need to understand what they are. When we are finished, we will also want to examine reasons why you want to stay alive, which I assume to be present because you are here talking to me. Advantages and disadvantages exist, and it is crucial that we closely examine both if you are to make a sound decision." The clinician will of course (a) worry that the client will be biased toward advantages of suicide to the neglect of disadvantages and (b) will naturally (hopefully!) have a corresponding bias toward the disadvantages of suicide and advantages of staying alive. This complementarity adds to the collaborative nature of the process. However, it is crucial that the conversation not devolve into a debate or argument; remaining collaborative is key.

We should point out that a similar perspective has been promoted for many years by Motivational Interviewing (Miller & Rollnick, 2013), which now enjoys substantial empirical support (Burke, Arkowitz, & Menchola, 2003). The MI process entails spending time with the client exploring the therapy agenda (such as quitting substance abuse), and sincerely exploring advantages of changing versus not changing behavior. This includes exploring (though not preaching) the importance of various goals (e.g., being a positive role model for one's children), as well as various obstacles that interfere with attaining such goals (such as strong urges to use drugs) and how these might be managed. Thus, motivation is constructed via a respectful, evolving relationship, rather than through persuasion, argument, moralizing, or guilt-inducement.

Build a partnership toward the *shared* goals

As has been suggested throughout this chapter, it cannot be overemphasized that an intervention attempted without agreement on goals is likely to fail, whether the goal is quitting smoking, losing weight, or refraining from self-harm. The suicidal person is in essentially the same boat as the individual who "knows" the family wants him to quit smoking, "knows" quitting is the logical thing to do, but either is not fully invested in quitting, or (more common) has tried to quit numerous times and has no hope that another quit attempt will succeed. A major difference in the case of suicide is that the suicidal person typically is experiencing suffering that he or she cannot tolerate and feels desperate to bring to an end. The task of finding common ground between helper and the suicidal individual is a significant challenge, success of which must not be taken for granted just because an individual is in the helper's office.

We recommend that helpers take a cue from the theory and practice of Acceptance and Commitment Therapy (Hayes, 2005) and resist any temptation to set goals without first identifying cherished personal values. ACT theory emphasizes the centrality of suffering to the human condition and the harm that results from desperate attempts to avoid suffering (including drug abuse and suicide). However, a simple "tough it out" message ("Stay alive and just accept the fact that suffering is part of being human.") is doomed to fail, because a clear vision of exactly *why* one should tolerate such (often severe) suffering is essential. Values clarification (e.g., McKay et al., 2010) is a critical aspect of this work. In the above example, the helper recognizes that the "politically correct" goal of quitting smoking (together with the difficult work of overcoming an addiction) will remain half-hearted until and unless it is connected with the person's heartfelt values. This can vary widely from one individual to another, from love for children, to saving money, to a teenager's concern about bad breath or "looking stupid"! Regardless, it is the values of *the individual, not the helper,* that matter here, and it is crucial for the helper to guide the individual to a point where quitting matters to him or her, not just to the helper or significant others.

In the case of suicidality, this is where "the rubber meets the road" and where helpers and clients often struggle; for the client is often suicidal precisely because nothing seems to matter. Goals often have been set repeatedly (such as in careers or important relationships) only to result in failure and disappointment. The question arises, "Why should I get excited about new goals, only to be disappointed yet again? It makes more sense to give up and get out." This kind of hopelessness can be contagious to therapists and loved ones alike, for the harsh realities may be indisputable; yet it is essential to recognize that, even in the context of great adversity, hopelessness is a feeling and not necessarily a fact.

More precisely, as Aaron Beck has observed for years, hopelessness is not actually an emotion, but an appraisal of the future (Beck, Steer, Beck, & Newman, 1993); and appraisals are subject to bias, particularly when one is depressed. In other words, a depressed, suicidal individual often is literally unable to access positive memories (e.g., past successes), and therefore bases future predictions on memories of failure. It is also important to recognize that many if not most people (least of all an individual in the midst of a suicidal episode) are unable to articulate core values clearly. However, it is a mistake to conclude that an individual has no values; in fact, it can be argued that it is precisely because strong values (such as interpersonal connection) have not been fulfilled that an individual is so distraught.

The ACT approach is not naïve about harsh realities of life, and there is no assumption that clarifying one's values will magically lead to said values being fulfilled. Indeed, the work of therapy, ACT or otherwise, entails a dual agenda of addressing (a) "How can we work together to help you pursue your values and create a life worth living?" and (b) "Let's work together on skills to manage painful emotions when bad things happen, so that you will have options other than self-harm or death for relief of suffering." Those familiar with Dialectical Behavior Therapy will recognize this as an agenda eloquently and thoroughly described by Marsha Linehan in her landmark volume first describing DBT (Linehan, 1993).

Develop a safety plan to allow time for this work to be accomplished

Next comes the crucial work of enhancing chances that the individual will survive long enough to benefit from treatment. Of course, a large body of literature exists describing various approaches to crisis intervention with suicidal individuals (e.g., Simon & Hales, 2012), so we need not summarize it here. However, it behooves us to cover one issue in this area that captures like no other the crucial nature of the therapeutic alliance: the no-suicide harm "contract." Widely panned in the literature (e.g., Rudd, Mandrusiak, & Joiner, 2006), such contracts remain stubbornly imbedded in conventional care, and may in some respects even be considered "standard of care." Such contracts call on the patient to sign a form stating that he or she promises not to kill or harm himself or herself, at least during the course of treatment. As noted above (HB), these contracts are easily detected by the patient as more for the helper's anxiety than patient protection, and even as a thinly disguised attempt to protect the helper from liability. Needless to say, such perceptions do little to facilitate (and even cause harm to) the development of a trusting working alliance. For more detailed critiques of the conventional no-suicide contract, see Garvey, Penn, Campbell, Esposito-Smythers, and Spirito (2009) and Rudd et al. (2006).

A preferable and highly practical approach to enhancing safety with a suicidal individual is safety planning. Promoted most prominently by Barbara Stanley and Greg Brown (Stanley & Brown, 2012), safety planning, by design, is a collaborative process of structured brainstorming with a suicidal individual to identify warning signs of a suicidal crisis and make written lists of internal and external coping resources that may be utilized when needed. Here, the helper takes a firm stance indicating that verbal assurances are a good starting point, but that concrete plans are required in a life-and-death situation (cf. fire drills). It has been my (TE) experience that, once the individual feels "on the same page" with a helper who has validated suffering and addressed frustrated needs, a natural flow into ensuring survival follows. A structured, collaborative, form-based process of identifying warning signs and listing various coping options that are tailor-made for the individual provides a solid foundation for an evolving working relationship between a suicidal individual and a helper. We should note that, while the traditional no-suicide contract has little if any empirical support (Rudd et al., 2006), early studies of the safety planning approach appear quite promising (Bryan et al., 2017).

Collaboratively implement evidence-based, suicide-specific therapeutic strategies

It is important to note that to emphasize one's "stance" and the importance of a collaborative working relationship is by no means presented "instead of" clinical interventions, but "together with." As noted above, multiple randomized trials in recent years have shown clearly that interventions designed for suicidality as a problem unto itself, rather than as a symptom of illness, result in significantly superior outcomes relative to conventional treatments (Brown et al., 2005; Ellis, Rufino, & Allen, 2017; Rudd et al., 2015). Table 8.1 presents a list of sample interventions from various suicide-specific therapies with significant empirical support.

Table 8.1 Examples of suicide-specific interventions.

Maintenance of an up-to-date safety plan[a]
Collaborative means management (e.g., stockpiled medications, firearms, etc.)
Hope Kit[b]
Detailed study of how suicidal episodes unfold (DBT behavioral chain analysis)[c]
Ongoing use of a Suicide Status Form (CAMS)[d]
Consistently teaching and practicing coping alternatives to self-harm[e]
Regularly exploring core factors underlying suicidality (stress, hopelessness, emotional pain, etc.)[f]
Problem-solving training[g]
Coping cards[h]
Behavioral activation (systematically planning and/or implementing rewarding activities)[i]
Exploring reasons for living and dying[j]
Clarifying personal values to help inform reasons for living[k]
Exploring "the one thing that would make me no longer suicidal"[l]
Imaginal rehearsal (re: coping with future adversity)[m]
Development/enhancement of social connection (e.g., resumption of community involvement)[n]

[a]Stanley and Brown (2012).
[b]Wenzel et al. (2009).
[c]Linehan (1993).
[d]Jobes (2016).
[e]Ellis and Newman (1996).
[f]Jobes (2016).
[g]Nezu, Nezu and D'Zurilla (2013).
[h]Wenzel et al. (2009)
[i]Hopko et al. (2016).
[j]Ellis and Newman (1996).
[k]McKay et al. (2010).
[l]Jobes (2016).
[m]Wenzel et al. (2009)
[n]Hopko et al. (2016).

These include Dialectical Behavior Therapy (DBT) (Linehan, Comtois, & Ward-Ciesielski, 2012), cognitive therapy for suicide prevention (CT-SP; Wenzel, Brown, & Beck, 2009), brief cognitive therapy (Rudd et al., 2015), and the Collaborative Assessment and Management of Suicidality (CAMS; Jobes, 2016).

Although research has not yet identified specific "active ingredients" within these interventions, clinical experience does allow for some educated guesses. For example, it has been striking to me (TE) how, contrary to the concerns of some clinicians, clients rarely object to a specific focus on suicide when this agenda is proposed in an empathic and collaborative manner. To the contrary, it is common to hear from the client how refreshing and validating it is to be able to talk directly and openly about what previously had been viewed as a taboo, even dangerous topic.

Second, although the quality of the therapeutic relationship is commonly recognized as a powerful influence on therapeutic outcomes (Norcross & Lambert, 2011), suicidal people often manifest vulnerabilities that must be addressed lest the need for the therapeutic relationship should continue indefinitely. These vary widely from one individual to another, and may include deficient problem-solving skills (Reinecke, 2006), emotional dysregulation (Rufino, Ellis, Clapp, Pearte, & Fowler, 2017), dysfunctional cognitive patterns (Jager-Hyman et al., 2014), and over-generalized autobiographical memory (Williams, Barnhofer, Crane, & Duggan, 2006), among others. The strategies listed in Table 8.1 are derived from these interventions, as well as from clinical experience.

Finally, there seems to be no substitute in the context of suicide for the restoration of hope. Hopelessness is recognized as a crucial mediator between depression and suicide risk (Beck et al., 1993) that can and should be addressed specifically in therapy. Importantly, this requires more than the mere "pep talks" that the suicidal individual has heard many times, to no avail, but working specifically on how hope becomes lost – and how it can be sustained – during times of adversity. The development of the Hope Box by Brown and colleagues (Wenzel et al., 2009) is one of many possible examples of ways to take restoration of hope beyond the superficial level. This creative yet simple exercise invites the client to start a collection (in a physical box, envelope, or in digital form) of reminders of inspiration, meaning, and hope. Clients are often highly creative in choosing what to include in such a collection, including photos of loved ones and pets, inspirational spiritual passages and poems, invigorating music, certificates of achievement earned through the years, anecdotes of "heroes" who have overcome adversity, and so forth. The hope box is added to over time and kept on hand, to be built during good times and utilized during dark times.

Conclusion

It is an uncommon challenge to move toward an alternative approach to a life-threatening situation that seemingly requires abandoning "common sense" and an instinctual inclination to "save a person from himself." Such an approach may work on occasion, perhaps while pulling a person back from the ledge of a tall building. A similar argument may be made regarding involuntary hospitalization (although we hasten to note that empirical evidence for the effectiveness of hospitalization is severely lacking (Linehan et al., 2006)). But such emergency situations are fundamentally different from working in a non-emergency situation with an individual who may still be in crisis, but whose risk of suicide is longer-term.

Following the lead of such approaches as Motivational Interviewing and Acceptance and Commitment Therapy more effectively accommodates the realities of the individual's experience, as expressed eloquently by individuals with lived experience of suicide. Such an approach helps the helper to re-orient from his or her own anxiety about the prospect of losing a client to suicide to an empathic connection with the suicidal individual that reduces resistance (reactance) and sets that stage for a partnership that produces needed energy from both parties to invest in the difficult work of solving complex problems. In the process, both parties recognize that suicidality occurs for understandable reasons and that what may appear to be insurmountable problems can be addressed through the synergy of collaboration.

References

Allen, J. G. (2013). *Mentalizing in the development and treatment of attachment trauma.* London: Karnac Books.

Beck, A. T., Steer, R. A., Beck, J. S., & Newman, C. F. (1993). Hopelessness, depression, suicidal ideation, and clinical diagnosis of depression. *Suicide and Life-Threatening Behavior, 23*(2), 139–145. http://doi.org/10.1111/j.1943-278X.1993.tb00378.x.

Bernard, M. E., Froh, J. J., DiGiuseppe, R., Joyce, M. R., & Dryden, W. (2010). Albert Ellis: Unsung hero of positive psychology. *The Journal of Positive Psychology, 5*(4), 302–310. http://doi.org/10.1080/17439760.2010.498622.

Brehm, J. W., & Brehm, S. S. (1983). *Psychological reactance: A theory of freedom and control.* San Diego, CA: Academic Press.

Brown, G. K., Ten Have, T., Henriques, G. R., Xie, S. X., Hollander, J. E., & Beck, A. T. (2005). Cognitive therapy for the prevention of suicide attempts: A randomized controlled trial. *JAMA, 294*(5), 563–570. http://doi.org/10.1001/jama.294.5.563.

Bryan, C. J., Mintz, J., Clemans, T. A., Leeson, B., Burch, T. S., Williams, S. R., et al. (2017). Effect of crisis response planning vs. contracts for safety on suicide risk in U.S. Army soldiers: A randomized clinical trial. *Journal of Affective Disorders, 212*, 64–72. http://doi.org/10.1016/j.jad.2017.01.028.

Burke, B. L., Arkowitz, H., & Menchola, M. (2003). The efficacy of motivational interviewing: A meta-analysis of controlled clinical trials. *Journal of Consulting and Clinical Psychology, 71*(5), 843–861. http://doi.org/10.1037/0022-006X.71.5.843.

Ellis, A. (1994). *Reason and emotion in psychotherapy: Revised and updated.* New York: Birch Lane Press.

Ellis, T. E. (2004). Collaboration and a self-help orientation in therapy with suicidal clients. *Journal of Contemporary Psychotherapy, 34*(1), 41–57. http://doi.org/10.1023/B:JOCP.0000010912.99125.6a.

Ellis, T. E., & Newman, C. (1996). *Choosing to live: How to defeat suicide through cognitive therapy*. Oakland, CA: New Harbinger.

Ellis, T. E., & Rufino, K. A. (2016). Change in experiential avoidance is associated with reduced suicidal ideation over the course of psychiatric hospitalization. *Archives of Suicide Research, 20*(April), 426–437. http://doi.org/10.1080/13811118.2015.1093983.

Ellis, T. E., Rufino, K. A., & Allen, J. G. (2017). A controlled comparison trial of the collaborative assessment and management of suicidality (CAMS) in an inpatient setting: Outcomes at discharge and six-month follow-up. *Psychiatry Research, 249*, 252–260. http://doi.org/10.1016/j.psychres.2017.01.032.

Ellis, T. E., & Rutherford, B. (2008). Cognition and suicide: Two decades of progress. *International Journal of Cognitive Therapy, 1*(1), 47–68. http://doi.org/10.1680/ijct.2008.1.1.47.

Frankl, V. E. (1959). *Man's search for meaning*. New York: Washington Square Press.

Garvey, K. A., Penn, J. V., Campbell, A. L., Esposito-Smythers, C., & Spirito, A. (2009). Contracting for safety with patients: Clinical practice and forensic implications. *The Journal of the American Academy of Psychiatry and the Law, 37*(3), 363–370. Retrieved from http://www.ncbi.nlm.nih.gov/pubmed/19767501.

Hayes, S. C. (2005). *Get out of your mind and into your life: The new acceptance and commitment therapy*. Oakland, CA: New Harbinger.

Hopko, D. R., Ryba, M. M., Mclndoo, C., & File, A. (2016). *Behavioral activation. The Oxford handbook of cognitive and behavioral therapies*. Retrieved from http://ovidsp.ovid.com/ovidweb.cgi?T=JS&PAGE=reference&D=psyc13&NEWS=N&AN=2015-53617-014.

Jager-Hyman, S., Cunningham, A., Wenzel, A., Mattei, S., Brown, G. K., & Beck, A. T. (2014). Cognitive distortions and suicide attempts. *Cognitive Therapy and Research, 38*(4), 369–374. http://doi.org/10.1007/s10608-014-9613-0.

Jamison, K. R. (1995). *An unquiet mind: A memoir of moods and madness*. New York: Vintage.

Jamison, K. R. (1999). *Night falls fast: Understanding suicide*. New York: Knopf.

Jobes, D. A. (2016). *Managing suicidal risk: A collaborative approach* (2nd ed.). New York: Guilford.

Linehan, M. M. (1993). *Cognitive therapy for borderline personality disorder*. New York: Guilford.

Linehan, M. M., Comtois, K. A., Murray, A. M., Tutek, D. A., Reynolds, S. K., & Lindenboim, N. (2006). Two-year randomized controlled trial and follow-up of dialectical behavior therapy vs therapy by experts for suicidal behaviors and borderline personality disorder. *Archives of General Psychiatry, 63*, 757–766.

Linehan, M. M., Comtois, K. A., & Ward-Ciesielski, E. F. (2012). Assessing and managing risk with suicidal individuals. *Cognitive and Behavioral Practice, 19*(2), 218–232. http://doi.org/10.1016/j.cbpra.2010.11.008.

Linehan, M. M., Goodstein, J. L., Nielsen, J., & Chiles, J. A. (1983). Reasons for staying alive when you are thinking of killing yourself: The reasons for living inventory. *Journal of Consulting and Clinical Psychology, 51*(2), 276–286.

McKay, M., Forsyth, J. P., & Eifert, G. H. (2010). *Your life on purpose: How to find what matters and create the life you want*. Oakland, CA: New Harbinger.

Michel, K., & Jobes, D. A. (2011). In K. Michel, & D. A. Jobes (Eds.), *Building a therapeutic alliance with the suicidal patient*. Washington, DC: American Psychological Association.

Miller, W. R., & Rollnick, S. (2013). *Motivational interviewing: Helping people change*. New York: Guilford.

Nezu, A. M., Nezu, C. M., & D'Zurilla, T. J. (2013). *Problem-solving therapy: A treatment manual*. New York: Springer Publishing Co.

Norcross, J. C., & Lambert, M. J. (2011). Psychotherapy relationships that work II. *Psychotherapy, 48*(1), 4–8. http://doi.org/10.1037/a0022180.

Orbach, I. (2001). Therapeutic empathy with the suicidal wish: Principles of therapy with suicidal individuals. *American Journal of Psychotherapy, 55*(2), 166–184.

Plath, S. (1971). *The bell jar*. New York: Harper & Row.

Reinecke, M. A. (2006). Problem solving: A conceptual approach to suicidality and psychotherapy. In T. E. Ellis (Ed.), *Cognition and suicide - theory, research, and therapy* (pp. 237–260). Washington, DC: American Psychological Association.

Rudd, M. D., Bryan, C. J., Wertenberger, E. G., Peterson, A. L., Young-McCaughan, S., Mintz, J., et al. (2015). Brief cognitive-behavioral therapy effects on post-treatment suicide attempts in a military sample: Results of a randomized clinical trial with 2-year follow-up. *American Journal of Psychiatry, 172*(5), 441–449. http://doi.org/10.1176/appi.ajp.2014.14070843.

Rudd, M. D., Mandrusiak, M., & Joiner, T. E. (2006). The case against no-suicide contracts: The commitment to treatment statement as a practice alternative. *Journal of Clinical Psychology*. http://doi.org/10.1002/jclp.20227.

Rufino, K. A., Ellis, T. E., Clapp, J., Pearte, C., & Fowler, J. C. (2017). Variations of emotion dysregulation in borderline personality disorder: A latent profile analysis approach with adult psychiatric inpatients. *Borderline Personality Disorder and Emotion Dysregulation, 4*(1), 17. http://doi.org/10.1186/s40479-017-0068-2.

Simon, R. I., & Hales, R. E. (2012). *The American psychiatric publishing textbook of suicide assessment and management* (2nd ed.). Washington, DC: American Psychiatric Publishing.

Stanley, B., & Brown, G. K. (2012). Safety planning intervention: A brief intervention to mitigate suicide risk. *Cognitive and Behavioral Practice, 19*(2), 256–264. http://doi.org/10.1016/j.cbpra.2011.01.001.

Styron, W. (1990). *Darkness visible: A memoir of madness*. New York: Vintage Books.

Wenzel, A., Brown, G. K., & Beck, A. T. (2009). *Cognitive therapy for suicidal patients: Scientific and clinical applications*. New York: Guilford.

Williams, J. M. G., Barnhofer, T., Crane, C., & Duggan, D. S. (2006). The role of over-general memory in suicidality. In T. E. Ellis (Ed.), *Cognition and suicide: Theory, research, and therapy* (pp. 173–192). Washington, DC: American Psychological Association.

CHAPTER 9

The "alternatives to suicide" approach: a decade of lessons learned

Sera Davidow, Caroline Mazel-Carlton
Western Massachusetts Recovery Learning Community, Holyoke, MA, United States

In the United States (US) and most other Westernized nations, where considerations of killing one's self are concerned, risk assessment serves as the primary 'intervention' (sometimes masquerading under the guise of 'prevention'). In turn, containment comprises a large slice of the front line 'treatment'. It is an approach that at least implies that those who are likely to die by suicide will readily present themselves through implementation of a brief questionnaire under a watchful eye, and that we somehow magically become clear at that point on 'what to do' with those for whom suicide is most imminently at hand. If only that were true.

The latest international initiative in the Suicide Prevention arena is one called "Zero Suicide", but it is largely the same old thing under little more than a new name. In the US, this effort is organized by the Suicide Prevention Resource Center (SPRC) as primarily funded by the Substance Abuse and Mental Health Services Administration (SAMHSA), a governmental agency that seems to have fully bought in to the project's objectives. These objectives start with creating buy-in toward reduction in rates of suicide, training the workforce, and "identifying" people who are at risk (Zero Suicide, 2018).

The first point (reduction in rates) is certainly not a hard sell, but the rest bears furthers examination. However, these objectives are presented uncritically by SPRC and others in spite of the fact that there are copious reports and studies citing the utter lack of efficacy of any assessment tool currently in existence. For example, in 2016, the American Psychological Association published an article in which Joseph Franklin of Harvard University was quoted as follows:

> *Our analyses showed that science could only predict future suicidal thoughts and behaviors about as well as random guessing. In other words, a suicide expert who conducted an in-depth assessment of risk factors would predict a patient's*

Alternatives to Suicide
ISBN 978-0-12-814297-4
https://doi.org/10.1016/B978-0-12-814297-4.00009-1

> *future suicidal thoughts and behaviors with the same degree of accuracy as someone with no knowledge of the patient who predicted based on a coin flip... This was extremely humbling — after decades of research, science had produced no meaningful advances in suicide prediction.*
>
> ***American Psychological Association (2016).***

Strangely, though, Franklin nonetheless warned that risk guidelines should not be abandoned. He suggested, "As most of these guidelines were produced by expert consensus, there is reason to believe that they may be useful and effective." This is a bold statement given it directly followed his quote about such tools proving no better than flipping a coin.

How odd that within moments of declaring failure, the very same individual may nonetheless reject that failure simply on the basis that what failed also happens to align with the dominant paradigm and those prominent figures that tout it. Moreover, this article does not exist in isolation. It is one of many, including a 2016 article, "*The futility of risk prediction in psychiatry*" in which the authors offer that "the evidence suggests that risk categorization may be of limited value, or worse, potentially harmful, confusing clinical thinking" (Mulder, Newton-Howes, & Coid, 2016). In fact, a 52% rate of accurate prediction seems to be the highest rate of accuracy currently on record. This rate was reported in a study published in 1983 in the *Archives of General Psychiatry* using what were considered to be the 20 best predictors available. It involved the correct prediction that 35 of 67 individuals would eventually die by their own hand, though not how soon that would occur or what might have helped to prevent it. Even the report's author, Alex Pokorny, indicated that he found no item or combination of items to be useful in identifying who would come to die by suicide (Pokorny, 1983).

Yet, challenging what is claimed in the name of 'science' is hard, especially when several industries (healthcare, pharmaceutical, suicidology, and so on) have organized their very existence around particular beliefs. In fact, there is a well-established bias against even publishing papers that are seen as 'negative' or counter to what is already purported to be truth (ScienceBlog, 2009). And, as we see above, even when studies do get published, many thought leaders are quite adept at the mental contortions required to nonetheless disregard what is said.

Unfortunately, it is this sort of thinking that also appears to drive much of the 'treatment' of people who are deemed at risk for dying by their own hand. This includes hospitalization, considered to be a front line defense designed to keep people 'safe'. In May of 2017 the Journal of the American Medical Association's Psychiatry division published an international meta-analysis looking at suicide rates of individuals who had been hospitalized. What they found was a fairly clear message: Suicide risk remains very high after psychiatric hospitalization. Specifically, they identified that individuals hospitalized for thoughts of suicide were 200 times more likely than the general population to die by suicide within three months post-discharge. Perhaps even more interestingly, individuals hospitalized for reasons unrelated to suicide also saw a post-discharge bump of 100 times increased risk. And, even years after discharge, individuals who had spent time on an inpatient psychiatric unit were still about 30 times more likely to kill themselves (American Psychiatric Association, 2017).

Ultimately, and in spite of the fact that the preceding information is readily available, most of us continue to be wrapped up in systems where ineffective assessment tools are used to inaccurately identify who should be held (sometimes against their will) on psychiatric units to prevent their death in the moment, thereby increasing the likelihood that they will eventually kill themselves. It is a set up that appears to force providers to section people into two distinct groups: The people we need to immediately contain because they appear to be at high risk of self-inflicted death, and those we may (more or less) ignore because they are not. And, it is a particularly peculiar set up given that we also have research that tells us that as many as 95% of individuals put in the 'high risk' pot will not die by suicide, and that about 50% of suicides happen within the group that it seemed safe to ignore (Murray & Devitt, 2017). Ultimately, it is a framework that is designed to make the provider feel comfortable that they have done what is recommended; they have practiced the standard of care. The impact on the individual supported appears to be secondary, at least once they are out of sight.

Clearly, there is a great deal to be unpacked here. For example, if assessment tools are not useful, what should we do instead? And, is there ever *any* call for hospitalization when someone is contemplating suicide? If so, then what are those circumstances, and what precisely would be helpful about a hospital environment? (And, could what would be helpful be replicated in an environment that does not also include all the harmful elements?) Finally, if not hospitalization, then what else can we do that would more genuinely support people through some of their darkest times?

The *Alternatives to Suicide* approach was developed in 2008 by the Western Massachusetts Recovery Learning Community (RLC) with financial support from local suicide prevention entities. It was a response — at least in part — to some of the aforementioned quandaries. This was an unusual collaboration, particularly since the *Alternatives to Suicide* approach has been described as intentionally not being 'suicide prevention' at all. Of course, some are startled by that claim, and hear it to mean that people involved with developing and sustaining *Alternatives to Suicide* have not had a vested interest in supporting people to stay alive. Quite the contrary.

The founders of *Alternatives to Suicide* realized early on that the blind spots endemic to the world of Suicide Prevention were causing harm (by encouraging force, etc.) and counter-productive to the stated goal of preventing suicide. Rather, they felt it was essential to let go of any agenda that required taking responsibility for keeping everyone alive, and instead to focus on making space for people to come to a place where they want to do that for themselves. As such, understanding the differences between being responsible *for* (keeping people alive, etc.) versus being responsible *to* (being with one another through dark times) rose up as the primary aim. People choosing not to die by suicide was and continues to be a side-effect of that aim done well (Western Massachusetts Recovery Learning Community, 2018).

Piloted in group format, the intent was to identify leaders who had themselves struggled with thoughts of suicide or suicide attempts, and who wanted to be a part of supporting others to share their thoughts openly, and without looming threat of negative consequences (i.e., any unwanted intervention) as a result. Unlike other efforts that involved someone who had first-hand experience with suicide, no clinicians were involved as co-facilitator. This was for several reasons including how difficult it can be for most clinicians to unlearn what they have been taught in school and work about how they should respond to what they perceive as a 'crisis', and some of the extra complications that can arise from involving someone with a clinical license. However, the top reason was because many people would find the presence of a clinician silencing (even if the clinician was able to overcome all other obstacles and had the greatest of intents), thus defeating the whole purpose of gathering at all.

For a brief period at the start, the initial funder did require a quarterly clinical consult with facilitators. Yet, after several consecutive meetings where the assigned clinician proclaimed that he was learning more than he was teaching or consulting (and because the RLC did not want to give appearances that clinical support was needed when in fact it was not particularly being utilized at all), that element was discontinued. There were several other components that were considered or tested out during this period that also did not stick over the long-term. These included operating as closed groups with an 'intake' of sorts to make sure someone was a good fit for the group, and following a group structure that required 'check ins' from each attendee. (Both were quickly done away with because it was found to be essential that the groups be accessible on a timeline and for reasons defined by the individual considering attending, and because it was also essential that they self-determined how they would participate once there).

Although the initial start-up process was led almost entirely by people who had struggled with thoughts of suicide themselves, they also sought to include as much input from as many other people who had 'been there' themselves as possible. One method for gathering input was through a community forum to ask people what had actually been helpful (and harmful) to them in the past. However, the founders of this approach were well aware of the tensions between failing to include many voices, and asking people (especially people subsisting on fixed incomes and living in poverty) to work for free. Individuals who have been in the system often get taken advantage of in research, or asked to share what they have learned on advisory boards and so on with no compensation by employees who are getting paid (Davidow, 2017b). As such, care was taken to be transparent about how information would be used, and to provide a monetary thank you to each participant. This gathering resulted in a 'Supporting Conversations Around Suicide' handout that has been evolving ever since (Western Mass Recovery Learning Community, 2015).

In spite of any bumps and shifts already noted, there were many starting elements that did come to constitute the foundation of the *Alternatives to Suicide* approach. For example, the approach has always focused on the idea that no one would exist in immovable 'fixer' or 'fixee' roles. This is a concept that seems simple, but is often misunderstood. One of the beauties of it is that it makes space for facilitators to truly participate in the groups, even if they themselves are struggling. In 2015, *Alternatives to Suicide* founders attended a conference in New York State in the United States where they unexpectedly crossed paths with presenters claiming to be running groups based on the *Alternatives to Suicide* approach. However, upon further examination, the New York group was found to have implemented rules and limitations such as that facilitators needed to have been free of any thoughts of suicide for at least one year before taking on the facilitator role. This alone is inconsistent with the idea of breaking down boundaries between 'fixer' and 'fixee'. While facilitators must be present enough to be able to help hold the values of the space and work with their co-facilitator to address issues as they arise, the very idea that one cannot be capable of these things while also sometimes struggling runs counter to key ideology. Furthermore, this approach accepts that moving in and out of questioning one's purpose, life, and place in the world is normal for many people, and thus the idea that one would need to be 'cured' from such contemplations makes very little sense at all.

Other components that have held since the beginning include an emphasis on curiosity and mutual exploration, as well as looking for opportunities to maintain or create threads not just with another solitary individual, but with the communities that might help keep someone tethered to this earth. Similarly, the groups have also always centered around honesty, and not treating each other as fragile, although what 'not treating each other as fragile' truly means and looks like was another area that expanded over time. For example, although the earliest groups believed wholeheartedly that there was room to challenge and be upfront with one another, they nonetheless still subscribed to the "no graphic detail" limitation that so many clinical groups and programs have in place. However, over time, those guiding the growth of *Alternatives to Suicide* came to realize that such a rigid approach does little more than act as another way to suppress people's stories (Davidow, 2019). Sometimes people need to have the fullness and rawness of their experiences heard, and if there is not space for that in the groups, it may not exist anywhere. Additionally, they realized that telling people that what they had been through was "too much" for others to hear sent a strong message to some that it must also be "too much" for them to survive. That and the idea that they might "trigger" others just by the telling of it all also served to replicate the idea that big feelings are bad, and should be avoided. Thus, over time, the 'no graphic detail' term was replaced with an expectation that graphic detail could be shared, and that individuals could be trusted to step out if something touched them too deeply in the moment. Now, if someone has a big response to another person's story, the assumption is not that it was wrong for that story to be told, but that it has potentially helped uncover something that would be useful for someone else to talk about, too.

Alternatives to Suicide groups in their current and longstanding form are intentionally very different from support groups found in clinical environments. This intentionality begins with the environment itself. The choice of non-clinical environment mitigates the fact that many folks who have had thoughts of suicide have experienced institutional trauma including forced drugging, confinement and coercion. Some of the settings used for *Alternatives to Suicide* groups include Quaker Meeting houses, synagogues, community centers, coffee shops and spaces used exclusively for peer support. Consideration is given around factors such as lighting, chairs, cushions, and so on. The intent is to do as much as possible to create a space that conveys the non-clinical values of the groups before facilitators ever say a word of introduction.

Most of the framework of *Alternatives to Suicide* groups is also now defined by the *Alternatives to Suicide* Group Charter. The charter was modeled after the Hearing Voices Group Charter (Hearing Voices USA, 2008). Its purpose is to clearly define the framework of what makes an *Alternatives to Suicide* group, without dictating each moment or eliminating opportunity for differences based on culture, geography, and so on. As indicated in the charter, there is no assessment, referral or "red tape" to attend *Alternatives to Suicide* groups. Individuals are invited to just show up as works for them. Participants are asked to meet one and only one criteria in order to attend: Believing that they might have something to personally gain in their own human struggle by being present for group conversations about the challenges of life, contemplation of death, and all that may follow from that.

Alternatives to Suicide groups are also explicitly not solely "attempt survivor" groups. Spaces are open to all who want to share about suicidal thoughts and experiences. The idea that a facilitator may check someone at the door for whether or not they have attempted already, and tell them to "come back when they have tried it" is seen as darkly absurd. It is little more than a bizarre replication of a mental health system that commonly offers little to no support until a certain level of crisis has been achieved.

Facilitators arrive well in advance of the group so that when a new person joins they can be sure to welcome them, offer relevant information, and answer any questions. On some occasions, people come to the group thinking that it is for "suicide loss survivors" (i.e., people who have lost someone else to suicide). In those instances, facilitators clarify that while many people in the group may be grieving losses of various kinds, the ultimate purpose is to voice and explore personal thoughts around suicide.

Rare occurrences of loss survivors using the group to ask participants to explain to them why their loved one chose suicide have sometimes stirred up feelings of shame, guilt, anger and other responses that have been counter-productive and inhibited the meeting from serving its stated purpose. Hence, separate resources for "loss survivors" are important.

Unlike many groups in clinical settings, there is no long list of rules posted on the wall. Groups are begun on-time by an introduction that focuses on values over prohibitions. Typically, groups are introduced by sharing a bit about the history and why it felt important to develop groups like this in the first place. Often facilitators will use the introduction as a time to share some of their own story. For example, they might share ways that they were treated in other spaces when the topic of suicide arose. This is done for many reasons, including how important it is to demonstrate that this is not yet another group where participants will be asked to share their deepest thoughts and feelings to fellow humans who share nothing of themselves back.

There is no written preamble used to introduce an *Alternatives to Suicide* group. This allows for personal experience, vulnerability, community needs and cultural values to infuse the space from the very first words. It also conveys an authenticity to the conversation and typically encourages people to pay closer attention than they would have if words were just being read off a page. Copies of the *Alternatives to Suicide* charter are generally made available to refer to if needed in the group as well as any additional community value statements such as the Western Mass Recovery Learning Community's Defining Principle (Western Mass Recovery Learning Community, 2012). An example of a group introduction may look as follows:

> *Welcome everyone to the Springfield meeting of Alternatives to Suicide. When we come together at this time it is very special because it is a meeting of one of the only true peer-to-peer support groups around the topic of suicide in the world. These groups started in Western Massachusetts in 2008 when members of the community noticed that there were very few places that they could have supportive conversation around the topic of suicide. They noticed that they experienced judgment when talking about suicide. They heard things like "a real man wouldn't think those thoughts" or "mothers who have these types of thoughts or selfish." Other folks like myself experienced things like forced hospitalization or being told they were "mentally ill" when they brought up the topic of wanting to die. In Alternatives to Suicide groups one of our Charter values is "no assumption of illness" but that does not mean "no assumption of struggle". What that means*

is we can talk about the many diverse experiences and emotions that might be leading us to consider leaving this world. We can also name for ourselves the things that help us stay in it, even if that just means staying alive to see the next season of "Empire". No one here is in a clinical role. All facilitators have had thoughts of suicide themselves. No one will be taking notes or reporting on anyone for thinking about suicide. This is a social group so typically when someone shares something another person might ask them more about it or speak to what they relate to. However, if you just want to share something and have the group immediately move on to another topic that is fine, too. Just let us know.

In an effort to convey the collectively held nature of the group, facilitators will typically invite non-facilitators to share in their own words some of the values of *Alternatives to Suicide* groups and what they mean to them personally. For example one young man once shared that the group "was a place where people ask 'how are you doing?' and I can actually tell the truth."

Another way that *Alternatives to Suicide* groups differ from more clinical groups or 12 step meetings is (as aforementioned) the lack of formal check-in after the introduction. In a typical group, participants go around in a circle only once in order to share with the community how they want to be referred to in the space both by name and pronouns, as well as any accessibility needs. It is emphasized that participants do not have to use the same name and pronouns in the group that they might use in other spaces. There is also no assumption that the name and pronoun used at the last group will be what a person uses in the current meeting. While the invitation to share pronouns can be controversial to or uncomfortable for some, it is prioritized in these groups because of the growing body of research that tells us that transgender and gender non-binary individuals (those who identify as neither fully male or female) are attempting suicide at alarmingly high rates (Toomey, Syversten, & Shramko, 2018), and that one of the most effective ways to reduce that trend is to hear and accept the name and pronouns that they ask others to use (Russell, Pollitt, Li, & Grossman, 2018). In fact, groups can be a place where people experiment with different identities including identities around gender, culture, societal roles, voice hearing experiences, and more. After everyone has shared how they want to be referred to, the conversation then begins.

Because the *Alternatives to Suicide* Charter is explicit that groups are social and non-clinical, value is placed on organic conversation arising and supporting a free-flowing dialogue around topics that are normally taboo or may lead to punitive responses under the umbrella justification of "safety". Facilitators do not respond to other group members in a formulaic way, nor are they encouraged to respond to every person who shares. This helps avoid creating a dynamic that conveys that the facilitator holds all the answers.

Conversations in *Alternatives to Suicide* groups can be incredibly diverse. Instead of determining risk factors or focusing on IF someone is going to end their lives, the discussion focuses more on WHY people are having thoughts of suicide. Quite a few participants have come from spending weeks on inpatient units because of a suicide attempt without having ever been asked why they wanted to die in the first place throughout the duration of their stay. For example, on more than one occasion, a young college student has arrived to the group after a hospital stay for a suicide attempt, and having not been asked what happened that led to the attempt, only to find out they had recently been sexually assaulted or raped. Sometimes, the student has also been involuntarily placed on leave or expelled from school due to the hospitalization and the school's fears of liability, which is an all too common occurrence itself (Klugman, 2018).

Conversations may center around traumatic events recent and in the past. Other common topics include lack of resources or purpose. A great deal of time is also spent unpacking some of the negative messages people have received from society at large about gender roles, race or immigrant status, or about worth being centered on people's economic output or relationship status. People can share fears of inadequacy, of not being enough, or of being "too much". More often than not, they will also hear those fears echoed by other people in the group. Several participants have reported that the group is one of the only places they can talk about experiences of sexism, racism or transphobia without these experiences being denied or shut down.

While the *Alternatives to Suicide* framework does not constitute 'rocket science', it is so fundamentally different than how most of us are taught to respond to someone who is talking about their own death, that it requires significant unlearning and practice in order to implement it well. Hence, the Western Mass Recovery Learning Community has developed a facilitator training to help people along that path. Of course, unlearning one concrete approach is much simpler, if there is another concrete approach being used as a replacement. One of the greatest challenges of teaching people to implement the *Alternatives to Suicide* approach, however, is that the very point is to replace a concrete approach with one that is flexible, and more abstract and exploratory. This presents a substantial hurdle for many students who have continued to ask *Alternatives to Suicide* trainers for a formula of some sort.

In 2018, in a best effort to straddle the lines of formula and abstraction, the following was developed by Caroline Mazel-Carlton: Validation + Curiosity + Vulnerability + Community (VCVC). This formula is meant as a touchstone for facilitators (and all others attempting to practice the *Alternatives to Suicide* approach); something to bear in mind when sitting in figurative darkness with others, and as a check-in point when things feel stuck or off track.

The formula is not meant to indicate the order in which these components must come into play. Rather, in conversation, all pieces should be kept in mind and brought in as makes sense, sometimes in combination with one another. That said, validation (the first 'V') is indeed often a good place to start. Validation of difficulties is emphasized over fixing. In clinical models, emotions and experiences around the topic of suicide typically go unrecognized because of the quickness to which clinicians are required to turn to risk assessment protocols. While this may seem inconsequential to some, it is through validation that we signal to people that we have truly seen and heard them. And, for someone who has walked through this world feeling unseen and unheard for so long, that may be precisely what is driving them to seek permanence where their seeming invisibility is concerned. After all, it seems not unreasonable to conclude that feeling so invisible may be far less painful if one, in fact, does not exist.

Thus, finding words that communicate genuinely seeing one another are prioritized, as is identifying and doing away with common and well-intended phrases that may unintentionally have the opposite effect. For example, facilitators are taught to avoid asking people if they have taken a pill for their distress, telling someone they are wrong to feel a certain way, or saying things such as "it could always be worse". Meanwhile, examples of statements that can serve as validation include:

- That sounds really hard
- It makes so much sense that you would feel [furious/sad/scared/etc.]
- The world can be such a scary place
- It seems like you are holding so much right now
- Thank you so much for being able to express your anger around that issue

Validation can be useful (and essential) even in the most stuck moments. As Brené Brown offers in her short video on empathy (https://bit.ly/1d7dG0H), something like "*I don't even know what to say right now. I'm just so glad you told me*", can make all the difference in signaling to someone that you are with them, and that they count (Brown, 2013). Ultimately, *Alternatives to Suicide* groups emphasize the power of individual pain shifting to a collectively held and seen issue. This means that there is a meaningful role even for those who may choose not to speak into the room for the duration of a group, as there is great power and value in being present to bear witness. Participants often report the sensation of a "weight being lifted" when they are able to share secretly held emotions or experiences with the group and be told that they make sense.

Curiosity (the first 'C') often walks hand-in-hand with validation. For example, it would be commonplace to hear someone say something like, "Wow. That sounds like it would be so scary. What was it like for you?" Similarly, if someone comes in to the group describing themselves in clinical terms (e.g., diagnostic labels like 'bipolar', behavioral labels like 'decompensating', 'manic', etc.), they are likely to be asked, "What does that look like for you?" Other curiosity questions include:

- How long have you felt this way?
- Is there something in your life that you need to let go of or let 'die'?
- What makes you feel strong?
- Where do you think that message that you're not 'good enough' comes from? Whose voice is it?
- Have you felt like this before?

Some of these questions have important implications for aiding us to break out of our more typical responses. For example, one woman spoke of how scared she was when speaking to another woman who was sharing her thoughts of suicide. She stopped being as scared when she simply asked, "How long have you felt suicidal", and the woman responded, "Oh, about 30 years". Many questions also help get at the idea that thoughts of one's own death may represent something very different than an actual desire to die. Perhaps those overwhelming thoughts of wanting to be gone are really about a relationship, job, or housing situation that needs to be eliminated instead. This is something Caroline Mazel-Carlton spoke so eloquently to in a keynote address at the 2018 World Hearing Voices Congress in the Netherlands:

> *I remember one of the times in my life where one of the voices I hear was just insistent that I needed to kill myself. Over and over telling me I needed to die. I was 29 years old at the time and since I had been involved with psychiatry since I*

> *was 8, I knew the consequences for telling someone this. My solution to resist the voice was that I would buy a ticket to see a movie and sit in the theater all day because I figured I couldn't kill myself there. Finally, I said to my voice in desperation 'Fine. You right. I should be dead. And I will kill myself. But first I have to read every word of the Lord of the Rings trilogy.' I wish I could say there was some deep symbolism to this choice. But honestly, no offense to fans of Tolkien, I just knew there was probably no way I was going to read those books. My voice didn't know this however, and it bought me some peace and space. Of course, ultimately, what I had to do to move forward was to listen to the voice's message. To realize that when I am hearing a voice that is telling me to kill myself, that there usually is something in my life that needs to die. Not that my literal heart needs to stop beating. But that there is a role, a relationship, a conception of myself that needs to END for me to go on living.*
>
> ***Mazel-Carlton (2018).***

It is precisely these sorts of questions that replace the more standard "Do you have a plan" oriented ones that often signal to people that someone is trying to figure out what to "do" with them. They also help discourage people from jumping to "problem-solve" as this can get in the way of the power of simply having the opportunity to speak and be heard.

It is this curiosity 'C' that also centers the idea that people are the experts on themselves. Sometimes people make the mistake of hearing this as equivalent to saying that people already know what to do, and do not need anyone else. Rather, it means that no one else could possibly know them better, but that they may need some support to raise the most relevant knowledge to the surface and put the various pieces together. In some instances, this process can even be silent. For example, one woman shared that just by being in the space created by the group and listening to others make meaning of their experience, her mind seemed to find the permission to make sense of what she had been through in a way that she had simply never been able to before. Specifically, she had been seeing visions about death and encouraging her to take certain harmful actions. She had been too afraid to share all that with any other human being for fear of the consequences, but during a group, was able to determine that the visions were a message about how she was still blaming herself for the past. That realization was what allowed her to regain some sense of power over the situation, and eventually those visions faded away.

This focus also provides space for inquiries such as "What are the reasons that you have chosen not to die?" These types of conversations often get to the heart of important issues around meaning, purpose, spirituality, and valued relationships. The most common response is that people have chosen to stay alive because of a pet or child. Another critical question (especially for someone who is insistent that suicide is the right choice) might be "Are there things that you want to do before you die?" This type of question helps break out of any power struggle that could be ensuing, and creates space for a totally different sort of conversation. For example, one man who was absolutely determined to die by his own hand had a conversation with a supporter about the art show he wanted to create and be remembered by. They talked about the photographs he already had, and where he wanted to go to take more. They talked about where the show might happen, and how he would want his pictures to be framed. And, by the end of that conversation (which lasted about two weeks), he did not want to die anymore because he has reconnected with something so meaningful to him. It is here in these sorts of situations where we may most strongly be called upon to accept that "the key to saving someone is to admit you are powerless to save anyone at all" (Davidow, 2018a, 2018b). Sometimes, it is only by letting go of any agenda that one is able to have the conversations that helps another person reconnect with their own internal spark. Thus, exploring these topics is just as valuable as discussing problems or traumatic events.

The second 'V' speaks not only to vulnerability, but also to the transparency that is required to bring that to life. This is where facilitators are encouraged to share deeply about their own experiences, but also to be honest about their fears and worries in the moment. It is where they get to say that they are scared for someone else, or unsure what to do, and ask others in the room to be with them in that uncertainty. It is also where they get to be honest about their limits (for example, not promising to be there all night with someone, if they have a child to pick up at 5 p.m.). A common statement heard in groups is from people sharing they have not spoken about "suicidal thoughts" in months or even years. Typically they will share that they stopped speaking about the thoughts after some negative clinical intervention or interaction with law enforcement or university authorities. Yet, no participant has ever voiced that they stopped HAVING thoughts of suicide after these responses; Simply that they stopped speaking of them out loud and started struggling in silence. It is often this second 'V' that paves the way for them to start speaking again.

Most group participants report some form of institutional trauma, coercion or force before attending groups. Therefore, it is often not enough to simply state in the group introduction that the space differs from clinical models. Facilitators of the group must model through their own shares that difficult experiences can be named without negative consequences. Also, because most of the mental health system is based on correcting individual brain pathology, it is also incumbent on facilitators to introduce the freedom to examine the context of thoughts of suicide. Examples of this include naming how rigid gender roles or messages that worth is linked to economic status or skin color have influenced their thoughts of wanting to die. The Charter freedom to "challenge social norms" is often modeled first by facilitators but powerful group discussions typically arise as many participants weigh in on how it impacted them to hear things like "boys don't cry" or "your people are lazy". The groups provide a space where a wider definition of trauma (beyond combat or sexual assault) is acknowledged. Frequently, after the acknowledgment and finding out others have shared experiences, people begin to feel less distress.

Individual expressions of culture, language and spirituality are welcomed in the group. Facilitator training contains modules exploring the impact of colonization not only on rates of suicide but also on the language used to define human struggle and the ways forward. Potential facilitators are encouraged to examine their own culture and to stretch to find language to describe a difficult moment in their life beyond "mental illness". During the course of the exercise, they also explore methods they used to move through the time of struggle beyond psychiatric drugs.

That brings us to the final 'C': Community. The clinical system is often designed in a manner that creates dependence on one clinician or team or service. While this can be a step toward something better, it also contributes to people getting stuck within and sometimes building their identities around the mental health system and their relationship to it. In 2017, the Massachusetts Department of Mental Health released an age demographic chart that told a very clear story about this fact. It showed a moderate influx of individuals entering the system in their 20s and 30s, followed by a spike of representation of people in their 40s, and a steep drop off beginning in the 50s. This is no accident. What it means is that people enter the system in their 20s and 30s, get stuck in the system, and then begin dying (much earlier than people outside of the system) or being transferred to nursing homes in their 50s (Davidow, 2017a). It is the rare provider organization that does a good job not just of providing support and whatever services that it offers, but also supporting people to connect to the broader world. And, so, the community 'C' in VCVC is meant as a prominent reminder that we are to be bridges, and not life rafts.

This looks like many things. It may mean simply making space for people to share about spiritual communities, sports teams, book clubs, and other places where they are making connections in the world, including how they got connected and how others might do the same. However, it also may look like creating an on-line group or email list so people who attend the group can stay connected, or participants (rather than facilitators) stepping in to stay late if someone is having a hard time and wants more support. In more than one instance, when facilitators have not been available (due to a holiday or some other reason), regular attendees have made plans to have the group meet at a local mall or coffee shop and carried on without them. Regardless of what it looks like, this 'C' is about making sure the power is shared, that each person holds a piece of it (especially where their own lives are concerned), and that the focus is on co-creation rather than looking to someone else to make things okay.

Groups are always co-facilitated (with both co-facilitators not only identifying as having their own experience with suicidal thoughts, but also being willing to share about that). The co-facilitation model helps bring diversity to group discussions about the many reasons a person may consider suicide, make meaning of difficulties they face, and move through them. Before holding group space, potential facilitators participate in a training exercise called "Mapping a Moment". In this exercise, they share with a partner the many factors that were impacting their life during one single moment where they were very close to choosing death. With their partner, they are encouraged to take turns sharing about the impact of past adversity (trauma), social factors, lack of resources, oppression, emotional states and how they were experienced personally. For many potential facilitators, it may be the first time they have explored these issues out loud with another person.

It is an important goal to have *Alternatives to Suicide* groups accessible to every person who wants them. However it would be naive to suggest that this will be enough. Even in places where *Alternatives to Suicide* groups have existed for a decade, participants are arriving all the time wounded and frustrated by experiences in the conventional mental health system. Many are dying before ever having found out that such spaces exist. To create broader change, the adoption of an *Alternatives to Suicide* approach that can be used by all individuals is needed. Early success has been had with the development of a "When Conversation Turns to Suicide" curriculum that passes on many of the lessons of the group space to people in clinical roles, family members, clergy, and whoever else may be interested in attending.

Unfortunately, change is not easy nor accepted with wide open arms in most instances. Moreover, alternative approaches tend to be judged through a much more critical lens for any apparent failures or weaknesses than more standard interventions that are in line with the dominant paradigm. This is perhaps doubly true when it comes to the tricky topic of suicide. Yet, it is hard to argue with the feedback of those who have actually attended. In 2018, the Western Mass Recovery Learning Community undertook the first efforts toward looking at outcomes for those who have attended groups. Although the research is ongoing, initial results tell us that the number one reason (cited by over 90% of respondents) that groups are helpful is because attendees "knew [they] could talk openly about suicide and other taboo topics without negative consequences." (Unsurprisingly, the next most popular reason was that attendees could "listen to how others were making meaning or moving through their distress.") The vast majority of respondents (over 85%) felt that at least one area of their life had improved as a result of attending groups, with the greatest area of improvement (95%) falling into the area of increased sense of connection to community (followed next by "improved understanding" of why suicidal thoughts sometimes rise up). Specific feedback included:

> *I have come to see thoughts about suicide and dying as a basic part of human experience, and that I don't have to be afraid to talk about it, even if sometimes it feels scary*

> *The group has plugged me into a community that continues to help me move forward and grow stronger. My life is better than I ever imagined it could be, and my thoughts of suicide have decreased a lot. This is largely because of the support of the group, which helped me to work through the thoughts and reduce their power*

> *I know for certain that this is the single most astonishing and optimistic change that I have found in my life in the last 2 years.*

> *The groups make me feel less crazy and less alone. I have not gone into the hospital since going to the groups, and now for the first time in my life I don't think I'm going to be hospitalized again because I have a place where I can talk about what's going on and have people ask me why I'm feeling that way, rather than assuming I feel the way I do because I'm sick and because there's something wrong with me.*

> *I believe that [Alternatives to Suicide] has helped me stay alive, but (more importantly), has helped me become more of the kind of person I am ok living with.*

I really appreciate that I can talk about things by name without having to be euphemistic and assuming that the other people in the group were too fragile to hear what I was going to say. This is the only group (except other RLC groups) where I can actually say the word "rape" and not have anyone tell me that that's "too triggering" and that I can't say that.

Nonetheless, as the approach gains traction and even as positive outcomes and feedback continue to roll in, many fear-based questions also continue to rise up. One such question about *Alternatives to Suicide* is whether or not the groups are simply a place for people to go to learn how to 'do it' (i.e., kill themselves) better. One individual in Australia, in fact, asked if the groups might be seen as a "college of suicide". This is a fear that comes out of the clinical system, and has been applied to all sorts of topics from hearing voices to problems with food (typically referred to as "eating disorders") to suicide. Whatever the topic, it is rooted in the idea that it is not only bad, but downright dangerous, for struggling people to talk to anyone who is not trained to help them. However, there simply is no foundation for this fear within any context. We need only look at the thriving Hearing Voices Movement (through which hundreds of thousands of voice hearers have joined internationally to hold conferences, groups, trainings, and more) to demonstrate that fact.

Another common question is how many attendees have died by suicide. This is rooted in the fear that unsupervised suicidal people will be even more likely to die by their own hand, but the answer should do a great deal to put both this and the prior question to rest. Of the hundreds upon hundreds of people who have attended *Alternatives to Suicide* groups, only two deaths by suicide are known. Both were people who had moved out of range of the support groups they had been attending in the Northeast region of the United States. Another commonality between these two individuals is that both worked in roles in the conventional mental health system. It is not out of the ordinary for clinicians to attend *Alternatives to Suicide* groups and report that the groups are one of the only options they have to receive support. When given space to share about their struggles, they will often name the demands of the provider role itself which expects them to take full responsibility for "fixing" the problems of others while at the same time remaining silent about their own. On the other hand, an *Alternatives to Suicide* approach is one that acknowledges that the distinct binary between "helper versus helped" or "sick versus well" has been ineffective in reducing suicide rates at best, and life-threatening on both sides of the divide at worst.

Yet another question that inevitably comes up in just about every training or talk about *Alternatives to Suicide* is "What do you do if someone tries to run in front of a truck", or "off a cliff", or "shows up to group having overdosed on pills" or "stands on the roof in a lightning storm". (Yes, at least one person — and often more than one — has asked each of those questions. The honors for the creativity of the last example go to a conference attendee in Denmark.) Some even misunderstand the philosophy of no risk assessment and no forced interventions for suicidal thoughts to mean that an *Alternatives to Suicide* facilitator would be expected to stand by and watch someone die. However, here is the thing: Suicidal thoughts are not a medical issue, and as indicated at the start of this chapter, the medical system seems to have really poor outcomes when trying to address this non-medical issue. On the other hand, our medical systems have quite good outcomes when it comes to addressing actual medical emergencies, whether they are brought on by a suicide attempt or other causes. No, the *Alternatives to Suicide* approach does not suggest standing by and watching someone die, whether by heart attack or overdose. That would not be fair to anyone involved. Non-consensually bearing witness to another person's death can be traumatizing. Yes, if a facilitator (or anyone else involved with the approach) sees someone racing to jump in front of a truck or off a cliff, it would be seen as perfectly okay to knock them over along their way. But, such an intervention would not be called 'treatment'. It would simply be called being human, and not wanting to watch a fellow human die.

The systems around us continue to make the mistake of pointing to 'suicide' as 'the problem' to be stamped out, often by any means necessary. Yet suicide is not 'the problem'. It is a solution. It may be a very desperate solution that we hope people will not choose, but it is a solution nonetheless. Treating it as 'the problem' is what has led us to this point. It renders the actual problems invisible, and lulls us into thinking we don't need to look any further. In fact, people say the words "I feel suicidal" for so many reasons, from not having a place to sleep tonight and knowing the hospital has a warm bed to having been trained by the system that's what one needs to say in order to get someone's attention to "I really want to die". And, if someone really wants to die, there's even more potential reasons why (Davidow, 2016).

Advocacy organizations argue that there is a 'stigma' surrounding suicide that is preventing people from seeking treatment. Yet, the true 'stigma' seems to lie within the hands of a treatment system so quick to take away someone's power should they utter thoughts of their own death (Davidow, 2018a, 2018b). Instead, *Alternatives to Suicide* argues that we must hear each other more clearly than ever before. We must acknowledge what we don't know, and accept that the answers will only be found if each of our voices has a place in the dialogue. We must accept our own powerlessness to control each other, in order to open up new possibilities for finding ways to co-exist. Perhaps the hardest reality that we must learn to accept is that we will always lose people, and that nothing we can do will ever prevent that. But, we lose more people when we try too hard to contain them, rather than working with them to figure out how to go on living. The greatest challenge of all is to figure out how to "hold each other with our arms wide open" (Davidow, 2018a, 2018b). And, this is precisely what the *Alternatives to Suicide* approach seeks to do.

References

American Psychiatric Association. (2017). *All patients at risk for suicide after psychiatric facility discharge, study finds.* [online] Available at https://psychnews.psychiatryonline.org/doi/full/10.1176/appi.pn.2017.7a17.

American Psychological Association. (2016). *After decades of research, science is no better able to predict suicidal behaviors.* [online] Available at https://www.apa.org/news/press/releases/2016/11/suicidal-behaviors.aspx.

Brown, B. (2013). *Brené Brown on empathy.* [online] Available at https://youtu.be/1Evwgu369Jw.

Davidow, S. (2016). *Suicidal tendencies, part I: I'm suicidal because I'm mentally ill because I'm suicidal. Mad in America.* [online] Available at https://www.madinamerica.com/2016/01/suicidal-tendencies-part-i-im-suicidal-because-im-mentally-ill-because-im-suicidal/.

Davidow, S. (2017a). *Dear Boston Globe, part VI: Congratulations. Bad things happen. Mad in America.* [online] Available at https://www.madinamerica.com/2017/04/dear-boston-globe-part-vi-congratulations-bad-things-happen/.

Davidow, S. (2017b). *Peer respite handbook: A guide to understanding, developing and supporting peer respites. Western Mass Recovery Learning Community.* Denver: Outskirts Press, 2017.

Davidow, S. (2018a). *Suicidal tendencies, part II: The real 'stigma' of suicide. Mad in America.* [online] Available at https://www.madinamerica.com/2018/03/suicidal-tendencies-part-ii-real-stigma-suicide/.

Davidow, S. (2018b). *Suicidal tendencies, part III: So, when do I get to call the cops? Mad in America.* [online] Available at https://www.madinamerica.com/2018/08/suicidal-tendencies-part-iii/.

Davidow, S. (2019). *No Graphic Detail: The Injustice of Being Silenced. Mad in America.* [online] Available at https://www.madinamerica.com/2019/08/no-graphic-detail/.

Hearing Voices USA. (2008). *HVN-USA charter.* [online] Available at http://www.hearingvoicesusa.org/hvn-usa-charter.

Klugman, M. (2018). Campus mental health. In *Presentation given at the National Association for Rights Protection and Advocacy Conference, Baltimore, Maryland, USA.*

Mazel-Carlton, C. (2018). Human rights: Expanding the conversation. In *Talk given at the 10th world hearing Voices Congress, The Hague, Netherlands.*

Mulder, R., Newton-Howes, Giles, & Coid, J. (2016). The futility of risk prediction in psychiatry. *The British Journal of Psychiatry: The Journal of Mental Science, 209*, 271–272. https://doi.org/10.1192/bjp.bp.116.184960.

Murray, D., & Devitt, P. (2017). *Suicide risk assessment doesn't work*. Scientific American. [online] Available at https://www.scientificamerican.com/article/suicide-risk-assessment-doesnt-work/.

Pokorny, A. D. (1983). Prediction of suicide in psychiatric patients report of a prospective study. *Archives of General Psychiatry, 40*, 249–257.

Russell, S., Pollitt, A., Li, G., & Grossman, A. (2018). Chosen name use is linked to reduced depressive symptoms, suicidal ideation, and suicidal behavior among transgender youth. *The Journal of Adolescent Health, 63*(4), 379–380. https://doi.org/10.1016/j.jadohealth.2018.02.003.

ScienceBlog. (2009). *Clinical trials: Unfavorable results often go unpublished*. [online] Available at https://scienceblog.com/18271/clinical-trials-unfavorable-results-often-go-unpublished/.

Toomey, R., Syversten, A., & Shramko, M. (2018). Transgender adolescent behavior. *Pediatrics, 142*(4).

Western Massachusetts Recovery Learning Community. (2012). *Defining principles*. [online] Available at http://www.westernmassrlc.org/defining-principles.

Western Massachusetts Recovery Learning Community. (2015). *Possible questions, statements & strategies for supporting conversations around suicide*.

Western Massachusetts Recovery Learning Community. (2018). *Alternatives to suicide*. [online] Available at http://www.westernmassrlc.org/alternatives-to-suicide.

Zero Suicide in Health and Behavioral Health Care. (2018). *Screening for and assessing suicide risk*. [online] Available at https://zerosuicide.sprc.org/toolkit/identify/screening-and-assessing-suicide-risk#footnote1_aoqsrk2.

CHAPTER 10

Psychological resilience to suicidal experiences

Patricia Gooding, Kamelia Harris
School of Health Sciences, Division of Psychology and Mental Health, University of Manchester, Manchester, United Kingdom

Key points

1. Resilience lacks conceptual clarity, but the key issue is what people with mental health problems, including suicidal experiences, mean by resilience from their personal perspectives.
2. Research exploring resilience to mental health problems is relatively scant although growing.
3. There are at least five approaches to researching resilience which may overlap, and which need to be applied to suicide research.
4. There needs to be a sustained effort across different mental health services to develop psychological interventions which aim to amplify resilience to mental health problems, including suicidal experiences, across the lifespan.
5. Those who are Experts By Experience should be involved in all research investigating psychological resilience to suicide.
6. It should be noted that Gooding has lived experience of suicidality.

Suicidal thoughts, behaviors, and deaths are of substantial personal, public, and societal concern worldwide (CDC, 2012, 2016; EU, 2012). The prevalence rates of death by suicide reflect one death every 40 s (WHO, 2017). There is robust evidence that the probability of death by suicide is considerably raised in those with experiences of severe mental health problems (Bolton, Gooding, Kapur, Barrowclough, & Tarrier, 2007; Caldwell & Gottesman, 1990; Cohen, Lavelle, Rich, & Bromet, 1994; Hawton, Sutton, Haw, Sinclair, & Deeks, 2005; Saha, Chant, & McGrath, 2007). It has been reported that in approximately 90% of all suicide fatalities the individuals who died had severe mental health problems, for example, schizophrenia, bipolar disorder, personality disorders, and anxiety disorders, including PTSD, Obsessive Compulsive Disorder and Body Dysmorphic

Alternatives to Suicide
ISBN 978-0-12-814297-4
https://doi.org/10.1016/B978-0-12-814297-4.00010-8

Disorder (Angelakis, Gooding, & Panagioti, 2016; Angelakis, Gooding, Tarrier, & Panagioti, 2015; Hawton, Casanas i Comabella, Haw, & Saunders, 2013; Hawton et al., 2005; Hawton & van Heeringen, 2009; Panagioti, Gooding, & Tarrier, 2012; Panagioti, Gooding, Triantafyllou, & Tarrier, 2015).

Although preventing suicide deaths is paramount, it is also vitally important to consider the distress that people experience when they have suicidal thoughts, make suicidal plans, experience suicidal urges, and attempt suicide. For instance, in those who have mental health problems on the schizophrenia spectrum, up to 50% experience suicidal ideation at any point in time or have a history of previous suicide attempts (Fialko et al., 2006; Hawton et al., 2005; Palmer, Pankratz, & Bostwick, 2005). Furthermore, having suicidal thoughts is a strong risk factor for death by suicide (Chapman et al., 2015; DeVylder, Lukens, Link, & Lieberman, 2015).

However, some people with severe mental health problems do not experience suicidal thoughts, plans, or urges and do not attempt, or die by, suicide. It is imperative to understand i. why some individuals do not develop suicidal thoughts when they experience numerous adversities, ii. why some people who have suicidal thoughts do not, then, form concrete plans to die by suicide, and iii. why some people who have concrete suicide plans do not attempt suicide or die by suicide. In other words, the obverse of identifying risk factors for suicidal experiences needs to be pro-actively addressed and explored. We need to understand why and how some people who have many risk factors for suicidal experiences seem to develop psychological resilience to some forms of suicidality. Research studies which focus on examining resilience to suicidal thoughts and acts are relatively scant, especially compared to the plethora of work examining risk factors for suicide (Johnson & Wood, 2017; Johnson, Wood, Gooding, Taylor, & Tarrier, 2011). There needs to be a better balance between investigating risk factors and investigating resilience factors with respect to understanding and addressing suicidal experiences.

The case of Jane: psychological resilience to suicidal thoughts and acts

Jane is in her mid 50's. Growing up as a small child, she experienced daily physical violence from her grandmother. Her grandparents acted as primary caregivers during a period when Jane was 5–7 years of age. The physical abuse abated as Jane grew older and as she entered her teenage years. Jane also experienced sexual abuse from the partner of her mother when she was about

The case of Jane: psychological resilience to suicidal thoughts and acts—cont'd

7, with the perpetrator attempting to continue this abuse until she was around 14. Her mother colluded with the sexual abuser and also physically and emotionally abused Jane. Jane has experienced mental health problems, including having suicidal thoughts, for most of her life. She has a concrete suicide plan which gives her a sense of relief because it seems a viable escape route for her. Recently, Jane feels she is being bullied at work which reminds her of the abuse she experienced when growing up. Having this escape route of suicide helps her get through the bullying. Jane perceives herself as a survivor but doesn't feel she is really living her life. Although Jane has thoughts of suicide and has a concrete suicide plan, she has not attempted suicide.

What has enabled Jane to survive? How has Jane managed to be resilient? Does Jane perceive herself as resilient?

Some people facing severe negative stressors do not experience suicidal thoughts or urges. Still others take no action to translate suicidal thoughts into plans and/or to translate a concrete plan into attempting suicide, as in the case of Jane described above. So, why do some people seem to have psychological resilience to developing suicidal thoughts, formulating plans of suicide and attempting to, or taking, their own lives? Addressing this question and acquiring this understanding about resilience to suicidal experiences is important at levels which include the political, societal, organizational, community and, of course, the individual (Wickham, Taylor, Shevlin, & Bentall, 2014). It has been suggested that targeting resilience represents a paradigm shift away from a focus on pathophysiology and that the emphasis on resilience operates at cognitive-emotional levels and also neurobiological levels (Kalisch, Müller, & Tüscher, 2015). This paradigm shift is fundamentally important.

Recent discussions with colleagues (e.g., clinical psychologists, therapists, social workers, community psychiatric nurses, support workers) working in mental health services (i.e., the National Health Service, UK) and in UK mental health charities (e.g., Mind, The Samaritans, Self Help & The Big Life Group) highlighted the need for strong commitment at policy, political, societal and community levels to address psychological resilience. It was pointed out that resilience is eroded by multifaceted dysfunctional interactions between financial, employment, and housing crises; that there is a lack of resources to help ameliorate physical and mental health issues in general; and that there are numerous problems with navigating complex health and social care systems which seem to inhibit, rather than to facilitate, the abilities of mental health professionals to nurture and encourage people to build, maintain, and sustain resilience. It was also pointed out that there can be a, somewhat, insidious view in some sectors of society that if an individual has a mental health problem, then they are not resilient, and that this may be seen as a personal failing undeserving of resource and undeserving of care.

The case of Peter: the undeserving, non-resilient

Peter has Type 1, insulin dependent, diabetes which he has had for just over 25 years. Peter sometimes has hypoglycemic episodes where his blood-glucose levels drop dangerously low and he loses consciousness. In these instances, his body can push out adrenalin and make his muscles twitch which results in a glucose out-flow and this helps him regain consciousness. However, when regaining consciousness he lacks motor co-ordination to a severe extent, and he can also experience visual hallucinations which are threatening to him. Peter has been feeling depressed about his diabetes for many years and hasn't been managing his condition well consequently. Sometimes, Peter thinks that death by suicide is a welcome option. Peter was recently admitted to Accident and Emergency (A&E) services at his local National Health Service hospital in the UK because he had a hypoglycemic episode, which he collapsed from, at a bus station in the city centre where he lives. He felt that the paramedics treated him well. On arrival at the A&E department, the nurse receiving him told him that he had failed to take care of himself properly and that he shouldn't be allowed to take up time needed by those who were 'really ill'. Peter knew that this type of judgment was unacceptable but felt too vulnerable to make a complaint. He also knew all too fully that hypoglycemia can be fatal. In hospital, he started to have suicidal thoughts which continued when he was discharged. Peter felt undeserving and a burden to society.

What were the key factors about the interaction between the nurse and Peter, when Peter arrived in hospital, which were detrimental to him? What should be done when following up, not only Peter, but also the nurse who received him onto the ward? How could Peter's psychological resilience be boosted?

Feeling a burden, for example, to family, friends, communities and society in general, is a key risk factor for having suicidal experiences, including death by suicide (Van Orden et al., 2010). This view, expressed by some health professionals, of the 'undeserving non-resilient' as in the case of the nurse receiving Peter onto the ward, described above, can be contrasted with an opposing view that is often a key principle of mental health charities. This opposing view is that everyone is resilient. Everyone is deserving, and a fundamental goal is to boost that resilience, and then work with everyone collaboratively to find ways of maintaining and amplifying resilience. In the case of Peter, he had been dealing with a physically/physiologically demanding and psychologically depleting condition for two-and-a-half decades. Hence, Peter can be seen as being exceptionally resilient. Identifying, enhancing and maintaining resilience is embraced by many mental health charities, and, indeed, by many individuals working in the mental health field. Key principles are that no-one should feel excluded from receiving mental health care; no-one should feel abandoned by mental health care services; and no-one should lose sight of their own resilience and potential for resilience. Understanding the psychological mechanisms which underlie resilience to suicidal thoughts and acts is crucial in promoting the development of psychological therapies and psychological approaches which enhance and maintain resilience to suicidal thoughts, plans, urges, acts and behaviors.

What is psychological resilience?

Psychological resilience is considered to be a set of skills or mechanisms which operate in the face of negative stressors or negative life events to return an individual to, or maintain, optimal psychological functioning (Bonanno, 2004; Masten, 2001). Such negative stressors can be internal, for example hearing criticizing voices ("you'll always be bad; you'll always be a failure; why are you still here; you shouldn't be here"), or external, for example, facing redundancy or other financial pressures, bereavement, a relationship break-up, being bullied, being excluded for many reasons and facing numerous types of stigmatization.

In the psychological literature, resilience has been investigated across a number of domains including elite sports performance (Golby & Sheard, 2004; Jones, Hanton, & Connaughton, 2002), military effectiveness (Bartone, 2006; King, King, Vogt, Knight, & Samper, 2006), academic achievement (Martin & Marsh, 2008; Nota, Soresi, & Zimmerman, 2004), homelessness (Kidd & Shahar, 2008), attitudes and coping abilities in those experiencing chronic illnesses (Hampel, Rudolph, Stachow, Labeta-Lentzsch, & Petermann, 2005; Moskowitz & Wrubel, 2005; Rabkin, Remien, Katoff, & Williams, 1993), in response to traumatic events

(Bonanno, 2005; Gold et al., 2000) and in minority groups, such as, sexual minorities (Kwon, 2013).

The problem with conceptualizations of resilience is that they lack definitional clarity and precision. A recent narrative systematic review (Ayed, Toner, & Priebe, 2018) based on 31 publications investigated resilience in adults with mental health problems. The review concluded that there were two broad ways of conceptualizing psychological resilience. The first was as a process and the second was as personal characteristics of an individual. Processes included three concepts: i. Immunity, such as, being able to resist; ii Bouncing Back, defined as returning to a state of stability; and iii Growth, implying positive transformation as a function of adversity. Characteristics of individuals encompassed i. having Personal Resources and ii. having Social Resources both of which were seen as having the potential to be protective. Examples of personal resources included developing coping skills, using positive emotions, acceptance, courage, and having hope for the future. Examples of social resources included the power of communities to aid recovery, having well-functioning and meaningful social networks, and having prompt access to well-resourced health and social services. It is a notable strength that the studies included in this systematic review used a range of methods, e.g., reviews, mixed methods, and qualitative and quantitative designs.

Thinking about resilience as both a set of processes and having personal and social resources offers the greatest potential for developing and sustaining resilience across a number of different levels, e.g., societal, community and individual. In other words, resilience may be determined by a range of modifiable psychosocial factors (Chmitorz et al., 2018; Kalisch et al., 2015). That such psychosocial factors are adaptable offers the potential for developing psychological approaches and techniques which can maximize and sustain resilience.

In order to determine the starting points for developing psychological interventions and techniques for nurturing resilience, it is important to explore what resilience means, personally, to individuals with severe mental health problems. In a qualitative study (Gooding, Littlewood, Owen, Johnson, & Tarrier, 2017), we were privileged to gain responses from 21 people with non-affective psychosis (e.g., hearing negative voices) and suicidality, together with experiencing external stressors (e.g., losing their job) to the question 'what does resilience meant to you?' Around 80% of the sample said that they understood the term resilience, and these were some of their responses:

"you can come to terms with everything" [ID = J25 ii]

"not caving in under pressure" [ID = J35 ii]

" is sort of keeping going, erm, a sense of not being defeated" [ID = J18 ii]

"Try to put something off, put something away, you know. Erm, don't know. Put something away, push something aside, so it doesn't matter." [ID = J16]

"you're tough" [ID = J30 ii]

"being able to kind of bounce back from something." [ID = J27 ii]

"energy to fight back" [ID = J19 ii]

"Well... to people... it would mean like how they cope with things... erm... yeah, just like that." [ID = J15 ii]

As depicted in Fig. 10.1 below, there were three overarching themes which described the responses of our participants. These were i. Acceptance, ii. Resistance and iii. Active strategies.

Only a small number of participants (three) expressed the meaning of resilience in terms of Acceptance. This seemed to encapsulate an idea of being reconciled with stressful or negative events and not having to challenge or fight against those events. The majority of participants endorsed resilience as a form of Resistance which was emotionally, psychologically and/or pragmatically seen as protective against a range of negative stressors. This protection was thought to act in three ways. First, to withstand pressure and 'keep going'. Second, to develop inner strength and form a 'thick skin'. Third, to be self-reliant. Resilience conceived of as an Active response to stressors captured the idea that difficulties in life could be challenged or over-come by not being defeated, rebounding, and

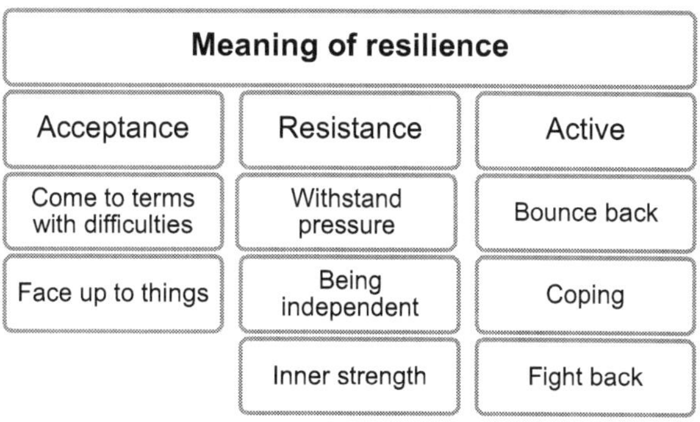

Fig. 10.1 The meaning of resilience as depicted by individuals with experiences of psychosis, and suicidal thoughts/behaviors.

finding the energy to fight back. It is interesting that the systematic review described above (Ayed et al., 2018) and our qualitative study converged in identifying resilience factors which were i. immunity/resistance, ii. bouncing back/rebounding, iii. acceptance and iv. developing coping skills.

Psychological resilience to suicidal experiences: a mixed methods approach

Suicidal experiences have been described as being on a continuum in which suicidal thoughts lead to suicidal intent, then the formation of a concrete suicide plan, and then suicidal acts e.g., suicide attempts. This continuum view of suicidality can, of course, be challenged because these sorts of experiences (Tarrier et al., 2013) are not necessarily perceived as being linear and can be experienced as cyclical or spiraling (Wyder & De Leo, 2007). That said, it is important to know how to stop suicidal thoughts from occurring in the first place, and/or escalating; how to stop the formation of suicidal plans; and how to prevent a suicide attempt.

In order to investigate these issues further, we presented a vignette to 36 people with a diagnosis of non-affective psychosis who had suicidal experiences (Gooding, Sheehy, & Tarrier, 2013). The vignette described a protagonist called 'Poppy' in which there was an escalation of her suicidal experiences from thoughts to plans and then to actively preparing to kill herself. Participants were asked what would stop Poppy's suicidal thoughts, plans and active preparations. We used a mixed methods approach. Social support was seen as most protective against suicidal thoughts with psychological talking therapies viewed as being most helpful in terms of input from mental health professionals. Medication was considered important in ameliorating suicidal plans. Hospitalization, albeit for short-stays followed up with counseling/talking therapy, was highlighted as the best approach for preventing suicidal acts.

This is the vignette that we developed. We'd like to invite you to consider how to reduce or weaken Poppy's suicidal thoughts and plans, and then lessen her active engagement with those plans. Perhaps, we can ask the question as to how resilience could be nurtured in Poppy in both the short and long term based on your experiences?

> *Poppy is in her early 30s. She has two small children, a demanding part-time job and difficult family commitments, particularly with her in-laws. Poppy is now expecting a third child. The first half of her pregnancy has gone as expected. However, she now feels constantly tired and increasingly inert. She literally feels*

as though a black cloud is swallowing her up and she becomes ever more withdrawn from her friends and family. She catches herself looking up at airplanes in the sky willing them to crash down on her. She begins to hear voices telling her that she is not fit to have another child and that she will give birth to the devil. She feels she is carrying a monster inside her.

You can find Poppy's evolving story here (Gooding et al., 2013).

Before we can consider how to nurture resilience in Poppy with respect to her suicidal experiences, we need to identify the different models or approaches that we can use to best understand psychological resilience to mental health problems, including suicidality. Only by identifying and specifying these models, can we begin to challenge, test and further develop our understanding of resilience to suicidal experiences.

A multi-componential mechanistic approach to understanding psychological resilience to suicidal experiences

The main problem with probing the meaning of resilience and examining factors which can stop suicidal thoughts, urges, plans and acts is that the definitions which have been generated and the factors which have been suggested are highly descriptive (Ayed et al., 2018). In order to understand how resilience to suicidal experiences can be developed and maintained, we need to comprehend the psychological mechanisms which underpin resilience to such experiences. Mechanisms which explain resilience to suicidality can only really be captured by a multi-componential dynamic approach (Johnson et al., 2011; Johnson, Gooding, Wood, & Tarrier, 2010; Johnson & Wood, 2017; Kalisch et al., 2015).

A case study of Nathan and Charlotte: a multi-componential approach

Nathan is in his 50's. He married his wife, Charlotte, about 18 years ago. Both are nurses working in mental health. Nathan works with people who live in the community. Charlotte works on inpatient psychiatric wards. Nathan has often had to take time off work due to work stress manifested as general anxiety which has been building up over the past 12 months. He often feels depressed because of his work. He also has suicidal thoughts because of the accumulative

Continued

A case study of Nathan and Charlotte: a multi-componential approach—cont'd

stressors that he experiences. That said, Nathan enjoys creative writing and has joined an on-line creative writing forum. Others on the forum have asked Nathan to submit a creative writing blog he has developed to a competition. Nathan doubts his abilities but feels encouraged by the people on the forum. He has also started mindfulness meditation classes at his local community centre which he feels are reducing his levels of anxiety related to work. However, he feels little improvement in his depression and still has suicidal thoughts. In his spare time Nathan volunteers for a dog rescue centre. He has always resonated with animals and, although he finds working with rescue dogs can be stressful and upsetting for many reasons, he very much values this work. He feels this is a core value for him. Whilst working on psychiatric inpatient wards is equally as stressful as working in the community, albeit in different ways, Charlotte does not feel that her work is detrimental to her mental health. However, Charlotte cannot have children due to medical reasons, but she does want to bring-up children. Charlotte discusses with Nathan whether they may be able to be 'foster parents' and may be able adopt in the future. Charlotte perceives that she cannot fulfill her role as a woman and that she does not fit into society unless she is able to bring-up children and thinks she is becoming depressed as a consequence. Nathan feels able to support Charlotte in whichever direction she wants to explore with respect to having a family. Because of Nathan's support, and reflecting and exploring her situation, Charlotte finds her sense of being a woman returning. In fact, she thinks that her sense of being a woman is stronger than it has ever been, even before she felt depressed about this issue.

What are the sources of resilience for Nathan and Charlotte? How might these sources of resilience intertwine for them as a couple? If you were a clinician working with Nathan and/or Charlotte what would be your 'gut reaction' with respect to working with their resilience individually, and then as a couple? What was the source of your gut reaction?

Five ways of modeling a dynamic approach to understanding psychological resilience can be identified. As we examine each of the five modeling approaches it might be helpful to consider them by reflecting on the case of Nathan and Charlotte as described above.

The unidimensional 'two poles' approach

This approach conceptualizes resilience as at one end of a pole (e.g., feeling socially supported) with risk factors at the other end of the pole (e.g., feeling socially defeated). To take the example of Nathan, if work-related stress and anxiety were risk factors for suicidal thoughts and acts, then resilience would be a lack of those risk factors, that is, not experiencing work-related stress and anxiety. The problem with this approach is that not experiencing a stressor or a risk factor does not equate to developing and maintaining resilience. Similarly, being resilient, does not equate to not experiencing risk factors. In the example above, if the stress and anxiety experienced by Nathan were not present, then Nathan could be seen as resilient. Clearly, there are two issues to consider in this situation. Is Nathan no longer exposed to the stress and anxiety, and, therefore, is he showing resilience because the stressor or stressors simply no longer exist? Or do the stressors exist, but Nathan can buffer or counter, those stressors?

The two-dimensional, buffering, approach

Two-dimensional conceptualizations of resilience expand the unidimensional approach. Such two-dimensional approaches suggest that risk and resilience are best considered as independent, albeit interacting, dimensions, such that the presence of one dimension, e.g., risk, does not imply the lack of the other, e.g., resilience. In the vignette, Nathan can experience risk factors for suicidality (e.g., stress and anxiety) and also evidence resilience to those risk factors at the same time. The buffering approach to resilience makes this idea more concrete. Resilience as a buffer focuses on being able to rebut negative stressors by weakening associations between stressors/risk factors and a negative outcome, such as, suicidal experiences (Johnson et al., 2011; Johnson & Wood, 2017). For instance, there may be a strong and positive association between financial pressures and developing suicidal thoughts but having a solid sense of being connected to others may weaken, or buffer, that association (Stone, Luo, Lippy, & McIntosh, 2015; You, Van Orden, & Conner, 2011). In the example in the vignette above, Nathan finds that the mindfulness meditation classes are positively acting on, i.e., weakening, the associations he is experiencing between work stress and anxiety. In other words, mindfulness meditation is a protective or buffering factor. This fits with the buffering hypothesis which suggests that resilience factors moderate or buffer the relationship between suicide risk factors, or triggers for suicidal experiences, and negative outcomes (Johnson et al., 2011).

Recovery

In the recovery model of resilience, a factor or function which has been lost is perceived as being regained. This model identifies adverse events and stressors; the subsequent adverse deviations from functioning caused by these events and stressors; and then the extent to which these deviations are alleviated (Goubert & Trompetter, 2017). This type of recovery process is sometimes conceptualized as rebounding or bouncing back to health (Tugade & Fredrickson, 2004). In the above vignette, Charlotte was losing her sense of being a woman because she was unable to have children which was negatively affecting her mental health. Through support from Nathan, she not only recovered her sense of being a woman but found that this sense had returned more strongly. This example illustrates that recovery can be allied to an experience of personal growth as a result of coming through negative experiences (Jacob, 2015; Sumskis, Moxham, & Caputi, 2016).

Psychological immunity

In the psychology immunity model, negative stressors do not have a detrimental effect on well-being (Davydov, Stewart, Ritchie, & Chaudieu, 2010). In other words, individuals seem resistant to negative events and negative stressors. In the vignette above, Charlotte seemed immune to work stressors having a detrimental effect on her mental health which could be contrasted with the experiences of her husband, Nathan. Of course, it is important to understand how individuals develop and maintain psychological immunity to factors which can be triggers for mental health problems, both in acute periods of their lives and over the longer time-course of their lives.

Maintenance

The maintenance approach to resilience encapsulates the ability to sustain a positive outlook in the face of negative experiences and stressors, sometimes over a long time period. This approach is closely linked to the positive psychology movement which examines how individuals thrive and flourish across different domains of their lives (Wood & Tarrier, 2010). The ability to maintain meaningful activities and values, despite adversity, is a key feature of the Maintenance model (Goubert & Trompetter, 2017). An important point is that this approach to resilience does not depend on recovery, nor a weakening of mental health problems due to a buffer, nor immunity. A positive outlook to life may be observed despite no improvement in mental health problems. It has been suggested that this positive outlook may hinge upon identifying key values which deflect focus away from mental health problems (Goubert & Trompetter, 2017). In the vignette, although Nathan's anxiety had been helped by mindfulness, he still experienced depression and suicidal thoughts. However, this was off-set by the work he did with the animal rescue center, exemplifying an important value held by him.

Evaluating the five resilience models

There are several important points to consider when evaluating these five resilience models. First, they are not necessarily mutually exclusive. For example, there may be buffering or protective factors which subsequently result in recovery and/or personal growth. Similarly, maintenance factors may exist alongside mechanisms which are protective or promote recovery. Second, and relatedly, the influence of the components of these five models, and the interactions between the five models, may differ across the lifespan. Hence, it is important to adopt a 'life-span' approach to understanding resilience. Third, all models resonate with the idea that resilience factors can be developed and nurtured which is a crucial underpinning for the development of psychological resilience interventions and a 'positive action' based approach to mental health problems including suicidal experiences. Fourth, the models have the potential to be adaptable to diverse cultures and diverse belief systems. Fifth, the five models are situated at an individual level of understanding rather than broader community, societal, and political levels which could be considered a weakness. That said, the principles intrinsic to these five models have the potential to be applied across different levels of understanding, including broader societal and political contexts. Finally, there are four contemporary psychological theories which have been developed to aid the understanding of suicidal experiences (see below). A key question is how to optimally develop these theories of suicide so that they can i. examine pathways to suicidal experiences and ii. the converse of that which is to examine and understand pathways to resilience to suicidal experiences across multiple domains.

Theoretical models of psychological resilience to suicidal experiences

There are four recent psychological theories which seek to explain the pathways to suicidal experiences. The first of these contemporary models of suicide is the Schematic Appraisal Model of Suicide, i.e., the SAMS (Johnson, Gooding, & Tarrier, 2008). The second is the Interpersonal

Theory of Suicide (Van Orden et al., 2010). The third is the Integrated Motivational-Volitional model of suicide (O'Connor, 2011). The most recent is the Three Step Theory (Klonsky & May 2015). Although all of these models can be adapted to consider psychological resilience to suicidal experiences, only the SAMS was explicitly developed to explain psychological resilience to suicidal experiences.

In order to develop all four theories of suicidal experiences with respect to resilience, it is necessary to i. evaluate the evidence pertaining to the five dynamic resilience to suicide approaches in general; and ii. determine the extent to which the evidence supports, refutes, and extends the contemporary models which attempt to understand pathways involved in suicidal thoughts and behaviors.

Evidence pertaining to the five dynamic suicide resilience models

It is not within the scope of this chapter to evaluate the evidence in detail which sheds light on which of the five resilience models are best supported. This caveat also applies to exploring which current psychological theories attempting to elucidate the pathways to suicidality are the most optimal for studying resilience to suicidal thoughts and acts. However, work from suicide researchers at the University of Manchester, UK, have found that feeling socially supported; perceptions of being able to regulate emotions; and feeling able to problem solve, especially inter-personally, seem important resilience factors in people who do and do not experience mental health problems e.g., PTSD (Panagioti, Gooding, Taylor, & Tarrier, 2014), psychosis (Gooding et al., 2017; Johnson, Gooding, Wood, & Tarrier, 2010; Johnson, Gooding, Wood, Taylor, et al., 2010) and bipolar disorders (Owen, Gooding, Dempsey, & Jones, 2017).

One point which should be emphasized is that the requisite methodological diversity doesn't exist in the literature to enable us to evaluate which of the five models of, or approaches to, resilience to suicidality are the most promising. For example, much of the research examining resilience to suicidal experiences in people with non-affective psychosis has simply taken a unidimensional, two-poles, approach, using very basic correlational designs. To explore buffering, recovery, immunity, and maintenance approaches to resilience to suicidality, longitudinal designs are needed in which temporal precedence can be established. Indeed, longitudinal deigns are relatively scant in work examining pathways to suicidal experiences (but see Panagioti, Gooding, & Tarrier, 2015). A potentially interesting question to consider is to what extent longitudinal designs using time points comprising months and years converge with findings using micro-longitudinal experience sampling designs where individuals are asked about their thoughts and feelings over the course of each day, across several days (Littlewood et al., 2019; Myin-Germeys et al., 2009). It is also the case that the vast majority of resilience research adopts quantitative designs. Qualitative work in this area is essential because we are only just beginning a journey which seeks to understand suicide resilience, and we need to understand the experiences of individuals who are, or have been suicidal, from their perspectives, in order to make progress. Qualitative work should be used in a way that is convergent with quantitative data, including using mixed methods. A neglected area which could offer in-depth insights is to meld, or nest, qualitative designs with experience sampling designs.

A final point is that it is very important to understand not only the views of people experiencing suicidality with respect to psychological resilience but also the views of mental health professionals working with those individuals. This is because, in order to design psychological interventions which are both efficacious and effective in developing and maintaining resilience to suicidal experiences, we need to evaluate the overlap in views and perceptions between mental health professionals and people experiencing suicidality, but we also need to investigate where there is divergence and the origin of that diversity (Awenat et al., 2017). An important issue to consider when examining convergent and divergent views is the extent to which mental health professionals receive requisite support which builds their resilience when working with people with severe mental health problems (Hall et al., 2018; Johnson et al., 2018). This is particularly important because many mental health professionals may also have/have had suicidal experiences.

References

Angelakis, I., Gooding, P., & Panagioti, M. (2016). Suicidality in body dysmorphic disorder (BDD): A systematic review with metaanalysis. *Clinical Psychology Review, 49*, 55–66.

Angelakis, I., Gooding, P., Tarrier, N., & Panagioti, M. (2015). Suicidality in obsessive compulsive disorder (OCD): A systematic review and meta-analysis. *Clinical Psychology Review, 39*, 1–15. https://doi.org/10.1016/j.cpr.2015.03.002.

Awenat, Y., Peters, S., Shaw-Nunez, E., Gooding, P., Pratt, D., & Haddock, G. (2017). Staff experiences and perceptions of working with in-patients who are suicidal: Qualitataive analysis. *The British Journal of Psychiatry, 211*(2), 103–108. https://doi.org/10.1192/bjp.bp.116.191817.

Ayed, N., Toner, S., & Priebe, S. (2018). Conceptualizing resilience in adult mental health literature: A systematic review and narrative synthesis. *Psychological Psychotherapy*. https://doi.org/10.1111/papt.12185.

Bartone, P. T. (2006). Resilience under military operational stress: Can leaders influence hardiness. *Military Psychology, 18*(Suppl. 1), S131–S148.

Bolton, C., Gooding, P., Kapur, N., Barrowclough, C., & Tarrier, N. (2007). Developing psychological perspectives of suicidal behaviour and risk in people with a diagnosis of schizophrenia: We know they kill themselves but do we understand why? *Clinical Psychology Review, 27*(4), 511–536.

Bonanno, G. A. (2004). Loss, trauma, and human resilience: Have we underestimated the human capacity to thrive after extremely aversive events? *American Psychologist, 59*(1), 20–28.

Bonanno, G. A. (2005). Resilience in the face of potential trauma. *Current Directions in Psychological Science, 14*(3), 135–138.

Caldwell, C. B., & Gottesman, I. I. (1990). Schizophrenics kill themselves too - a review of risk-factors for suicide. *Schizophrenia Bulletin, 16*(4), 571–589.

CDC. (2012). *Centers for disease control and prevention: Morbidity and mortality weekly report 2012*. Retrieved from http://www.cdc.gov/mmwr/preview/mmwrhtml/mm6101a6.htm?s_cid=mm6101a6_w.

CDC. (2016). *National suicide statistics*. Retrieved from https://www.cdc.gov/nchs/fastats/suicide.htm.

Chapman, C. L., Mullin, K., Ryan, C. J., Kuffel, A., Nielssen, O., & Large, M. M. (2015). Meta-analysis of the association between suicidal ideation and later suicide among patients with either a schizophrenia spectrum psychosis or a mood disorder. *Acta Psychiatrica Scandinavica, 131*(3), 162–173. https://doi.org/10.1111/acps.12359.

Chmitorz, A., Kunzler, A., Helmreich, I., Tuscher, O., Kalisch, R., Kubiak, T., et al. (2018). Intervention studies to foster resilience - a systematic review and proposal for a resilience framework in future intervention studies. *Clinical Psychology Review, 59*, 78–100. https://doi.org/10.1016/j.cpr.2017.11.002.

Cohen, S., Lavelle, J., Rich, C. L., & Bromet, E. (1994). Rates and correlates of suicide attempts in first-admission psychotic-patients. *Acta Psychiatrica Scandinavica, 90*(3), 167–171.

Davydov, D., Stewart, R., Ritchie, K., & Chaudieu, I. (2010). Resilience and mental health. *Clinical Psychology Review, 30*(5), 479–495. https://doi.org/10.1016/j.cpr.2010.03.003.

DeVylder, J. E., Lukens, E. P., Link, B. G., & Lieberman, J. A. (2015). Suicidal ideation and suicide attempts among adults with psychotic experiences data from the collaborative psychiatric epidemiology surveys. *JAMA Psychiatry, 72*(3), 219–225. https://doi.org/10.1001/jamapsychiatry.2014.2663.

EU. (2012). *Death due to suicide by gender*.

Fialko, L., Freeman, D., Bebbington, P. E., Kuipers, E., Garety, P. A., Dunn, G., et al. (2006). Understanding suicidal ideation in psychosis: Findings from the psychological prevention of relapse in psychosis (PRP) trial. *Acta Psychiatrica Scandinavica, 114*(3), 177–186.

Golby, J., & Sheard, M. (2004). Mental toughness and hardiness at different levels of rugby league. *Personality and Individual Differences, 37*(5), 933–942.

Gold, P. B., Engdahl, B. E., Eberly, R. E., Blake, R. J., Page, W. F., & Frueh, B. C. (2000). Trauma exposure, resilience, social support, and PTSD construct validity among former prisoners of war. *Social Psychiatry and Psychiatric Epidemiology, 35*(1), 36–42.

Gooding, P., Littlewood, D., Owen, R., Johnson, J., & Tarrier, N. (2017). Psychological resilience in people experiencing schizophrenia and suicidal thoughts and behaviours. *Journal of Mental Health*, 1–7.

Gooding, P., Sheehy, K., & Tarrier, N. (2013). Perceived stops to suicidal thoughts, plans, and actions in persons experiencing psychosis. *Crisis-The Journal of Crisis Intervention and Suicide Prevention, 34*(4), 273–281. https://doi.org/10.1027/0227-5910/a000194.

Goubert, L., & Trompetter, H. (2017). Towards a science and practice of resilience in the face of pain. *European Journal of Pain, 2*(8), 1201–1305.

Hall, L. H., Johnson, J., Heyhoe, J., Watt, I., Anderson, K., & O'Connor, D. B. (2018). Strategies to improve general practitioner well-being: Findings from a focus group study. *Family Practice, 35*(4), 511–516. https://doi.org/10.1093/fampra/cmx130.

Hampel, P., Rudolph, H., Stachow, R., Labeta -Lentzsch, A., & Petermann, F. (2005). Coping among children and adolescents with chronic illness. *Anxiety, Stress and Coping: An International Journal, 18*(2), 145–155.

Hawton, K., Casanas i Comabella, C., Haw, C., & Saunders, K. (2013). Risk factors for suicide in individuals with depression: A systematic review. *Journal of Affective Disorders, 147*(1–3), 17–28. https://doi.org/10.1016/j.jad.2013.01.004.

Hawton, K., & van Heeringen, K. (2009). Suicide. *Lancet, 373*(9672), 1372–1381.

Hawton, K., Sutton, L., Haw, C., Sinclair, J., & Deeks, J. J. (2005). Schizophrenia and suicide: Systematic review of risk factors. *British Journal of Psychiatry, 187*, 9–20.

Jacob, K. S. (2015). Recovery model of mental illness: A complementary approach to psychiatric care. *Indian Journal of Psychological Medicine, 37*(2), 117–119.

Johnson, J., Gooding, P., & Tarrier, N. (2008). Suicide risk in schizophrenia: Explanatory models and clinical implications, the schematic appraisal model of suicide (SAMS). *Psychology and Psychotherapy: Theory, Research and Practice, 81*, 55–77.

Johnson, J., Gooding, P. A., Wood, A. M., & Tarrier, N. (2010). Resilience as positive coping appraisals: Testing the schematic appraisals model of suicide (SAMS). *Behaviour Research and Therapy, 48*(3), 179–186. https://doi.org/10.1016/j.brat.2009.10.007.

Johnson, J., Gooding, P. A., Wood, A. M., Taylor, P. J., Pratt, D., & Tarrier, N. (2010). Resilience to suicidal ideation in psychosis: Positive self-appraisals buffer the impact of hopelessness. *Behaviour Research and Therapy, 48*(9), 883–889.

Johnson, J., Hall, L. H., Berzins, K., Baker, J., Melling, K., & Thompson, C. (2018). Mental healthcare staff well-being and burnout: A narrative review of trends, causes, implications, and recommendations for future interventions. *International Journal of Mental Health Nursing, 27*(1), 20–32. https://doi.org/10.1111/inm.12416.

Johnson, J., & Wood, A. M. (2017). Integrating positive and clinical psychology: Viewing human functioning as continua from positive to negative can benefit clinical assessment, interventions and understandings of resilience. *Cognitive Therapy and Research, 41*(3), 335–349. https://doi.org/10.1007/s10608-015-9728-y.

Johnson, J., Wood, A. M., Gooding, P., Taylor, P. J., & Tarrier, N. (2011). Resilience to suicidality: The buffering hypothesis. *Clinical Psychology Review, 31*(4), 563–591. https://doi.org/10.1016/j.cpr.2010.12.007.

Jones, G., Hanton, S., & Connaughton, D. (2002). What is this thing called mental toughness? An investigation of elite sport performers. *Journal of Applied Sport Psychology, 14*(3), 205–218.

Kalisch, R., Müller, M. B., & Tüscher, O. (2015). A conceptual framework for the neurobiological study of resilience. *Behavior and Brain Sciences, 38*(e92). https://doi.org/10.1017/S0140525X1400082X.

Kidd, S., & Shahar, G. (2008). Resilience in homeless youth: The key role of self-esteem. *American Journal of Orthopsychiatry, 78*(2), 163–172.

King, L. A., King, D. W., Vogt, D. S., Knight, J., & Samper, R. E. (2006). Deployment risk and resilience inventory: A collection of measures for studying deployment-related experiences of military personnel and veterans. *Military Psychology, 18*(2), 89–120.

Klonsky, E. D., & May, A. M. (2015). The three-step theory (3ST): A new theory of suicide rooted in the "ideation-to-action" framework. *International Journal of Cognitive Therapy, 8*(2), 114–129.

Kwon, P. (2013). Resilience in lesbian, gay, and bisexual individuals. *Personality and Social Psychology Review, 17*(4), 371–383. https://doi.org/10.1177/1088868313490248.

Littlewood, D., Kyle, S., Carter, L.-A., Peters, S., Pratt, D., & Gooding, P. (2019). Short sleep duration and poor sleep quality predict next-day suicidal ideation: An ecological momentary assessment study. *Psychological Medicine, 49*(3), 403–411. https://doi.org/10.1017/s0033291718001009.

Martin, A. J., & Marsh, H. W. (2008). Academic buoyancy: Towards an understanding of students' everyday academic resilience. *Journal of School Psychology, 46*(1), 53–83.

Masten, A. S. (2001). Ordinary magic: Resilience processes in development. *American Psychologist, 56*(3), 227–238.

Moskowitz, J. T., & Wrubel, J. (2005). Coping with HIV as a chronic illness: A longitudinal analysis of illness appraisals. *Psychology and Health, 20*(4), 509–531.

Myin-Germeys, I., Oorschot, M., Collip, D., Lataster, J., Delespaul, P., & van Os, J. (2009). Experience sampling research in psychopathology: Opening the black box of daily life. *Psychological Medicine, 39*(9), 1533–1547.

Nota, L., Soresi, S., & Zimmerman, B. J. (2004). Self-regulation and academic achievement and resilience: A longitudinal study. *International Journal of Educational Research, 41*(3), 198–215.

O'Connor, R. C. (2011). The Integrated Motivational-Volitional model of suicidal behavior. *Crisis-The Journal of Crisis Intervention and Suicide Prevention, 32*(6), 295–298. https://doi.org/10.1027/0227-5910/a000120.

Owen, R., Gooding, P., Dempsey, R., & Jones, S. H. (2017). The reciprocal relationships between social factors and the experience of bipolar disorder: A qualitative investigation. *Clinical Psychology and Psychotherapy, 24*(4).

Palmer, B. A., Pankratz, V. S., & Bostwick, J. M. (2005). The lifetime risk of suicide in schizophrenia - a reexamination. *Archives of General Psychiatry, 62*(3), 247–253.

Panagioti, M., Gooding, P., & Tarrier, N. (2012). A meta-analysis of the association between Posttraumatic Stress Disorder (PTSD) and suicidality: The role of comorbid depression. *Comprehensive Psychiatry, 53*(7), 915–930. https://doi.org/10.1016/j.comppsych.2012.02.009.

Panagioti, M., Gooding, P. A., & Tarrier, N. (2015). A prospective study of suicidal ideation in posttraumatic stress disorder: The role of perceptions of defeat and entrapment. *Journal of Clinical Psychology, 71*(1), 50–61. https://doi.org/10.1002/jclp.22103.

Panagioti, M., Gooding, P. A., Taylor, P. J., & Tarrier, N. (2014). Perceived social support buffers the impact of PTSD symptoms on suicidal behavior: Implications into suicide resilience research. *Comprehensive Psychiatry, 55*(1), 104–112. https://doi.org/10.1016/j.comppsych.2013.06.004.

Panagioti, M., Gooding, P. A., Triantafyllou, K., & Tarrier, N. (2015). Suicidality and posttraumatic stress disorder (PTSD) in adolescents: A systematic review and meta-analysis. *Social Psychiatry and Psychiatric Epidemiology, 50*(4), 525–537. https://doi.org/10.1007/s00127-014-0978-x.

Rabkin, J. G., Remien, R., Katoff, L., & Williams, J. B. (1993). Resilience in adversity among long-term survivors of AIDS. *Hospital and Community Psychiatry, 44*(2), 162–167.

Saha, S., Chant, D., & McGrath, J. (2007). A systematic review of mortality in schizophrenia. Is the differential mortality gap worsening over time? *Archives of General Psychiatry, 64*(10), 1123–1131.

Stone, D. M., Luo, F., Lippy, C., & McIntosh, W. L. (2015). The role of social connectedness and sexual orientation in the prevention of youth suicide ideation and attempts among sexually active adolescents. *Suicide and Life-Threatening Behavior, 45*(4), 415–430. https://doi.org/10.1111/sltb.12139.

Sumskis, S., Moxham, L., & Caputi, P. (2016). Meaning of resilience as described by people with schizophrenia. *International Journal of Mental Health Nursing*. https://doi.org/10.1111/inm.12268.

Tarrier, N., Gooding, P., Pratt, D., Kelly, J., Awenat, Y., & Maxwell, J. (2013). *Cognitive behavioural prevention of suicide in psychosis: A treatment manual*. London, UK: Routledge.

Tugade, M. M., & Fredrickson, B. L. (2004). Psychological resilience and positive emotional granularity: Examining the benefits of positive emotions on coping and health. *Journal of Personality, 7*(6), 1161–1190.

Van Orden, K. A., Witte, T. K., Cukrowicz, K. C., Braithwaite, S. R., Selby, E. A., & Joiner, T. E. (2010). The interpersonal theory of suicide. *Psychological Review, 117*(2), 575–600.

WHO. (2017). *Suicide data*. Retrieved from http://www.who.int/mental_health/prevention/suicide/suicideprevent/en/.

Wickham, S., Taylor, P., Shevlin, M., & Bentall, R. P. (2014). The impact of social deprivation on paranoia, hallucinations, mania and depression: The role of discrimination social support, stress and trust. *PLoS One, 9*(8). https://doi.org/10.1371/journal.pone.0105140.

Wood, A. M., & Tarrier, N. (2010). Positive clinical psychology: A new vision and strategy for integrated research and practice. *Clinical Psychology Review, 30*(7), 819–829. https://doi.org/10.1016/j.cpr.2010.06.003.

Wyder, M., & De Leo, D. (2007). Behind impulsive suicide attempts: Indications from a community study. *Journal of Affective Disorders, 104*(1–3), 167–173. https://doi.org/10.1016/j.jad.2007.02.015.

You, S., Van Orden, K. A., & Conner, K. R. (2011). Social connections and suicidal thoughts and behavior. *Psychology of Addictive Behaviors, 25*(1), 180–184. https://doi.org/10.1037/a0020936.

CHAPTER 11

Textual analysis of suicide notes: how a new approach could yield fresh insights?

David Lawrence[a], Phoebe Carrington-Jones[a], Michael J. Kyron[b]
[a]Graduate School of Education, The University of Western Australia, Perth, WA, Australia; [b]School of Psychological Science, University of Western Australia, Perth, WA, Australia

Empirical study of suicide has been challenging, from a statistical point of view, because of the relatively low frequency of suicide deaths. This means that prospective studies require a very large cohort size which in turn limits the breadth and depth of information that can be collected from cohort members. Retrospective studies, such as psychological autopsy studies, are limited to information pieced together or reconstructed after the event which limits the breadth and scope of information that is available to inform suicide prevention research. In particular, no information can be collected from the deceased other than from what they leave behind, such as in the form of a suicide note. As O'Connor and Leenaars (2004) note, "A suicide note is the closest we get to the suicidal mind, often written minutes before death." Relatively few studies have conducted thematic and semantic analysis of suicide notes. Of those that have, none have taken a protective factors approach. The primary use of suicide notes has been to understand the motivation for suicidal action, and understanding the precipitating life circumstances and risk factors. Numerous studies exist identifying risk factors within suicide notes, yet there is not one study we are aware of that has sought to identify the potential weakening of protective factors within the notes. Many people experience suicidal impulses and difficult life circumstances (Nock et al., 2008). From the perspective of suicide prevention, understanding any positive factors that a person might be encouraged to cling to in order to "choose life" or the absence of any such factors may be as important as understanding the circumstances that lead to suicidal risk. This is an important omission in the literature, as the bolstering of protective factors in order to facilitate a 'choose life' perspective may be effective in counteracting suicide risk factors.

Alternatives to Suicide
ISBN 978-0-12-814297-4
https://doi.org/10.1016/B978-0-12-814297-4.00011-X

Researching suicide and its antecedents

The interpersonal theory of suicide (Van Orden et al., 2010; Joiner, 2005) has been proposed by its authors with the intent of fostering scientific inquiry by proposing testable hypotheses, and with the hope of stimulating the collection of new types of information in suicide research. There are many suicide registers or databases of completed suicides across the world (Adjacic-Gross et al., 2008). A key feature common to almost all of these registers is collection of information regarding the nature of the death, particularly cause of death, type of incident, and mechanisms used. This is reflected in the classification of suicide deaths in the International Classification of Diseases (World Health Organization, 2004), which primarily focuses on the method used to end life. This classification of suicide deaths has been useful in supporting research into methods of suicide, and this research has identified that restriction of access to some means of suicide has resulted in reductions in suicide rates (Gunnell, Middleton, & Frankel, 2000). For instance, restricting the availability of barbiturate sedatives from the late 1960s onwards saw a substantial reduction in suicide rates, particularly among females (Lester & Abe, 1989; Oliver & Hetzel, 1973). However it is not feasible to restrict access to all possible means of suicide, and other approaches to suicide prevention are also required (Hawton, 2007).

Epidemiological research has identified a number of risk factors for suicide, including mental disorders (particularly depression, bipolar disorder, and psychoses), substance abuse, and terminal physical illness (Franklin et al., 2017). Psychological autopsy studies have also identified traumatic events and exposure to risk factors that are associated with suicide such as being a victim of child abuse or domestic violence, relationship breakup, loss of someone close, job or financial loss (Franklin et al., 2017). Because of the high prevalence of these risk factors compared to the number of completed suicides, to date this knowledge has not been useful for developing a predictive model of suicide or identifying individuals for direct suicide prevention interventions (Franklin et al., 2017).

To make progress toward developing an approach to predicting individual suicide risk that could be useful in clinical or prevention settings, research into risk factors for suicide may need to identify either more specific risk factors or groups of risk factors, or may need to look at other aspects of the context or individual in order to understand suicide risk. For instance, the interpersonal theory of suicide proposes thwarted belongingness and perceived burdensomeness as core pathways to feelings of hopelessness and suicidal intent (Van Orden et al., 2010). Further, the theory proposes acquired capability as a pathway from suicidal ideation to action. For example, a difficult relationship breakup may give rise to the sense of loneliness and self-hate that is postulated to be associated with thwarted belongingness and perceived burdensomeness. However, the overwhelming majority of people who go through a difficult breakup do not take their life. Are there other ways that register-based or psychological autopsy data could be collected and used to better understand the antecedents of risk among those who do take their lives after experiencing such a loss?

Research using suicide notes

To try and understand the circumstances relating to a suicide death, coroners, police investigators, and researchers undertaking psychological autopsy studies have to piece together the events preceding the death, and the deceased's state of mind from the available information. This may include interviews with people who knew the deceased, including family members, friends and service providers who may have had contact with the deceased. Where a suicide note is left, Shneidman (1996) has suggested, "our best route to understanding suicide is not through the study of the structure of the brain, nor the study of social statistics, nor the study of mental diseases, but directly through the study of human emotions described in plain English, in the words of the suicidal person." However, research on suicide notes has been limited because of the relatively small number of collections of suicide notes in existence. More jurisdictions are digitizing suicide notes and related materials as part of their data collections, suggesting that research on suicide notes should become more feasible and widespread in coming years.

Suicide notes can take many forms ranging from very short communications confirming suicidal intent to extended collections of writings, diaries and audio or video recordings. As there is no typical structure to a suicide note and as their form and content can vary greatly, there is considerable flexibility in how to analyze this textual information.

Suicide note research to date has largely focused on why individuals choose to take their life, rather than what might have kept them from doing so. Overlooking positive aspects limits an understanding of which factors can be directly targeted during clinical interventions to minimize suicide risk. One such factor is whether the person delayed the decision to end their life. Several studies provide evidence that positive affect is common in suicide notes. Pestian et al. (2012) assessed nearly 1300 suicide notes for emotional content. While the most frequently identified emotion was hopelessness, a comparable amount of notes indicated either love or hopefulness. The focus on negative factors may overlook how positive factors influence the decision to suicide. For instance, an individual may indicate a desire to escape from distress in their life through suicide, yet may have delayed the process due to an unwillingness to emotionally damage a loved one. Such a situation suggests they had something to cling to which deterred suicidal behaviors, and should be bolstered during clinical interventions. Future research should look to examine differences in positive affect in suicide notes between those who attempt suicide, and those who complete suicide.

Importance of interpersonal relationships

We undertook a narrative review of research using suicide notes to examine the types of approaches that have been taken to analyzing suicide notes and the types of information typically extracted from suicide notes (Green, Johnson, & Adams, 2006). One of the most common approaches taken has been to document or classify the reasons why the person has made a decision to end their life. Other approaches, such as looking at emotional content of notes and interpersonal features have been conducted and are the focus of this review. Cohen and Fiedler (1974) analyzed the emotional content and meaning of 195 suicide notes, and found a significant proportion of notes included positive emotional content. Almost half of the notes (43%) expressed positive affect and no hostility and another 15% expressed both positive affect and hostility. Almost 20% of all statements in the notes were considered to express love or other positive affect.

Examples of positive affect in suicide notes can be seen in popular culture. In an excerpt from a suicide note written by American NFL footballer Aaron Hernandez to his fiancée, Shayanna Jenkins-Hernandez, in 2017, there are clear expressions of love and positive affect:

> *Shay, you have always been my soul-mate and I want you to live life and know I'm always with you. I told you what was coming indirectly! I love you so much and know you are an angel!*

Even earlier, Osgood and Walker (1959) analyzed 100 suicide notes. While the primary focus of their study was on motivation for suicide, they identified that over half of notes included positive statements about or directed to the deceased's spouse, and one in three included positive statements about children of the deceased. This early research indicated that suicide does not solely occur in the absence of positive interpersonal relationships, and understanding suicide may not be only about understanding the triggers and reasons for suicide.

More recent research has more directly applied the interpersonal theory of suicide to suicide notes. Sanger and McCarthy Veach (2008) specifically set out to identify interpersonal themes in suicide notes. Due to difficulties accessing notes, their analysis was restricted to a corpus of suicide notes dating from the 1950s and 1960s. They identified that over half of the notes included evidence of positive relationships including love, praise, and gratitude for people close to the deceased. They also noted positive relationship themes more frequently than negative relationship themes. Additionally, they looked for evidence of perceived burdensomeness, and found that one in four suicide notes included either explicit or implicit statements of burdensomeness, while about one in five include statements attempting to minimize the impact their death will have on others, and about one in three asked forgiveness for the act of suicide or more generally.

Concern for others suggests that many individuals who complete suicide do have positive relationships in their lives, or at least have relationships with some positive aspects or that were positive at some time in their lives. Exploring and supporting positive relationships may therefore be useful when working with individuals who express suicidal intent (Sanger & McCarthy Veach, 2008). Developing our understanding of the interpersonal aspects of suicide through note research may help identify specific targets for suicide prevention. As Shneidman (1996) noted, people contemplating suicide are often highly ambivalent about the decision. A better understanding of the positive aspects of people's relationships and lives might be a useful adjunct to our understanding of the negative life events and circumstances that increase suicide risk.

The work of Sanger and McCarthy Veach (2008) seems to be the primary application of the interpersonal theory of suicide to a textual analysis of suicide notes. This work was limited by difficulties the authors experienced accessing suicide notes, resulting in the use of a modest sized sample of notes from over 50 years ago. There is potential benefit of using this approach on a larger and more contemporary collection of suicide notes.

From one of the largest collections of suicide notes used in research, Leenaars (1988) identified eight clusters of concepts underpinning suicidal motivations. Three of these clusters related to interpersonal factors: *interpersonal factors,* where the deceased expressed motivations relating to difficulties either establishing or maintaining relationships; *rejection-aggression,* where the deceased was responding to significant relationship loss and redirecting their anger or aggression toward themselves; and *identification-egression,* where the deceased describes being motivated by intense attachment to a lost or rejecting person. Each of these clusters is potentially related in the interpersonal theory of suicide. While this research did identify interpersonal factors as being the primary motivation for suicide in a proportion of cases, it did not specifically investigate the interplay between interpersonal factors and other potential motivators. O'Connor and Leenaars (2004) applied the same clusters to a comparison of suicide notes from Northern Ireland and the United States, and found that interpersonal components were more commonly identified in suicide notes from Northern Ireland, suggesting that culture and context are important factors.

Recent developments in methods for digitally analyzing unstructured textual data, including linguistic analysis, are starting to be used on digitized collections of suicide notes. Fernández-Cabana, Ceballos-Espinoza, Mateos, Alves-Perez, and Garcia-Caballero (2015) used digital text classification methods to analyze a collection of 80 suicide notes from Chile, searching for risk factors as proposed in the interpersonal theory of suicide. They identified one or both of thwarted belongingness and perceived burdensomeness in 60% of notes, with thwarted belongingness identified most frequently (in 42% of notes).

Another area of research inquiry based on suicide notes has been comparison of genuine and simulated suicide notes (Schneidman & Farberow, 1957), and comparison of notes from completed suicides and attempted suicides (Handelman & Lester, 2007). Comparison to simulated suicide notes has so far yielded few insights, as creating simulated suicide notes is methodologically challenging. Research on attempted versus completed suicide notes has yielded valuable insights into the consistently found qualitative differences between the two. Overall, studies have consistently identified more positive affect within the notes of completed suicides (Brevard & Lester, 1991; Handelman & Lester, 2007; Livermore, 1985). The notes of completed suicides are also more likely to be addressed to someone, express apology and have a lower total isolation score (summed from relevant interpersonal characteristics). For example, an excerpt from the suicide note written by Jessica Edens in 2017 provides an example of expression of apology and interpersonal connection:

> *For my parents and sister: I am so sorry for the pain I am causing all of you. You've always been there for me and I love you all so much. I know that what I have done is selfish, but I cannot live with this pain any longer.*

An additional, noteworthy common feature of notes from completed suicides is indication of the 'cognitive deconstruction' described in Baumeister's (1990) escape theory of suicide. These notes had significantly less metaphysical references than those of suicide attempters (Handelman & Lester, 2007). There is evidently merit in the study of notes of individuals who have completed suicide, as they appear to be unique to suicide, and can therefore provide us with insight into this specific state of mind.

The reasons for these counterintuitive findings are unclear, although insights could be gleaned from the interpersonal theory of suicide. This theory suggests that it is perceptions of interpersonal adversity, rather than the objective presence of interpersonal relationships that are of particular importance. Despite positive relationships in their lives, completers may still perceive themselves to be a burden or feel they do not belong. As a pre-requisite for feelings of perceived burdensomeness is some form of human connection, burden may be lower among attempters due to an absence of meaningful interpersonal relationships (Van Orden et al., 2010). Despite significant interpersonal relationships evident among completers, they may only be protective insofar as they are perceived positively (i.e., without associated perceptions of burden and thwarted belonging).

Positive affect associated with the notes of suicide completers may also indicate an acceptance of life circumstances, and the only remaining option being suicide. This indicates a preparedness and willingness to die by suicide potentially that may increase the likelihood of attempting and completing suicide. The negative affect within the notes of those attempting suicide may indicate a degree of aggression-specific impulsiveness surrounding an attempt, with prior research noting this may be linked to interpersonal conflict (Simon et al., 2001). Impulsive attempters are just as likely to leave behind clues (i.e., notes, phone calls), but are less likely to consider alternative methods of suicide and expect to die with their attempt than those who plan (Simon et al., 2001). Note research, in conjunction with quantitative assessments, could look to further explore these notions.

Classification of suicide deaths

Our understanding of suicide may be improved by seeking to expand the range of information we seek and classify regarding suicide. As an analogy, improvements in outcomes for some physical diseases have resulted from developing more detailed classifications and focusing on more specific solutions. For instance, coding of causes of death was originally done with a single cause assigned to each death. Understanding of the pathology that leads to death was increased when multiple causes of death were considered (Goldacre, Duncan, Cook-Mozaffari, & Griffith, 2003). It is not uncommon for a death following a chronic illness to directly result from pneumonia or heart failure while a cancer, say, may have been the underlying cause. In the case of suicide deaths, the underlying cause of death is coded as the mechanism or method of suicide. A focus on identifying the pathology, mechanism or circumstance that leads to taking the decision to take one's life as an alternative approach may have added value. Currently no standard classifications exist for classifying pathways to suicide attempt. Similarly prevention efforts may be enhanced by statistical reporting and research with greater focus on antecedents to suicidal thoughts and actions rather than on methods of death. As an example, cancer survival has been enhanced by subdividing into different classes and developing improved treatments and preventions for individual classes of cancer. Survival from acute lymphoblastic leukemia has dramatically improved in recent decades, not as a result of a single breakthrough, but rather improved subtyping of these cancers and more targeted interventions for each subtype (Hunger et al., 2012). A single unifying theory such as the interpersonal theory may be too ambitious an aim if there are multiple pathological pathways to suicidal action. The ability to refine and enhance existing theoretical models would be improved by having systematic data collection of all the relevant components of these theories. Being able to routinely extract and classify information relating to positive factors and interpersonal factors as well as risk exposures may facilitate such research.

Expanding our understanding and classification of pathways to suicidal thoughts and actions could be helpful even when our current understanding of predictors are not sufficient to build useful predictive models. For example, studies in developed countries consistently identify that a high proportion (often around half) of suicides occur in people who have received psychiatric treatment (Franklin et al., 2017). Clearly mental illness is a significant risk factor for suicide. One potential area of focus for suicide prevention would be on improving the quality of mental health care to reduce the number of people who fall out of mental health care while still unwell and at high risk of suicide. As is widely reported in the literature, type or severity of mental illness is not in and of itself a strong enough predictor of suicidal risk in order to identify which patients are at high risk and thus in need of higher quality of care (Franklin et al., 2017). Even among people with severe depression, psychotic disorders, and alcohol/drug comorbidities, the majority do not complete suicide. However, despite the fact that there are effective treatments available for most mental disorders, the quality of mental health care delivered at the population level remains low (Sawyer et al., 2018). Substantial proportions of people with mental disorders do not seek or receive treatment, and out of those who do seek treatment only a small minority receive a sustained and appropriate level of care that could be considered minimally adequate (Wang, Demler, & Kessler, 2002). Further complicating the delivery of mental health care is the variety of different treatments available for most disorders, most of which are effective for some rather than all patients. Identifying the appropriate treatment for an individual with mental disorder may require trial and error, requiring persistence on the part of the patient if the initial treatment does not yield positive results (Fernandes et al., 2017). People with mental disorders may be more prone to becoming discouraged or give up help seeking if their initial attempts to seek help are unsuccessful. Because of its low predictive ability for suicide, improving the quality of psychiatric care may not be indicated purely as a suicide prevention measure. Improving the quality of psychiatric care is justified from the perspective of reducing distress and suffering and the economic and social burden of mental illness in society, and any concomitant reduction in suicide rates may be a positive by-product.

The number of people who attempt suicide is substantially higher than the number of completed suicides, and the number of people who express suicidal ideation is an order of magnitude greater again, to the extent that expressing suicidal ideation within a health care setting is not in and of itself a strong enough predictor of suicide risk. As a result, in the emergency department setting it is common for the number of people who present with suicidal ideation to exceed the resources of the hospital to provide support for, resulting in emergency departments having protocols for assessing suicide risk (Tragum et al., 2014; NSW Health, 2004). While the proportion of people with mental disorders who complete suicide is low, the presence of suicidal ideation in a person with mental illness is indicative of a level of distress inconsistent with successful treatment and recovery. Improving our mental health care models so that people experiencing high levels of distress can get the help they need, and receive a co-ordinated continuity of care through the recovery process even if this requires multiple therapies is warranted to alleviate suffering associated with mental illness even if the number of people treated is substantially greater than the number of suicides prevented.

One path to reducing suicide rates is to reduce the prevalence of factors associated with suicide such as the prevalence of mental illness. The science of mental health prevention is much less advanced than mental health treatment, and the prevalence of mental disorders has not declined suggesting that what limited prevention efforts have been implemented to date have had a minimal impact (Jorm, Patten, Brugha, & Mojtabai, 2017). Again, while reducing the prevalence of mental illness would need to prevent a substantial number of cases of mental illness for each suicide prevented, it is still warranted to alleviate suffering and costs to individuals and society associated with mental illness.

Limitations of suicide note research and directions for future research

Many studies have noted the interpersonal nature of suicide notes. However, the act of leaving behind a suicide note is in itself an interpersonal action, with the intent of communicating to other parties (Barrett et al., 2016). Learnings from suicide notes will not necessarily apply to those who do not leave notes. Research has consistently found significant qualitative differences between the individual characteristics and the suicides of those who leave notes, in comparison to those who do not. Paraschikas, Michopoulos, Douzenis, Christodoulou, Koutsaftis, & Lykouras (2012) conducted a two-year study in Greece to identify whether significant differences existed between the individuals and the suicides of those who left notes and those who did not. They found that individuals who left notes all died by hanging or shooting (which is consistent with Chynoweth's (1977) Australian study, which suggested note-writers died predominantly by shooting), had no history of psychiatric illness, or recent psychiatric hospitalization. These differences appear to vary as a function of culture (see Paraschakis et al., 2012, for discussion), however the notion of significant differences between the two groups remains constant. Note-leaving itself varies as a function of region and culture, with notes left in 3%—42% of cases (Paraschakis et al., 2012). While the rate of note-leaving fluctuates, in all studies the majority of those who die by suicide do not leave a note. In conjunction with the findings that suicide note-leavers differ significantly from those who do not leave notes, this means that conclusions drawn from suicide notes may not be able to be validly extrapolated to the whole population of individuals who have completed suicide. Suicide note research should be supplemented by qualitative assessments of suicide attempters, comparing factors involved in the decision between those who leave behind a note and those who do not.

There is an important counterpoint to focusing on suicide notes in that what a person contemplating suicide writes is going to reflect their state of mind and cognitive state at the time. Mental illness, particularly depression, is common in people who die by suicide. Impaired mental state associated with acute depression may be an important factor in what gets communicated in a suicide note. Constriction of thought is commonly seen in suicidal individuals, where individuals are unable to perceive solutions to the problems facing them even though an independent observer may feel otherwise, or do not perceive hope that potential options could be effective (Lester, 2012). For instance, if suicide note text is analyzed from the perspective of identifying the presence of protective factors or relationships, it may be difficult to distinguish their absence from a suicide note due to a depressed individual's inability to perceive the positive things around them from their genuine absence from their lives.

Hand coding themes in suicide notes can be very time consuming, and there can be a degree of inconsistency with thematic and emotional coding of content. A potential way to mitigate this issue is through the use of machine learning algorithms, which show some promise in accurately identifying those who are at risk of suicide and those who are not (Braithwaite, Giraud-Carrier, West, Barnes, & Hanson, 2016). Pestian et al. (2012) compared the accuracy of psychiatric trainees, mental health professionals and machine learning algorithms in discriminating between notes from suicide completers and elicited notes from healthy control groups. Results suggested that machine learning on average performed better than humans. This approach has been replicated in a number of other studies to identify the emotional content of suicide notes. Despite the promising capabilities of machine learning, in its current state it is not perfect and struggles in identification of rarer themes/emotions, although advances in technology should reduce this issue over time. However, machine learning and automation allows for a large quantity of notes to be assessed, and inform high level analysis which can explore how factors may interact.

Conclusion

Suicide notes provide rare insight into the minds of those who complete suicide. Despite common misconceptions, those who complete suicide often indicate positive emotions and relationships in their lives. Focusing simply on negative factors may overlook important nuances of suicide, particularly as having reasons to live has been identified as protective against suicidal thoughts and behaviors in quantitative assessments (Bakhiyi, Calati, Guillaume, & Courtet, 2016). However, the existence of positive factors in those who complete suicide suggests they may not be sufficient in themselves to protect an individual from suicide. Despite the objective presence of positive relationships, an individual may still be capable of perceiving that they are a burden to others and feeling that they do not belong. This may be a factor in completed suicides. How positive and negative factors interrelate is a question for future suicide note research. Examining positive and negative aspects of suicide notes could act to enhance understanding of why people choose suicide, and also how suicide risk can be assessed. Given that many who attempt suicide receive some sort of mental health care prior, there is often some opportunity to address mental health issues prior to suicide attempts. Based on current information available form suicide note research, clinical interventions should focus on increasing coping skills and distress tolerance, and simultaneously bolster interpersonal relationships.

References

Adjacic-Gross, V., Weiss, M. G., Ring, M., Hepp, U., Bopp, M., Gutzwiller, F., et al. (2008). Methods of suicide: International suicide patters derived from the WHO mortality database. *Bulletin of the World Health Organization, 86*, 726–732.

Bakhiyi, C. L., Calati, R., Guillaume, S., & Courtet, P. (2016). Do reasons for living protect against suicidal thoughts and behaviors? A systematic review of the literature. *Journal of Psychiatric Research,* 77, 92–108. https://doi.org/10.1016/j.jpsychires.2016.02.019.

Barrett, J. R., Lee, W., Shetty, H., Broadbent, M., Corss, S., Hotopf, M., et al. (2016). 'He left me a message on Facebook': Comparing the risk profiles of self-harming patients who leave paper suicide notes with those who leave messages on new media. *BJPsych Open, 2*, 217–220. https://doi.org/10.1192/bjpo.bp.116.002832.

Baumeister, R. F. (1990). Suicide as escape from self. *Psychological Review, 97*, 90–113.

Braithwaite, S. R., Giraud-Carrier, C., West, J., Barnes, M. D., & Hanson, C. L. (2016). Validating machine learning algorithms for Twitter data against established measures of suicidality. *JMIR Mental Health, 3*, e21. https://doi.org/10.2196/mental.4822.

Brevard, A., & Lester, D. (1991). A comparison of suicide notes written by completed and attempted suicides. *Annals of Clinical Psychiatry, 3*, 43–45.

Chynoweth, R. (1977). The significance of suicide notes. *Australian and New Zealand Journal of Psychiatry, 11*, 197–200.

Cohen, S. L., & Fiedler, J. E. (1974). Content analysis of multiple messages in suicide notes. *Suicide and Life-Threatening Behavior, 4*, 75–95.

Fernandes, B. S., Williams, L. M., Steiner, J., Leboyer, M., Carvalho, A. F., & Berk, M. (2017). The new field of 'precision psychiatry'. *BMC Medicine, 15*, 80. https://doi.org/10.1186/s12916-017-0849-x.

Fernández-Cabana, M., Ceballos-Espinoza, F., Mateos, R., Alves-Perez, M. T., & Garcia-Caballero, A. A. (2015). Suicide notes: Clinical and linguistic analysis from the perspective of the interpersonal theory of suicide. *European Journal of Psychiatry, 29*, 293–308. https://doi.org/10.4321/S0213-61632015000400006.

Franklin, J. C., Ribeiro, J. D., Fox, K. R., Bentley, K. H., Kleiman, E. M., Huang, X., et al. (2017). Risk factors for suicidal thoughts and behaviors: A meta-analysis of 50 years of research. *Psychological Bulletin, 143*, 187–232. https://doi.org/10.1037/bul0000084.

Goldacre, M. J., Duncan, M. E., Cook-Mozaffari, P., & Griffith, M. (2003). Trends in mortality rates comparing underlying-cause and multiple-cause coding in an English population 1979-1998. *Journal of Public Health, 25*, 249–253. https://doi.org/10.1093/pubmed/fdg058.

Green, B. N., Johnson, C. D., & Adams, A. (2006). Writing narrative literature reviews for peer-reviewed journals: Secrets of the trade. *Journal of Chiropractic Medicine, 5*, 101–117. https://doi.org/10.1016/S0899-3467(07)60142-6.

Gunnell, D., Middleton, N., & Frankel, S. (2000). Method availability and the prevention of suicide. A re-analysis of secular trends in England and Wales 1950-1975. *Social Psychiatry and Psychiatric Epidemiology, 37*, 437–443.

Handelman, L. D., & Lester, D. (2007). The content of suicide notes from attempters and completers. *Crisis, 28*, 102–104. https://doi.org/10.1027/0227-5910.28.2.102.

Hawton, K. (2007). Restricting access to methods of suicide: Rationale and evaluation of this approach to suicide prevention. *Crisis, 28*, 4–9. https://doi.org/10.1027/0227-5910.28.S1.4.

Hunger, S. P., Lu, X., Devidas, M., Camitta, B. M., Gaynon, P. S., Winick, N. J., et al. (2012). Improved survival for children and adolescents with acute lymphoblastic leukemia between 1990 and 2005: A report from the children's oncology group. *Journal of Clinical Oncology, 30*, 1663–1669. https://doi.org/10.1200/JCO.2011.37.8018.

Joiner, T. E. (2005). *Why people die by suicide*. Cambridge, MA: Harvard University Press.

Jorm, A. F., Patten, S. B., Brugha, T. S., & Mojtabai, R. (2017). Has increased provision of treatment reduced the prevalence of common mental disorders? Review of the evidence from four countries. *World Psychiatry, 16*, 90–99. https://doi.org/10.1002/wps.20388.

Leenaars, A. A. (1988). *Suicide notes: Predictive clues and patterns*. New York: Human Sciences Press, Inc.

Lester, D. (2012). The role of irrational thinking in suicidal behavior. *Comprehensive Psychology, 1*, 8. https://doi.org/10.2466/12.02.07.16.CP.1.8.

Lester, D., & Abe, K. (1989). The effect of controls on sedatives and hypnotics on their use for suicide. *Journal of Toxicology: Clinical Toxicology, 27*, 299–303.

Livermore, A. (1985). Forty suicide notes. In R. Cohen-Sandler (Ed.), *Proceedings of the 18th annual meeting* (pp. 47–49). Denver, CO: American Association of Suicidology.

Nock, M. K., Borges, G., Bromet, E. J., Alonso, J., Angermeyer, M., Beutrais, A., et al. (2008). Cross-national prevalence and risk factors for suicidal ideation, plans and attempts. *British Journal of Psychiatry, 192*, 98–105.

NSW Health. (2004). *Suicide risk assessment and management: Emergency department.* Sydney: NSW Department of Health.

O'Connor, R. C., & Leenaars, A. A. (2004). A thematic comparison of suicide notes drawn from Northern Ireland and the United States. *Current Psychology, 22*, 339–347.

Oliver, R. G., & Hetzel, B. S. (1973). An analysis of recent trends in suicide rates in Australia. *International Journal of Epidemiology, 2*, 91–101.

Osgood, C. E., & Walker, E. G. (1959). Motivation and language behavior: A content analysis of suicide notes. *Journal of Abnormal Psychology, 59*, 58–67.

Paraschakis, A., Michopoulos, I., Douzenis, A., Christodoulou, C., Koutsaftis, F., & Lykouras, L. (2012). Differences between suicide victims who leave notes and those who do not: A 2-year study in Greece. *Crisis: The Journal of Crisis Intervention and Suicide Prevention, 33*, 344–349. https://doi.org/10.1027/0227-5910/a000150.

Pestian, J. P., Matykiewicz, P., Linn-Gust, M., South, B., Uzuner, O., Wiebe, J., et al. (2012). Sentiment analysis of suicide notes: A shared task. *Biomedical Informatics Insights, 5*(Suppl. 1), 3–16.

Sanger, S., & McCarthy Veach, P. (2008). The interpersonal nature of suicide: A qualitative investigation of suicide notes. *Archives of Suicide Research, 12*, 352–365.

Sawyer, M. G., Reece, C. E., Sawyer, A. C. P., Johnson, S. E., Hiscock, H., & Lawrence, D. (2018). Access to health professionals by children and adolescents with mental disorders: Are we meeting their needs? *Australian and New Zealand Journal of Psychiatry*. https://doi.org/10.1177/0004867418760713.

Schneidman, E. S., & Farberow, N. L. (1957). *Clues to suicide*. New York: McGraw-Hill.

Simon, T. R., Swann, A. C., Powell, K. E., Potter, L. B., Kresnow, M. J., & O'Carroll, P. W. (2001). Characteristics of impulsive suicide attempts and attempters. *Suicide and Life-Threatening Behavior, 32*(Supplement to Issue 1), 49–59.

Shneidman, E. S. (1996). *The suicidal mind*. New York: Oxford University Press.

Tragum, S. D., Friedman, F., & Pacheco, M. N. (2014). Assessment of suicidal behavior in the emergency department. *Innovations in Clinical Neuroscience, 11*, 194–200.

Van Orden, K. A., Witte, T. K., Cukrowicz, K. C., Braithwaite, S. R., Selby, E. A., & Joiner, T. E. (2010). The interpersonal theory of suicide. *Psychological Review, 117*, 575–600. https://doi.org/10.1037/a0018697.

Wang, P. S., Demler, O., & Kessler, R. C. (2002). Adequacy of treatment for serious mental illness in the United States. *American Journal of Public Health, 92*, 92–98.

World Health Organization. (2004). *International statistical classification of diseases and related health problems. Tenth revision* (2nd ed.). Geneva: World Health Organization.

PART 4

Suicide and a life worth living from indigenous and refugee perspectives

CHAPTER 12

Self-determination and strengths-based Aboriginal and Torres Strait Islander suicide prevention: an emerging evidence-based approach

Pat Dudgeon[a], Abigail Bray[b], Roz Walker[c]
[a]Professor, Poche Centre for Indigenous Health, School of Indigenous Studies, University of Western Australia, Crawley, Perth, WA, Australia; [b]Research Consultant School of Indigenous Studies, University of Western Australia, Crawley, Perth, WA, Australia; [c]Associate Professor, Poche Centre for Indigenous Health, School of Indigenous Studies, University of Western Australia, Crawley, Perth, WA, Australia

Introduction

Aboriginal and Torres Strait Islander peoples (hereon respectfully referred to as Indigenous Australians) are custodians of one of the oldest harmonious, culturally diverse and environmentally sustainable democratic societies. Their society was a highly ordered and unified democracy that spans a land mass twice the size of Europe. Indigenous Australians possessed complex, all-encompassing knowledge systems which have been appropriated and suppressed since the British Empire invaded in 1788. Since then, generations of Aboriginal and Torres Strait Islander people have been subjected to human rights abuses from genocide to assimilation. The significant health gap between Indigenous and non-Indigenous Australians is widely recognised to be symptomatic of these lengthy and ongoing traumatic impacts which have also resulted in high Indigenous suicide rates. As a 2018 Senate Inquiry into Australian Rural Mental Health concluded, Indigenous suicide is related to 'despair caused by the history of dispossession combined with the social and economic conditions in which Aboriginal and Torres Strait islander peoples live' (2018, p. 128). Indeed, a profound and deep-seated loss of control over life and land is recognised as the cause of pathogenic and fatal levels of despair for Indigenous peoples across the world (Duran & Duran, 1995), a despair which has resulted in high levels of Indigenous youth suicide (Lawson-Te Aho & Liu, 2010). A central focus of Indigenous suicide prevention research has been about

Alternatives to Suicide
ISBN 978-0-12-814297-4
https://doi.org/10.1016/B978-0-12-814297-4.00012-1

restoring and reiterating the life-affirming knowledge systems which supported the flourishing of Indigenous peoples prior to colonisation and which are recognised as the source of strengths-based, culturally safe therapeutic practices today. While Indigenous suicide has unique social and cultural determinants, Indigenous concepts of 'flourishing' are also culturally unique around the world.

As article 5 of The Turamarama Declaration (on Maori suicide) states: 'we believe that the will to 'live well' is strong when the human mauri is strong; 'living well' means being able to live as Maori, as indigenous peoples, and as citizens of the world' (Durie, 2017, p. 67). Indigenous knowledge systems about 'living well' (or flourishing) can be understood as forms of spiritual or ecocentric therapeutic governance which are founded on a life-affirming and custodial kinship *with* the earth, and respectful and loving human and more-than-human relationships. For the Cree people, for example, *miyupimaatisiiun* (being alive well) 'serves both to organize social life and create a sense of collective identity' (Adelson, 2000; Kirmayer, Brass, & Tait, 2000, p. 612). There are also a number of Native American Medicine Wheel teachings (Roundtree & Smith, 2016) which describe systems of strengths-based ecocentric therapeutic governance. Indigenous discourses of flourishing, wellbeing, or living well, can be understood to be centered on a respectful and responsive relationship to the life force which has also been described as Raw Law (Watson, 2016) — 'the law is filled with the spirit of creation' (Watson, 1998, p. 1) — and describes what might be termed an axiology of wellbeing, or an ethics of flourishing as a whole way of life (Yap & Yu, 2016; Dudgeon & Bray, 2019).

In the international cross-disciplinary field of Indigenous suicide research there is a broad consensus that Indigenous suicide is the 'culmination of "cultural wounds" inflicted on whole communities and whole ways of life' (Chandler & Dunlop, 2018, p. 147) while the remedy for these cultural wounds is collective, community-based 'cultural medicine', or cultural healing and community driven empowerment solutions (Wexler & Gone, 2012). This is an evidence-based position. Longitudinal studies of *self-determining* Indigenous communities with high levels of agency have provided clear evidence that restoring community control over the conditions of everyday life results in few or no youth suicides (Radford et al., 1990; Chandler & Lalonde, 1998; Barker, Goodman, & DeBeck, 2017; Chandler & Dunlop, 2018, pp. 147–160; Prince, 2018). Further, Barker et al., 2017 explore the emerging evidence base for "culture as treatment" — to prevent suicide, emphasizing the 'significance of interconnectedness in healing, and revitalization of traditional values to reclaim community wellness' (2017, e208). Within Australia, an Aboriginal and Torres Strait Islander strengths-based suicide prevention practice founded on strengthening community self-determination and Social and Emotional Wellbeing (SEWB) within individuals, families and communities has emerged as a key evidence-based, and culturally safe, solution to overcoming the multiple complex factors which contribute to despair and suicide (Dudgeon et al., 2016; Prince, 2018).

This chapter is divided into three broad sections. The first section presents an overview of the global incidence of suicide among colonised Indigenous peoples, the international literature on historical trauma, and evidence-based solutions which have been produced by Indigenous experts, communities and their allies. The second section discusses Aboriginal and Torres Strait Islander suicide, key research in the field, and provides a detailed overview of the central issues within Australia. The third section continues the focus on Aboriginal and Torres Strait Islander suicide, explores an evidence-informed, strengths-based approach to prevention, the role of self-determination and the importance of strengthening the inter-relationships between the seven Indigenous knowledge domains which compose SEWB. Importantly, understanding this complex Indigenous *core concept* (SEWB) is vital to any work in Indigenous health and mental health. Finally, the chapter concludes by affirming the scientific and experiential innovations coming from the field of Indigenous suicide prevention.

Cultural continuity and self-determination: healing collective trauma

"Across sectors and countries, Indigenous peoples have called for suicide prevention strategies that are community-led, strengths-based, and trauma-informed, and that redress intersecting forms of structural discrimination, social inequity, and their downstream consequences. Global efforts to reduce suicide rates among Indigenous peoples must include actions focused on communities that experience the most profound disparities, while also seeking to promote population mental health and improve health equity (Pollock, Naiker, Loro, Mulay, & Colman, 2018, p. 16)".

Cross-disciplinary research into Indigenous suicide prevention founded on and guided by Indigenous knowledge systems is leading critical analysis in a number of fields including Indigenous psychology, psychiatry, suicidology, cross-cultural psychology, medical anthropology, population health studies, and critical race studies. This research has decolonised Western methodologies and paradigms and re-centred Indigenous epistemologies producing a plethora of conceptual and methodological innovations (Dudgeon, Bray, Walker, & Darlastone-Jones, 2019). Such approaches include community-led suicide prevention initiatives.

Moving beyond dominant biomedical deficit-based interpretations of suicide that focus on individual pathologies which 'encourage individual and group stigmatization' (Wexler et al., 2015, p. 894), a strengths-based Indigenous analysis of suicide has emerged which explores the complex interactions between families and communities and the contemporary and historical social and cultural determinants of health (Dudgeon et al., 2016). Such approaches amplify the role of protective factors, are culturally safe, asset-based, engage with community capabilities and capacity building (self-determination), focus on resilience, critically address cultural and social determinants, and are governed by Indigenous knowledge systems and methodologies (Dudgeon et al., 2016; Fogarty, Lovell, Langenberg, & Heron, 2018). Indigenous concepts of wellbeing tend to be holistic, eco-centric, and relational and informed by complex, culturally specific Indigenous therapeutic systems. Significantly, self-determination within comprehensive primary health care services and the practice of holistic Indigenous therapeutic systems are recognised as best practice solutions to strengthening wellbeing (Oster et al., 2014; Dudgeon et al., 2016; King, Smith & Gracey, 2009; Prince, 2018). The creation of 'sustainable communities' and 'conditions which enable people to take control of their lives' (Marmot, 2011, pp. 512—13) has been identified as central to the flourishing of Indigenous peoples. Robust quantitative and qualitative evidence gathered over decades has confirmed the knowledge of Indigenous Elders and their communities about the protective role of *culture* in the restoration of collective empowerment and wellbeing (Colquhoun & Dockery, 2012; Galliher, Jones, & Dahl, 2011; Jones & Galliher, 2007; LaFromboise, Hoyt, Oliver, & Whitbeck, 2006; Pittenger, 1998; Whitesell, Mitchell, Kaufman & Spicer, 2006; Whitesell, Mitchell, & Spicer, 2009). Indeed, recent Indigenous advances in the field of neuroscience have found that cultural healing practices enhance trauma recovery (Yellow Bird, 2013; Sasakamoose, Bellegarde, Sutherland, Pete, & McKay-McNabb, 2017; Sasakamoose, Scerbe, Wenaus, & Scandrett, 2016).

Colonisation and trauma

"Our Country and people have suffered many traumas since colonisation, the magnitude of which is beyond words. Looking through trauma is like being trapped in the back of a mirror, there is no reflection of self. It is like being trapped in darkness, unable to see where to go or what is there, surrounded by 'not knowing', paralyzed by fear..." (Milroy, 2007).

The 1997 *Bringing Them Home: Report of the National Inquiry into the Separation of Aboriginal and Torres Strait Children from their Families* is one of the most extensive records of the traumatic impact of colonisation on Indigenous peoples, and the evidence gathered demonstrated that Aboriginal and Torres Strait Islander people have been subjected to genocide as defined by international law (Wilkie, 1997). The Report meticulously documents how generations of children were forcibly taken from their families and subjected to abusive forms of assimilation in what 'has been tantamount to a continuing cultural and spiritual genocide both as an individual and a community experience' (Wilkie, 1997, p.171). The national investigation concluded that this genocidal process of assimilation 'has been the single most significant factor in emotional and mental health problems which in turn have impacted on physical health' (ibid.). The process of colonisation has traumatised generations of Indigenous people. Some of this includes direct actions such as massacres; the forced removal of children; exposure to individual, cultural and institutional racism; dispossession from Country; forced labor; and the outlawing and suppression of culture. These are all cultural wounds inflicted on whole communities and whole ways of life. Extensive research into the specific forms of trauma endured by Indigenous peoples has drawn attention to intergenerational impacts. For example, Hartman and Gone (2014) use the term 'historical trauma' to describe the combination of four significant factors: colonial injury; collective experience; cumulative effects and, cross-generational impacts. There is now a substantial literature on historical trauma and the role of Indigenous therapeutic healing (Yellow Horse Brave Heart, 1998; Milroy, Dudgeon, & Walker, 2014; Atkinson, 2002; Atkinson Nelson, Brooks, Atkinson and Ryan 2014; Pihama, Smith, C., Reynolds, Smith, L. and Te Nana, 2014; Waitoki, Nikora, Harris, and Levy, 2014; Lawson-Te Aho, 2014).

While forms of historical trauma can be transmitted through individuals, families and communities over generations, it is important to recognise that for many Indigenous people, ongoing colonisation is also a form of ongoing trauma leading to forms of complex and compounding trauma (Atkinson et al., 2014). Structurally entrenched social disadvantage and marginalisation, higher imprisonment rates, health and income inequities, discrimination across housing, education, employment, health services and judicial systems, for example, expose already traumatised people to systemic and chronic forms of *traumatising racism*. Increasingly, evidence over the last few decades has found that exposure to individual, institutional and cultural racism greatly impairs physical and psychological health (Paradies, 2016; Williams, Lawrence, & Davis, 2019). Exposure to chronic and enduring forms of racism can lead to cumulative trauma (Atkinson et al., 2014; Kanter et al., 2017). In the light of this important research on the pathogenic and traumatising impact of colonisation and racism, culturally safe suicide prevention services are clearly essential to best practice to reduce suicide. Moreover, and equally importantly, *culturally safe communities*, ones which are able to practice cultural healing and self-determination — or *multi-sectorial Indigenous governance* — have been found to reduce Indigenous suicide (Chandler & Dunlop, 2018, pp. 147—160; Prince, 2018).

Self-continuity and cultural-continuity

There is considerable literature on the ways in which the strengthening of 'self-continuity' — 'the sense that past, present, and future time-slices of one's identity are meaningfully connected' (Becker et al., 2017, p. 2) supports resilience, psychosocial stability and motivation (Sedikides, Wildschut, Routledge, & Arndt, 2015). Threats to self-continuity are linked to a range of destructive effects, 'negative personal and societal outcomes, including low self-esteem, dissociation, negative intergroup attitudes, and *suicidality*' (Becker et al., 2017, p. 3, emphasis added). Indeed, a lack of positive affective attachment to the past (nostalgia, pride, for example) appears to foreclose the future: a 'lack of past-to-present self-continuity is associated with suicidality — implying an ultimate level of disregard for one's future self (Ball & Chandler, 1989; Sokol & Eisenheim, 2016) (Becker et al., 2017, p. 4). As Indigenous social scientists have pointed out for some time, Indigenous concepts of 'self' move beyond dominant western concepts of the individual — Indigenous self-continuity is collective, relational, multidimensional, and connected to strong cultural continuity to the past, present, and the future (Kirmayer et al., 2000). Yet, it is this very fabric of Indigenous self-continuity which has been targeted and eroded by colonialism.

In a comprehensive overview of the relevant scientific literature in the field it was found that Indigenous people in higher income countries have substantially elevated suicide rates (Pollack, Naiker, Loro, Mulay & Colman 2018). However, given that the majority of Indigenous populations live in middle- and low-income counties, where coronial records are unreliable and limited, accurate global data about Indigenous suicide is not available. Furthermore, it is important to recognise that '[s]uicide rate disparities between Indigenous and non-Indigenous populations are substantial in some settings but not universal' (Pollack et al., 2018, p. 1). In Australia, since 1990 there is evidence that strengthening cultural integrity of Indigenous communities is linked to fewer mental health problems and suicides while Indigenous people who had been 'displaced from their traditional living areas' (i.e. their own Country) experienced a 'higher incidence of self-destructive behavior' (Radford et al., 1990, p. 8; Prince, 2018), and greater levels of grief and loss (Zubrick et al., 2014). In Canada, the literature on Indigenous suicide prevention, and Indigenous wellbeing in general, has found that low to non-existence suicide rates are found in communities that have evidence of both 'cultural continuity' and self-governance (Chandler & Lalonde, 1998).

The concept of 'cultural continuity' was first used in a significant international study by Chandler and Lalonde (1998) which showed that suicide rates among Indigenous youth were unevenly distributed among First Nation bands in two hundred communities across Canada. In many First Nation bands, no Indigenous youth had died by suicide. A longitudinal study of those same communities found similar evidence fifteen years later. Such communities are:

> *Marked by multiple community-level efforts to achieve a high level of ownership of their own cultural past, and an elevated success in controlling their own civic futures. In particular, this means that Indigenous communities with low-to-absent rates of youth suicide tend to be characterised by such things as self-government and active involvement in attempts to restore title to traditional lands, to preserve Indigenous languages and culture, and to restore the historic place of women in tribal governance. In more foreword-reaching ways, such communities have also made special strides in regaining control of their own educational practices and child-protection services as well as their former dominion over judicial and community safety matters, and have assumed critical responsibility for ensuring the safety of their own health and welfare. Whenever all of these of what we have called 'cultural continuity' are present, the aggregated level of youth suicide drops to zero. Whenever such ambitions have been frustrated, the youth suicide rate is heartbreakingly high.*
>
> ***(Chandler & Dunlop, 2018, p. 158)***

As the quote above explains, cultural continuity is not simply a matter of restoring language or engaging in cultural practices, but also strengthening community sovereignty and Indigenous control, or self-determination, over everyday existence and, importantly, being able to create a future. This means, in effect, as Wexler & Gone argue in their analysis of culturally responsive Indigenous suicide prevention, engaging in *decolonisation* (Wexler & Gone, 2012).

Similarly, Tiessen, Taylor, and Kirmayer (2009) in their study with two Indigenous communities in Manitoba found that Aboriginal youth who perceived higher levels of cultural control experienced greater feelings of individual control which in turn was associated with greater psychological well-being. Increasingly, culture is recognised as central to the wellbeing of Indigenous people. A comprehensive review of recent literature (Bourke et al., 2018) on the role of Indigenous culture for health and wellbeing found evidence of positive connections in both quantitative and qualitative studies of the relationship between land and caring for land, Indigenous language use, self-determination, family and kinship, cultural knowledge, beliefs and expression and the strengthening of health and wellbeing. Within Australia in the last two decades, Indigenous suicide prevention practice and research has also highlighted a holistic strengths-based SEWB approach which addresses the cultural and social determinants of wellbeing and restores healthy connections between the seven domains of Indigenous wellbeing — Country, culture, spirituality, community, family and kinship, mind and emotions, and body (Gee, Dudgeon, Schultz, Hart, & Kelley, 2014; Zubrick et al., 2014). The next section discusses Indigenous suicide in Australia and some emerging challenges.

Aboriginal and Torres Strait Islander suicide

Suicide is an urgent population health issue in Australia, although it is particularly high for Indigenous Australians (who comprise only 3% of the population). The Australian Bureau of Statistics stated: '[i]n 2017, suicide was the leading cause of death among people aged between 15 and 44 years. [...] In 2017, suicide remained the leading cause of death of children between 5 and 17 years of age, with 98 deaths occurring in this age group. This represents a 10.1% increase in deaths from 2016' (ABS, 2017).

Indigenous cultures in Australia were governed by complex Laws which covered all aspects of life and yet there were no cultural protocols or stories about suicide and no known words for suicide within the numerous language groups. Instances of suicide began to be reported in the late 1980s. Reports of Indigenous men found hung to death within prisons in Australia sparked the 1991 Royal Commission into Aboriginal Deaths in Custody (Hunter, Reser, Baird, & Reser, 1999). Since the late-1980s Indigenous suicide rates have increased. Comprehensive and entrenched patterns of socio-economic disadvantage, the continuation of punitive levels of 'cultural exclusion' (Brody, 1966; Hunter & Milroy, 2006), and barriers to culturally safe and sustainable social and emotional wellbeing services have all contributed to high suicide levels. For example, the 2016 Steering Committee for the Review of Government Service Provision found that Indigenous Australians die by suicide twice as often as non-Indigenous Australians, and younger Indigenous people, including children, are significantly more likely to die by suicide (Dudgeon, Calma & Holland, 2017a) than other children. Moreover, it has been found that Indigenous Australians are exposed to more stressful life events than non-Indigenous Australians (ABS, 2013), and that increased exposure to such events is strongly linked to higher levels of psychological distress and suicidal ideation (Dudgeon, Watson & Holland, 2017b). In addition there are health service gaps between the Indigenous and non-Indigenous population, and a lack of culturally safe comprehensive primary health care and mental health services remain an ongoing symptom of health inequity in colonial Australia (De Leo, Sveticic, Milner, & Mackay, 2011).

Indigenous communities and their leaders have consistently called for governments to address both the socio-economic conditions which result in ill health and despair and to decolonise the mental health and primary health care systems, by establishing culturally safe practices and recognising Indigenous knowledge systems which support SEWB (People Culture Environment, 2014). This is understood as a strengths-based cultural determinants approach. The focus on suicide prevention is recognised as a national priority area which has resulted in a raft of policies and community innovations. A central innovation in the field has been the development of therapeutic, strengths-based Indigenous knowledge systems which are relational, holistic, and culturally appropriate and prioritise SEWB. Health is a holistic concept that 'encompasses everything important in a person's life, including land, environment, physical body, community, relationships, and law' (Burns, Maling, & Thomson, 2010, p. 1).

Strengths-based Aboriginal and Torres Strait Islander suicide prevention

One result of the Indigenous self-determination movement in Australia has been the development of nine guiding principles of Aboriginal and Torres Strait Islander Social and Emotional Wellbeing. In brief, the 1989 National Aboriginal Health Strategy identified nine engagement principles which were developed by the landmark *Ways Forward* (Swan & Raphael, 1995), and also contained in the National Strategic Framework for Aboriginal and Torres Strait Islander Peoples Mental Health and Social and Emotional Wellbeing 2004–2009. These nine principles inform a central text in the field, *Working Together: Aboriginal and Torres Strait Islander Mental Health and Wellbeing: Principles and Practice* (Dudgeon, Milroy & Walker 2014). The revised 2017–2023 national SEWB Framework also promotes these principles which are underpinned by a recognition that self-determination in the health sector is the solution to over-coming the complex burdens of colonisation (Dudgeon, Bray, D'Costa & Walker, 2017c). These nine guiding principles embody a holistic and whole-of-life view of health held by Aboriginal and Torres Strait Islander people, and emphasise that SEWB is a strengths-based understanding of health.

In 2013 based on extensive community consultation, the first National Aboriginal and Torres Strait Islander Suicide Prevention Strategy (NATSISPS) was launched with six action areas:

- Building strengths and capacity in Aboriginal and Torres Strait Islander communities
- Building strengths and resilience in individual and families
- Targeted suicide prevention services
- Co-ordination of approaches to prevention
- Building the evidence base and disseminating information
- Standards and quality in suicide prevention (Dudgeon et al., 2016, p. 11).

Although the NATSISPS was subsumed into the Fifth Mental Health Plan the legacy of a strength-based approach remains important as a way of de-stigmatising, and reducing traumatic levels of racism. A strength-based approach is important for moving beyond entrenched deficit discourses about Indigenous people which too often result in misinformation and misunderstandings of complex issues and disregard the solutions that exist within communities. As the research by Chandler and LaLonde demonstrated, strong Indigenous communities with high levels of wellbeing are more common than generally recognised by a dominant society with a vested interest in negative stereotypes about the 'lacking' Indigenous Other.

Between 2014 and 2016, the *Aboriginal and Torres Strait Islander Suicide Prevention Project* (ATSISPEP) was conducted to identify successful factors in Indigenous suicide prevention. The overall focus of ATSISPEP was to refine the evidence base for Indigenous suicide prevention in Australia from an Indigenous stand-point, using Indigenous methodologies and knowledge systems, and to develop a cultural framework for prevention services and programs. The team conducted six community roundtables across Australia with numerous Indigenous experts-by-experience and Indigenous experts in a range of disciplines and services connected to suicide prevention (Milroy, Dudgeon, Cox, Georgatos, Bray, 2017). Central to ATSISPEP is a recognition of a strengths-based SEWB discourse which is widely recognised as a culturally appropriate Indigenous health model (Dudgeon et al., 2017c). This holistic model was refined by Gee (2014), after substantial community consultations, and further developed by Dudgeon and Walker (2015) and informs important state and federal health policies and strategies such as the *National Strategic Framework for Aboriginal and Torres Strait Islander Peoples' Mental Health and Social and Emotional Wellbeing 2017–2023*. The Indigenous concept of SEWB is not only a core concept within the field of Indigenous suicide prevention but more broadly is a reiteration of one of the earth's oldest and most powerful knowledge systems which has provided a guide to harmonious, healthy and environmentally sustainable living for tens of thousands of years.

One important result of the extensive work conducted by ATSISPEP over this time is *Solutions That Work: What the Evidence and Our People Tell Us Report* (Dudgeon et al., 2016). This report stressed holistic solutions and self-determination as key solutions, and in particular 'partnerships with community organisations and ACCHSs, employment of community members/peer workforce, indicators for evaluation, cross agency collaboration, data collections and dissemination of learnings' as central (Dudgeon et al., 2016., p. 16). Another vital outcome from ATSISPEP was a report conducted with the support of the Healing Foundation, *Stories from Community: How Suicide Rates Fell in Two Indigenous Communities* (Prince, 2018). This report, much like Chandler and Lalonde's (1998) research into First Nation bands in Canada with reduced youth suicide rates, discusses two case studies detailing the success of the Tiwi Islands (Queensland) and Yarrabah (Northern Territory) communities which have worked constistently to reduce high levels of suicide by practicing self-determination and cultural-continuity. Moreover, within the case histories gathered, the theme of memory emerged as a protective factor. As Prince (2018) observes 'both Tiwi and Yarrabah created, through community empowerment, a new narrative and have consciously sought to embed this narrative in the community as a means to protecting those still challenged with suicide ideation not to further contemplate, plan or act on such ideation' (2018, p.14). Creating a strengths-based positive narrative was also described as making 'good memories' about the community and for the community so that young people have (to refer to the term discussed earlier) a sense of collective self-continuity (ibid.).

The following factors have been identified by community experts-by-experience, and the ATSISPEP team, as important to on the ground, whole-of-community and whole-of-government suicide prevention.

Key success factors for indigenous suicide prevention

Universal/indigenous community wide

- Primordial prevention (ie the prevention of risk factors themselves): addressing community challenges, racism, poverty, social and cultural determinants of health
- Cultural elements (i.e. strengthening SEWB by going on Country, connecting with Elders, learning about skin groups, understanding kinships systems, building a strong cultural identity through sharing stories and participating in cultural activities which strengthen loving relationship between individuals, families and communities.
- Alcohol/drug use reduction
- Primary prevention
- Indigenous-specific Gatekeeper training (ie Training for individuals who have significant roles and regular contact with people in their community (i.e. 'gatekeepers') to recognise and respond to people at potential risk of suicide, and to support those who are bereaved by suicide or attempted suicide previously.
- Awareness-raising programs about suicide risk/use of DVDs with no assumption of literacy
- Reducing access to lethal means of suicide
- Training of frontline staff/groups in detecting depression and suicide risk
- E-heath services/services/crisis call lines and chat service
- Responsible suicide reporting by the media

Selective - at risk groups

School age

- Peer-to-peer support and mental health literacy programs
- Aboriginal Cultures being taught in schools (i.e. Indigenous knowledge systems, history, language, and law appropriate to place so that children can strengthen their identity and sense of self-continuity)

Young people

- Peer-to-peer mentoring, and education and leadership on suicide prevention
- Programs to engage/divert, including sport
- Connecting to culture, history, country, and Elders
- Providing education and hope for the future — preparing for employment

Indicated - at risk individual

- Clinical elements including culturally safe screening, diagnosis and treatment
- Access to counsellors/mental health support
- 24/7 availability of culturally safe counsellors and emergency services
- Awareness of critical risk periods and responsiveness at those times
- Crisis response teams after a suicide/prevention
- Continuing care/assertive outreach post Emergency Department discharge after a suicide attempt
- Clear referral pathways
- Recognition and observance of time protocols (ie take time to establish trust and relationship)
- High-quality and culturally appropriate treatments (ie culturally safe healing, this may involve traditional healers, smoking ceremonies as well as or in place of medication)
- Cultural competence of staff/mandatory training requirements

Common elements

- Community leadership/cultural framework
- Community empowerment, development, ownership-community-specific responses
- Involvement of Elders
- Cultural framework

Provider

- Partnerships with community organisations and ACCHS

- Employment of community members/peer workforce
- Indicators for evaluation
- Cross-agency collaboration
- Data collections
- Dissemination of learning (Prince, 2018, p. 37) adapted from ATSIS-PEP Report, Dudegon et al., 2016 p. 64.

In November 2018 the second National Aboriginal and Torres Strait Islander Suicide Prevention and the second World Indigenous Suicide Prevention Conferences were held back to back between the 20th to 23rd November in Perth, Western Australia. Hosted by the Center of Best Practice in Aboriginal and Torres Strait Islander Suicide Prevention (CBPATSISP), Poche Center for Indigenous Health, University of Western Australia, both Conferences were designed so that Indigenous people owned and directed the discussions taking place. Over 500 delegates from across Australia and the world gathered with policy makers and researchers to share experiences and collaborate on solutions that work in Indigenous suicide prevention. Conference Patron and keynote speaker, Professor Tom Calma AO reminded delegates that the story of Indigenous suicide is a global phenomenon with many other countries experiencing similar Indigenous suicide rates to that in Australia – about twice the mainstream population. As the research in this chapter confirms, and as Indigenous peoples at both Conferences asserted, the process of recovery from colonisation is a globally shared agenda. The gathering of International Indigenous Elders, leaders, youth and community members enabled discussions about the issues, challenges and potential solutions predicated on the notions of hope, healing and recovery.

Conclusion

This chapter presents a strong case for the need for both self-determination and decolonisation as discourses, strategies and essential conditions to create hope and sustainable futures for Indigenous peoples. Self-determination in the field of Indigenous suicide prevention means control over the process of prevention, diagnosis and healing. It also requires data sovereignty and control over community level data on the determinants and environmental factors influencing suicide. Such data is essential to: inform culturally responsive suicide prevention activities; provide a new approach to evaluation led by community rather than external agencies; and, understand and progressively improve suicide prevention programs. An Indigenous suicide prevention practice recognises that restoring SEWB by building strong relationships between the seven domains of wellbeing and addressing the social and cultural determinants of wellbeing is the key to protecting people from the enduring psychological, social, and economic assault of ongoing colonisation. Conference participants made a resounding call for recognition of the history of colonisation and subsequent trauma, including the ongoing disadvantage, marginalisation and lack of action by government on Aboriginal and Torres Strait Islander issues, particularly suicide prevention. They called for a national and community level recovery and healing process for community, which recognises truth as the basis for moving forward, and reiterated the need for suicide prevention policy, plans, services and programs to be based on the principles of Aboriginal and Torres Strait Islander community control, empowerment and self-determination. This in turn means Aboriginal and Torres Strait Islander suicide prevention needs to build the capacity and capability of Aboriginal and Torres Strait Islander service providers, by: increasing the Indigenous suicide prevention workforce, ensuring that the mainstream workforce is culturally competent and services are culturally safe; and, embedding the role of Elders and cultural healers in mainstream and community controlled services. Elders are crucial to foster culture and family connections to ensure that each generation knows who they are and that their identity is not lost, and to: 'instil a strong cultural identity within our younger generation so that they come to realise that life is spirit and spirit is life' (CBPATSIP 2019).

References

Adelson, N. (2000). *Being alive well: Health and the politics of Cree well-being*. Toronto: University of Toronto Press, University of Toronto Press.

Atkinson, J. (2002). *Trauma trails, recreating song lines: The transgenerational effects of trauma in Indigenous Australia*. Melbourne: Spinifex Press.

Atkinson, J., Nelson, J., Brooks, R., Atkinson, C., & Ryan, K. (2014). Addressing individual and community transgenerational trauma. Chapter 17. In P. Dudgeon, H. Milroy, & R. Walker (Eds.), *Working together: Aboriginal and Torres Strait islander health and wellbeing principles and practice* (2nd ed., pp. 289–305). Canberra: Australian Government of the Department of the Prime Minister and Cabinet.

Australian Bureau of Statistics 'Psychological Distress' Australian Aboriginal and Torres Strait Islander Health Survey, First Results, 2012, 2013, ABS cat. no. 4727.0.55.001, Retrieved from. www.abs.gov.au/ausstats/abs@.nsf/Lookup/9F3C9BDE98B3C5F1CA257C2F00145721?opendocument.

Australian Bureau of Statistics. (2016). *Causes of death*. Australia, 2016. Retrieved February 1, 2018, from http://www.abs.gov.au/AUSSTATS/abs@.nsf/DetailsPage/3303.02016?OpenDocument.

Australian Bureau of Statistics. (2017). *Causes of death*. Australia, 2017, 3303.0 http://www.abs.gov.au/ausstats/abs@.nsf/Lookup/by%20Subject/3303.0~2017~Main%20Features~Intentional%20self-harm,%20key%20characteristics~3.

Ball, L., & Chandler, M. (1989). Identity formation in suicidal and non-suicidal youth. *Development & Psychopathology, 1*(3), 257–275. https://doi.org/10.1017/S0954579400000444.

Barker, B., Goodman, A., & DeBeck, K. (2017). Reclaiming Indigenous identities: Culture as strength against suicide among Indigenous youth in Canada. *Canadian Journal of Public Health, 108*(2), e208–e210.

Becker, M., et al. (2017). Being oneself through time: Bases of self-continuity across 55 cultures. *Self and Identity*, 1–18.

Bourke, S., Wright, A., Jill, G., Russell, L., Dunbar, T., & Lovett, R. (2018). Evidence review of Indigenous culture for health and wellbeing. *The International Journal of Health, Wellness and Society, 8*(4), 11–27.

Brody, E. B. (1966). Cultural exclusion, character and illness. *American Journal of Psychiatry, 122*(8), 852–858.

Burns, J., Maling, C. M., & Thomson, N. (2010). *Summary of indigenous women's health, JMt Lawley*. WA: Australian Indigenous HealthInfoNet.

Centre for Best Practice in Aboriginal and Torres Strait Islander Suicide Prevention (CBPATSIP) Summary and Recommendations from the 2nd national Aboriginal and Torres Strait Islander suicide prevention and the 2nd world Indigenous suicide prevention Conferences, 2019.

Chandler, M., & Dunlop, W. L. (2018). Cultural wounds demand cultural medicine. In M. Greenwood, S. De Leeuw, & N. M. Lindsay (Eds.), *Determinants of Indigenous peoples health: 2nd ed.: Beyond the social.*

Chandler, M. J., & Lalonde, C. E. (1998). Cultural continuity as a hedge against suicide in Canada's First Nations. *Transcultural Psychiatry, 35*(2), 193–219.

Colquhoun, S., & Dockery, A. M. (2012). *The link between Indigenous culture and wellbeing: Qualitative evidence for Australian Aboriginal peoples. CLMR discussion.* Perth: Curtin University, Centre for Labour Market Research and School of Economics and Finance. Paper Series 2012/01.

De Leo, D., Sveticic, J., Milner, A., & Mackay, K. (2011). *Suicide in Indigenous populations of Queensland. Australian institute of suicide research and prevention. National Centre of excellence in suicide prevention and WHO collaboration Centre for research and training in suicide prevention Brisbane*. Australia: Australian Academic Press.

Dudgeon, P., Bray, A., Walker, R., & Darlastone-Jones, D. (2020). Aboriginal Participatory Action Research: An Indigenous methodology promoting social and emotional wellbeing and decolonisation. In B. Hokowhitu, A. Moreton-Robinson, L. Tuhiwai Smith, S. Larkin, & C. Anderson (Eds.), *The Routledge Handbook of Critical Indigenous Studies*. New York & London: Routledge (in press).

Dudgeon, P., Calma, T., & Holland, C. (2017a). The context and causes of the suicide of Indigenous people in Australia. *Journal of Indigenous Wellbeing: Te Mauri-Pimatisiwin, 2*(1), 5–15.

Dudgeon, P., Watson, M., & Holland, C. (2017b). Trauma in the Aboriginal and Torres Strait Islander population. *Australian Clinical Psychologist, 3*(1), 6–18.

Dudgeon, P., Bray, A., D'Costa, B., & Walker, R. (2017c). Decolonising psychology: Validating social and emotional wellbeing. *Australian Psychologist, 52*, 316–325.

Dudgeon, P., Milroy, J., Calma, T., Luxford, Y., Ring, I., Walker, R., Cox, A., Georgatos, G., & Holland, C. (2016). *Solutions that Work: What the Evidence and Our People Tell us: Aboriginal and Torres Strait Islander Suicide Prevention Evaluation Project Report. Perth: Aboriginal and Torres Strait Islander Suicide Prevention Evaluation Project.* School of Indigenous Studies, University of Western Australia.

Dudgeon, P., & Walker, R. (2015). Decolonising Australian psychology: Discourses, strategies, and practice. *Journal of Social and Political Psychology, 3*(1), 276–297. https://doi.org/10.5964/jspp.v3i1.126.

Dudgeon, P., Milroy, H., & Walker, R. (2014). Working Together: Aboriginal and Torres Strait Islander mental health and wellbeing principles and practice (2nd ed). *Canberra: Department of the Prime Minister and Cabinet.*

Dudgeon, P., Cox, A., Walker, R., Scrine, C., Kelly, K., Blurton, D., Boladeras, J., … Woods, C. (2014a). *Voices of the peoples: The national empowerment Project research report 2015.* Perth: National Empowerment Project, University of Western Australia.

Dudgeon, P., Walker, R., Scrine, C., Shepherd, C. C. J., Calma, T., & Ring, I. (2014b). Effective strategies to strengthen Aboriginal and Torres Strait Islander mental health and wellbeing. In *Closing the gap clearinghouse series.* Canberra: Australian Institute of Health and Welfare & Melbourne: Australian Institute of Family Studies.

Dudgeon, P., Wright, M., Paradies, Y., Garvey, D., & Walker, I. (2014c). Aboriginal social, cultural and historical contexts. In P. Dudgeon, H. Milroy, & R. Walker (Eds.), *Working together: Aboriginal and Torres Strait Islander mental health and wellbeing principles and practice* (2nd ed., pp. 3–24). Canberra: Department of the Prime Minister and Cabinet.

Duran, E., & Duran, B. (1995). *Native American postcolonial psychology.* Albany, NY: State University of New York Press.

Durie, M. (2017). Indigenous suicide: The Turamarama declaration. *Journal of Indigenous wellbeing: Te Mauri -Pimatisiwin, 2*(2), 59–67.

Fogarty, W., Lovell, M., Langenberg, J., & Heron, M.-J. (2018). *Deficit discourse and strengths-based approaches: Changing the narrative of Aboriginal and Torres Strait Islander health and wellbeing.* Carlton South VIC: Lowitija Institute.

Galliher, R. V., Jones, M. D., & Dahl, A. (2011). Concurrent and longitudinal effects of ethnic identity and experiences of discrimination on psychosocial adjustment of Navajo adolescents. *Developmental Psychology, 47*, 509–526.

Gee, G., Dudgeon, P., Schultz, C., Hart, A., & Kelley, K. (2014). Understanding social and emotional wellbeing and mental health from an Aboriginal and Torres Strait Islander perspective. In P. Dudgeon, H. Milroy, & R. Walker (Eds.), *Working together: Aboriginal and Torres Strait islander health and wellbeing principles and practice* (2nd ed.). Canberra: Australian Government of the Department of the Prime Minister and Cabinet.

Hartman, W. E., & Gone, J. (2014). American Indian historical trauma: Community perspectives from Two Great Plains Medicine Men. *American Journal of Community Psychology, 54*(3–4), 274–288.

Hunter, E., Reser, J., Baird, M., & Reser, P. (1999). *An analysis of suicide in Indigenous communities of north Queensland; The historical, cultural and symbolic landscape.* Canberra, Australia: Publications (Public Affairs, Parliamentary and Access Branch) Commonwealth apartment of Health and Aged Care.

Hunter, E., & Milroy, H. (2006). Aboriginal and Torres Strait Islander suicide in context. *Archives of Suicide Research, 10*(2), 141–157.

Jones, M. D., & Galliher, R.((2007). Navajo ethnic identity: Predictors of psychosocial outcomes in Navajo adolescents. *Journal of Research on Adolescence, 17*, 683–696.

Kanter, J. W., Williams, M. T., Kuczynski, A. M., Manbeck, K. E., Debreaux, M., & Rosen, D. C. (2017). A preliminary report on the relationship between microaggressions against black people and racism among white college students. *Race and Social Problems, 9*(4), 291–299.

King, M., Smith, A., & Gracey, M. (2009). Indigenous health part 2: the underlying cause of the health gap. *Lancet, 374*, 76–85.

Kirmayer, L. J., Brass, G. M., & Tait, C. L. (2000). The mental health of Aboriginal peoples: Transformations of identity and community. *Canadian Journal of Psychiatry, 45*(7), 607–616.

LaFromboise, T. D., Hoyt, D. R., Oliver, L., & Whitbeck, L. B. (2006). Family, community and school influences on resilience among American Indian adolescents in the upper Midwest. *I, 34*, 193–209. https://doi.org/10.1002/jcop.20090.

Lawson-Te Aho, K., & Liu, J. H. (2010). Indigenous suicide and colonisation: The legacy of violence and the necessity of self-determination. *International Journal of Computer Vision, 4*(1), 124–133. IS THI 2014???

Lawson-Te Aho, K. (2014). The healing is in the pain: Revisiting and re-narrating trauma as a starting point for healing. *Psychology and Developing Societies, 26*(2), 181–212. https://doi.org/10.1177/0971333614549139.

Marmot, M. (2011). Social determinants and the health of Indigenous Australians. *Medical Journal of Australia, 194*, 512–513.

Milroy, H. (2007). *Note accompanying artwork 'restoring life and spirits: Recovery from trauma' by Prof. Helen Milroy, Aboriginal and Torres Strait Islander social justice commissioner, human rights and equal opportunity commission report 2007*. https://www.humanrights.gov.au/publications/social-justice-report-2007-about-report-credits.

Milroy, H., Dudgeon, P., & Walker, R. (2014). Community life and development programs - pathways to healing. In *Working Together: Aboriginal and Torres Strait Islander Mental Health and Wellbeing Principles and Practice* (2nd ed., pp. 419–436). Canberra: Australian Government Department of the Prime Minister and Cabinet (Chapter 24) in Dudgeon P, Milroy H & Walker R. 2014.

Milroy, J., Dudgeon, P., Cox, A., Georgatos, G., & Bray, A. (2017). What the people said: Findings from the regional roundtables of the Aboriginal and Torres Strait Islander Suicide Prevention Evaluation Project. *Journal of Indigenous Wellbeing, 2*(1), 16–32.

Oster, R., Grier, A., Lightning, R., Mayan, M. J., & Toth, E. L. (2014). Cultural continuity, traditional Indigenous language, and diabetes in Alberta First Nations: A mixed methods study. *International Journal for Equity in Health, 13*(92). Retrieved from https://equityhealthj.biomedcentral.com/articles/10.1186/s12939-014-0092-4.

Paradies, Y. (2016). Colonisation, racism and Indigenous health. *Journal of Population Research, 33*(1), 83–96.

People Culture Environment. (2014). *The Elder's report into preventing Indigenous self-harm & youth suicide*. Melbourne: People Culture Environment. Retrieved from http://www.cultureislife.org/bepartofthehealing/EldersReport.pdf.

Pihama, L., Reynolds, P., Smith, C., Reid, J., Tuhiwai Smith, L., & TeNana, R. (2014). Positioning historical trauma within Aotearoa New Zealand. *Alternative, 10*(3), 248–262.

Pittenger, S. M. (1998). The relationship between ethnic identity, self-esteem, emotional well-being and depression among Lakota/ Dakota Sioux adolescents (Doctoral dissertation). *Dissertation Abstracts International: Section B: Sciences and Engineering, 60*(3-B), 1311.

Pollock, N. J., Naiker, K., Loro, A., Mulay, S., & Colman, I. (2018). Global incidence of suicide among Indigenous peoples: A systematic review. *BMC Medicine, 16*, 145. https://doi.org/10.1186/s12916-018-1115-6.

Prince, D. (2018). *Stories from community: How suicide rates fell in two Indigenous communities The Healing Foundation*. Canberra, Australia.

Radford, A. J., Harris, R. D., Brice, G. A., van der Byl, M., Monten, H., Matters, D., Neeson, M., Bryan, L., & Hassan, R. J. (1990). *Taking control: A joint study of Aboriginal social health in Adelaide with particular reference to stress and destructive behaviours, 1989-1989*. South Australia, Adelaide: Department of Primary Health Care, Flinders University. Monograph 7.

Roundtree, J., & Smith, A. (2016). Strength-based well-being indicators for Indigenous children and families: A literature review of Indigenous communities identified wellbeing indicators (Online); Aurora *American Indian and Alaska Native Mental Health Research, 23*(3), 206–220 https://doi.org/10.5820/aian.2303.2016.206.

Sasakamoose, J., Bellegarde, T., Sutherland, W., Pete, S., & McKay-McNabb, K. (2017). Miýo-pimatisiwin developing Indigenous cultural responsiveness theory (ICRT): Improving Indigenous health and well-being. *The International Indigenous Policy Journal, 8*(4).

Sasakamoose, J., Scerbe, A., Wenaus, I., & Scandrett, A. (2016). First nation and Metis youth perspectives of health: An Indigenous qualitative Inquiry. *Qualitative Inquiry*, 1–15.

Sedikides, C., Wildschut, T., Routledge, C., & Arndt, J. (2015). Nostalgia counteracts self-discontinuity and restores self-continuity. *European Journal of Social Psychology, 45*, 52–61. https://doi.org/10.1002/ejsp.2073.

Senate community affairs references committee. (2018). *Accessibility and quality of mental health service in rural and remote Australia*. Canberra: Senate Printing Unit, Parliament House.

Social Health Reference Group. (2004). *Social and emotional well being framework: A national strategic framework for Aboriginal and Torres Strait Islander mental health and social and emotional wellbeing 2004-2009*. Canberra: Australian Government.

Sokol, Y., & Eisenheim, E. (2016). The relationship between continuous identity disturbances, negative mood, and suicidal ideation. *Primary Care Companion CNS Disord, 18*(1). https://doi.org/10.4088/PCC.15m01824.

Swan, P., & Raphael, B. (1995). *Ways forward: National Aboriginal and Torres Strait Islander mental health policy national consultancy report*. Canberra: Department of Health and Ageing.

Tiessen, M., Taylor, D., & Kirmayer, L. J. (2009). A key individual-to- community link: The impact of perceived collective control on Aboriginal youth well-being. Pimatisiwin: A journal of Aboriginal & Indigenous community health. *Fall*, 7(2), 241–267, 27pp. 2.

Waitoki, W., Nikora, L. W., Harris, P. E. T. K., & Levy, M. P. (2014). *Maori experiences of bipolar disorder: Pathways to recovery. Maori and Psychology Research Unit, University of Waikato; Te Pou o te Whakaaro Nui*. Hamilton, New Zealand: The National Centre of Mental Health Research, Information and Workforce Development.

Watson, I. (1998). Naked peoples: Rules and regulations. *Law Text Culture, 4*, 1–17.

Watson, I. (2016). *Raw Law: Aboriginal peoples, colonialism and international law*. New York: Routledge.

Wexler, L., Chandler, M., Gone, J. P., Cwik, M., Kirmayer, L. J., LaFrombois, T., Brockie, T., O'Keefe, V., Walkup, J., & Allen, J. (2015). Advancing suicide prevention research with rural American Indian and Alaska Native Populations. *American Journal of Public Health, 105*(5), 891–899.

Wexler, L. M., & Gone, J. P. (2012). Culturally responsive suicide prevention in Indigenous communities: Unexamined assumptions and new possibilities. *American Journal of Public Health, 102*(5), 800–806.

Whitesell, N. R., Mitchell, C. M., Kauffman, C. E., & Spicer, P. (2006). Developmental trajectories of personal and collective self-concept among American Indian adolescents. *Child Development, 77*, 1487–1503.

Wilkie, M. (1997). *Bringing them home: Report of the National Inquiry into the Separation of Aboriginal and Torres Strait Children from their Families*. Canberra: Human Rights and Equal Opportunity Commission.

Williams, D. R., Lawrence, J. A., & Davis, B. A. (2019). Racism and health: Evidence and needed research. *Annual Review of Public Health, 40*, 14.1–14.21.

Yap, M., & Yu, E. (2016). *Community wellbeing from the ground up: A yawuru example*. Bankwest Curtin Economics Center Research Report 3/16 August.

Yellow Bird, M. (2013). Neurodecolonization: Applying mindfulness research to decolonizing social work. In M. Gray, J. Coates, M. Yellow Bird, & T. Hetherington (Eds.), *Decolonizing social work* (pp. 293–310). Surrey, UK: Ashgate.

Yellow Horse Brave Heart, M. Y. H. (1998). The return to the sacred path: Healing from historical trauma and historical unresolved grief among the Lakota. *Smith College Studies in Social Work, 68*, 287–305.

Zubrick, S. R., Shepherd, C. C. J., Dudgeon, P., Gee, G., Paradies, Y., Scrine, C., & Walker, R. (2014). Social determinants of social and emotional wellbeing. In P. Dudgeon, H. Milroy, & R. Walker (Eds.), *Working together: Aboriginal and Torres Strait Islander mental health and wellbeing principles and practice* (2nd ed., pp. 93–112). Canberra: Department of the Prime Minister and Cabinet.

CHAPTER 13

Refugees and suicide: when the quest for a better life becomes thwarted

Shraddha Kashyap, Amy Joscelyne
School of Psychology, University of New South Wales (UNSW), Sydney, NSW, Australia

Introduction

According to the office of the United Nations High Commissioner for Refugees (UNHCR), a refugee is "... someone who is unable or unwilling to return to their country of origin owing to a well-founded fear of being persecuted for reasons of race, religion, nationality, membership of a particular social group, or political opinion ..." (UNHCR, 2010). Asylum seekers are individuals who have fled their country of origin, and have applied (or intend to apply) for asylum in another country, but whose applications are still pending a decision (UNHCR, 2016). This chapter will review how the experiences of forced migrants may influence suicide risk and resilience, from the perspective of the Interpersonal Theory of Suicide.

The Interpersonal Theory of Suicide (IPTS) posits that the *desire* and the *capability* to engage in suicidal behavior are separate constructs (Joiner et al., 2009; Van Orden et al., 2010). It argues that suicidal thoughts can emerge from individuals not feeling connected to other people in their lives (thwarted belongingness) and feeling like a burden (perceived burdensomeness; Van Orden et al., 2010). Further, the IPTS posits that suicidal ideation alone is not enough for people to act on those thoughts (Van Orden et al., 2010). It suggests that the capability to engage in suicidal behavior needs to be acquired through repeated exposure to painful and fear-inducing experiences (Hamza, Stewart, & Willoughby, 2012; Van Orden et al., 2010). While factors proposed by the IPTS have not been measured widely among asylum seekers and refugees; we propose that this theory provides a useful framework to explore what may corrode resilience and contribute to suicide risk in this population.

We suggest that despite the will to live, which drives the process of seeking asylum; individuals living in sustained displacement and facing

Alternatives to Suicide
ISBN 978-0-12-814297-4
https://doi.org/10.1016/B978-0-12-814297-4.00013-3

uncertain futures can develop a sense of hopelessness and thwarted belongingness. Furthermore, barriers to attaining basic needs such as housing, food security, and employment during sustained displacement may be associated with perceived burdensomeness. Preliminary evidence for this theory with refugee populations is provided by one study where results suggested there were significant associations between thwarted belongingness, perceived burdensomeness, and suicidal ideation among Bhutanese refugees resettled in the USA (Ao et al., 2012). Moreover, this theory seems particularly relevant to the refugee experience given that repeated exposure to fear inducing and painful events (e.g. trauma) is a defining feature of the refugee experience. In other words, forced migrants are faced with the kinds of experiences that may result in an acquired capability to engage in suicidal behavior (Ellis et al., 2015).

In this section we will briefly discuss the reported prevalence rates and correlates of psychological disorders among forced migrants; including pre- and post-migration stressors; as a basis for exploring how these factors may influence suicide risk and resilience. Indeed, higher rates of psychological distress were found among forced migrants compared to voluntary migrants and the general population (Beiser & Hou, 2017; Browne et al., 2017; Fazel, Wheeler, & Danesh, 2005).

Prevalence of psychopathology

Reported prevalence rates of mental health disorders within the population of forced migrants are highly variable. For example, one meta-analysis found rates of posttraumatic stress disorder (PTSD) ranging from 0 to 99%, with a weighted prevalence rate of 30.6%; and depression ranging from 3 to 85.5%, with a weighted prevalence of 30.8% (Steel et al., 2009). More recently, a review among refugees using clinical diagnostic assessments reported a 15.4% prevalence rate of PTSD, and 17.3% of depression (Steel et al., 2009; WHO, 2013). Another review of mental health disorders among forced migrants up to five years post-displacement, found that rates of PTSD ranged from 4.4 to 86%, depression ranged from 2.3 to 80%, and anxiety ranged from 20.3% to 88% (Bogic, Njoku, & Priebe, 2015). Authors argued that higher quality studies tended to report lower prevalence rates (Bogic et al., 2015). These findings suggest that not all forced migrants experience sustained, clinically significant psychological disorders. Therefore, when trying to understand resilience to stress and suicide risk, we need to consider what factors may lead to these variable reports of psychological wellbeing.

The variability in rates of psychological disorders could be due to interactions between exposure to stress and individual factors which protect against psychopathology. These may include positive perceived social support, hope, faith/religiosity (Kroo & Nagy, 2011; Orton, Griffiths, Green, & Waterman, 2012; Shakespeare-Finch, Schweitzer, King, & Brough, 2014; Tippens, 2017), optimism, connectedness to culture (Pieloch, McCullough, & Marks, 2016) and a sense of belongingness (Nuttman-Shwartz, Dekel, & Tuval-Mashiach, 2011). These associations between resilience and belongingness, hope, optimism, and perceived social support are consistent with the interpersonal antecedents of suicidal desire causally implicated by the IPTS. For example, the lack of hopelessness, thwarted belongingness and perceived burdensomeness demonstrated by individuals stating that they feel hopeful, connected to others and as if they belong could be protecting them from suicide risk and psychopathology (Ellis et al., 2015). By the same token, some of the variability in rates of psychological disorders could be attributed to individuals without permanent/secure immigration status often reporting higher rates of mental health disorders (Crumlish & Bracken, 2011; Iversen & Morken, 2004; Nickerson, Steel, Bryant, Brooks, & Silove, 2011), related to different kinds of post-migration stressors, associated with more insecurity (Crumlish & Bracken, 2011; McColl, McKenzie, & Bhui, 2008). This insecurity could then be related to higher thwarted belongingness, and this might be more corrosive to resilience.

Finally, the variability in prevalence rates of psychopathology could be associated with methodological differences between studies and culturally heterogeneous samples; together with measuring both clinical and non-clinical populations, and whether or not individuals were exposed to certain stressors, such as torture (Bogic et al., 2015; Johnson & Thompson, 2008).

Factors associated with psychological distress

Psychological distress is a consistent correlate of suicide risk in non-refugee populations (May & Klonsky, 2016) and has often been associated with suicide risk in forced migrant populations (e.g. Cohen, 2008; Goosen et al., 2011; Rahman & Hafeez, 2003). Therefore, we will briefly outline factors associated with significant psychological distress among forced migrants.

Fig. 13.1 shows examples of pre- and post-migration stressors faced by forced migrants. Emerging evidence suggests that post-migration stressors may impact on the ongoing mental health of asylum seekers and refugees

PRE-MIGRATION STRESSORS*

- **Exposure to war, imprisonment, genocide, homelessness, physical and sexual violence, lack of access to food and healthcare, and separation from family**
- **Exposure to more trauma is associated with increasingly worse mental health outcomes**

POST-MIGRATION STRESSORS**

- **Socioeconomic stress, such as denial of or restricted employment rights**
- **Social isolation, due to factors such as perceived discrimination and low social participation**
- **Immigration procedure stress, including delayed asylum application processing, and prolonged detention**
- **Poor access to health care and services; worry about family back home, and being unable to return home in an emergency**

Figure 13.1 Pre- and Post-migration stressors. *Note:* *(Johnson & Thompson, 2008; Lerner, Bonanno, Keatley, Joscelyne, & Keller, 2016; McColl et al., 2008; Porter & Haslam, 2005; Schweitzer, Brough, Vromans, & Asic-Kobe, 2011; Steel et al., 2009); (Johnson & Thompson, 2008; Mollica et al., 1998; Neuner et al., 2004); **(Bogic et al., 2012; Bogic et al., 2015; Chen, Hall, Ling, & Renzaho, 2017; McColl et al., 2008; Mölsä, Kuittinen, Tiilikainen, Honkasalo, & Punamäki, 2017; Nickerson et al., 2017; Porter & Haslam, 2005; Schick et al., 2016; Silove, Steel, McGorry, & Mohan, 1998; Steel et al., 2011).

over and above pre-migration stress (Chen et al., 2017; Li, Liddell, & Nickerson, 2016; Morgan, Melluish, & Welham, 2017). Consequently, since most asylum seekers and refugees worldwide have not been permanently resettled, those without permanent immigration status may be more likely to suffer from distress related to this insecure situation, and associated problems (McColl et al., 2008; Steel et al., 2006). For example, the temporary and uncertain nature of insecure immigration status has been associated with significant hopelessness (Procter, Kenny, Eaton, & Grech, 2018), and in turn, hopelessness has been consistently implicated with increased suicide risk (Ribeiro, Huang, Fox, & Franklin, 2018; Van Orden et al., 2010). In this way, it could be that the drive to live and seek a better life is corroded by hopelessness.

Further, one study found that permanently resettled Bhutanese refugees in the USA experienced thwarted belongingness and perceived burdensomeness (Ellis et al., 2015). Refugees leave their broader communities and social networks behind, often resulting in social isolation. Isolation combined with obstacles to finding meaningful employment such as language barriers, discrimination, or not being able to transfer qualifications to host communities; may lead to both thwarted belongingness and perceiving themselves to be a burden to their family and communities (Ellis et al., 2015). Indeed, results of this study suggest that both individual and resettlement factors were associated with thwarted belongingness and perceived burdensomeness (Ellis et al., 2015). For example, for both men and women; poor health, together with perceived lack of access to health and mental health services were associated with thwarted belongingness and perceived burdensomeness (Ellis et al., 2015). While socioeconomic stress was associated with perceived burdensomeness among both men and women; for men, unemployment was more strongly associated with perceived burdensomeness; while for women, being illiterate in English or Nepali and the lack of choice over their future was associated with feeling like a burden as well as thwarted belongingness (Ellis et al., 2015). Therefore, among forced migrants with both permanent and non-permanent status, pre and post migration stressors can lead to exacerbations in perceived burdensomeness and thwarted belongingness.

Studies also suggest that forced migrants who have been permanently resettled report more positive wellbeing than those living in sustained displacement. For example, one study found that while asylum seekers and refugees reported similar levels of pre-migration trauma exposure; asylum seekers were more likely than refugees to endorse distress related to the immigration status determination process (e.g. interviews by immigration officials, fear of being sent home); health, welfare and asylum problems (e.g. poor access to health care and services); and family problems (e.g. worry about family back home, and being unable to return home in an emergency; Silove et al., 1998). Moreover, after controlling for age, gender, pre-migration trauma and length of residency; ongoing temporary protection and past detention were independent contributors to poorer mental health in a sample of refugees and asylum seekers, with both temporary and permanent protection in Australia (Steel et al., 2006). Results of another study comparing resettled Syrian refugees in the Netherlands, to those living in camps for internally displaced peoples (IDP) in Syria, suggested that individuals living in IDP camps reported significantly poorer wellbeing (Al Ibraheem, Kira, Aljakoub, & Al Ibraheem, 2017). The temporary nature of their situation could be associated with reduced optimism about the future, and any associated hopelessness may in part erode the resilience associated with looking for a new life.

However, resettled refugees reported higher depression than those in IDP camps (Al Ibraheem et al., 2017). Indeed, one study with 64 forced migrants in Sweden, found no significant difference in levels of psychopathology or rates of suicidal behaviors between resettled refugees, and asylum-seekers (Ferrada-Noli & Sundbom, 1996). The authors suggested that PTSD severity could be a larger contributor to suicidality than immigration status (Ferrada-Noli & Sundbom, 1996). Still, given the small sample size and the heterogeneous cultural backgrounds of participants in the latter study (Ferrada-Noli & Sundbom, 1996), the generalisability and validity of these findings may be limited. Finally, while it is possible that asylum seekers might exaggerate reported levels of distress, it is plausible that these heightened symptoms reflect the ongoing instability and obstacles they face (Silove et al., 1998; Steel et al., 2006).

Moreover, a longitudinal study found that individuals on temporary protection visas reported higher rates of depression, anxiety, and traumatic stress; together with lower social integration and lower English language skills, compared to those with permanent protection (Steel et al., 2011). It could be that poorer social integration and language skills are related to lower access to services which provide help with these issues, which in turn may be associated with a non-permanent visa status (Steel et al., 2011). Therefore, results of the above studies point to factors related to insecure futures, and factors which could arguably be related to thwarted belongingness, and perceived burdensomeness. For example, fear of being sent home (Silove et al., 1998), temporary protection (Steel et al., 2006), living in temporary IDP camps (Al Ibraheem et al., 2017) and poor social integration (Steel et al., 2011) may be associated with a sense of thwarted belongingness and hopelessness related to a future life worth living. The lack of security could also be related to a sense of perceived burdensomeness where factors such as poor language skills (Steel et al., 2011) could hinder finding employment and the opportunity to build a new life independently. Therefore, when trying to understand suicide risk and resilience among asylum seekers and refugees, it is important to recognize the different challenges faced by individuals living in different circumstances, and that those who have not been permanently resettled could be at higher risks of experiencing difficulties than those who have (Al Ibraheem et al., 2017; Steel et al., 2006). Interactions between post-migration stressors, which may be associated with hopelessness, thwarted belongingness and perceived burdensomeness; could then have a negative impact on resilience, and the prospect of a future life worth living.

Measuring these factors among forced migrants would improve our understanding of what influences resilience and suicide risk.

The asylum/refugee status determination process and psychological distress

As described above, psychological distress among asylum seekers and refugees is associated with both pre- and post-migration stressors. Here, we will briefly outline the empirical evidence which identified stressors specifically related to seeking asylum among forced migrants in the post-migration environment, and suggest how exposure to these stressors could lead to experiencing hopelessness, thwarted belongingness and perceived burdensomeness, which, according to the IPTS would increase suicide risk among forced migrants. These include the process of seeking asylum, and prolonged detention.

First, the process of applying for asylum, and associated issues have been identified as a significant source of stress for asylum seekers (Crumlish & Bracken, 2011). The uncertainty associated with the process of seeking asylum, together with exposure to common post-migration stressors such as social isolation (e.g. perceived discrimination, boredom, loneliness) may lead to thwarted belongingness and socioeconomic stress (e.g. unemployment), and the inability to stand on their own feet, could lead to perceived burdensomeness. Psychological distress associated with these factors may then be associated with increased suicide risk via reduced resilience and increased hopelessness about the future. Indeed, a review of the empirical literature studying asylum seekers in Western countries over 20 years, suggests there is a high risk of psychopathology among asylum-seekers (Ryan, Kelly, & Kelly, 2009). The review proposes that their mental health can deteriorate while waiting for a decision, and then improve following a positive outcome (Ryan et al., 2009). For example, among Iraqi asylum seekers in the Netherlands, it was found that a longer asylum procedure was associated with higher incidences of psychopathology (Laban, Gernaat, Komproe, Schreuders, & de Jong, 2004; Laban, Komproe, Gernaat, & de Jong, 2008). Further, among all the post-migration stressors measured; unemployment, stress related to family issues (e.g. missing and worrying about family back home), and the asylum procedure itself (e.g. uncertain visa status, fear of being sent away) had the strongest associations with psychopathology (Laban, Gernaat, Komproe, van der Tweel, & De Jong, 2005). These factors, identified by asylum seekers as stressful, are consistent with the IPTS. That is, not being able to work and provide for themselves and family could be conceived as perceived burdensomeness (e.g. as was found in Ellis et al., 2015), and fear of being sent away could be viewed as a sense of not belonging to the host community.

Indeed, among 40 asylum seekers in Australia; greater exposure to pre-migration trauma, delays in processing, difficulties with immigration procedures, obstacles to employment, perceived discrimination, boredom and loneliness (i.e. factors which may impede a sense of belonging, and hinder independent living) were significantly associated with psychopathology (Silove, Sinnerbrink, Field, Manicavasagar, & Steel, 1997). However, the cross-sectional nature of studies with small and culturally heterogeneous samples, are limitations to existing studies (Ryan et al., 2009). Therefore, prospective research framed by factors put forward by the IPTS may help confirm these findings, and inform evidence-based interventions to address stressors associated with seeking asylum and help boost resilience.

Finally, a negative impact of prolonged detention on the psychological wellbeing of forced migrants has been reported (Filges, Montgomery, & Kastrup, 2018; Robjant, Hassan, & Katona, 2009). According to recent reviews of the literature, there is evidence for an independent adverse effect of prolonged detention on the mental health of asylum seekers (Filges et al., 2018; Robjant et al., 2009). Indeed, one review analyzed studies which compared detained asylum seekers to those living in the community and found worse mental health outcomes among those who were detained (Filges et al., 2018). Viewing these findings from the lens of the IPTS would suggest that prolonged detention might be associated with thwarted belongingness as detained individuals are not permitted to live (or belong) in the wider community. Living in institutional detention for extended periods of time also prevents forced migrants from living independently, which may lead to a sense of perceived burdensomeness. Finally, prolonged detention, where the length of detention is unknown, is likely associated with significant hopelessness about the future (Procter et al., 2018), and according to the IPTS, these factors would be associated with increased suicide risk, by eroding the possibility of a future life that is worth living. However, small sample sizes, difficulties in isolating the effects of detention from the stressors faced by asylum seekers before, during and after detention; and that all studies reviewed were based on samples from only three high income countries (Australia, USA, and UK; Robjant et al., 2009) are limitations. Nevertheless, the existing research is consistent in finding poor wellbeing among detained asylum seekers (Robjant et al., 2009).

Summary

While the pre- and post-migration stressors faced by asylum-seekers and refugees are well documented, research relating to the prevalence and correlates of psychological disorders in this population is more variable. Variable prevalence rates could be due to the interaction between exposure to stressors and resilience among forced migrants, and/or methodological differences between studies. Emerging research also suggests that forced migrants without permanent immigration status are at higher risks of experiencing poorer wellbeing compared to those who are permanently resettled. It is possible that challenges related to temporary or insecure status are associated with increased levels of hopelessness, thwarted belongingness and perceived burdensomeness. These in turn could corrode the resilience which allowed individuals to brave perils to leave their homes and seek asylum, and challenge the idea of a future life worth living, thereby increasing suicide risk. However, not all studies find differences in psychological distress between those with and without secure immigration status. This could be because even permanently resettled refugees experience thwarted belongingness and perceived burdensomeness (Ellis et al., 2015), which was associated with suicidal ideation (Ao et al., 2012). Finally, factors described by the IPTS need to be empirically measured more widely among forced migrants before strong conclusions can be drawn, but the case for viewing results of existing studies through the lens of the IPTS is compelling, and this theory can be used as a framework to inform intervention and future research.

Within the context of pre- and post-migration stressors faced by forced migrants, and the sometimes-mixed findings around reported mental health consequences of dealing with these stressors; the rest of this chapter aims to review and discuss what the current peer-reviewed, empirical literature tells us about suicide risk in particular, among asylum seekers and refugees. We will then outline suggestions by researchers and clinicians who work in this field regarding what can be done to improve our understanding of the situation, and provide recommendations for future research and clinical work, to improve the quality of life for forced migrants worldwide.

Prevalence of suicidal behavior

In this section, we will outline the current literature regarding prevalence rates of suicidal ideation, self-injury, and suicide attempts/deaths by suicide among forced migrants. The prevalence of suicidality (including suicidal ideation and behaviors) was previously reported to range between 3% and 34% (Vijayakumar & Jotheeswaran, 2010, pp. 195–210). Here, we will discuss suicidal ideation, and suicidal behaviors (self-injury and suicide attempts/deaths) separately, due to the ideation-to-action framework outlined by the IPTS (Van Orden et al., 2010). That is, as described in the introduction, the IPTS views suicidal ideation and behaviors as separate constructs, where acting on suicidal thoughts requires individuals to have acquired the capability to hurt themselves (Van Orden et al., 2010). This capability can be acquired through exposure to painful or provocative events (Van Orden et al., 2010), and habituation to physical pain via behaviors such as non-suicidal self-injury (Hamza et al., 2012). For these reasons, non-suicidal self-injury will be discussed as well as suicide attempts, when possible, to try to paint a clearer picture of suicide risk, and potential correlates among asylum seekers and refugees.

Suicidal ideation

This section will divide recent studies that measured suicidal ideation among permanently resettled refugees only; non-permanently resettled asylum seekers and refugees only; and studies which either do not specify immigration status, or compare rates of suicidal ideation between permanently and non-permanently resettled samples living in host communities. Studies are divided in this manner due to the differences in stressors faced by these populations, where those with insecure status often report worse psychological wellbeing (Crumlish & Bracken, 2011; McColl, 2008; Steel et al., 2011). Indeed, it is likely that permanent resettlement can address key risk factors implicated in theories of suicide (e.g. hopelessness, belongingness, the ability to contribute and live independently and not feel like a burden), and so resilience among those permanently resettled may not be challenged to the same degree as those who are still displaced.

Permanently resettled populations

Based on four samples (see Table 13.1), the prevalence of reported suicidal ideation among permanently resettled refugees appears to range between 3% and 34.4%. Three of four studies reported between 3% and 11% of individuals experiencing suicidal ideation, which is generally lower than rates seen among non-permanently resettled populations (see Table 13.1). We would expect rates to be lower among permanently resettled populations due to the likelihood of lower levels of thwarted belongingness (as they have a permanent home), perceived burdensomeness (as they are more

Table 13.1 Prevalence of suicidal ideation.

Paper	Sample	Measures	Prevalence of suicidal ideation
Permanently resettled populations			
Ao et al. (2016)	423 Bhutanese refugees resettled in the USA between 2009 and 2012	19-item measure: Based on the suicidality module of the world Mental health composite international diagnostic interview, the scale for suicidal ideation, and the disability injury survey	3%
Bhui et al. (2003)	180 Somali refugees resettled in the UK	Beck depression inventory	34.40%
Jankovic et al. (2013)	854 refugees from former yugoslavia resettled in Western Europe	MINI international neuropsychiatric interview	10.20%
Jensen, Skardalsmo, & Fjermestad (2014)	75 unaccompanied refugee minors, with 12 backgrounds, resettled in Norway	Hopkins symptom checklist-37 A for adolescents	11%
Non-permanently resettled populations			
Refugee camps			
Rahman & Hafeez (2003)	297 Afghan mothers residing in a refugee camp in Pakistan	Self-reporting questionnaire (SRQ-20)	32%
Al-Modallal (2012)	300 women attending health care centers in refugee camps in Jordan	Yes/No questions: had suicidal thoughts, and/or had attempted a suicidal action.	13.6%

Continued

Table 13.1 Prevalence of suicidal ideation.—cont'd

Paper	Sample	Measures	Prevalence of suicidal ideation
Permanently resettled populations			
Falb, McCormick, Hemenway, Anfinson, & Silverman (2013)	873 women (majority Karen) residing across three refugee camps along the Thai-Burma border	Yes/no outcome, derived from a single item: "In the past four weeks, has the thought of ending your life been on your mind?"	7.4% (However, among women who reported experiencing both intimate partner violence, and conflict related victimisation; 50% reported experiencing suicidal ideation)
Akinyemi, Atilola, & Soyannwo (2015)	444, both male and female refugees of mostly Liberian background, living in camps in Nigeria	MINI international neuropsychiatric interview	27.3%
Vijayakumar et al. (2017)	1303 Tamil speaking sri Lankans residing in refugee camps in southern India	21-item Beck's scale for suicidal ideation	1.2%
Immigration detention			
Keller et al. (2003)	70 detained asylum-seekers in the USA	Hopkins symptom Checklist-25	26%
Zachary Steel et al. (2004)	Retrospective, self-report study among 10 families detained in Australia (14 adults and 20 children)	Structured psychiatric interviews	93% of adults and 55% of children described experiencing suicidal ideation while in detention

Table 13.1 Prevalence of suicidal ideation.—cont'd

Paper	Sample	Measures	Prevalence of suicidal ideation
Permanently resettled populations			
Mares & Jureidini (2004)	16 adults and 20 children in immigration detention in Australia, who were referred for psychological assessment and treatment	Comprehensive clinical assessment, multiple interviews	10 children aged 6–17 years met criteria for major depression and suicidal ideation
Permanent and non-permanently resettled populations living in host communities			
Ferrada-Noli & Sundbom (1996)	32 asylum-seekers and 32 individuals with refugee status matched on age and gender, residing in Sweden	Modified checklist produced by the national Board of health and welfare	42%
Sarkardi et al. (2017)	46 unaccompanied refugee minors in Sweden	Montgomery—Åsberg depression rating scale self-report	48%
Lerner, Bonanno, Keatley, Joscelyne, & Keller (2015)	267 asylum-seekers and refugee survivors of torture residing in New York city	Clinical intake interviews	29.20%

likely to have the opportunity to live independently) and hopelessness (due to higher chances of a future life worth living), given their secure status. Variability in prevalence within permanently resettled refugees, could then be due to differences in the environments between samples, where perhaps different levels of post-migration stressors are faced, as well as differences in individual resilience factors. The highly variable cultural backgrounds, sample sizes, and differences in ages between participants in these studies may also account for the differences in prevalence rates. Furthermore, in one study, individuals who reported only thoughts about suicide, without methods/plans or previous attempts were not included as "suicidal" and excluded from the percentage of people described as endorsing suicidality (Jankovic et al., 2013). Therefore, variation in how suicidal ideation was defined may account for differences in prevalence rates. Finally, heterogeneity in the kinds of instruments used to measure suicidal ideation in these studies, including clinical interviews (Bhui et al., 2003; Jankovic et al., 2013), and structured questionnaires (Jensen et al., 2014) may also explain these differences.

Non-permanently resettled populations

Refugee camps

Reported rates of suicidal ideation among refugees residing in camps are also variable between samples (1.2%–32%). Indeed, only 16 individuals (1.2%) reported experiencing suicidal ideation in a refugee camp in Southern India, while a larger number (80) individuals (6.1%), in that same population reported past suicide attempts (Vijayakumar et al., 2017). The authors suggested that the low levels of reported suicidal ideation among the Tamil Sri Lankans (1.2%) in these camps could be due to cultural stigma around discussing mental health problems, and suicide; as well as potential worry about maintaining confidentiality in a refugee camp, and/or worry that reporting suicidality may adversely impact on resettlement opportunities (Vijayakumar et al., 2017). Viewing these findings from the lens of the IPTS would suggest that the very desire to obtain permanent status, or to belong somewhere, may result in underreporting of suicidal desire. That is, it appears that a non-permanent status, or insecure future not only has the potential to directly impact on the exacerbation factors thought to be causally related to suicide risk, but may even lead to not reporting suicidal ideation for fear that it may hinder chances of obtaining a secure future life worth living.

Immigration detention

Reported rates of suicidal ideation among detained asylum-seekers, in two high income countries, (Australia and USA) range between 26% and over 90% (see Table 13.1). These prevalence rates are higher than for permanently resettled and non-detained samples, and are concurrent with the IPTS. For example, as discussed earlier, prolonged detention is associated with significant psychological distress and potentially associated with hopelessness, thwarted belongingness and perceived burdensomeness.

Other

Finally, two studies which compared rates of suicidal ideation between asylum seekers and refugees in Sweden (Ferrada-Noli & Sundbom, 1996), and asylum seekers and permanent residents in Switzerland (Premand et al., 2018); report non-significant differences between those with permanent and non-permanent immigration status. However, not having applied for refugee status was associated with higher odds of reporting suicidal ideation among torture survivors in the USA (Lerner et al., 2015). Again, it could be that a higher risk of suicidal ideation is associated with non-permanent visa status, but the three studies described above suggest that the literature is not conclusive.

In summary, reported rates of suicidal ideation generally appear to be highest among detained forced migrants, followed by non-permanently resettled and permanently resettled forced migrants. These differences in suicidal desire lend support to the notion that an insecure future, coupled with the inability to build independent lives worth living, plus restricted movements (among detained forced migrants) may be associated with higher levels of suicidal ideation, potentially via hopelessness, thwarted belongingness and perceived burdensomeness. Belongingness and burdensomeness need to be measured more widely among forced migrants to test this hypothesis, but the link between living conditions, psychological distress and suicidal ideation is compelling. Furthermore, preliminary evidence for an association between thwarted belongingness, perceived burdensomeness and suicidal ideation in a refugee sample does exist, as shown in a study that found such an association among Bhutanese refugees living in the USA (Ao et al., 2012).

It is also important to acknowledge that rates of suicidal ideation varied within the permanently, non-permanently and detained samples. Different definitions and approaches to data collection between studies could affect these findings. Future research would benefit from more uniform measures of suicidal ideation among asylum seekers and refugees, which have been validated across as many cultural groups as possible.

The next section will report prevalence rates of suicidal behaviors (including suicide attempts and self-injury).

Suicidal behaviors (self-injury, suicide attempts, and deaths by suicide)

This section will also be divided according to the kind of population measured in each study (i.e. permanently resettled only, non-permanently resettled only; and studies which use mixed samples or compare samples). Eleven of the studies describe reported suicidal behavior which occurred post-displacement, and during the resettlement period (for both permanently and non-permanently resettled samples). The remaining (nine) studies (Al-Modallal, 2012; Allodi & Cowgill, 1982; Ferrada-Noli, Asberg, Ormstad, et al., 1998; Ferrada-Noli & Sundbom, 1996; Flaskerud & Anh, 1988; Kira et al., 2017; Madianos et al., 2011; Ssenyonga et al., 2013; Tousignant et al., 1999) report prevalence of suicidal behavior at time of assessment, and it is unclear whether this includes pre-migration suicide attempts. Therefore, these studies may confound pre- and post-displacement suicide risk. Nevertheless, they still provide some indication of the level of suicidality in each sample in their post-migration environment.

Permanently resettled populations

Studies of permanently resettled refugees report rates of suicidal behavior ranging from 2.78% to 13.7% (see Table 13.2). However, one study conducted with Vietnamese refugees living in the USA, which reported a 7% prevalence rate (Flaskerud & Anh, 1988), did not measure suicidal thoughts separately to behavior, and so the 7% may include both suicidal ideation and behavior (see Table 13.2).

Non-permanently resettled populations

Refugee camps

According to three studies, the prevalence of suicidal behavior among individuals residing in refugee camps appears to range between 0.5% and 29.2% (see Table 13.2). This large variability could be due to several factors, including cultural heterogeneity, sample size, distribution of genders (e.g. one study measured women only; Al-Modallal, 2012); and the likelihood that camps in India, Jordan and Uganda would likely be different environments and have access to different resources. Nevertheless, compared to permanently resettled refugees, these rates have a higher upper limit (see Table 13.2). This is consistent with the IPTS, as individuals living in refugee camps have a less certain future compared to those with permanent status, living in host communities. Furthermore, individuals in refugee camps could be at ongoing risk of being exposed to more painful or fear inducing events (e.g. violence within refugee camps; Crisp, 2000), potentially leading to higher acquired capability to engage in suicidal behavior.

Immigration detention

Among detained asylum seekers in the UK, the rate of suicide deaths increased from 1997 to 2005 (see Table 13.2), and authors suggest this could be due to increasing numbers of people in detention. Moreover, the

Table 13.2 Prevalence of suicidal behaviors.

Paper	Sample	Measures	Prevalence of suicidal behaviors
Permanently resettled populations			
Ao et al. (2012)	579 Bhutanese refugees resettled in the USA between 2008 and 2011	Psychological autopsies	16 (2.8%) confirmed deaths by suicide after arriving in the USA
Flaskerud & Anh (1988)	81 Vietnamese refugees living in the USA	Clinical records	**7%** of participants reported suicidal thoughts, wishes or attempts at time of assessment (not measured separately)
Allodi & Cowgill (1982)	41 Latin American refugees (torture survivors) living in Canada	Clinician interview	4 participants **(9.8%)** attempted suicide following torture
Tousignant et al. (1999)	203 adolescents from refugee families, 35 different backgrounds	Diagnostic interview schedule for children Version 2.25 (DISC-2.25)	12 month prevalence rate, **3%** of participants reported suicide attempts
Kira, Shuwiekh, Rice, Al Ibraheem, & Aljakoub (2017)	196 syrian refugees living in Egypt	The post-cumulative trauma-related disorders measure	**13.7%** suicidal plans or attempts
Non-permanently resettled populations			
Refugee camps			
Vijayakumar et al. (2017)	1303 Tamil speaking sri Lankans residing in refugee camps in southern India	Self-report "ever attempted suicide"	Reported past suicide attempts was 6.1%, 7 deaths by suicide during study period **(0.5%)**; 5 at baseline; 2 post-intervention

Continued

Table 13.2 Prevalence of suicidal behaviors.—cont'd

Paper	Sample	Measures	Prevalence of suicidal behaviors
Permanently resettled populations			
Al-Modallal (2012)	300 women attending health care centers in refugee camps in Jordan	Yes/No questions: had suicidal thoughts, and/ or had attempted a suicidal action.	**7.3%** suicide attempts
Ssenyonga, Owens, & Olema (2013)	89 congolese refugees residing in the nakivale refugee camp in Uganda	MINI psychiatric interview	**29.2%**; moderate to high risk of suicidal behavior
Immigration detention			
Cohen (2008)	1806 asylum-seekers detained in immigration removal centers (IRC) in the UK	Clinical records	231 ***(12.79%)*** reported incidents of ***self-harm***; **deaths by suicide**: Prevalence rates were found to increase from **1997-8 (42 per 100,000) to 2003 −5 (211 per 100,000)**
CCJDP (2002); Dudley (2003)	Australian immigration detention centers (IDCs), between 1 March 2001 and 30 October 2001	IDC records	**264** incidents of self-harm; **estimated** prevalence rates of self-harm for men were **12,343 per 100,000**; and for women, **estimated** rates were **10,227 per 100,000**

Table 13.2 Prevalence of suicidal behaviors.—cont'd

Paper	Sample	Measures	Prevalence of suicidal behaviors
Permanently resettled populations			
(Hedrick, 2017)	Australian immigration detention centers (IDCs), between October 2009 and May 2011	IDC records	959 reported self-harm incidents while in detention; based on **estimated** 4269 detainees, reported prevalence rate was **22%**, or **224 per 1000:** Male to female self-harm ratio of 12:1
Keller et al. (2003)	70 detained asylum-seekers in the USA	Hopkins symptom Checklist-25	2 out of 70 **(2.9%)** detained asylums seekers reported attempting suicide while in detention
Steel et al. (2004)	Retrospective, self-report study among 10 families detained in Australia (14 adults and 20 children)	Structured psychiatric interviews	**36%** of adults and **5%** of children retrospectively reported engaging in self-harm while in detention
Mares & Jureidini (2004)	16 adults and 20 children in immigration detention in Australia, who were referred for psychological assessment and treatment	Comprehensive clinical assessment, multiple inter views	8 children **(40%)** reported engaging in self-harm while detained
Permanent and non-permanently resettled populations living in host communities			
Cohen (2008)	Asylum-seekers living in detention and the community in the UK	Clinical records	38 known deaths by suicide after arriving in the UK

Continued

Table 13.2 Prevalence of suicidal behaviors.—cont'd

Permanently resettled populations

Paper	Sample	Measures	Prevalence of suicidal behaviors
Goosen et al. (2011)	Participants included those in all the asylum-seeker reception centers in The Netherlands between 2002 and 2007	Asylum reception center clinical records.	35 deaths by suicide and 290 cases of suicidal behavior after arriving in The Netherlands; **suicide deaths**, male asylum seekers: **25.6/ 100,000 per year**; female asylum seekers: **4/1000,000 per year**; ***other suicidal behaviors: 199.2/100,000 per year*** (males) and ***188.2/ 100,000 per year*** (females)
Van Oostrum, Goosen, Uitenbroek, Koppenaal, & Stronks (2011)	Study explored mortality rates among asylum-seekers and the Dutch population between 2002 and 2005	Community health services (CHS) for asylum seekers clinical records.	Of 193 deaths among male asylum seekers during this period, 22 **(11.4%)** were known suicides; and of the 138 deaths among female asylum seekers, 3 **(2%)** were known suicides
Ferrada-Noli, Asberg, Ormstad, Lundin, & Sundbom (1998)	149 forced migrants (23 with refugee status), in Sweden	Modified checklist produced by the national Board of health and welfare	**16.7%** of participants reported having made at least one suicide attempt while in Sweden

Table 13.2 Prevalence of suicidal behaviors.—cont'd

Permanently resettled populations

Paper	Sample	Measures	Prevalence of suicidal behaviors
Ferrada-Noli & Sundbom (1996)	32 asylum-seekers were compared to 32 refugees living in Sweden	Modified checklist produced by the national Board of health and welfare	**46%** previous suicide attempt
Madianos, Sarhan, & Koukia (2011)	Palestinians living in the west Bank, following exposure to violence, **31.2%** of sample were refugees	Clinical interviews	76 **(8.3%)** reported having attempted suicide

average suicide rate among detained asylum seekers between 1997 and 2005 was reported as 122 per 100,000, compared to a UK national rate of 9 per 100,000 during this same time; suggesting a higher suicide rate among asylum seekers than the general population (Cohen, 2008). This higher rate of suicide compared to the host community lends further support to the IPTS, where for detained asylum seekers; not living within or belonging to the host community (thwarted belongingness), together with not being able to live independently (perceived burdensomeness), combined with exposure to refugee trauma (acquired capability) may be associated with an increased risk of suicide compared to the host population. However, these rates are based on small numbers (12 known deaths by suicide) in this time frame, and so, these data should be interpreted with care (Cohen, 2008).

In Australian Immigration Detention Centers (IDCs), the prevalence of self-harm and suicide were reported to be 41 times (males) and 26 times (females) the rates among non-refugee/asylum seeker community populations (Dudley, 2003). These numbers suggest large differences in rates of self-harm and suicidal behaviors between detained asylum seekers and the host population. Furthermore, updated information suggests a male to female self-harm ratio of 12:1 (Hedrick, 2017), and this difference in risk between males and females was also found among asylum seekers living in the community in the UK (Cohen, 2008) and the Netherlands (Goosen, Kunst, Stronks, van Oostrum, & Uitenbroek, 2011; Van Oostrum et al., 2011). These gender differences are discussed further in the next section.

However, these numbers are based on estimates of the number of asylum seekers in detention in 2001 (Dudley, 2003), and a reported lack of systematic collection of data about self-injury in IDCs (Dudley, 2003; Hedrick, 2017) means that we may not have an accurate idea of the prevalence. Nonetheless, studies do consistently suggest that there are higher rates of self-harm and suicidal behaviors among detained asylum seekers compared to host populations (which would be consistent with the IPTS), and among male compared to female asylum seekers.

Permanently and non-permanently resettled populations living in host communities

Cohen (2008) reported that between 2000 and 2005, there were a total of 38 known deaths by suicide among asylum seekers including those in detention and living in the community in the UK Of the 38 individuals who died by suicide, 35 were male, and 3 were female (Cohen, 2008). Two studies which examined data about self-injury and suicide among asylum seekers living in the Netherlands also found higher rates of suicidal behavior among males than females (see Table 13.2). First, based on data about suicide deaths and hospital treated suicidal behaviors (non-suicidal self-injury, and suicide attempts) from all the asylum reception centers in the Netherlands, males were found to engage in more suicidal behavior than females, with a ratio of 10:1 (Goosen et al., 2011). Second, a study that looked at mortality rates among asylum-seekers and the Dutch population between 2002 and 2005, reports 22 deaths by suicide among male asylum seekers and 3 among female asylum seekers (Van Oostrum et al., 2011).

Therefore, one consistent finding is that male asylum seekers engaged in more suicidal behaviors than females (Cohen, 2008; Goosen et al., 2011; Hedrick, 2017; Van Oostrum et al., 2011). These findings add to the broader literature wherein suicide rates are typically higher among males compared to females, possibly due to the higher lethality of methods employed during a suicide attempt (Freeman et al., 2017). Interpreting these results from the perspective of the IPTS would suggest that males experienced higher levels of thwarted belongingness, perceived burdensomeness and had higher acquired capability to engage in suicidal behavior. It could also be that there is more stigma around discussing emotional problems among male forced migrants (e.g. De Anstiss & Ziaian, 2010) and this may lead to fewer males seeking help for mental health problems, thereby eroding resilience and increasing suicide risk. Future research would need to measure these factors among forced migrants to better understand why these gender differences exist.

Notably, researchers advise caution about interpreting prevalence rates due to the possibility that not all suicide deaths are known to be suicides, and due to the small number of incidents (Cohen, 2008; Goosen et al., 2011). Furthermore, it is also unclear whether the rate of suicidal behaviors among asylum seekers and refugees in general is higher than host populations. Some studies report higher incidences of suicidality (including ideation and behaviors) among asylum seekers/refugees (e.g., Cohen, 2008; Dudley, 2003; Jankovic et al., 2013; Staehr & Munk-Andersen, 2006; Westman et al., 2003), and some find no differences (e.g., Falb et al., 2013; Madianos et al., 2011; Norredam et al., 2012; Tousignant et al., 1999). This discrepancy could be due to methodological and practical constraints inherent to conducting research among forced migrants (described in detail at the end of this section). There may also be specific factors associated with suicide risk which lead to differing results. One of these factors could be exposure to pre-migration trauma. Pre-migration correlates of suicide risk among asylum seekers and refugees will therefore be described below.

Pre-migration stressors and suicide risk

Emerging research reports links between particular types of pre-migrations stressors and increased suicide risk. For example, among Somali refugees living in the USA, suicidal ideation was related to pre-migration food shortage, feeling close to death, and being seriously injured (Bhui et al., 2003). In addition, one study found significant associations between the manner in which individuals were tortured, and their methods of attempting suicide (Ferrada-Noli, Asberg, & Ormstad, 1998). More specifically, it was reported that those tortured via blunt-force were more likely to jump from a height or in front of trains; water torture was associated with drowning, and sharp force torture was associated with self-cutting or stabbing (Ferrada-Noli, Asberg, & Ormstad, 1998). The results of both of these studies could be associated with the acquired capability construct, proposed by the IPTS as a causal factor for increased suicidality (Ellis et al., 2015). That is, the IPTS argues that exposure to painful, or fear inducing events may increase the risk of engaging in suicidal behavior among those experiencing suicidal ideation (Van Orden et al., 2010). Habituation to physical pain has also been implicated in increased acquired capability for suicidal behavior (Hamza et al., 2012). Therefore, the associations between feeling close to death, being seriously injured, and suicidality, and that the method of torture was related to the method of self-injury lends support to this idea. Furthermore, among a group of refugees from former Yugoslavia, exposure to war related imprisonment and traumatic war experiences were associated with higher suicidality (Jankovic et al., 2013). Another study found that exposure to sexual violence was significantly associated with increased odds of reporting suicidal ideation among torture survivors in the USA, before they received any psychosocial intervention (Lerner et al., 2015). This finding is consistent with meta-analyses in non-refugee populations, which report sexual abuse as a reliable correlate of suicide risk (Beghi, Rosenbaum, Cerri, & Cornaggia, 2013; May & Klonsky, 2016).

Therefore, there appears to be a consistent pattern of pre-migration adverse events which are associated with increased suicidality. Relationships between exposure to fear inducing and painful events such as traumatic war experiences (Jankovic et al., 2013), sexual violence (Lerner et al., 2015), feeling close to death (Bhui et al., 2003), specific methods of injury which may be related to methods of self-injury (Ferrada-Noli, Asberg, & Ormstad, 1998); and increased suicidality can also be viewed via the IPTS. That is, the IPTS would categorise these pre-migration traumatic events as increasing the acquired capability for individuals to engage in suicidal behavior, when coupled with thwarted belongingness and perceived burdensomeness, which may also exist among forced migrants in the post-migration environment (Ellis et al., 2015). It may then be a combination of these factors which corrode resilience in this population.

Limitations

Overall, a lack of systematic data collection about suicidal thoughts and behaviors among forced migrants (Cohen, 2008; Hedrick, 2017), small numbers of known suicidal behaviors; small samples (Mares & Jureidini, 2004) and cultural differences pertaining to mental health (e.g. stigma; Vijayakumar et al., 2017) limit our understanding of suicidality among forced migrants. Indeed, reported difficulties in accessing clinical information among asylum seekers and refugees (Cohen, 2008; Robjant et al., 2009; Vijayakumar, 2016; Vijayakumar et al., 2017); and the possibility that deaths by suicide among asylum-seekers and refugees are not always known to be suicides (Cohen, 2008), make it difficult to determine accurate prevalence rates of suicidal behavior in this population. For example, it was reported that in the UK, if an asylum seeker in the community dies by suicide, information about their asylum/refugee status is not systematically recorded by coroners (Cohen, 2008). These practical and methodological issues may also explain the highly variable prevalence rates reported.

Summary

Notwithstanding limitations, in this section, we provided examples of studies that reported numbers of asylum seekers and refugees, in various circumstances, who reported suicidal ideation, and/or engaged in suicidal behavior. Differences in the prevalence of rates of suicidality could be due to methodological differences between studies, or the association between exposure to pre-migration adverse events and suicidality. The IPTS would argue that exposure to those painful and fear inducing events could lead to an increased acquired capability for engaging in suicidal behavior. We suggest that when viewing the evidence through the lens of the IPTS, this potential acquired capability, together with thwarted belongingness and perceived burdensomeness potentially experienced in the post-migration environments (to different extents, depending on the level of security, hope, and ability to live independently); would work together to erode the drive to live shown by individuals who leave their home to seek asylum.

Correlates of suicide risk among asylum-seekers and refugees

Research among non-refugee populations suggests that links between demographic and psychosocial factors such as age, gender and education, with increased suicide risk were not strong (May & Klonsky, 2016). Conversely, psychological distress was more consistently associated with suicide risk (Beghi et al., 2013; May & Klonsky, 2016). Since these findings apply to non-refugee/asylum seeker populations, can we apply these conclusions to forced migrants (Vijayakumar, 2016)? There is a smaller body of research examining relationships between psychological distress, psychosocial factors and suicide risk among forced migrants compared to other populations (Vijayakumar, 2016). However, the available research does suggest that psychological distress and suicide risk are related among forced migrants. For example, 82% of asylum seekers who died by suicide in detention in the UK (Cohen, 2008), and 80% of asylum seekers who engaged in suicidal behavior in the Netherlands (Goosen et al., 2011), had a history of mental health problems.

Since we have already outlined factors associated with psychological distress which likely corrode resilience (i.e. pre- and post-migration stressors, and stressors associated with the refugee/asylum determination process); in this section we will provide examples of relevant empirical studies that identified relationships between environmental and psychosocial factors, and suicide risk specifically among forced migrants. These will also be reviewed from the perspective of the IPTS.

Substance abuse and suicide risk

Two studies found associations between substance abuse and suicide risk; one among Somali refugees in the USA (Bhui et al., 2003) and the other among asylum seekers in the Netherlands (Goosen et al., 2011). However, substance abuse was not a factor among asylum seekers with high suicide risk in the UK (Cohen, 2008), and a review found that there is not enough evidence to suggest that there is a relationship between forced displacement and substance abuse (Weaver & Roberts, 2010). Therefore, while it should be studied further, we cannot yet draw conclusions about the relationship between substance abuse and suicide risk among forced migrants.

Sexuality, gender identity and suicide risk

Emerging research suggests that LGBTQ identifying forced migrants may be at elevated risks of suicidality. For example, among survivors of torture seeking treatment in a clinic for asylum seekers and refugees in the USA, the 57% of clients who were persecuted due their LGBTQ identity reported significantly higher rates of suicidal ideation than non LGBTQ survivors of torture, matched by country of origin and sex (Hopkinson et al., 2017). Indeed, LGBTQ clients were found to report higher incidences of sexual violence, earlier ages of first trauma, and more persecution by family members than their matched counterparts (Hopkinson et al., 2017). Another study used 26 qualitative interviews among individuals who obtained refugee status in Canada or the USA on the basis of their LGBTQ identity (Alessi, Kahn, & Chatterji, 2016). Thematic analysis revealed associations between reported abuse, psychological distress and increased suicidality in this sample (Alessi et al., 2016).

The increased risk of suicidality among LGBTQ identifying refugees and asylum seekers is consistent with non-refugee populations (King et al., 2008). However, since LGBTQ asylum-seekers and refugees report increased or earlier onset of abuse by members of their own family and community, they often migrate alone (Hopkinson et al., 2017; Portman & Weyl, 2013). Clinicians in this field therefore argue that LGBTQ forced migrants may be more socially isolated than their non-LGBTQ counterparts as they could be segregated from their own (country of origin) community, *and* be less likely to disclose their sexual/gender identity to host services, due to past experiences of persecution (Shidlo & Ahola, 2013). This would likely increase the chances of experiencing thwarted belongingness, which may then be aggravated by the hesitation to disclose and openly embrace their identity, leading to them missing out on developing belongingness in their post-migration environment. Therefore, the significant social isolation, and potential thwarted belongingness may require tailored interventions for this population (Portman & Weyl, 2013; Shidlo & Ahola, 2013). Social isolation has also been linked with increased risk of suicidality among asylum seekers and refugees in general and will be discussed below.

Social factors and suicide risk

Studies suggest that factors such as social isolation, religiosity, unemployment, and relationship problems are associated with suicide risk among forced migrants.

Social isolation

Among Bhutanese refugees living in the USA, perceived low social support, a perceived lack of care, lack of resettlement services, separation from family, an "erosion" of social networks, and low integration, were associated with an elevated suicide risk (Ao et al., 2016; Chase & Sapkota, 2017; Hagaman et al., 2016). Social isolation was also associated with higher suicide risk among asylum seekers in the UK (Cohen, 2008). Furthermore, relationship problems were a commonly reported stressor related to self-injury among asylum-seekers in the Netherlands (Goosen et al., 2011), and family conflict was associated with higher rates of suicidal ideation among Bhutanese refugees in the USA (Ao et al., 2016). These findings are consistent with the idea that thwarted belongingness would be associated with increased suicidality, indeed, among the Bhutanese refugee population, measures of thwarted belongingness and perceived burdensomeness were significantly associated with higher suicidal ideation (Ao et al., 2012).

Religiosity

While religiosity has sometimes been associated with resilience among forced migrants (Kroo & Nagy, 2011), the association between religion and suicide risk is less clear (Lawrence, Oquendo, & Stanley, 2016). One review suggests that religion is associated with lower suicide risk (Gearing & Lizardi, 2009). Another systematic review suggests that religiosity may protect against suicide attempts but not suicidal ideation (Lawrence et al., 2016). However, the extent to which religious affiliation protects against suicide attempts, may depend on the cultural specific implications of being affiliated with that religion (Gearing & Lizardi, 2009; Lawrence et al., 2016). For example, members of minority religions may be more socially isolated (Lawrence et al., 2016), and social isolation was found to be associated with higher suicide risk (see above). Further, these results may also be influenced by the religious or cultural taboo surrounding discussing suicide (Vijayakumar, John, Pirkis, & Whiteford, 2005). Therefore, when considering religion in the context of suicide risk among culturally diverse populations such as forced migrants, it is important to be aware of what an individual's religious and cultural beliefs are regarding suicide, and any stigma around discussing this.

Unemployment

Suicidal ideation among Bhutanese refugees was associated with not being able to provide for their family (Ao et al., 2016), and suicide deaths were associated with disappointment with current employment (Hagaman et al., 2016). Another study using this Bhutanese sample also found that among men in particular, unemployment was associated with perceived burdensomeness (Ao et al., 2012). Furthermore, unemployment back home was related to higher suicidal ideation among Somali refugees in the USA (Bhui et al., 2003). All of these findings lend support to the idea that not being able to provide for family, or to live independently (i.e. perceived burdensomeness) may corrode resilience, and are associated with higher suicide risk.

The refugee determination process and suicide risk

Time since arrival

Studies report varying time frames for a "high risk" period for suicidal behaviors among asylum-seekers and refugees after arriving in host countries.

Refugees. The median time from arrival in the USA to death was 4.2 months for Bhutanese refugees who died by suicide (Hagaman et al., 2016). In one study, all suicide attempts in a sample of Indochinese refugees occurred within one year of resettlement in the USA (Alley, 1982).

This could reflect an initial culture shock, or thwarted belongingness among newly arrived asylum seekers. However, Somali refugees who had been living in the USA for over 7 years were more likely to report suicidal ideation, and authors suggest that persistent difficulties with resettlement such as long term unemployment and financial strain may account for this finding (Bhui et al., 2003). Therefore, the relationship between time in host country and suicide risk could be non-linear, where both the initial social isolation *and* long-term difficulties are associated with thwarted belongingness and perceived burdensomeness. Again, these factors need to be measured among forced migrants in a prospective manner to check for any changes in suicide risk over time since arrival.

Asylum-seekers. Like with refugees, a large number of suicide attempts among asylum seekers in Denmark (44%) occurred soon after their arrival (within 6 months; Staehr & Munk-Andersen, 2006). Furthermore, among 88 asylum seekers who were treated for suicide attempts in Sweden; 24.1% made the registered suicide attempt early in the process, before hearing about their final decision (Sundvall, Tidemalm, Titelman, Runeson, & Baarnhielm, 2015). Conversely, Cohen (2008) found no relationship between the stage of the asylum process and suicide risk among asylum-seekers in the UK Differences between these studies could be due to the lack of information in coroners' reports related to which stage in the asylum process any individual was, or indeed whether an individual was an asylum seeker (Cohen, 2008). Therefore, similar to refugee samples, there appears to be a pattern of higher suicide risk during the early stages of seeking asylum. This may be related to hopelessness about their future; plus thwarted belongingness, and perceived burdensomeness in their new environment. Measuring the IPTS variables among asylum seeker populations may increase our understanding and help inform interventions to enhance resilience and reduce suicide risk.

Applying for asylum

Rejection of asylum applications. Rejection of asylum applications has been linked with suicidality. For example, among asylum seekers presenting to acute psychiatric emergency care in Denmark, during a three month period, 60% reported suicide ideation/behaviors and those at the highest risk often had rejected asylum applications (Reko, Bech, Wohlert, Noerregaard, & Csillag, 2015). Further, in Sweden, among asylum seekers treated for suicidal behavior, 39.1% of individuals attempted suicide following the recent rejection of an asylum claim (Sundvall et al., 2015).

In addition, in a sample of 70 immigrants (including voluntary and forced migrants) admitted to hospital for suicide attempts in Switzerland, 6 (8.57%) individuals reported a rejected asylum-application as their reason for attempting suicide (Yilmaz & Riecher-Rossler, 2012). These links between rejected asylum applications and increased suicide risk can be viewed as a direct/real experience of thwarted belongingness (and not just perceived, which according to the IPTS would be sufficient to increase the risk of suicidal desire; Van Orden et al., 2010). However, we do not know how many people in this Swiss sample were asylum seekers, and the first two studies described in this section (Reko et al., 2015; Sundvall et al., 2015) only included individuals who presented to acute care. Therefore, we do not know how many asylum seekers with rejected claims did not attempt suicide or require acute care, or how many asylum seekers who may have attempted suicide were not treated by these services.

Detention and long waiting times. It was reported that the rate of self-harm and suicidal behaviors among asylum seekers in detention was higher than the UK national average (Cohen, 2008), and it was estimated that male asylum seekers residing in detention in Australia engaged in suicidal behavior at 1.8 times the rate of male prisoners (Dudley, 2003). Further, one study among asylum seekers in Denmark suggested that long waiting times together with rejection of applications may increase suicide risk (Staehr & Munk-Andersen, 2006). From the perspective of the IPTS, the difference between prison inmates and detained asylum seekers is that prison inmates would know the duration of their incarceration. Therefore, asylum seekers may lose hope the longer they are in detention without a favourable outcome, and this hopelessness could erode resilience and drive suicidal desire (Van Orden et al., 2010).

Summary

In this section we described correlates of suicide risk among forced migrants. These included substance abuse, sexuality and gender identity, social factors (social isolation, religiosity and unemployment), and the refugee/asylum determination process (time since arrival, rejected asylum applications, detention, and long waiting times). We suggest that all of these factors could be interpreted through the IPTS, where problems with social connectedness caused by several factors could be related to thwarted belongingness; unemployment could be related to perceived burdensomeness (Ellis et al., 2015), and the process of applying for asylum itself may be associated with both. For example, a rejected asylum application can be seen as an objective rejection of belongingness, and living in detention would prevent individuals from living independently and may lead to them perceiving themselves as a burden. Finally, the process of seeking asylum is uncertain, and this, together with longer waiting times could be associated with significant hopelessness (Procter et al., 2018). Therefore, all of these post-migration stressors, when combined with the potential acquired capability to engage in self-injury gained via exposure to pre-migration trauma, may explain the reduced drive to live among forced migrants facing uncertain futures.

Conclusions and future directions

People with refugee backgrounds face significant stressors in both their pre- and post-migration environments. Pre-migration stressors include exposure to war, genocide, sexual violence and torture (Johnson & Thompson, 2008; McColl et al., 2008; Steel et al., 2009). Post-migration stressors include social isolation, financial stress, perceived discrimination, and prolonged detention (Bogic et al., 2012; Filges et al., 2018; McColl et al., 2008; Nickerson et al., 2017; Porter & Haslam, 2005) These stressors have been well documented and are associated with mental health disorders such as PTSD and depression (Li et al., 2016; Porter & Haslam, 2005; Steel et al., 2009) and may be associated with a corrosion of resilience (Sundram & Ventevogel, 2017). However, the prevalence of clinically significant psychopathology among forced migrants is less clear. Recent estimates based on diagnostic criteria suggest the rate of PTSD to be 15.4%, and depression to be 17.3% (WHO, 2013). Therefore, not all forced migrants suffer from sustained, psychological disorders following exposure to trauma. Psychological interventions to reduce suicide risk may then need to be tailored toward individuals at the highest risk of experiencing psychopathology, encompassing diverse cultural groups, living in different circumstances. One way of tailoring interventions to reduce suicide risk and enhance resilience could be via the IPTS (Van Orden et al., 2010). The variability in prevalence of psychological distress and suicidality between populations could be partly explained by factors such as thwarted belongingness, perceived burdensomeness and acquired capability to engage in suicidal behavior. Preliminary evidence for the validity of these variables among Bhutanese refugees (Ao et al., 2012; Ellis et al., 2015) suggests that this is a compelling avenue of research to pursue.

However, barriers to conducting research among forced migrants have been identified. Researchers report difficulties in accessing clinical information for representative samples of forced migrants living in different environments (Cohen, 2008; Vijayakumar et al., 2017). This lack of access to information, together with using measures which may not be validated for diverse cultural groups, small sample sizes, a lack of longitudinal research, and a lack of comparable research in low-middle income countries which host the most asylum seekers and refugees; limit the conclusions we can draw (McColl et al., 2008; Robjant et al., 2009; Ryan et al., 2009; Vijayakumar, 2016). Given the immense number of displaced peoples worldwide facing pre-, post-migration stressors, and uncertain futures (UNHCR, 2017); there is an urgent need for more knowledge about what might corrode resilience and increase suicide risk among forced migrants. This is especially the case for low-middle income countries, which host the majority of forced migrant (85%; UNHCR, 2017) and among children and adolescents who make up 51% of displaced peoples (Vijayakumar, 2016).

This research can be guided by the IPTS, where if high levels of thwarted belongingness, perceived burdensomeness, and acquired capability are found, then these factors can inform treatment targets to enhance or abate the corrosion of resilience. For example, to the best of our knowledge, empirical studies measuring psychological outcomes among forced migrants who sought asylum in Australia, and currently reside in offshore detention have not yet been conducted. Studying how resilience can be corroded is especially relevant among individuals in this population, as media reports suggest that suicidality is a significant issue (Doherty & Vasefi, 2018). Apart from suicidality, reports of "resignation syndrome" among child asylum seekers and refugees living with uncertain immigration status have been made in Sweden (Sallin et al., 2016) and in Australian offshore detention centers (Newman, 2018). This syndrome involves children withdrawing from fundamental aspects of living by not eating, drinking, or being responsive; potentially in response to exposure to trauma as well as hopelessness in the context of a lengthy, strenuous and uncertain process (Newman, 2018; Sallin et al., 2016). From the perspective of the IPTS, this withdrawal could be seen as a form of giving up on life where the prospect of a future life worth living becomes hopeless from the child's perspective. The IPTS therefore provides a theoretical framework for empirical research that could attempt to elucidate the causal factors that contribute to suicide risk among refugees and asylum seekers, laying the foundation for the development of interventions that target these factors.

By the same token, knowing more about factors affecting the wellbeing of forced migrants living in immigration detention in various host countries, may help to reduce suicide risk. Do they experience high levels of thwarted belongingness, perceived burdensomeness and do they have an acquired capability to engage in suicidal behavior? If this is the case, then interventions to reduce these factors can be implemented. Still, significant obstacles to providing psychological interventions for detained asylum-seekers have been identified (Brooker, Albert, Young, & Steel, 2016). These may include ongoing deterioration related to confinement and insecure visa status, substance use, self-harm and alleged sexual violence (Brooker et al., 2016). These issues, together with a lack of a robust evidence base to guide treatment in such situations present a challenge to clinicians. However, strategies such as encouraging engagement, acquiring coping skills, connecting with the self and others, and identifying future support have been identified as potentially helpful in managing distress (Brooker et al., 2016). These strategies are consistent with reducing thwarted belongingness, perceived burdensomeness and increasing hope for the future. Furthermore, among individuals facing long waiting times for asylum decisions, including the "legacy caseload" in Australia; it has been reported that there were 11 known suicides since June 2014 (Procter et al., 2018). Clinicians and researchers posit that a sense of "lethal hopelessness" may be associated with increased suicide risk in this population (Procter et al., 2018). This is also consistent with the IPTS. Empirical studies which explore the concept of lethal hopelessness, and its association with well-being and suicide risk using the IPTS as a theoretical framework may help clinicians design evidence-based interventions to provide support in these circumstances.

Broader recommendations to mitigate stress and improve wellbeing among asylum-seekers and refugees living in different contexts have also been made, and these recommendations appear to be consistent with reducing the causal factors of suicide risk implicated by the IPTS. These include providing early emotional support at the time of arrival and relocation; early education about language and culture of host community (this may improve integration and a sense of belongingness); early provisions for economic activity (this may reduce perceived burdensomeness); and allowing connections between forced migrants with NGOs, family, and any potential sources of support (Vijayakumar, 2016). In addition, asylum-seekers and refugees should have equitable access to appropriate specialised health and mental health care (McColl et al., 2008; Sundvall et al., 2015). Since poor access to health services was associated with thwarted belongings and perceived burdensomeness among Bhutanese refugees (Ellis et al., 2015), this is also consistent with the IPTS. Encouraging engagement with services by targeting issues which may act as barriers to seeking help (e.g. stigma around mental illness; Vijayakumar et al., 2017) may also help improve wellbeing. Indeed, service provision itself may be improved when trained interpreters are used, and asylum seekers and refugees are well informed (Cohen, 2008; Eytan et al., 2002). Emerging evidence also suggests that involving community members in interventions may be beneficial (Ao et al., 2016), which may again counter thwarted belongingness. Finally, service providers should increase their awareness of any issues related to specific populations, such as LGBTQ identifying asylum-seekers and refugees (Portman & Weyl, 2013).

Overall, we do not yet have a robust, evidence-based clinical model to inform interventions to reduce suicide risk and enhance resilience, specifically for asylum seeker and refugees from diverse backgrounds, living in various circumstances (McColl et al., 2008). The consensus thus far is that provision of interventions should be trauma-informed and culturally sensitive; and that they should consider the complexity of the influences of pre- and post-migration stress on wellbeing (Turner & Herlihy, 2009; Vijayakumar, 2016). A framework for research into suicide risk based around the IPTS would be consistent with the available research pointing to factors associated with a corrosion of resilience and suicide risk. That is, giving up on life or failing to re-engage with life when facing significant adversity as a refugee or asylum seeker could be aggravated by the uncertainty of a life in "limbo". In a situation where there is no life worth living that forced migrants can return to, together with decreasing hope that they can move toward a life which they perceive as worth living in the future; the corrosion of resilience may be more likely to occur than among non-refugee populations. This, together with a possible acquired capability to act on suicidal thoughts gained via exposure to pre-migration trauma may contribute to the elevated suicide risk among forced migrants.

Despite often overcoming significant adversity to seek refuge, the process of beginning a new life can be challenging. As clinicians and researchers, our role is to gain a good understanding of factors which are involved, and design evidence-based interventions to alleviate stress and help boost resilience, when required.

References

Akinyemi, O., Atilola, O., & Soyannwo, T. (2015). Suicidal ideation: Are refugees more at risk compared to host population? Findings from a preliminary assessment in a refugee community in Nigeria. *Asian J Psychiatr, 18*, 81–85.

Al Ibraheem, B., Kira, I. A., Aljakoub, J., & Al Ibraheem, A. (2017). The health effect of the Syrian conflict on IDPs and refugees. *Peace and Conflict: Journal of Peace Psychology, 23*(2), 140–152.

Al-Modallal, H. (2012). Patterns of coping with partner violence: Experiences of refugee women in Jordan. *Public Health Nursing, 29*(5), 403–411.

Alessi, E. J., Kahn, S., & Chatterji, S. (2016). The darkest times of my life': Recollections of child abuse among forced migrants persecuted because of their sexual orientation and gender identity. *Child Abuse & Neglect, 51*, 93–105.

Alley, J. C. (1982). Life-threatening indicators among the Indochinese refugees. *Suicide and Life-Threatening Behavior, 12*(1), 46–51.

Allodi, F., & Cowgill, G. (1982). Ethical and psychiatric aspects of torture: A Canadian study. *Canadian Journal of Psychiatry/La Revue canadienne de psychiatrie, 27*(2), 98–102.

Ao, T., Shetty, S., Sivilli, T., Blanton, C., Ellis, H., Geltman, P. L., et al. (2016). Suicidal ideation and mental health of Bhutanese refugees in the United States. *Journal of Immigrant and Minority Health, 18*(4), 828–835. https://doi.org/10.1007/s10903-015-0325-7.

Ao, T., Taylor, E., Lankau, E., Sivilli, T. I., Blanton, C., Shetty, S., et al. (2012). *An investigation into suicides among Bhutanese refugees in the us 2009–2012 stakeholders report*. Center for Disease Control and Prevention.

Beghi, M., Rosenbaum, J. F., Cerri, C., & Cornaggia, C. M. (2013). Risk factors for fatal and nonfatal repetition of suicide attempts: A literature review. *Neuropsychiatric Disease and Treatment, 9*, 1725.

Beiser, M., & Hou, F. (2017). Predictors of positive mental health among refugees: Results from Canada's General Social Survey. *Transcultural Psychiatry, 54*(5–6), 675–695.

Bhui, K., Abdi, A., Abdi, M., Pereira, S., Dualeh, M., Robertson, D., et al. (2003). Traumatic events, migration characteristics and psychiatric symptoms among Somali refugees: Preliminary communication. *Social Psychiatry and Psychiatric Epidemiology, 38*(1), 35–43.

Bogic, M., Ajdukovic, D., Bremner, S., Franciskovic, T., Galeazzi, G. M., Kucukalic, A., et al. (2012). Factors associated with mental disorders in long-settled war refugees: Refugees from the former Yugoslavia in Germany, Italy and the UK. *The British Journal of Psychiatry, 200*(3), 216–223. https://doi.org/10.1192/bjp.bp.110.084764.

Bogic, M., Njoku, A., & Priebe, S. (2015). Long-term mental health of war-refugees: A systematic literature review. *BMC International Health and Human Rights, 15*, 29. https://doi.org/10.1186/s12914-015-0064-9.

Brooker, S., Albert, S., Young, P., & Steel, Z. (2016). *Challenges to providing mental health care in immigration detention*. Geneva: Global Detention Project.

Browne, D. T., Kumar, A., Puente-Duran, S., Georgiades, K., Leckie, G., & Jenkins, J. (2017). Emotional problems among recent immigrants and parenting status: Findings from a national longitudinal study of immigrants in Canada. *PLoS One, 12*(4), e0175023. https://doi.org/10.1371/journal.pone.0175023.

CCJDP. (2002). *Damaging kids – children in department of immigration and multicultural affairs' immigration detention centres* (Retrieved from Melbourne).

Chase, L., & Sapkota, R. P. (2017). In our community, a friend is a psychologist": An ethnographic study of informal care in two Bhutanese refugee communities. *Transcultural Psychiatry, 54*(3), 400–422. https://doi.org/10.1177/1363461517703023.

Chen, W., Hall, B. J., Ling, L., & Renzaho, A. M. (2017). Pre-migration and post-migration factors associated with mental health in humanitarian migrants in Australia and the moderation effect of post-migration stressors: Findings from the first wave data of the BNLA cohort study. *The Lancet Psychiatry, 4*(3), 218–229.

Cohen, J. (2008). Safe in our hands?: A study of suicide and self-harm in asylum seekers. *J Forensic Leg Med, 15*(4), 235–244. https://doi.org/10.1016/j.jflm.2007.11.001.

Crisp, J. (2000). A state of insecurity: The political economy of violence in Kenya's refugee camps. *African Affairs, 99*(397), 601–632.

Crumlish, N., & Bracken, P. (2011). Mental health and the asylum process. *Irish Journal of Psychological Medicine, 28*(2), 57–60.

De Anstiss, H., & Ziaian, T. (2010). Mental health help-seeking and refugee adolescents: Qualitative findings from a mixed-methods investigation. *Australian Psychologist, 45*(1), 29–37.

Doherty, B., & Vasefi, S. (2018). *Iranian asylum seeker dies by suicide on Nauru. The Guardian Australia.* Retrieved from https://www.theguardian.com/world/2018/jun/15/iranian-asylum-seeker-dies-by-suicide-on-nauru.

Dudley, M. (2003). Contradictory Australian national policies on self-harm and suicide: The case of asylum seekers in mandatory detention. *Australasian Psychiatry, 11*(Suppl. 1), S102–S108.

Ellis, B., Lankau, E. W., Ao, T., Benson, M. A., Miller, A. B., Shetty, S., et al. (2015). Understanding Bhutanese refugee suicide through the interpersonal-psychological theory of suicidal behavior. *American Journal of Orthopsychiatry, 85*(1), 43–55.

Eytan, A., Bischoff, A., Rrustemi, I., Durieux, S., Loutan, L., Gilbert, M., et al. (2002). Screening of mental disorders in asylum-seekers from Kosovo. *Australian and New Zealand Journal of Psychiatry, 36*, 499–503.

Falb, K. L., McCormick, M. C., Hemenway, D., Anfinson, K., & Silverman, J. G. (2013). Suicide ideation and victimization among refugee women along the Thai-Burma border. *Journal of Traumatic Stress, 26*(5), 631–635. https://doi.org/10.1002/jts.21846.

Fazel, M., Wheeler, J., & Danesh, J. (2005). Prevalence of serious mental disorder in 7000 refugees resettled in western countries: A systematic review. *Lancet, 365*(9467), 1309–1314. https://doi.org/10.1016/S0140-6736(05)61027-6.

Ferrada-Noli, M., Asberg, M., & Ormstad, K. (1998). Suicidal behavior after severe trauma. Part 2: The association between methods of torture and of suicidal ideation in post-traumatic stress disorder. *Journal of Traumatic Stress, 11*(1), 113–124.

Ferrada-Noli, M., Asberg, M., Ormstad, K., Lundin, T., & Sundbom, E. (1998). Suicidal behavior after severe trauma. Part 1: PTSD diagnoses, psychiatric comorbidity and assessments of suicidal behavior. *Journal of Traumatic Stress, 11*(1), 103–112.

Ferrada-Noli, M., & Sundbom, E. (1996). Cultural bias in suicidal behaviour among refugees with post-traumatic stress disorder. *Nordic Journal of Psychiatry, 50*(3), 185–191.

Filges, T., Montgomery, E., & Kastrup, M. (2018). The impact of detention on the health of asylum seekers: A systematic review. *Research on Social Work Practice, 28*(4), 399–414.

Flaskerud, J. H., & Anh, N. T. (1988). Mental health needs of Vietnamese refugees. *Hospital & Community Psychiatry, 39*(4), 435–437.

Freeman, A., Mergl, R., Kohls, E., Székely, A., Gusmao, R., Arensman, E., et al. (2017). A cross-national study on gender differences in suicide intent. *BMC Psychiatry, 17*(1), 234.

Gearing, R. E., & Lizardi, D. (2009). Religion and suicide. *Journal of Religion and Health, 48*(3), 332–341.

Goosen, S., Kunst, A., Stronks, K., van Oostrum, I., & Uitenbroek, D. (2011). *Suicide death and hospital-treated suicidal behaviour in asylum seekers in.*

Goosen, S., Kunst, A. E., Stronks, K., van Oostrum, I. E., Uitenbroek, D. G., & Kerkhof, A. J. (2011). Suicide death and hospital-treated suicidal behaviour in asylum seekers in The Netherlands: A national registry-based study. *BMC Public Health, 11*, 484. https://doi.org/10.1186/1471-2458-11-484.

Hagaman, A. K., Sivilli, T. I., Ao, T., Blanton, C., Ellis, H., Cardozo, B. L., et al. (2016). An investigation into suicides among Bhutanese refugees resettled in the United States between 2008 and 2011. *Journal of Immigrant and Minority Health, 18*(4), 819–827.

Hamza, C. A., Stewart, S. L., & Willoughby, T. (2012). Examining the link between nonsuicidal self-injury and suicidal behavior: A review of the literature and an integrated model. *Clinical Psychology Review, 32*(6), 482–495. https://doi.org/10.1016/j.cpr.2012.05.003.

Hedrick, K. (2017). Getting out of (self-) harm's way: A study of factors associated with self-harm among asylum seekers in Australian immigration detention. *J Forensic Leg Med, 49*, 89–93. https://doi.org/10.1016/j.jflm.2017.05.014.

Hopkinson, R. A., Keatley, E., Glaeser, E., Erickson-Schroth, L., Fattal, O., & Nicholson Sullivan, M. (2017). Persecution experiences and mental health of LGBT asylum seekers. *Journal of Homosexuality, 64*(12), 1650–1666.

Iversen, V. C., & Morken, G. (2004). Differences in acute psychiatric admissions between asylum seekers and refugees. *Nordic Journal of Psychiatry, 58*(6), 465–470.

Jankovic, J., Bremner, S., Bogic, M., Lecic-Tosevski, D., Ajdukovic, D., Franciskovic, T., et al. (2013). Trauma and suicidality in war affected communities. *European Psychiatry, 28*(8), 514–520.

Jensen, T. K., Skardalsmo, E. M. B., & Fjermestad, K. W. (2014). Development of mental health problems-A follow-up study of unaccompanied refugee minors. *Child and Adolescent Psychiatry and Mental Health, 8*, 2014, ArtID 29, 8.

Johnson, H., & Thompson, A. (2008). The development and maintenance of post-traumatic stress disorder (PTSD) in civilian adult survivors of war trauma and torture: A review. *Clinical Psychology Review, 28*(1), 36–47.

Joiner, T. E., Jr., Van Orden, K. A., Witte, T. K., Selby, E. A., Ribeiro, J. D., Lewis, R., et al. (2009). Main predictions of the interpersonal–psychological theory of suicidal behavior: Empirical tests in two samples of young adults. *Journal of Abnormal Psychology, 118*(3), 634.

Keller, A. S., Rosenfeld, B., Trinh-Shevrin, C., Meserve, C., Sachs, E., Leviss, J. A., et al. (2003). Mental health of detained asylum seekers. *Lancet, 362*(9397), 1721–1723. https://doi.org/10.1016/S0140-6736(03)14846-5.

King, M., Semlyen, J., Tai, S. S., Killaspy, H., Osborn, D., Popelyuk, D., et al. (2008). A systematic review of mental disorder, suicide, and deliberate self harm in lesbian, gay and bisexual people. *BMC Psychiatry, 8*, 70. https://doi.org/10.1186/1471-244X-8-70.

Kira, I. A., Shuwiekh, H., Rice, K., Al Ibraheem, B., & Aljakoub, J. (2017). A threatened identity: The mental health status of Syrian refugees in Egypt and its etiology. *Identity: An International Journal of Theory and Research, 17*(3), 176–190.

Kroo, A., & Nagy, H. (2011). Posttraumatic growth among traumatized Somali refugees in Hungary. *Journal of Loss & Trauma, 16*(5), 440–458.

Laban, C. J., Gernaat, H. B., Komproe, I. H., Schreuders, B. A., & de Jong, J. T. (2004). Impact of a long asylum procedure on the prevalence of psychiatric disorders in Iraqi asylum seekers in The Netherlands. *The Journal of Nervous and Mental Disease, 192*(12), 843–851.

Laban, C. J., Gernaat, H. B., Komproe, I. H., van der Tweel, I., & De Jong, J. T. (2005). Postmigration living problems and common psychiatric disorders in Iraqi asylum seekers in The Netherlands. *The Journal of Nervous and Mental Disease, 193*(12), 825–832. https://doi.org/10.1097/01.nmd.0000188977.44657.

Laban, C. J., Komproe, I. H., Gernaat, H. B., & de Jong, J. T. (2008). The impact of a long asylum procedure on quality of life, disability and physical health in Iraqi asylum seekers in The Netherlands. *Social Psychiatry and Psychiatric Epidemiology, 43*(7), 507–515. https://doi.org/10.1007/s00127-008-0333-1.

Lawrence, R. E., Oquendo, M. A., & Stanley, B. (2016). Religion and suicide risk: A systematic review. *Archives of Suicide Research, 20*(1), 1–21.

Lerner, E., Bonanno, G. A., Keatley, E., Joscelyne, A., & Keller, A. S. (2015). Predictors of suicidal ideation in treatment-seeking survivors of torture. *Psychol Trauma.* https://doi.org/10.1037/tra0000040.

Lerner, E., Bonanno, G. A., Keatley, E., Joscelyne, A., & Keller, A. S. (2016). Predictors of suicidal ideation in treatment-seeking survivors of torture. *Psychological Trauma: Theory, Research, Practice, and Policy, 8*(1), 17.

Li, S. S., Liddell, B. J., & Nickerson, A. (2016). The relationship between post-migration stress and psychological disorders in refugees and asylum seekers. *Current Psychiatry Reports, 18*(9), 82. https://doi.org/10.1007/s11920-016-0723-0.

Madianos, M. G., Sarhan, A. L., & Koukia, E. (2011). Posttraumatic stress disorders comorbid with major depression in West bank, Palestine: A general population cross sectorial study. *The European Journal of Psychiatry, 25*(1), 19–31.

Mares, S., & Jureidini, J. (2004). Psychiatric assessment of children and families in immigration detention—clinical, administrative and ethical issues. *Australian & New Zealand Journal of Public Health, 28*(6), 520–526.

May, A. M., & Klonsky, E. D. (2016). What distinguishes suicide attempters from suicide ideators? A meta-analysis of potential factors. *Clinical Psychology: Science and Practice, 23*(1), 5–20. https://doi.org/10.1111/cpsp.12136.

McColl, H., McKenzie, K., & Bhui, K. (2008). Mental healthcare of asylum-seekers and refugees. *Advances in Psychiatric Treatment, 14*(6), 452–459.

Mollica, R. F., McInnes, K., Pham, T., Fawzi, M. C. S., Murphy, E., & Lin, L. (1998). The dose-effect relationships between torture and psychiatric symptoms in Vietnamese ex-political detainees and a comparison group. *The Journal of Nervous and Mental Disease, 186*(9), 543–553.

Mölsä, M., Kuittinen, S., Tiilikainen, M., Honkasalo, M.-L., & Punamäki, R.-L. (2017). Mental health among older refugees: The role of trauma, discrimination, and religiousness. *Aging & Mental Health, 21*(8), 829–837. https://doi.org/10.1080/13607863.2016.1165183.

Morgan, G., Melluish, S., & Welham, A. (2017). Exploring the relationship between postmigratory stressors and mental health for asylum seekers and refused asylum seekers in the UK. *Transcultural Psychiatry, 54*(5–6), 653–674. https://doi.org/10.1177/1363461517737188.

Neuner, F., Schauer, M., Karunakara, U., Klaschik, C., Robert, C., & Elbert, T. (2004). Psychological trauma and evidence for enhanced vulnerability for posttraumatic stress disorder through previous trauma among West Nile refugees. *BMC Psychiatry, 4*(1), 34.

Newman, L. (2018). What is resignation syndrome and why is it affecting refugee children? *The Conversation.* https://theconversation.com/explainer-what-is-resignation-syndrome-and-why-is-it-affecting-refugee-children-101670.

Nickerson, A., Liddell, B., Asnaani, A., Carlsson, J., Fazel, M., Knaevelsrud, C., et al. (2017). *Trauma and mental health in forcibly displaced populations: An international society for traumatic stress studies briefing paper* (Retrieved from).

Nickerson, A., Steel, Z., Bryant, R., Brooks, R., & Silove, D. (2011). Change in visa status amongst mandaean refugees: Relationship to psychological symptoms and living difficulties. *Psychiatry Research, 187*(1–2), 267–274. doi:S0165-1781(10)00783-3 [pii]. https://doi.org/10.1016/j.psychres.2010.12.015.

Norredam, M., Olsbjerg, M., Petersen, J. H., Laursen, B., & Krasnik, A. (2012). Are there differences in injury mortality among refugees and immigrants compared with native-born? *Injury Prevention*. injuryprev-2012-040336.

Nuttman-Shwartz, O., Dekel, R., & Tuval-Mashiach, R. (2011). Post-traumatic stress and growth following forced relocation. *British Journal of Social Work, 41*(3), 486–501. https://doi.org/10.1093/bjsw/bcq124.

Orton, L., Griffiths, J., Green, M., & Waterman, H. (2012). Resilience among asylum seekers living with HIV. *BMC Public Health, 12*(1), 926.

Pieloch, K. A., McCullough, M. B., & Marks, A. K. (2016). Resilience of children with refugee statuses: A research review. *Canadian Psychology/Psychologie canadienne, 57*(4), 330.

Porter, M., & Haslam, N. (2005). Predisplacement and postdisplacement factors associated with mental health of refugees and internally displaced persons: A meta-analysis. *Journal of the American Medical Association, 294*, 602–612. https://doi.org/10.1001/jama.294.5.602.

Portman, S., & Weyl, D. (2013). *LGBT refugee resettlement in the US: Emerging best practices*. Retrieved from http://www.fmreview.org/sogi.html.

Premand, N., Baeriswyl-Cottin, R., Gex-Fabry, M., Hiller, N., Framorando, D., Eytan, A., et al. (2018). Determinants of suicidality and of treatment modalities in a community psychiatry sample of asylum seekers. *The Journal of Nervous and Mental Disease, 206*(1), 27–32.

Procter, N. G., Kenny, M. A., Eaton, H., & Grech, C. (2018). Lethal hopelessness: Understanding and responding to asylum seeker distress and mental deterioration. *International Journal of Mental Health Nursing, 27*(1), 448–454. https://doi.org/10.1111/inm.12325.

Rahman, A., & Hafeez, A. (2003). Suicidal feelings run high among mothers in refugee camps: A cross sectional survey. *Acta Psychiatrica Scandinavica, 108*(5), 392–393.

Reko, A., Bech, P., Wohlert, C., Noerregaard, C., & Csillag, C. (2015). Usage of psychiatric emergency services by asylum seekers: Clinical implications based on a descriptive study in Denmark. *Nordic Journal of Psychiatry, 69*(8), 587–593.

Ribeiro, J. D., Huang, X., Fox, K. R., & Franklin, J. C. (2018). Depression and hopelessness as risk factors for suicide ideation, attempts and death: Meta-analysis of longitudinal studies. *The British Journal of Psychiatry, 212*(5), 279–286.

Robjant, K., Hassan, R., & Katona, C. (2009). Mental health implications of detaining asylum seekers: Systematic review. *British Journal of Psychiatry, 194*(4), 306–312. doi:194/4/306 [pii] 10.1192/bjp.bp.108.053223.

Ryan, D. A., Kelly, F. E., & Kelly, B. D. (2009). Mental health among persons awaiting an asylum outcome in western countries. *International Journal of Mental Health, 38*(3), 88–111. https://doi.org/10.2753/imh0020-7411380306.

Sallin, K., Lagercrantz, H., Evers, K., Engström, I., Hjern, A., & Petrovic, P. (2016). Resignation syndrome: Catatonia? Culture-bound? *Frontiers in Behavioral Neuroscience, 10*, 7.

Sarkardi, A., Adahl, K., Stenvall, E., Ssegonja, R., Batti, H., Gavra, P., et al. (2017). Teaching recovery techniques: Evaluation of a group intervention for unaccompanied refugee minors with symptoms of PTSD in Sweden. *European Child & Adolescent Psychiatry, 27*, 467–479. https://doi.org/10.1007/s00787-017-1093-9.

Schick, M., Zumwald, A., Knopfli, B., Nickerson, A., Bryant, R. A., Schnyder, U., et al. (2016). Challenging future, challenging past: The relationship of social integration and psychological impairment in traumatized refugees. *European Journal of Psychotraumatology, 7*, 28057. https://doi.org/10.3402/ejpt.v7.28057.

Schweitzer, R. D., Brough, M., Vromans, L., & Asic-Kobe, M. (2011). Mental health of newly arrived Burmese refugees in Australia: Contributions of pre-migration and post-migration experience. *Australian and New Zealand Journal of Psychiatry, 45*(4), 299–307.

Shakespeare-Finch, J., Schweitzer, R. D., King, J., & Brough, M. (2014). Distress, coping, and posttraumatic growth in refugees from Burma. *Journal of Immigrant & Refugee Studies, 12*(3), 311–330.

Shidlo, A., & Ahola, J. (2013). *Mental health challenges of LGBT forced migrants* (Retrieved from).

Silove, D., Sinnerbrink, I., Field, A., Manicavasagar, V., & Steel, Z. (1997). Anxiety, depression and PTSD in asylum-seekers: Associations with pre-migration trauma and post-migration stressors. *British Journal of Psychiatry, 170*, 351–357. https://doi.org/10.1192/bjp.170.4.351.

Silove, D., Steel, Z., McGorry, P., & Mohan, P. (1998). Trauma exposure, postmigration stressors, and symptoms of anxiety, depression and posttraumatic stress in Tamil asylum-seekers: Comparison with refugees and immigrants. *Acta Psychiatrica Scandinavica, 97*, 175–181.

Ssenyonga, J., Owens, V., & Olema, D. K. (2013). Posttraumatic cognitions, avoidance coping, suicide, and posttraumatic stress disorder among adolescent refugees. *Procedia - Social and Behavioral Sciences, 82*, 261–265. https://doi.org/10.1016/j.sbspro.2013.06.256.

Staehr, M. A., & Munk-Andersen, E. (2006). Suicide and suicidal behavior among asylum seekers in Denmark during the period 2001-2003. A retrospective study. *Ugeskrift for Laeger, 168*(17), 1650–1653.

Steel, Z., Chey, T., Silove, D., Marnane, C., Bryant, R. A., & van Ommeren, M. (2009). Association of torture and other potentially traumatic events with mental health outcomes among populations exposed to mass conflict and displacement: A systematic review and meta-analysis. *Journal of the American Medical Association, 302*(5), 537–549. doi:302/5/537 [pii]. https://doi.org/10.1001/jama.2009.1132.

Steel, Z., Momartin, S., Bateman, C., Hafshejani, A., Silove, D. M., Everson, N., et al. (2004). Psychiatric status of asylum seeker families held for a protracted period in a remote detention centre in Australia. *Australian & New Zealand Journal of Public Health, 28*(6), 527–536.

Steel, Z., Momartin, S., Silove, D., Coello, M., Aroche, J., & Tay, K. W. (2011). Two year psychosocial and mental health outcomes for refugees subjected to restrictive or supportive immigration policies. *Social Science & Medicine, 72*(7), 1149–1156. https://doi.org/10.1016/j.socscimed.2011.02.007.

Steel, Z., Silove, D., Brooks, R., Momartin, S., Alzuhairi, B., & Susljik, I. (2006). Impact of immigration detention and temporary protection on the mental health of refugees. *British Journal of Psychiatry, 188*, 58–64. https://doi.org/10.1192/bjp.bp.104.007864.

Sundram, S., & Ventevogel, P. (2017). The mental health of refugees and asylum seekers on Manus Island. *The Lancet.com, 390*, 2534–2535. https://doi.org/10.1016/S0140-6736(17)33051-9.

Sundvall, M., Tidemalm, D. H., Titelman, D. E., Runeson, B., & Baarnhielm, S. (2015). Assessment and treatment of asylum seekers after a suicide attempt: A comparative study of people registered at mental health services in a Swedish location. *BMC Psychiatry, 15*, 2015, ArtID 235, 15.

Tippens, J. A. (2017). Urban Congolese refugees in Kenya: The contingencies of coping and resilience in a context marked by structural vulnerability. *Qualitative Health Research, 27*(7), 1090–1103.

Tousignant, M., Habimana, E., Biron, C., Malo, C., Sidoli-LeBlanc, E., & Bendris, N. (1999). The quebec adolescent refugee project: Psychopathology and family variables in a sample from 35 nations. *Journal of the American Academy of Child & Adolescent Psychiatry, 38*(11), 1426–1432.

Turner, S. W., & Herlihy, J. (2009). Working with refugees and asylum seekers. *Psychiatry, 8*(8), 322–324.

UNHCR. (2010). *Convention and protocol relating to the status of refugees*. Retrieved from Communications and Public Information Service.

UNHCR. (2016). *Global trends in forced displacement in 2016*. Retrieved from Geneva, Switzerland http://www.humansecuritybrief.info/index.html.

UNHCR. (2017). *Global trends: Forced displacement in 2017*.

Van Oostrum, I. E., Goosen, S., Uitenbroek, D. G., Koppenaal, H., & Stronks, K. (2011). Mortality and causes of death among asylum seekers in The Netherlands, 2002–2005. *Journal of Epidemiology & Community Health, 65*, 376–383.

Van Orden, K. A., Witte, T. K., Cukrowicz, K. C., Braithwaite, S. R., Selby, E. A., & Joiner, T. E., Jr. (2010). The interpersonal theory of suicide. *Psychological Review, 117*(2), 575–600. April 2010.

Vijayakumar, L. (2016). Suicide among refugees - a mockery of humanity. *Crisis: The Journal of Crisis Intervention and Suicide Prevention, 37*(1), 1–4.

Vijayakumar, L., John, S., Pirkis, J., & Whiteford, H. (2005). Suicide in developing countries (2) risk factors. *Crisis, 26*(3), 112–119.

Vijayakumar, L., & Jotheeswaran, A. (2010). *Suicide in refugees and asylum seekers*. Mental health of refugees and asylum seekers.

Vijayakumar, L., Mohanraj, R., Kumar, S., Jeyaseelan, V., Sriram, S., & Shanmugam, M. (2017). CASP—An intervention by community volunteers to reduce suicidal behaviour among refugees. *International Journal of Social Psychiatry, 63*(7), 589–597.

Weaver, H., & Roberts, B. (2010). Drinking and displacement: A systematic review of the influence of forced displacement on harmful alcohol use. *Substance Use & Misuse, 45*(13), 2340–2355.

Westman, J., Hasselstrom, J., Johansson, S. E., & Sundquist, J. (2003). The influences of place of birth and socioeconomic factors on attempted suicide in a defined population of 4.5 million people. *Archives of General Psychiatry, 60*, 409–414.

WHO. (2013). *Guidelines for the management of conditions specifically related to stress* (Retrieved from Geneva).

Yilmaz, A., & Riecher-Rossler, A. (2012). Attempted suicide in immigrants from Turkey: A comparison with Swiss suicide attempters. *Psychopathology, 45*(6), 366–373.

PART 5

Epigenetics of suicidal behaviors

CHAPTER 14

Epigenetics of suicidal behaviors

Laura M. Fiori, Gustavo Turecki
McGill Group for Suicide Studies, Douglas Mental Health University Institute, McGill University, Montreal, QC, Canada

Introduction

Suicidal behaviors fall along a continuum, ranging from ideation, to death by suicide. Worldwide, nearly one million people die by suicide each year (Saxena, Krug, Chestnov, World Health Organization, & Department of Mental Health and Substance Abuse, 2014), with significantly higher numbers attempting suicide or experiencing suicidal ideation. Although the majority of people displaying suicidal behaviors have a history of psychiatric disorders, their transmission appears to be independent of suicide (Turecki & Brent, 2016), indicating that suicidal behavior is a distinct phenotype. Numerous twin (Voracek & Loibl, 2007), adoption (Wender et al., 1986), and family (Brent, Bridge, Johnson, & Connolly, 1996; McGirr et al., 2009) studies have demonstrated that suicidal behaviors possess a genetic component, with heritability estimated between 30% and 50% (Fu et al., 2002; McGuffin, Marusic, & Farmer, 2001; Statham et al., 1998; Turecki & Brent, 2016), with the remainder of the risk due to environmental factors. Over the years, it has become increasingly recognized that the effects of the environment on both behavioral development and psychopathology are mediated through epigenetic regulation of gene function (McGowan et al., 2009; Turecki, 2014; Weaver et al., 2004).

Epigenetics refer to processes that alter gene expression without changing the underlying DNA sequence. Numerous studies have investigated epigenetic differences in the context of psychiatric disorders, including mood disorders, anxiety disorders, schizophrenia, eating disorders, and substance use disorders (for recent reviews, see (Hoffmann, Sportelli, Ziller, & Spengler, 2017; Hubel, Marzi, Breen, & Bulik, 2019; Palmisano & Pandey, 2017)). Additionally, specific epigenetic alterations associated with the experience of early life adversity (ELA), defined as

Alternatives to Suicide
ISBN 978-0-12-814297-4
https://doi.org/10.1016/B978-0-12-814297-4.00014-5

childhood abuse and parental neglect, have been identified (for examples see (Jawahar, Murgatroyd, Harrison, & Baune, 2015; Lutz, Almeida, Fiori, & Turecki, 2015; Turecki & Meaney, 2016). These findings are notable, as ELA is also associated with increased rates of anxiety, depression, substance use disorders, and suicidal behaviors (Gilbert et al., 2009; McCauley et al., 1997; McLaughlin et al., 2010). Given the complex interplay between environmental experiences, psychopathology, and suicidal behaviors, it can be difficult, and likely impossible, to completely disentangle their effects. Nonetheless, a number of interesting findings relating epigenetic processes to suicidal behaviors have emerged.

In this chapter, we will first discuss basic concepts relating to two major epigenetic modifications, DNA methylation, and post-translational histone modifications. Secondly, we will summarize studies which have specifically investigated these epigenetic mechanisms in relation to suicidal behaviors, at both the candidate gene and epigenome-wide levels. Finally, we will discuss the implications of the findings to-date, as well as future directions for research in this field.

Fundamentals of epigenetics

DNA methylation

DNA methylation is the most well-characterized epigenetic modification, and involves the addition of a methyl group to the 5' position of cytosine nucleotides: most commonly at cytosine-guanine dinucleotides (CpG) in mammals (Maunakea et al., 2010). Additionally, both non-CpG methylation, and additional modifications, such as hydroxymethylation (5hmC), are observed, but have only recently begun to be investigated within a psychiatric context (Gross et al., 2017; Jang, Shin, Lee, & Do, 2017). Interestingly, these modifications appear to be particularly important in brain functioning (Lister et al., 2013).

DNA methylation patterns are created and maintained by DNA methyltransferases (DNMT). DNMT1, DNMT3a, and DNMT3b are all involved in maintenance functions, while DNMT3a and DNMT3b also play roles in *de novo* DNA methylation (Jin, Li, & Robertson, 2011). Canonically, DNA methylation is a repressive mark inversely related to gene expression (Klose & Bird, 2006). Methylation of CpG sites that fall within gene promoters can directly block transcription factor binding, or indirectly block transcription by recruiting proteins with methylated-DNA binding domains to modify chromatin structure (Baylin & Jones, 2011;

Curradi, Izzo, Badaracco, & Landsberger, 2002). Unlike gene promoter regions, gene body methylation has been associated with increased gene expression, and the use of alternative promoters (Jjingo, Conley, Yi, Lunyak, & Jordan, 2012; Maunakea et al., 2010; Zemach, McDaniel, Silva, & Zilberman, 2010). Interestingly, methylation and hydroxymethylation appear to have distinct effects (Lister et al., 2013; Wen et al., 2014). This is important to consider when attempting to predict functional consequences of altered methylation, as the majority of currently used molecular techniques are unable to distinguish between these marks.

DNA methylation has been investigated using either affinity-based or sequencing-based technologies. Affinity-based technologies involve the hybridization of DNA against pre-selected genomic sequences, and allow the relative levels of methylated and unmethylated cytosines at each site to be determined. The most commonly-used arrays are those produced by Illumina, with the most current build, the Infinium MethylationEPIC Beadchip, allowing the interrogation of >850 000 sites. Alternatively, custom-designed arrays against specific functional or genomic regions have also been used. Next-generation sequencing methods are also available, with the most information being derived from whole-genome bisulfite sequencing (WGBS), followed by less costly alternatives including reduced representation bisulfite sequencing (RRBS) and methyl-CpG binding domain sequencing (MBD-seq). Numerous techniques are also available for more focused investigations, including cloning or direct sequencing of specific genomic targets, pyrosequencing, high-resolution melt assays, and the EpiTYPER system (Sequenom).

Histone modifications

Genetic information is consolidated by histones and associated proteins into chromatin structures, where genomic DNA is condensed into numerous layers of higher organization. At the core of a chromatin unit is the nucleosome: an octamer of histone proteins wrapped tightly by DNA, with their N-terminal tails protruding outward from the core. Modification of histone tails, particularly at lysine (K) residues, alters chromatin structure and subsequently regulates downstream transcriptional processes through effects on DNA compaction and protein recruitment to the site of transcription (Kornberg & Lorch, 1999). Histone tails can be covalently modified by acetylation, methylation, phosphorylation, SUMOylation, and ubiquitinylation (Berger, 2007). The effect of these modifications on gene expression depends upon the histone protein (H2A, H2B, H3, H4), specific amino acid residue, the nature of the modification, and combination of modifications on the tail (Bannister & Kouzarides, 2011).

As histone modifications occur at the protein-level, the majority of methods employ chromatin immunoprecipitation (ChIP) techniques. Typically, DNA is first fragmented into nucleosomes, which are then incubated with an antibody that recognizes a specific histone modification. Complexes are purified, and the profile of the modification is determined by comparing pre- and post-immunoprecipitated samples. At the largest scale, ChIP-seq involves sequencing all DNA in both samples, then aligning reads back to the genome to identify regions (peaks) displaying an enrichment of that modification. At the more targeted level, differences in levels of a modification at a specific genomic region can be assessed using quantitative real-time polymerase chain reaction (qRT-PCR). As the specific effects of histone modifications on gene expression are related to combinations of various modifications (histone code), datasets assessing each modification separately can be combined to reveal overall chromatin states.

Epigenetic studies of suicidal behaviors

The majority of the studies investigating epigenetic modifications in relation to suicidal behaviors have been candidate gene studies, evaluating genes and biological pathways which have previously been associated with suicidal behaviors through other avenues. A summary of significant findings from targeted studies is shown in Table 14.1. In addition to candidate gene studies, larger scale studies, including epigenome-wide association studies (EWAS), have identified interesting new targets whose roles in suicide had not been previously suspected. These studies are shown in Table 14.2.

HPA axis

The hypothalamic-pituitary-adrenal (HPA) axis plays an essential role in regulating behavioral and physiological responses to stress, and dysregulated functioning of this pathway has been repeatedly demonstrated in psychiatric disorders (for examples, see (Belvederi Murri et al., 2014; O'Connor, Ferguson, Green, O'Carroll, & O'Connor, 2016; Zorn et al., 2017). The reactivity of this stress system has been consistently shown to be modified by the early life environment through epigenetic mechanisms, leading to behavioral changes across the lifespan (Francis, Diorio, Liu, & Meaney, 1999; Liu et al., 1997; Meaney & Szyf, 2005). Much of the work in

Table 14.1 Significant findings from targeted epigenetic studies in suicide.

Signficant Gene(s)	Significant findings	Phenotype	Tissue	Reference
NR3C1	Hypermethylation in abused suicides	Abuse and non-abuse, Suicide versus HC	Brain	McGowan et al., (2009)
NR3C1	Hypermethylation (exon 1B and 1C), hypomethylation (exon 1H)	Abuse and non-abuse, Suicide versus HC	Brain	Labonte et al., (2012a)
NR3C1	Hypermethylation of exon 1C in patients with suicidality	Bulimia with suicidality versus bulimia without suicidality versus HC	Blood	Steiger et al., (2013)
NR3C1, BDNF, FKBP5, CRHBP	Hypermethylation in suicide ideation	Suicide ideation versus non-ideation, MDD	Blood	Roy et al., (2017)
CRH	Hypomethylation in high-risk attempters	High-risk suicide attempt versus low-risk attempt	Blood	Jokinen et al., (2018)
SKA2	Methylation predicted suicide attempts	Suicide attempts, suicide ideation	Saliva, blood	Kaminsky et al., (2015)
SKA2	Methylation predicted suicide attempts and ideation	Suicide ideation and attempts	Blood	Sadeh et al., (2016)
BDNF	Hypermethylation in suicides	Suicide versus HC	Brain	Keller et al., (2010)
BDNF	Hypermethylation in attempters and ideators	Suicide attempts, suicide ideation	Blood	Kang et al., (2013)
BDNF	Hypermethylation in suicidal ideation	Suicide ideation, late life	Blood	Kim et al., (2014)
BDNF	Hypermethylation associated with suicidal ideation and depressive symptoms	Suicide ideation, breast cancer	Blood	Kim et al., (2015)

Continued

Table 14.1 Significant findings from targeted epigenetic studies in suicide.—cont'd

Signficant Gene(s)	Significant findings	Phenotype	Tissue	Reference
BDNF	Hypermethylation associated with suicidal ideation	Suicide ideation, acute coronary syndrome	Blood	Kang et al., (2018)
TrkB	Hypermethylation in suicides	Suicide versus HC	Brain	Ernst et al., (2009b)
TrkB	Increased H3K27me3 in suicides	Suicide versus HC	Brain	Ernst et al., (2009a)
TrkB	Hypermethylation in suicides	Suicide versus HC	Brain	Maussion et al. (2014)
AMD1, ARG2, OAZ1, OAZ2	Overall and site-specific differences in promoter methylation	Suicide versus HC	Brain	Gross et al. (2013)
OAZ1	Increased H3K4me3	Suicide versus HC	Brain	Fiori et al. (2012)
HTR2A	Hypermethylation in suicide attempters with schizophrenia	Schizophrenia and bipolar disorder, Suicide attempt versus non-attempt	Brain, blood	De Luca et al., (2009)
TPH2	Hypermethylation in suicide attempters	MDD, suicide attempt versus non-attempt	Blood	Zhang et al. (2015)
GABAA	Hypermethlation in suicide	Suicide versus HC	Brain	Poulter et al. (2008)
rRNA	Hypermethylation of rRNA promoters and 5′ regulatory regions	Abused suicide versus HC	Brain	McGowan et al. (2008)
CACNA1C	Significant differences in two CpG sites in suicide attempters	Suicide attempt versus non-attempt	Blood	Kim et al. (2017)
ELOVL5	Hypomethylation in downstream region, hypermethylation in upstream region	MDD, suicide attempt versus non-attempt	Blood	Haghighi et al. (2015)

Table 14.1 Significant findings from targeted epigenetic studies in suicide.—cont'd

Signficant Gene(s)	Significant findings	Phenotype	Tissue	Reference
Galanin, GALR3	Brain region- and gender-specific alterations in methylation	MDD-suicide versus HC	Brain	Barde et al. (2016)
Cx30, Cx43	Increased H3K9me3 in suicides	Suicide versus HC	Brain	Nagy, Torres-Platas, Mechawar, & Turecki (2017)
KOR	Hypomethylation in abused suicides compared to non-abused suicides or controls	Abuse and non-abuse Suicide versus HC	Brain	Lutz et al. (2018)

Table 14.2 EWAS which identified significant epigenetic differences related to suicidal behaviors.

Highlighted genes	Phenotype	Tissue	Reference
ALS2, DGKZ, HIST2H2AB, NR1D1, TAF5L	Abuse and non abuse Suicide versus HC	Brain	Labonte et al. (2012b)
NR2E1, CHRNB2, GRM7, DBH	Suicide versus HC	Brain	Labonte et al. (2013)
ATP8A1, KCNAB2, LOC153328, SKA2	Suicide, suicidal behaviors	Brain, blood	Guintivano et al. (2014)
EYA2, MEGF11, LMNA, GLUD1, ERBB3, SLC18A2	MDD-suicide versus HC	Brain	Haghighi et al. (2014)
BEGAIN, GRIK2	Suicide versus HC	Brain	Nagy et al. (2015)
LINGO3, POU3F1, ITGB1	Abuse and non-abuse Suicide versus HC	Brain	Lutz et al. (2017)
PSORS1C3, TAPBP, ATP5G2	MDD-suicide versus HC	Brain	Murphy et al. (2017)

psychiatry has focused specifically on its relationship with ELA, with particular focus on the glucocorticoid receptor (GR, NR3C1). Two studies specifically investigated the effects of ELA in suicide by comparing promoter methylation of NR3C1 in suicides with and without experience of childhood abuse. These studies examined NR3C1 expression in the hippocampus, and identified methylation differences which correlated with expression of several NR3C1 isoforms (exons 1B, 1C, and 1H), and were specific to abuse rather than suicide (Labonte et al., 2012a; McGowan et al., 2009). However, another study, in patients with bulimia nervosa, examined methylation of exons 1B, 1C, 1F, and 1H, and found that elevated methylation in exon 1C was significantly associated with suicidal behavior, but not childhood abuse (Steiger, Labonte, Groleau, Turecki, & Israel, 2013). These findings indicate that, at least under certain conditions, NR3C1 methylation is related to suicidal behaviors independently of abuse.

Two additional studies examined larger sets of stress and HPA-related genes, including NR3C1, to assess their relationship to suicidal behaviors, independently of abuse. Roy and colleagues examined the expression and methylation of five stress-related genes in the blood of patients with major depressive disorder (MDD) and healthy controls, and found four (brain-derived neurotrophic factor (BDNF), FK506 binding protein 5 (FKBP5), corticotropin releasing hormone binding protein (CRHBP), and NR3C1) that displayed hypermethylation in patients with suicidal ideation relative to patients without ideation, and healthy controls (Roy, Shelton, & Dwivedi, 2017). Additionally, hypermethylation was associated with decreased expression of BDNF, FKBP5, and NR3C1. They found no significant differences in methylation or expression of corticotropin releasing hormone receptor 1 (CRHR1). More recently, a study investigated methylation of corticotropin releasing hormone (CRH), CRHBP, CRHR1, CRHR2, FKBP5, and NR3C1 in the blood of suicide attempters (Jokinen et al., 2018). They identified signficant hypomethylation of CRH in patients with higher severity suicide attempts, and furthermore, one of these sites was hypermethylated in a cohort of adolescents at high risk of psychiatric disorders.

Several studies have identified epigenetic alterations in spindle and kinetochore associated complex subunit 2 (SKA2) in suicidal behaviors. This gene has been implicated in glucocorticoid receptor signaling (Rice et al., 2008), and was first highlighted in an EWAS study in the prefrontal cortex of individuals who died by suicide (Guintivano et al., 2014).

This study identified increased methylation at a specific cytosine residue in the 3′ untranslated region (3′ UTR) of SKA2, which was negatively correlated with gene expression in the brain and blood. Additionally, methylation at this site was significantly elevated in the blood of individuals displaying suicidal ideation, was associated with waking cortisol levels, and interacted with anxiety to influence suicide attempts and ideation. A follow-up study by the same group found that SKA2 methylation in saliva and blood interacted with trauma exposure to predict lifetime suicide attempts, and to mediate cortisol suppression in the dexamethasone suppression test (Kaminsky et al., 2015). Another group found that SKA2 methylation was associated with internalizing symptoms, and predicted rates of suicidal behaviors (Sadeh et al., 2016). Finally, a methylation biosignature including methylation at discoidin domain receptor tyrosine kinase 1 (DDR1), rho guanine nucleotide exchange factor 10 (ARHGEF10), and protein tyrosine phosphatase, non-receptor type 6 (SHP1), was found to interact with SKA2 methylation to predict suicidal ideation (Clive et al., 2016).

Brain-derived neurotrophic factor (BDNF) signaling

Similar to the HPA axis, the properties of the nerve growth factor BDNF and its receptor, neurotrophic receptor tyrosine kinase (NTRK2, TrkB), have repeatedly been shown to be involved in psychiatric disorders, particularly depression, and suicidal behaviors (for some reviews, see (Dwivedi, 2010; Hing, Sathyaputri, & Potash, 2018). The first study investigating BDNF in the brains of people who died by suicide focused on the promoter/exon IV region (Keller et al., 2010). They found it to be hypermethylated compared to non-suicide controls, and that methylation was inversely correlated with expression. A number of studies have also investigated BDNF methylation in the blood, in relation to suicide attempts and ideation. As mentioned in Section 3.1, BDNF was hypermethylated in the blood of patients with suicidal ideation relative to patients without ideation and healthy controls (Roy et al., 2017). Another study found hypermethylation of the BDNF promoter in patients with MDD who had previously attempted suicide, or who experienced suicidal ideation (Kang et al., 2013). Finally, several studies looking specifically at suicidal ideation found hypermethylation of BDNF in the elderly (Kim et al., 2014), and in patients with breast cancer (Kim et al., 2015), or acute coronary syndrome (Kang et al., 2018).

Several epigenetic studies have investigated TrkB in suicide, focusing on the TrkB.T1 isoform, which is specifically expressed in astrocytes. The first study found that methylation at specific sites in the promoter was elevated in the prefrontal cortex of suicides, and associated with decreased expression of this transcript (Ernst et al., 2009b). Additionally, hypermethylation was identified at several sites in the 3′ UTR of TrkB.T1, which correlated with expression in the prefrontal cortex (Maussion et al., 2014). These results appear to be brain-region specific, as no differences were found in the cerebellum (Ernst et al., 2009b) or Wernicke's area (Keller et al., 2011). Finally, a third study found increased histone 3 lysine 27 trimethylation (H3K27me3), which is associated with heterochromatin, in the promoter region of TrkB in the prefrontal cortex and it was inversely correlated with gene expression (Ernst, Chen, & Turecki, 2009a). These findings were also specific to the prefrontal cortex, as no differences were found in the cerebellum.

Polyamine system

Dysregulation of the polyamine system has been observed in a number of psychiatric disorders, including mood disorders, anxiety, and schizophrenia (Fiori & Turecki, 2008). The polyamine stress response (PSA) is activated after exposure to stressful stimuli, resulting in elevated levels of putrescine and agmatine in the brain and periphery (Fiori & Turecki, 2008; Limon, Mamdani, Hjelm, Vawter, & Sequeira, 2016; Turecki, 2014). The involvement of the polyamine system in suicidal behavior was first demonstrated by gene expression studies which found widespread downregulation of the catabolic enzyme spermidine/spermine N1-acetyltransferase (SAT1) in the brains of suicides (Sequeira et al., 2006). Since this time, a number of studies have investigated how epigenetic mechanisms may be involved in the altered expression of polyamine-related genes. Two studies investigated the promoter region of SAT1, and found no significant differences in methylation or levels of H3K27me3 in the brain (Fiori & Turecki, 2011; Guipponi et al., 2009). However, methylation and genetic variation at the 3' UTR in SKA2 was found to interact with methylation at a GR-binding site in the SAT1 promoter to associate with suicidal ideation, suggesting that epigenetic regulation of SAT1 may be stress-related (Guintivano et al., 2014).

In addition to SAT1, no significant differences were found in levels of methylation or H3K27me3 in the promoter regions of the catabolic enzymes spermine synthase (SMS) or spermine oxidase (SMOX) in the brain (Fiori & Turecki, 2010). However, epigenetic studies of anabolic enzymes identified methylation differences in the promoter regions of ornithine decarboxylase antizymes 1 (OAZ1) and 2 (OAZ2), arginase II (ARG2) and S-adenosylmethionine decarboxylase (AMD1), with methylation of ARG2 and AMD1 being significantly correlated with gene expression (Gross, Fiori, Labonte, Lopez, & Turecki, 2013). The levels of histone 3 lysine 4 trimethylation (H3K4me3), which is typically associated with active gene expression, were investigated in the same genes, and increased levels were found in the promoter region of OAZ1, which was positively correlated with expression (Fiori, Gross, & Turecki, 2012). No differences between suicides and controls were found for this modification in the promoters of AMD1, OAZ2, or ARG2.

Serotonin system

Serotonergic neurotransmission is the target of the majority of antidepressant therapies, and has been extensively investigated in psychiatry. Although a number of studies have examined epigenetic regulation of the serotonin transporter (SLC6A4) in relation to childhood adversity and depression (for examples, see (Booij et al., 2015; van der Knaap et al., 2015)), methylation of this gene has yet to be examined in relation to suicidality. A few epigenetic studies have looked at the serotonin 2A receptor (HTR2A), as a polymorphic site in exon 1 of this gene has been associated with suicidal behaviors (Wang et al., 2015). The first study examined methylation at a polymorphic site in exon 1 of HTR2A, and found no differences in brains of suicides (De Luca, Viggiano, Dhoot, Kennedy, & Wong, 2009). However, they observed significantly increased levels of methylation at this site in the blood of patients with schizophrenia who had attempted suicide relative to non-attempters, but no differences between attempters and non-attempters with bipolar disorder. In addition, they found no signficant differences in exon 1 methylation in white blood cells or saliva from suicide attempters with schizophrenia, or in the brains of people who died by suicide (Bani-Fatemi et al., 2016, 2017). One additional serotonin-related study examined methylation of tryptophan hydroxylase 2 (TPH2) in the blood of patients with MDD, and found significantly elevated methylation in patients who had previously attempted suicide, compared to non-attempters (Zhang et al., 2015).

Additional targeted studies

In addition to the studies described above, epigenetic alterations have been identified in genes outside of the "classical" suicide-related pathways. These studies are also shown in Table 14.1, and represent potential new avenues for suicide-related research. While in some cases, these findings appear to be related to ELA, rather than suicide (Lutz et al., 2018; McGowan et al., 2008), larger studies in additional clinical populations will be needed to fully characterize their relationship with suicidal behaviors.

Epigenome-wide association studies (EWAS)

While the majority of epigenetic studies have been restricted to targeted analyses, investigators have also utilized broader, epigenome-wide, approaches to identify epigenetic changes in genes which had not been previously implicated in suicide. Epigenome-wide studies which identified sites or regions which were significantly associated with suicidal behaviors are shown in Table 14.2. With the exception of the study described above by Guintvano and colleagues (Guintivano et al., 2014), the genes described in this section have yet to be replicated in additional cohorts.

The first EWAS investigating suicide used a custom-designed promoter tiling array to assess methylation differences in the hippocampi of abused suicide completers compared to non-suicide controls (Labonte et al., 2012b). This study identified 362 promoters which displayed significantly different levels of methylation, and a gene ontology analysis indicated an enrichment of genes related to neuronal plasticity. Among these genes, alsin (ALS2) was selected for further study. Methylation differences were found to be specific to neuronal cells, which showed hypermethylation at a specific CpG site in abused suicides compared to non-abused suicides and non-suicide controls. In vitro studies indicated that this site was in a regulatory region of the promoter, and that methylation decreased gene expression. Furthermore, analysis of gene expression in the hippocampus found that both abused and non-abused suicides had decreased expression of isoform 2 of this gene, suggesting that hypermethylation in the promoter may be responsible for the downregulation of this isoform in suicide.

A follow-up study was performed in a larger group of suicides and non-suicide controls, and identified 366 promoter regions which showed differential methylation in the hippocampus (Labonte et al., 2013). These findings were significant after controlling for a history of childhood adversity, indicating that this differential methylation was specifically related to suicide rather than ELA. A gene ontology analysis indicated an enrichment of genes related to cognitive processes and neuronal communication. The most significant methylation differences in this cluster were nuclear receptor subfamily 2 group E member 1 (NR2E1), cholinergic receptor nicotinic beta 2 subunit (CHRNB2), glutamate metabotropic receptor 7, (GRM7), and dopamine beta-hydroxylase (DBH). These genes were hypermethylated in suicides, and methylation of NR2E1 and GRM7 was inversely correlated with expression in the brain.

Finally, a third study was performed to investigate suicide and ELA, this time in the anterior cingulate cortex (ACC) (Lutz et al., 2017). In this study, RRBS was performed in the ACC of suicides with a history of childhood abuse and non-psychiatric controls. Numerous epigenetic changes were found in genes related to oligodendrocytes, as well as an impairment in transcription of myelin-related genes, and reduction in myelination in depressed suicides with a history of childhood abuse. The three most differentially methylated regions were in leucine rich repeat and Ig domain containing 3 (LINGO3), POU class 3 homeobox 1 (POU3F1), and integrin subunit beta 1 (ITGB1), each of which are related to myelin and oligodendrocytes. Methylation differences in LINGO3 and POU3F1 were found to be specific to an oligodendrocyte fraction of cells, with no changes in neuronal cells. Further, suicides without a history of childhood abuse had similar methylation levels to non-suicides in these cells, indicating that these effects are specific to ELA, rather than suicide.

Two EWAS have been performed to investigate suicide in the context of MDD. The first study investigated the orbital prefrontal cortex (Brodmann area (BA) 47) of suicides with MDD and non-psychiatric controls using the Illumina Infinium HumanMethylation27 BeadChip, which assesses methylation at 27 578 CpG sites across the genome (Haghighi et al., 2014). They identified a significant effect of age on methylation, and interestingly, found a significantly higher number of CpG sites influenced by age in the depressed suicide group compared to the non-suicide controls (136 vs. 17). A gene ontology analysis of these age-related genes found an enrichment for genes associated with behavior, cell cycle, cell death and survival, and cellular and embryonic development.

The second study examined two brain regions: the orbitofrontal cortex, and the subgenual anterior cingulate cortex (BA11 and BA25, respectively) (Murphy et al., 2017). This study used the Infinium HumanMethylation450K BeadChip Array, which interrogates over 485 000 sites in the genome, and compared depressed suicides with non-psychiatric controls. They identified three regions that were differentially methylated in both brain areas, mapping to the genes psoriasis susceptibility 1 candidate 3 (PSORS1C3), TAP binding protein (TAPBP), and ATP synthase membrane subunit c locus 2 (ATP5G2). Hypomethylation of PSORS1C3 was also observed in sorted neuronal cells from the prefrontal cortex of an independent sample of suicides. Additionally, for each sample, they generated polygenic risk scores (PRS) for MDD and suicide, and used weighted gene co-expression network analysis (WGCNA) to identify networks of co-methylated modules associated with the depressed suicides and the two PRS. In BA25, they found two modules which associated with a PRS score for suicide attempt, and gene ontology analyses showed an enrichment of processes relevant to MDD and suicide, including nervous system development and mitochondrial function.

A number of studies have suggested an important role of astrocytic dysfunction in suicide and mood disorders (Rajkowska & Stockmeier, 2013; Torres-Platas et al., 2011). To investigate how epigenetic differences may be involved in this effect in suicide, irrespective of psychiatric diagnosis, a sub-population of suicide completers was identified who displayed decreased levels of astrocytic markers in the prefrontal cortex, and performed methylation binding domain (MBD) enrichment followed by sequencing, to compare genome-wide methylation in these subjects with non-suicide controls (Nagy et al., 2015). This study found 115 differentially methylated regions between these two groups, with the majority being hypomethylated in suicides. Differential methylation was validated in the two most significant genes, glutamate ionotropic receptor kainate type subunit 2 (GRIK2), and brain enriched guanylate kinase associated (BEGAIN), which showed hypo- and hyper-methylation in suicides, respectively. Further, the study found that while methylation differences in GRIK2 were maintained in both neuronal and non-neuronal cells, hypermethylation of BEGAIN was only found in non-neuronal cells. Methylation of both genes was found to be inversely correlated with expression in the brain. Finally, in vitro studies showed that this region of BEGAIN has a regulatory function, which is impacted by methylation.

Three additional EWAS have been performed which did not identify significant epigenetic differences related to suicidal behaviors. The first study examined methylation in the prefrontal cortex of 6 suicides and 6 non-psychiatric controls using the Illumina 450K array (Schneider, El Hajj, Muller, Navarro, & Haaf, 2015). Overall, they found no significantly differentially methylated sites or regions. However, the sample size of this study was small, and was likely underpowered to detect the relatively small methylation differences typically observed in psychiatry.

The second study investigated 5hmC in the prefrontal cortex of depressed suicides and non-psychiatric controls (Gross et al., 2017). As mentioned earlier, most molecular techniques are unable to distinguish between methylation and hydroxymethylation, which can have opposing effects on gene transcription. This study was the first to fully characterize 5hmC in depressed suicides, and used a restriction enzyme (AbaS1)-based approach, followed by sequencing, to assess differences across the genome. Although no sites reached genome-wide significance, 550 sites showed suggestive differential hydroxymethylation. The elevated levels of 5hmC in two genes, myosin XVI (MYO16) and insulin-degrading enzyme (IDE) were validated by oxidative bisulfite sequencing (oxBS). Interestingly, while the expression of MYO16 was significantly increased, which was consistent with the canonical role of gene-body 5hmC, the levels of IDE were significantly decreased, indicating that, like methylation, the effects of 5hmC on transcription are not always straightforward.

Finally, while all the EWAS studies described above focused on methylation in the brain, a recent study investigated white blood cells from suicide attempters and non-attempters diagnosed with schizophrenia (Bani-Fatemi et al., 2018). This study used the Illumina 450K array, and found hypomethylation in coiled-coil domain containing 53 (CCDC53) in suicide attempters, although this did not reach genome-wide significance.

Conclusions and future perspectives

As seen in the previous sections, numerous genes and biological pathways have been shown to display epigenetic differences in relation to suicidal behaviors. Furthermore, in many cases, these differences have been linked to specific functional effects on gene expression, indicating clear functional roles of these suicide-associated regions.

To date, many of the results herein have been replicated across only a few studies. However, consistent findings regarding alterations to SKA2, and NR3C1 strongly suggest that epigenetic studies remain a promising avenue to pursue. Clearly, additional studies in larger, and better-characterized, cohorts are necessary. This is particularly important in epigenetic studies, as these effects are susceptible to subtle environment differences, and results can be easily confounded by clinical and socio-demographic factors such as gender, age, ELA, and psychiatric diagnosis. This is quite apparent in the case of NR3C1, whose relationship with suicidal behaviors appears to be largely, but not exclusively, mediated by ELA. While it is notable that the genes displaying significant differences in targeted studies have failed to emerge in EWAS, this is likely due to a lack of statistical power in these high-throughput studies. Nonetheless, the findings regarding SKA2, which was initially identified in an EWAS, indicate the utility of combining both epigenome-wide and targeted approaches in this field. This study also highlighted the potential for epigenetic findings in the brain to be translated into the blood, where they can serve as biomarkers for suicidal behaviors. This information could be especially useful in populations at risk for suicide, including people diagnosed with mood disorders or schizophrenia, or who have experienced childhood abuse. As such, additional studies combining different tissues are needed in order to determine the relationship between epigenetic differences in the brain and the blood. Moreover, it remains unclear which region of the brain represents the most meaningful site to investigate for suicide-related epigenetic changes, and more studies which examine multiple brain regions are needed.

The stability of suicide-related epigenetic differences over time has yet to be addressed, which it is especially relevant in the case of ELA. As many of the significant findings described in this chapter were observed in adults, who had experienced abuse decades earlier, many of these alterations do appear to persist over time. Nonetheless, it has not been conclusively demonstrated that these suicide-related epigenetic signatures in adulthood are identical to those that were present in childhood. Determining how these signatures develop and evolve over time would be invaluable, as it may allow for early identification of individuals at later risk for suicidality.

What is particularly promising are studies which have demonstrated that epigenetic-related processes can be modified by antidepressant treatments. Indeed, a number of studies have demonstrated differential methylation and histone modifications in the promoter regions of BDNF following antidepressant treatment (D'Addario et al., 2013; Lopez et al., 2013; Tadic et al., 2014). While histone modifications have been less well studied than methylation, levels of histone modification enzymes have also been found to be altered by antidepressant treatment (Iga et al., 2007).

Further, treatment with HDAC inhibitors has been shown to elicit antidepressant-like effects in animals (Covington et al., 2009; Hobara, Uchida, Otsuki, Yamagata, & Watanabe, 2010; Tsankova et al., 2006). As such, while studies of ELA have definitively demonstrated the adverse effects of early childhood experiences, it appears that these environmental influences on the epigenome have the potential to be reversed, thus representing potential new targets for treatment of suicidal behaviors.

In conclusion, the studies described in this chapter have demonstrated numerous epigenetic changes in relation to suicidal behaviors, which have been observed in both the brain and peripheral samples. As the epigenome is an integral system for mediating the effects of the environment on gene function, understanding its involvement in suicidal behaviors represents an important step toward elucidating the molecular mechanisms underlying their development, as well as for identifying novel targets for diagnosis and treatment.

References

Bani-Fatemi, A., Howe, A. S., Matmari, M., Koga, A., Zai, C., Strauss, J., et al. (2016). Interaction between methylation and CpG single-nucleotide polymorphisms in the HTR2A gene: Association analysis with suicide attempt in schizophrenia. *Neuropsychobiology, 73*, 10–15.

Bani-Fatemi, A., Jeremian, R., Wang, K. Z., Silveira, J., Zai, C., Kolla, N. J., et al. (2018). Epigenome-wide association study of suicide attempt in schizophrenia. *Journal of Psychiatric Research, 104*, 192–197.

Bani-Fatemi, A., Strauss, J., Zai, C., Wong, A. H. C., & de Luca, V. (2017). Multiple tissue methylation analysis of HTR2A exon I in suicidal behavior. *Psychiatric Genetics, 27*, 219–224.

Bannister, A. J., & Kouzarides, T. (2011). Regulation of chromatin by histone modifications. *Cell Research, 21*, 381–395.

Barde, S., Ruegg, J., Prud'homme, J., Ekstrom, T. J., Palkovits, M., Turecki, G., et al. (2016). Alterations in the neuropeptide galanin system in major depressive disorder involve levels of transcripts, methylation, and peptide. *Proceedings of the National Academy of Sciences of the United States of America, 113*, E8472–E8481.

Baylin, S. B., & Jones, P. A. (2011). A decade of exploring the cancer epigenome — biological and translational implications. *Nature Reviews Cancer, 11*, 726–734.

Belvederi Murri, M., Pariante, C., Mondelli, V., Masotti, M., Atti, A. R., Mellacqua, Z., et al. (2014). HPA axis and aging in depression: Systematic review and meta-analysis. *Psychoneuroendocrinology, 41*, 46–62.

Berger, S. L. (2007). The complex language of chromatin regulation during transcription. *Nature, 447*, 407–412.

Booij, L., Szyf, M., Carballedo, A., Frey, E. M., Morris, D., Dymov, S., et al. (2015). DNA methylation of the serotonin transporter gene in peripheral cells and stress-related changes in hippocampal volume: A study in depressed patients and healthy controls. *PLoS One, 10*, e0119061.

Brent, D. A., Bridge, J., Johnson, B. A., & Connolly, J. (1996). Suicidal behavior runs in families. A controlled family study of adolescent suicide victims. *Archives of General Psychiatry, 53*, 1145–1152.

Clive, M. L., Boks, M. P., Vinkers, C. H., Osborne, L. M., Payne, J. L., Ressler, K. J., et al. (2016). Discovery and replication of a peripheral tissue DNA methylation biosignature to augment a suicide prediction model. *Clinical Epigenetics, 8*, 113.

Covington, H. E., Maze, I., LaPlant, Q. C., Vialou, V. F., Yoshinori, O. N., Berton, O., et al. (2009). Antidepressant actions OF HDAC inhibitors. *Journal of Neuroscience : The Official Journal of the Society for Neuroscience, 29*, 11451–11460.

Curradi, M., Izzo, A., Badaracco, G., & Landsberger, N. (2002). Molecular mechanisms of gene silencing mediated by DNA methylation. *Molecular and Cellular Biology, 22*, 3157–3173.

D'Addario, C., Dell'Osso, B., Galimberti, D., Palazzo, M. C., Benatti, B., Di Francesco, A., et al. (2013). Epigenetic modulation of BDNF gene in patients with major depressive disorder. *Biological Psychiatry, 73*, e6–e7.

De Luca, V., Viggiano, E., Dhoot, R., Kennedy, J. L., & Wong, A. H. (2009). Methylation and QTDT analysis of the 5-HT2A receptor 102C allele: Analysis of suicidality in major psychosis. *Journal of Psychiatric Research, 43*, 532–537.

Dwivedi, Y. (2010). Brain-derived neurotrophic factor and suicide pathogenesis. *Annals of Medicine, 42*, 87–96.

Ernst, C., Chen, E. S., & Turecki, G. (2009a). Histone methylation and decreased expression of TrkB.T1 in orbital frontal cortex of suicide completers. *Molecular Psychiatry, 14*, 830–832.

Ernst, C., Deleva, V., Deng, X., Sequeira, A., Pomarenski, A., Klempan, T., et al. (2009b). Alternative splicing, methylation state, and expression profile of tropomyosin-related kinase B in the frontal cortex of suicide completers. *Archives of General Psychiatry, 66*, 22–32.

Fiori, L. M., Gross, J. A., & Turecki, G. (2012). Effects of histone modifications on increased expression of polyamine biosynthetic genes in suicide. *International Journal of Neuropsychopharmacology, 15*, 1161–1166.

Fiori, L. M., & Turecki, G. (2008). Implication of the polyamine system in mental disorders. *Journal of Psychiatry & Neuroscience, 33*, 102–110.

Fiori, L. M., & Turecki, G. (2010). Genetic and epigenetic influences on expression of spermine synthase and spermine oxidase in suicide completers. *International Journal of Neuropsychopharmacology, 13*, 725–736.

Fiori, L. M., & Turecki, G. (2011). Epigenetic regulation of spermidine/spermine N1-acetyltransferase (SAT1) in suicide. *Journal of Psychiatric Research, 45*, 1229–1235.

Francis, D., Diorio, J., Liu, D., & Meaney, M. J. (1999). Nongenomic transmission across generations of maternal behavior and stress responses in the rat. *Science, 286*, 1155–1158.

Fu, Q., Heath, A. C., Bucholz, K. K., Nelson, E. C., Glowinski, A. L., Goldberg, J., et al. (2002). A twin study of genetic and environmental influences on suicidality in men. *Psychologie Medicale, 32*, 11–24.

Gilbert, R., Widom, C. S., Browne, K., Fergusson, D., Webb, E., & Janson, S. (2009). Burden and consequences of child maltreatment in high-income countries. *Lancet, 373*, 68–81.

Gross, J. A., Fiori, L. M., Labonte, B., Lopez, J. P., & Turecki, G. (2013). Effects of promoter methylation on increased expression of polyamine biosynthetic genes in suicide. *Journal of Psychiatric Research, 47*, 513–519.

Gross, J. A., Pacis, A., Chen, G. G., Drupals, M., Lutz, P. E., Barreiro, L. B., et al. (2017). Gene-body 5-hydroxymethylation is associated with gene expression changes in the prefrontal cortex of depressed individuals. *Translational Psychiatry, 7*, e1119.

Guintivano, J., Brown, T., Newcomer, A., Jones, M., Cox, O., Maher, B. S., et al. (2014). Identification and replication of a combined epigenetic and genetic biomarker predicting suicide and suicidal behaviors. *American Journal of Psychiatry, 171*, 1287–1296.

Guipponi, M., Deutsch, S., Kohler, K., Perroud, N., Le Gal, F., Vessaz, M., et al. (2009). Genetic and epigenetic analysis of SSAT gene dysregulation in suicidal behavior. *American Journal of Medical Genetics, 150B*, 799–807.

Haghighi, F., Galfalvy, H., Chen, S., Huang, Y. Y., Cooper, T. B., Burke, A. K., et al. (2015). DNA methylation perturbations in genes involved in polyunsaturated Fatty Acid biosynthesis associated with depression and suicide risk. *Frontiers in Neurology, 6*, 92.

Haghighi, F., Xin, Y., Chanrion, B., O'Donnell, A. H., Ge, Y., Dwork, A. J., et al. (2014). Increased DNA methylation in the suicide brain. *Dialogues in Clinical Neuroscience, 16*, 430–438.

Hing, B., Sathyaputri, L., & Potash, J. B. (2018). A comprehensive review of genetic and epigenetic mechanisms that regulate BDNF expression and function with relevance to major depressive disorder. *American Journal of Medical Genetics, 177*, 143–167.

Hobara, T., Uchida, S., Otsuki, K., Yamagata, H., & Watanabe, Y. (2010). Molecular mechanisms of the antidepressant actions by histone deacetylase inhibitors. *Neuroscience Research, 68*(Suppl. 1), e316.

Hoffmann, A., Sportelli, V., Ziller, M., & Spengler, D. (2017). Epigenomics of major depressive disorders and schizophrenia: Early life decides. *International Journal of Molecular Sciences, 18*.

Hubel, C., Marzi, S. J., Breen, G., & Bulik, C. M. (2019). Epigenetics in eating disorders: A systematic review. *Molecular Psychiatry, 24*, 901–915.

Iga, J., Ueno, S., Yamauchi, K., Numata, S., Kinouchi, S., Tayoshi-Shibuya, S., et al. (2007). Altered HDAC5 and CREB mRNA expressions in the peripheral leukocytes of major depression. *Progress in Neuro Psychopharmacology & Biological Psychiatry, 31*, 628–632.

Jang, H. S., Shin, W. J., Lee, J. E., & Do, J. T. (2017). CpG and non-CpG methylation in epigenetic gene regulation and brain function. *Genes, 8*.

Jawahar, M. C., Murgatroyd, C., Harrison, E. L., & Baune, B. T. (2015). Epigenetic al terations following early postnatal stress: A review on novel aetiological mechanisms of common psychiatric disorders. *Clinical Epigenetics, 7*, 122.

Jin, B., Li, Y., & Robertson, K. D. (2011). DNA methylation: Superior or subordinate in the epigenetic hierarchy? *Genes & Cancer, 2*, 607–617.

Jjingo, D., Conley, A. B., Yi, S. V., Lunyak, V. V., & Jordan, I. K. (2012). On the presence and role of human gene-body DNA methylation. *Oncotarget, 3*, 462–474.

Jokinen, J., Bostrom, A. E., Dadfar, A., Ciuculete, D. M., Chatzittofis, A., Asberg, M., et al. (2018). Epigenetic changes in the CRH gene are related to severity of suicide attempt and a general psychiatric risk score in adolescents. *EBioMedicine, 27*, 123–133.

Kaminsky, Z., Wilcox, H. C., Eaton, W. W., Van Eck, K., Kilaru, V., Jovanovic, T., et al. (2015). Epigenetic and genetic variation at SKA2 predict suicidal behavior and post-traumatic stress disorder. *Translational Psychiatry, 5*, e627.

Kang, H. J., Bae, K. Y., Kim, S. W., Shin, I. S., Hong, Y. J., Ahn, Y., et al. (2018). BDNF methylation and suicidal ideation in patients with acute coronary syndrome. *Psychiatry Investig*, 0.

Kang, H. J., Kim, J. M., Lee, J. Y., Kim, S. Y., Bae, K. Y., Kim, S. W., et al. (2013). BDNF promoter methylation and suicidal behavior in depressive patients. *Journal of Affective Disorders, 151*, 679–685.

Keller, S., et al. (2010). Increased BDNF promoter methylation in the Wernicke area of suicide subjects. *Archives of General Psychiatry, 67*, 258–267.

Keller, S., Sarchiapone, M., Zarrilli, F., Tomaiuolo, R., Carli, V., Angrisano, T., et al. (2011). TrkB gene expression and DNA methylation state in Wernicke area does not associate with suicidal behavior. *Journal of Affective Disorders, 135*, 400–404.

Kim, J. M., Kang, H. J., Bae, K. Y., Kim, S. W., Shin, I. S., Kim, H. R., et al. (2014). Association of BDNF promoter methylation and genotype with suicidal ideation in elderly Koreans. *American Journal of Geriatric Psychiatry, 22*, 989–996.

Kim, J. M., Kang, H. J., Kim, S. Y., Kim, S. W., Shin, I. S., Kim, H. R., et al. (2015). BDNF promoter methylation associated with suicidal ideation in patients with breast cancer. *International Journal of Psychiatry in Medicine, 49*, 75–94.

Kim, Y. J., Park, H. J., Jahng, G. H., Lee, S. M., Kang, W. S., Kim, S. K., et al. (2017). A pilot study of differential brain activation to suicidal means and DNA methylation of CACNA1C gene in suicidal attempt patients. *Psychiatry Research, 255*, 42–48.

Klose, R. J., & Bird, A. P. (2006). Genomic DNA methylation: The mark and its mediators. *Trends in Biochemical Sciences, 31*, 89–97.

van der Knaap, L. J., Riese, H., Hudziak, J. J., Verbiest, M. M., Verhulst, F. C., Oldehinkel, A. J., et al. (2015). Adverse life events and allele-specific methylation of the serotonin transporter gene (SLC6A4) in adolescents: The TRAILS study. *Psychosomatic Medicine, 77*, 246–255.

Kornberg, R. D., & Lorch, Y. (1999). Twenty-five years of the nucleosome, fundamental particle of the eukaryote chromosome. *Cell, 98*, 285–294.

Labonte, B., Suderman, M., Maussion, G., Lopez, J. P., Navarro-Sanchez, L., Yerko, V., et al. (2013). Genome-wide methylation changes in the brains of suicide completers. *American Journal of Psychiatry, 170*, 511–520.

Labonte, B., Suderman, M., Maussion, G., Navaro, L., Yerko, V., Mahar, I., et al. (2012b). Genome-wide epigenetic regulation by early-life trauma. *Archives of General Psychiatry, 69*, 722–731.

Labonte, B., Yerko, V., Gross, J., Mechawar, N., Meaney, M. J., Szyf, M., et al. (2012a). Differential glucocorticoid receptor exon 1(B), 1(C), and 1(H) expression and methylation in suicide completers with a history of childhood abuse. *Biological Psychiatry, 72*, 41–48.

Limon, A., Mamdani, F., Hjelm, B. E., Vawter, M. P., & Sequeira, A. (2016). Targets of polyamine dysregulation in major depression and suicide: Activity-dependent feedback, excitability, and neurotransmission. *Neuroscience & Biobehavioral Reviews, 66*, 80–91.

Lister, R., et al. (2013). Global epigenomic reconfiguration during mammalian brain development. *Science, 341*, 1237905.

Liu, D., Diorio, J., Tannenbaum, B., Caldji, C., Francis, D., Freedman, A., et al. (1997). Maternal care, hippocampal glucocorticoid receptors, and hypothalamic-pituitary-adrenal responses to stress. *Science, 277*, 1659–1662.

Lopez, J. P., Mamdani, F., Beaulieu, M. M., Yang, J., Berlim, M. T., Ernst, C., et al. (2013). Epigenetic regulation of BDNF expression according to antidepressant response. *Molecular Psychiatry, 18*, 398–399.

Lutz, P. E., Almeida, D., Fiori, L. M., & Turecki, G. (2015). Childhood maltreatment and stress-related psychopathology: The epigenetic memory hypothesis. *Current Pharmaceutical Design, 21*, 1413–1417.

Lutz, P. E., et al. (2017). Association of a history of child abuse with impaired myelination in the anterior cingulate cortex: Convergent epigenetic, transcriptional, and morphological evidence. *American Journal of Psychiatry, 174*, 1185–1194.

Lutz, P. E., Gross, J. A., Dhir, S. K., Maussion, G., Yang, J., Bramoulle, A., et al. (2018). Epigenetic regulation of the Kappa opioid receptor by child abuse. *Biological Psychiatry, 84*, 751–761.

Maunakea, A. K., et al. (2010). Conserved role of intragenic DNA methylation in regulating alternative promoters. *Nature, 466*, 253–257.

Maussion, G., Yang, J., Suderman, M., Diallo, A., Nagy, C., Arnovitz, M., et al. (2014). Functional DNA methylation in a transcript specific 3'UTR region of TrkB associates with suicide. *Epigenetics, 9*, 1061–1070.

McCauley, J., Kern, D. E., Kolodner, K., Dill, L., Schroeder, A. F., DeChant, H. K., et al. (1997). Clinical characteristics of women with a history of childhood abuse: Unhealed wounds. *Jama, 277*, 1362–1368.

McGirr, A., Alda, M., Seguin, M., Cabot, S., Lesage, A., & Turecki, G. (2009). Familial aggregation of suicide explained by cluster B traits: A three-group family study of suicide controlling for major depressive disorder. *American Journal of Psychiatry, 166*, 1124–1134.

McGowan, P. O., Sasaki, A., D'Alessio, A. C., Dymov, S., Labonte, B., Szyf, M., et al. (2009). Epigenetic regulation of the glucocorticoid receptor in human brain associates with childhood abuse. *Nature Neuroscience, 12*, 342–348.

McGowan, P. O., Sasaki, A., Huang, T. C., Unterberger, A., Suderman, M., Ernst, C., et al. (2008). Promoter-wide hypermethylation of the ribosomal RNA gene promoter in the suicide brain. *PLoS One, 3*, e2085.

McGuffin, P., Marusic, A., & Farmer, A. (2001). What can psychiatric genetics offer suicidology? *Crisis, 22*, 61–65.

McLaughlin, K. A., Green, J. G., Gruber, M. J., Sampson, N. A., Zaslavsky, A. M., & Kessler, R. C. (2010). Childhood adversities and adult psychiatric disorders in the national comorbidity survey replication II: Associations with persistence of DSM-IV disorders. *Archives of General Psychiatry, 67*, 124–132.

Meaney, M. J., & Szyf, M. (2005). Maternal care as a model for experience-dependent chromatin plasticity? *Trends in Neurosciences, 28*, 456–463.

Murphy, T. M., Crawford, B., Dempster, E. L., Hannon, E., Burrage, J., Turecki, G., et al. (2017). Methylomic profiling of cortex samples from completed suicide cases implicates a role for PSORS1C3 in major depression and suicide. *Translational Psychiatry, 7*, e989.

Nagy, C., Suderman, M., Yang, J., Szyf, M., Mechawar, N., Ernst, C., et al. (2015). Astrocytic abnormalities and global DNA methylation patterns in depression and suicide. *Molecular Psychiatry, 20*, 320–328.

Nagy, C., Torres-Platas, S. G., Mechawar, N., & Turecki, G. (2017). Repression of astrocytic connexins in cortical and subcortical brain regions and prefrontal enrichment of H3K9me3 in depression and suicide. *International Journal of Neuropsychopharmacology, 20*, 50–57.

O'Connor, D. B., Ferguson, E., Green, J. A., O'Carroll, R. E., & O'Connor, R. C. (2016). Cortisol levels and suicidal behavior: A meta-analysis. *Psychoneuroendocrinology, 63*, 370–379.

Palmisano, M., & Pandey, S. C. (2017). Epigenetic mechanisms of alcoholism and stress-related disorders. *Alcohol, 60*, 7–18.

Poulter, M. O., Du, L., Weaver, I. C., Palkovits, M., Faludi, G., Merali, Z., et al. (2008). GABAA receptor promoter hypermethylation in suicide brain: Implications for the involvement of epigenetic processes. *Biological Psychiatry, 64*, 645–652.

Rajkowska, G., & Stockmeier, C. A. (2013). Astrocyte pathology in major depressive disorder: Insights from human postmortem brain tissue. *Current Drug Targets, 14*, 1225–1236.

Rice, L., Waters, C. E., Eccles, J., Garside, H., Sommer, P., Kay, P., et al. (2008). Identification and functional analysis of SKA2 interaction with the glucocorticoid receptor. *Journal of Endocrinology, 198*, 499–509.

Roy, B., Shelton, R. C., & Dwivedi, Y. (2017). DNA methylation and expression of stress related genes in PBMC of MDD patients with and without serious suicidal ideation. *Journal of Psychiatric Research, 89*, 115–124.

Sadeh, N., Wolf, E. J., Logue, M. W., Hayes, J. P., Stone, A., Griffin, L. M., et al. (2016). Epigenetic variation at Ska2 predicts suicide phenotypes and internalizing psychopathology. *Depression and Anxiety, 33*, 308–315.

Saxena, S., Krug, E. G., Chestnov, O., World Health Organization, & Department of Mental Health and Substance Abuse. (2014). *Preventing suicide : A global imperative*. Geneva: World Health Organization.

Schneider, E., El Hajj, N., Muller, F., Navarro, B., & Haaf, T. (2015). Epigenetic dysregulation in the prefrontal cortex of suicide completers. *Cytogenetic and Genome Research, 146*, 19–27.

Sequeira, A., Gwadry, F. G., Ffrench-Mullen, J. M., Canetti, L., Gingras, Y., Casero, R. A., Jr., et al. (2006). Implication of SSAT by gene expression and genetic variation in suicide and major depression. *Archives of General Psychiatry, 63*, 35–48.

Statham, D. J., Heath, A. C., Madden, P. A., Bucholz, K. K., Bierut, L., Dinwiddie, S. H., et al. (1998). Suicidal behaviour: An epidemiological and genetic study. *Psychologie Medicale, 28*, 839–855.

Steiger, H., Labonte, B., Groleau, P., Turecki, G., & Israel, M. (2013). Methylation of the glucocorticoid receptor gene promoter in bulimic women: Associations with borderline personality disorder, suicidality, and exposure to childhood abuse. *International Journal of Eating Disorders, 46*, 246–255.

Tadic, A., Muller-Engling, L., Schlicht, K. F., Kotsiari, A., Dreimuller, N., Kleimann, A., et al. (2014). Methylation of the promoter of brain-derived neurotrophic factor exon IV and antidepressant response in major depression. *Molecular Psychiatry, 19*, 281–283.

Torres-Platas, S. G., Hercher, C., Davoli, M. A., Maussion, G., Labonte, B., Turecki, G., et al. (2011). Astrocytic hypertrophy in anterior cingulate white matter of depressed suicides. *Neuropsychopharmacology, 36*, 2650–2658.

Tsankova, N. M., Berton, O., Renthal, W., Kumar, A., Neve, R. L., & Nestler, E. J. (2006). Sustained hippocampal chromatin regulation in a mouse model of depression and antidepressant action. *Nature Neuroscience, 9*, 519–525.

Turecki, G. (2014). The molecular bases of the suicidal brain. *Nature Reviews Neuroscience, 15*, 802–816.

Turecki, G., & Brent, D. A. (2016). Suicide and suicidal behaviour. *Lancet, 387*, 1227–1239.

Turecki, G., & Meaney, M. J. (2016). Effects of the social environment and stress on glucocorticoid receptor gene methylation: A systematic review. *Biological Psychiatry, 79*, 87–96.

Voracek, M., & Loibl, L. M. (2007). Genetics of suicide: A systematic review of twin studies. *Wiener Klinische Wochenschrift, 119*, 463–475.

Wang, J. Y., Jia, C. X., Lian, Y., Sun, S. H., Lyu, M., & Wu, A. (2015). Association of the HTR2A 102T/C polymorphism with attempted suicide: A meta-analysis. *Psychiatric Genetics, 25*, 168–177.

Weaver, I. C., Cervoni, N., Champagne, F. A., D'Alessio, A. C., Sharma, S., Seckl, J. R., et al. (2004). Epigenetic programming by maternal behavior. *Nature Neuroscience, 7*, 847–854.

Wender, P. H., Kety, S. S., Rosenthal, D., Schulsinger, F., Ortmann, J., & Lunde, I. (1986). Psychiatric disorders in the biological and adoptive families of adopted individuals with affective disorders. *Archives of General Psychiatry, 43*, 923–929.

Wen, L., et al. (2014). Whole-genome analysis of 5-hydroxymethylcytosine and 5-methylcytosine at base resolution in the human brain. *Genome Biology, 15*, R49.

Zemach, A., McDaniel, I. E., Silva, P., & Zilberman, D. (2010). Genome-wide evolutionary analysis of eukaryotic DNA methylation. *Science, 328*, 916–919.

Zhang, Y., Chang, Z., Chen, J., Ling, Y., Liu, X., Feng, Z., et al. (2015). Methylation of the tryptophan hydroxylase2 gene is associated with mRNA expression in patients with major depression with suicide attempts. *Molecular Medicine Reports, 12*, 3184–3190.

Zorn, J. V., Schur, R. R., Boks, M. P., Kahn, R. S., Joels, M., & Vinkers, C. H. (2017). Cortisol stress reactivity across psychiatric disorders: A systematic review and meta-analysis. *Psychoneuroendocrinology, 77*, 25–36.

Index

Note: 'Page numbers followed by "*f*" indicate figures and "*t*" indicate tables and "*b*" indicate boxes'.

B

C

D

E

F

G

H

Made in the USA
Las Vegas, NV
17 December 2022

63157802R00195